THE LIBRARY OF ADDICTIVE DRUGS

# Alcohol

## ITS HISTORY, PHARMACOLOGY, AND TREATMENT

MARK EDMUND ROSE, M.A.,
and
CHERYL J. CHERPITEL, DR.P.H.

HAZELDEN®

Hazelden
Center City, Minnesota 55012
hazelden.org

© 2011 by Hazelden Foundation
All rights reserved. Published 2011.
Printed in the United States of America

Library of Congress Cataloging-in-Publication Data

Rose, Mark Edmund.
    Alcohol : its history, pharmacology, and treatment / Mark Edmund Rose and Cheryl J. Cherpitel.
      p.   cm.
    Includes bibliographical references and index.
    ISBN 978-1-61649-147-5 (softcover) — ISBN 978-1-61649-403-2 (e-book)
    1. Drinking of alcoholic beverages—United States—History.   2. Alcoholism—Social aspects—United States.   3. Alcoholism—Psychological aspects—United States.   4. Alcoholism—Treatment—United States—History.   I. Cherpitel, Cheryl J. II. Title.
    HV5015.R67 2011
    616.86'1—dc23

                                                   2011037772

***Editor's note***

This publication is not intended as a substitute for the advice of health care professionals.

    Alcoholics Anonymous, AA, the Big Book, the *Grapevine, AA Grapevine,* and *GV* are registered trademarks of Alcoholics Anonymous World Services, Inc.

    Hazelden offers a variety of information on chemical dependency and related areas. The views and interpretations expressed herein are those of the authors and are neither endorsed nor approved by AA or any Twelve Step organization.

                  14  13  12  11       1  2  3  4  5  6

Cover design by Theresa Jaeger Gedig
Interior design by Madeline Berglund
Typesetting by BookMobile Design and Publishing Services

# CONTENTS

# ACKNOWLEDGMENTS

A funny thing happened along the way as I [Mark Rose] was preparing to enter treatment for drug and alcohol dependence. It was June 1983, and my grade point average at UC Santa Barbara had just slid below 2.0. I returned home for the summer and had several meetings with concerned professionals, which had been arranged by my parents. I agreed to go into treatment after finishing a summer class at UC San Diego, where an "A" would get me out of academic probation. Concluding that psychopharmacology was my best shot, I enrolled in a course taught by an unknown, entry-level instructor named George Koob, Ph.D. (now one of the top addiction scientists in the world). I became fascinated with learning about how therapeutic and recreational drugs acted on the brain to produce their effects, and I frequently visited with Dr. Koob. I took the final exam, entered treatment the next day, and got my "A."

I would sincerely like to thank Dr. Koob for igniting a passion; my former boss Mark Willenbring, M.D.; undergraduate mentor Harry Hoberman, Ph.D.; supervisor Warren Maas, L.P., J.D.; and friend Aviel Goodman, M.D., for their hugely influential role in helping me define and shape my professional interests and direction.

I would also like to express my gratitude to my parents for their unwavering love and support, my uncle Walt and grandmother Lilli (we called her Nana) for their incredible caring and emotional generosity while they were around, all my close friends along the way, and my sister Karen Rose Werner and friends Jonathan Rice, Seamus Mahoney, and Mark Mahowald, M.D., for their input while this book was being written. And finally, I would like to thank Aviel Goodman, M.D., for his time and invaluable peer review and critique of the chapter on the science of alcohol and alcoholism.

**The following authors and/or publishers have graciously granted permission to use material from their work:**

Coyhis, D. L., and W. L. White. 2006. *Alcohol Problems in Native America: The Untold Story of Resistance and Recovery.* Colorado Springs: White Bison, Inc.

DDA (Dual Diagnosis Anonymous). 1996. "12 Steps + 5: Original Concept Paper." Dual Diagnosis Anonymous of Oregon Inc. website. Accessed Apr. 8, 2011. www.ddaoregon.com/about.htm.

Dole, Vincent P. 1991. "Addiction as a Public Health Problem," *Alcoholism: Clinical and Experimental Research* 15 (5): 749–752. Published by John Wiley and Sons. © 1991, John Wiley and Sons.

Garland, E. L., S. A. Gaylord, C. A. Boettiger, and M. O. Howard. 2010. "Mindfulness Training Modifies Cognitive, Affective, and Physiological Mechanisms Implicated in Alcohol Dependence: Results of a Randomized Controlled Pilot Trial." *Journal of Psychoactive Drugs* 42:177–192.

Gorski, T. T., and M. Miller. 1982. *Counseling for Relapse Prevention.* Independence, MO: Independence Press. This material is copyrighted and proprietary information of Terence T. Gorski.

Harwood, H. 2000. *Updating Estimates of the Economic Costs of Alcohol Abuse in the United States: Estimates, Update Methods, and Data.* Report prepared by The Lewin Group for the National Institute on Alcohol Abuse and Alcoholism. Based on estimates, analyses, and data reported in Harwood, H., D. Fountain, and G. Livermore. 1998. *The Economic Costs of Alcohol and Drug Abuse in the United States 1992.* Report prepared for the National Institute on Drug Abuse and the National Institute on Alcohol Abuse and Alcoholism, National Institutes of Health, Department of Health and Human Services. NIH Publication No. 98-4327. Rockville, MD: National Institutes of Health.

Henderson, Elizabeth Connell. 2000. *Understanding Addiction.* Copyright 2000 by University Press of Mississippi.

Miller, W. R., and R. J. Harris. 2000. "Simple Scale of Gorski's Warning Signs for Relapse." *Journal of Studies on Alcohol* 61:759–765. Items reproduced with permission from Alcohol Research Documentation, Inc., publisher of the *Journal of Studies on Alcohol,* now the *Journal*

# Alcohol

*of Studies on Alcohol and Drugs* (www.jsad.com). This material is copyrighted and proprietary information of Terence T. Gorski.

White, William L. 2007. "In Search of the Neurobiology of Addiction Recovery: A Brief Commentary on Science and Stigma." www.facesandvoicesofrecovery.org/pdf/White/White_neurobiology _2007.pdf. (Also available at www.williamwhitepapers.com.)

WHO (World Health Organization). 2008. "Core Health Indicators: Per Capita Recorded Alcohol Consumption (Litres of Pure Alcohol) among Adults (>=15 Years)." Accessed Sept. 15, 2011. http://apps .who.int/whosis/database/core/core_select_process.cfm?strISO3 _select=ALL&strIndicator_select=AlcoholConsumption&intYear _select=latest&language=english.

The excerpts from the pamphlet *Three Talks to Medical Societies* are reprinted with permission of Alcoholics Anonymous World Services, Inc. ("AAWS"). Permission to reprint these excerpts does not mean that AAWS necessarily agrees with the views expressed herein. A.A. is a program of recovery from alcoholism *only*—use of these excerpts in connection with programs and activities which are patterned after A.A., but which address other problems, or in any other non A.A. context, does not imply otherwise.

# INTRODUCTION

Alcohol is unique among recreational drugs. On one hand, many people enjoy drinking alcohol and are able to do so without harming themselves or others. On the other hand, 15% of all persons who drink alcohol will develop an addiction to alcohol (also called alcoholism or alcohol dependence) (Anthony et al. 1994; Chen and Anthony 2004; Hughes et al. 2006).

The U.S. government estimates that 104 million adults in the U.S. are regular drinkers and that 18.2 million people currently have a diagnosable alcohol use disorder, which includes alcohol abuse and alcohol dependence (Centers for Disease Control and Prevention 2010; Hasin et al. 2007). Almost every American is affected by alcoholism. More than half of all adults have a family history of problem drinking or alcoholism, and families, communities, and society as a whole are enormously impacted (Centers for Disease Control and Prevention 2010; Hasin et al. 2007).

Alcohol abuse and alcoholism cost the U.S. economy approximately $235 billion each year (Thavorncharoensap et al. 2009), accounted for by alcohol-related accidents and injury, property destruction, and violent crime; illness, disease, and premature death; and worker impairment that results in elevated costs to the health care, criminal justice, and social service systems, and in lost worker productivity and industrial output. The emotional cost to the alcoholic, the family, the loved ones, and the innocent victims of alcohol-related physical and sexual assault, motor vehicle accidents, and ruined relationships cannot be calculated.

Fortunately, the last ten years have seen enormous advances in the understanding of alcoholism and its treatment. With tremendous scientific leaps in investigating and understanding the biological basis of alcoholism, the effectiveness of existing treatments, and the future direction of treatment development all may further improve treatment outcomes. Research has identified the drinking patterns among nonalcoholics that place them at highest risk for accidents, injuries, and medical problems. This information is already being used in prevention and risk-reduction efforts.

Much of the research addressed in this book has been funded by the U.S. government through the National Institute on Alcohol Abuse and Alcoholism (NIAAA), which is the branch of the National Institutes of Health (NIH) that addresses alcohol problems and alcoholism.

This book provides detailed, current information on the most important aspects of alcohol use, alcoholism, and its treatment. Preparation of this book involved an exhaustive review of the most recent research in areas of alcoholism important to professionals, students, alcoholics in recovery, concerned family members and loved ones of the alcoholic, and to anyone with an interest in the subject matter. Although some of the concepts are complex, we have made every effort to keep the material accessible and easy to understand for readers unfamiliar with addiction, while keeping it interesting and relevant for students and professionals in the field. Following is a chapter-by-chapter overview of the major topics covered in this book.

The historical background of alcohol use, alcohol problems, and treatment in the United States is examined in chapter 1. The chapter provides a context for understanding the origin of current treatment approaches and of the cyclical nature of attitudes toward alcoholics and alcohol problems. Many elements of the current understanding of alcoholism and addiction actually originated in the late 1800s, when the core features of alcoholism such as the genetic contribution, craving, tolerance, progression, and loss of control were identified. A history of the disease concept of alcoholism and an overview of the rise and fall of the temperance movements and self-help organizations in the 1800s are also provided. The founding of Alcoholics Anonymous in 1935 and the introduction of the Minnesota Model of alcoholism treatment in the late 1940s are discussed, as is their evolution to the present day.

Alcohol use is widespread among nearly all segments of American society, and no demographic group is immune to alcohol problems and alcoholism. Chapter 2 describes the latest statistics on alcohol use, alcohol problems and alcoholism, patterns of drinking that distinguish certain groups from others (e.g., college students), and those demographic groups that are especially susceptible to alcohol problems. Also discussed are the factors that place certain individuals at a much higher risk of developing alcoholism. Those factors include

- childhood stress and emotional trauma;
- genetic factors;
- the influence of family, culture, and the peer group;
- psychological and personality factors; and
- the interaction between genetic susceptibility and environmental stress.

The use of alcohol is linked to many harmful consequences not only for the drinker but also the family and friends of the drinker, and the community and society inhabited by the drinker. Some of the social harms associated with alcohol include crime, accidents and injuries, illness, disease and death, and disrupted school and work performance and productivity. The public health impact of alcohol use and alcoholism is discussed in chapter 3. The chapter includes the impact of alcohol use in special populations such as women, college students, and adolescents, and the contribution of drinking to crime, domestic abuse, and injuries, including traffic-related accidents and fatalities. The total economic cost of alcohol abuse is also discussed.

Chapter 4 explains the biological basis of alcoholism. While social drinking and occasional heavy drinking are not viewed as having a disease basis, a subset of drinkers will eventually develop alcohol dependence. Certain core symptoms of alcohol dependence reflect potential changes in the structure and function of key brain regions. Those symptoms are

- the inability to control one's drinking,
- the persistence in drinking despite harmful consequences,
- craving of alcohol,
- preoccupation over the next drink, and
- the need to drink more alcohol to achieve the desired effect.

These changes in brain function serve to perpetuate compulsive drinking and may make relapse likely since they may persist after drinking has stopped, forming the basis for defining alcohol dependence as a chronic disease. Alcoholism shares many similarities with other chronic diseases such as diabetes and high blood pressure. However, regarding alcoholism as a disease does not remove responsibility from the alcoholic for continuous self-care, any more than it does from the diabetic or hypertensive patient.

Starting in chapter 4, "Notes" in italic font may appear. Because some of the material related to the science of alcoholism and the pharmacology of drug therapies for alcoholism can be especially complex due to its language, the authors offer an additional explanatory note. In order to preserve the integrity while keeping the material accessible to the lay reader, a summary paragraph in italics is placed at the end of the more complex and technical sections.

Alcohol withdrawal develops shortly after a person with alcohol dependence abruptly stops drinking. The severity of withdrawal can vary from minor symptoms to hallucinations, seizures, permanent disability, or death. Alcohol withdrawal is discussed in chapter 5, including the signs and symptoms, the factors that influence the severity, and the medications that are used to manage alcohol withdrawal. Also described is post-acute withdrawal from alcohol, which reflects the symptoms of alcohol withdrawal that extend beyond the period of acute alcohol withdrawal. Post-acute withdrawal may last for months in some persons. It may consist of disturbances in mood, memory, stress tolerance, sleep, and energy level. Changes in brain function from chronic alcohol abuse can contribute to the symptoms of post-acute withdrawal, which may be reduced through active involvement in a recovery program such as Alcoholics Anonymous (AA).

Alcoholics Anonymous (AA) is the most widely available and successful recovery program for persons who want to quit drinking. In the past decade, a large volume of research has validated AA as a potentially essential and effective component of long-term recovery. Until fairly recently, the scientific evidence of AA success was much weaker, resulting in mixed feelings among some clinicians in referring clients, and in greater effort among researchers in investigating alternatives to AA.

Now, with the strength of scientific evidence, the focus of researchers has shifted, in part, to exploring ways to increase the attendance and retention of new members in AA. Special attention is given to those members referred from treatment settings. Chapter 6 discusses AA in depth and the different aspects of AA such as the demographic makeup of its members, the structure and organization, the Twelve Step program, and the spiritual framework. Also discussed are the specific elements that operate within AA that contribute to sobriety and the other benefits from involvement.

The concept of spirituality itself is confusing for many people, and this concept is explained to the reader from several different perspectives. Also discussed are the various self-help organizations that provide an alternative to AA for persons preferring a more tailored or secular approach, as well as the latest research on the effectiveness of these programs in promoting abstinence.

Professional treatment of alcohol dependence consists of psychological and medication approaches, and these are discussed in chapter 7. Medication therapy of alcohol dependence involves the use of drugs that are free of abuse potential, with the goal of reducing the craving for alcohol, irritability, and anxiety that plague many persons trying to stay sober. Medications are also used in persons who frequently relapse in order to block the pleasurable effects of alcohol and therefore the motivation to continue drinking if a relapse begins.

Effective medication therapy is the direct result of advances in the understanding of the brain biology of alcohol dependence. Research has identified abnormal functioning in several brain chemical systems that are associated with alcohol cravings and emotional distress in early recovery. Medications are used to target these systems to normalize their function, which in turn can reduce these symptoms and diminish the likelihood of relapse in early recovery. There is universal agreement that medications should never be used as the only source of therapy, and that medications will never replace self-help programs such as AA as the cornerstone of long-term sobriety. However, medications can play a vital role in blocking the obsession and craving to drink and in reducing the risk of relapse during early recovery when relapse risk is highest.

Psychological approaches to treating alcohol dependence address the problematic thinking, emotions, and behavior of alcoholics trying to achieve and maintain sobriety. These approaches consist of cognitive-behavioral therapy, behavioral therapies intended for the alcoholic or for the family or partner of the alcoholic, motivational enhancement interventions, and an approach that combines elements of several psychological treatment approaches to address relapse prevention.

Other aspects of professional treatment are also discussed. The average American has probably seen many television commercials for alcoholism treatment where a high "cure" rate is promised, which can raise questions about the actual success rates of alcohol treatment programs. Chapter 7 presents a discussion of the history of treatment outcome reporting, and how improvements in research methods have led to the more accurate evaluation of treatment outcome. The elements of successful recovery from alcoholism are also described, as well as the special treatment needs of older adults.

Meditation and prayer are important spiritual components of recovery for many alcoholics and are included in Step Eleven of AA. Although comprehensive coverage of prayer is beyond the scope of this book, chapter 8 gives a detailed discussion of meditation and the use of meditation throughout history to achieve greater closeness with the Divine. The meditation approaches most often used and their spiritual roots are also presented. Recent research provides us with an interesting account of positive changes in brain function and structure with regular meditation, and how these changes parallel the transformations in thought, emotion, behavior, and perception reported by practitioners. Many alcoholics entering sobriety have histories of emotional trauma, and a discussion is given of research demonstrating the benefits of meditation in persons recovering from post-traumatic stress.

Chapter 9 discusses current trends in a number of areas related to alcoholism treatment and recovery. Some include

- treatment development;
- the growth of informal community-based recovery communities and recovery advocacy organizations;

- the continued specialization of Twelve Step programs; and
- the growing influence of electronic communication as it relates to information sharing, treatment, and recovery support of alcoholism.

Also described is an emerging paradigm change in the approach to professional alcoholism treatment, where shortcomings in the current approach of treating alcoholism as an acute illness are leading to a movement calling for a long-term disease/recovery management approach.

In short, this book provides the reader with the most up-to-date, state-of-the-art knowledge and understanding of alcoholism and alcohol-related problems. A virtual explosion in the publication of high-quality, ground-breaking scientific research on alcohol use disorders and related problems has occurred in the last decade. This recent body of research is dramatically changing our understanding of the disease concept of alcoholism. The scientific process is guiding the development of future treatment and revealing how therapies currently available can be used more effectively.

We have reviewed hundreds of these research studies and present the scientific knowledge most likely to be helpful and interesting to the professional, clinician, and student working with alcoholic clients, the director or administrator of substance abuse treatment programs, as well as the person with a drinking problem, the concerned loved one of someone with an alcohol problem, and the recovering alcoholic.

CHAPTER 1

# History of Alcohol Use, Alcoholism, and Treatment in the United States

Alcohol has been one of the most widely used intoxicants throughout human history. Originally, alcohol was a powder and not a liquid. The word *alcohol* originates from the Arabic term *al-kuhul,* meaning *kohl,* a powder for the eyes, which later came to mean "finely divided spirit." From 3000 to 2000 BC, numerous cultures throughout the world (except in North and South America) described the use of alcohol for medicinal, social, religious, or recreational purposes. The following is a brief time-line of the discovery and use of alcohol throughout recorded history (Courtwright 2001; Walton and Glover 1999; Sherratt 1995; Escohotado 1999; McCarthy 1963).

# The History of Alcohol Use

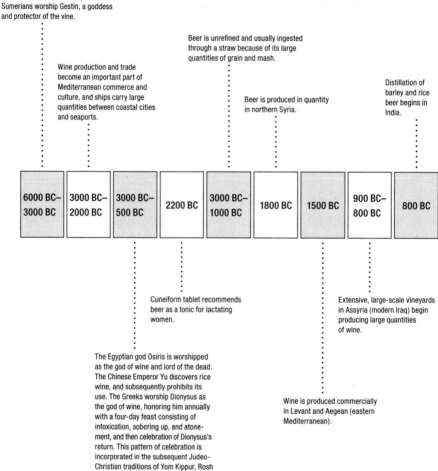

The selective cultivation of grape vines for making wine (termed *viticulture*) is believed to originate in the mountains between the Black and Caspian seas (modern Armenia). In Mesopotamia, the Sumerians worship Gestin, a goddess and protector of the vine.

Wine production and trade become an important part of Mediterranean commerce and culture, and ships carry large quantities between coastal cities and seaports.

Beer is unrefined and usually ingested through a straw because of its large quantities of grain and mash.

Beer is produced in quantity in northern Syria.

Distillation of barley and rice beer begins in India.

| 6000 BC–3000 BC | 3000 BC–2000 BC | 3000 BC–500 BC | 2200 BC | 3000 BC–1000 BC | 1800 BC | 1500 BC | 900 BC–800 BC | 800 BC |

Cuneiform tablet recommends beer as a tonic for lactating women.

Extensive, large-scale vineyards in Assyria (modern Iraq) begin producing large quantities of wine.

The Egyptian god Osiris is worshipped as the god of wine and lord of the dead. The Chinese Emperor Yu discovers rice wine, and subsequently prohibits its use. The Greeks worship Dionysus as the god of wine, honoring him annually with a four-day feast consisting of intoxication, sobering up, and atonement, and then celebration of Dionysus's return. This pattern of celebration is incorporated in the subsequent Judeo-Christian traditions of Yom Kippur, Rosh Hashanah, and Easter.

Wine is produced commercially in Levant and Aegean (eastern Mediterranean).

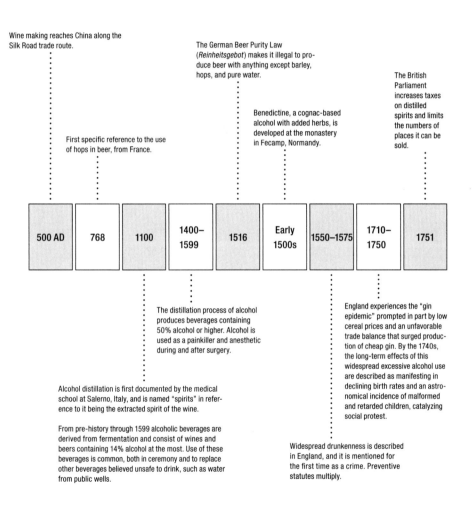

Wine making reaches China along the Silk Road trade route.

The German Beer Purity Law (*Reinheitsgebot*) makes it illegal to produce beer with anything except barley, hops, and pure water.

The British Parliament increases taxes on distilled spirits and limits the numbers of places it can be sold.

Benedictine, a cognac-based alcohol with added herbs, is developed at the monastery in Fecamp, Normandy.

First specific reference to the use of hops in beer, from France.

| 500 AD | 768 | 1100 | 1400–1599 | 1516 | Early 1500s | 1550–1575 | 1710–1750 | 1751 |

The distillation process of alcohol produces beverages containing 50% alcohol or higher. Alcohol is used as a painkiller and anesthetic during and after surgery.

England experiences the "gin epidemic" prompted in part by low cereal prices and an unfavorable trade balance that surged production of cheap gin. By the 1740s, the long-term effects of this widespread excessive alcohol use are described as manifesting in declining birth rates and an astronomical incidence of malformed and retarded children, catalyzing social protest.

Alcohol distillation is first documented by the medical school at Salerno, Italy, and is named "spirits" in reference to it being the extracted spirit of the wine.

From pre-history through 1599 alcoholic beverages are derived from fermentation and consist of wines and beers containing 14% alcohol at the most. Use of these beverages is common, both in ceremony and to replace other beverages believed unsafe to drink, such as water from public wells.

Widespread drunkenness is described in England, and it is mentioned for the first time as a crime. Preventive statutes multiply.

# Historical Per Capita Alcohol Use in the United States

The following table illustrates the estimated per capita (age 15 and older) consumption of alcohol from 1850 to 2007, based on gallons of pure alcohol per person per year (excerpted from NIAAA 2009).

Table 1.1

### Historical Per Capita
### Alcohol Consumption in the U.S.

| Year | Gallons of pure alcohol per person |
|---|---|
| 2007 | 2.31 |
| 2000 | 2.18 |
| 1990 | 2.45 |
| 1980 | 2.76 |
| 1970 | 2.52 |
| 1960 | 2.07 |
| 1950 | 2.04 |
| 1940 | 1.56 |
| 1934[1] | 0.97 |
| 1916–1919 | 1.96 |
| 1901–1905 | 2.39 |
| 1881–1890 | 1.99 |
| 1870 | 2.07 |
| 1850 | 2.10 |

1. *The year following the repeal of prohibition.*

## Alcohol Use in Colonial America

Settlers from northwest Europe brought alcohol to the New World when they first arrived in 1492, and with it the attitudes they harbored toward alcohol and its use. Alcohol was regarded as the "Good Creature of God"—a gift from the Almighty that was integrated into most aspects of colonial life. Men, women, and children drank alcohol on a daily basis, and not solely for the intoxicating effects (White 1999).

The disease and death that was spread by contaminated water earned alcohol its designation as *aqua vitae*—the water of life (Vallee 1998). Children as young as infant-age were given warmed alcohol with bread or other food, and young boys entered taverns to be taught by their fathers the arts of storytelling and drinking (Rorabaugh 1979; Steinsapir 1983). Although alcohol was valued in colonial America, drunkenness was condemned as a sinful misuse of this gift from God. These attitudes toward alcohol use were reflected by the numerous antidrunkenness laws, and also by the absence of laws that limited the age of access to alcohol (Mosher 1980; White 1999).

Cider, beer, and wine were the preferred alcoholic beverages. The Puritans believed alcohol was God's gift to man, and a test of his soul. This viewpoint is reflected in the Puritan aphorism "The wine is from God, but the drunkard is from the Devil." A group called Tithingmen, tax collectors overseeing ten-family units, monitored excessive drunkenness and reported it to the local Protestant minister. He in turn could punish first-time offenders. Repeated and chronic public inebriates were sent to the governor's representative for punishment (Dunlap 2006).

During the colonial era, the tavern was the center of the community. For the sake of convenience, the first colleges in America had breweries on campus for faculty and students. Even though the use of alcohol was pervasive, drunkenness remained highly stigmatized, and isolated cases of chronic drunkenness were viewed as a moral or criminal matter and not a medical or public health problem (White 2004).

## Alcohol and Native Americans

At the time of initial European contact, Native American tribes had a highly sophisticated knowledge of botanical psychopharmacology and used this understanding to ingest a broad spectrum of psychoactive drugs within a medicinal or religious context. There is very little pre-colonial evidence of recreational drug use or abuse among Native American tribes until distilled alcohol was introduced by European settlers (MacAndrew and Edgerton 1969; Mancall 1995; Westermeyer 1996; White 1999).

In a book entitled *Alcohol Problems in Native America* (2006), Coyhis and White offer the following perspective on the development of alcohol problems among Native Americans:

> There has yet to be definitive evidence that Native Peoples physically respond to alcohol differently than other races or possess a unique biological vulnerability to alcoholism . . . No gene has been identified that makes Native Americans more susceptible to alcoholism than other races. Differences of alcohol metabolism and genetic vulnerability to alcoholism are traits of individuals and families, not traits of racial and ethnic groups. There are as many differences in vulnerability to alcohol problems (and the choice to drink or not drink, the frequency and intensity of drinking, choices of alcoholic beverages, the locations of drinking, the purposes for drinking, and the effects of drinking) within and across Native tribes as between Native people as a whole and other racial/cultural groups.

The authors state that many factors contributed to the alcohol problems experienced by Native Americans since its introduction by Europeans in 1492, including the use of alcohol to facilitate the colonization and subjugation of Native Americans by Europeans and Americans alike. The authors conclude that the underlying cause of alcohol problems among

Native Americans stems from the suppression, oppression, and colonization of Native Americans by a radically different cultural group that also deliberately used alcohol as a weapon of colonization (Simonelli 2006).

## African Americans

Most Africans who were forced into slavery in the Americas came from West Africa where beer and wine had been incorporated into social and religious customs since antiquity among the non-Islamic (Islam prohibits alcohol use) African cultures. Moderate drinking was encouraged and drunkenness was stigmatized through drinking rituals, and alcohol problems, which seldom existed previously, rose in tandem with the colonization and deculturation of African tribes (Pan 1975; White and Sanders 2002).

Access to alcohol by African slaves was restricted due to concerns among slave owners over financial loss if a slave became injured or killed while intoxicated, and over fear that uncontrolled alcohol use could fuel a slave rebellion. The exception to this was the encouragement of slaves by their slave masters to drink heavily on Saturday nights, on holidays, and during harvest.

In his diary (1855), Frederick Douglass viewed this controlled promotion of alcohol intoxication on selective occasions, and through rituals that included drinking contests, as a way to keep the slave in "a state of perpetual stupidity" and "disgust the slave with his own freedom." Douglass further noted how the slave master's controlled promotion of drunkenness reduced the risk of slave rebellions since slaves were unlikely to plan an escape or insurrection while intoxicated. In contrast, a sober, thinking slave was the most dangerous threat to the established order (White, Sanders, and Sanders 2006).

Before emancipation, freed blacks often chose not to use alcohol, seeing sobriety as a prerequisite to personal safety and citizenship. When black people did drink, they did so moderately. The extent of their moderation led the medical community to believe that they were racially immune to the influence of alcohol (Herd 1985). Although drinking and intoxication among black people increased following emancipation, the most serious alcohol-related problem for black people in America was encountering intoxicated white people (Blassingame 1972; White and Sanders 2002).

## Rising Alcohol Use in the Early 1800s

It has been said that America went on an extended drunken binge in the decades following the Revolutionary War (Rorabaugh 1979). Between 1780 and 1830, the annual per capita alcohol consumption in America rose from 2.5 gallons to more than 7 gallons. Drinking preferences shifted from fermented beverages such as cider and beer to rum and whiskey (Rorabaugh 1979). During this period, the colonial tavern that was a community hub gave way to the urban saloon, which was regarded as a symbol of drunkenness and vice. Likewise, moderate drinking within a family context shifted to excessive drinking by unattached and unruly males.

These dramatic and alarming changes in drinking patterns, and the visible emergence of alcohol problems, prompted the beginning of a century-long temperance movement whose goal was the complete abolition of alcohol for the sake of preserving the well-being of children, families, communities, and the country (Cherrington 1920; Lender and Martin 1982; Rorabaugh 1979). Another byproduct of this rise in drinking and alcohol problems was the discovery of addiction (Levine 1978; White 2004).

## Temperance Movements and Mutual-Help Societies

As per capita alcohol use skyrocketed in America between 1780 and 1830, concern grew into alarm over the misuse of alcohol by children, especially among orphaned children. The emerging temperance movement responded with a series of actions that included (Mosher 1980)

- lobbying for a minimum drinking age and temperance education laws,
- publishing temperance literature aimed at young drinkers,
- including young people in temperance society activities, and
- suppressing drinking on college campuses.

Temperance societies of the nineteenth century included cadet branches for young inebriates. Many of these young alcoholics who recovered would join in the antidrinking outreach crusades to young drinkers (Foltz 1891). Young problem drinkers were also admitted to the first addiction treatment institutions in America, and alcoholics between the ages of 15 and 20 made up about 10% of admissions to inebriate homes and inebriate asylums. By the 1890s, patients as young as twelve were being admitted to hospitals for detoxification (White 1998).

Religiously oriented urban rescue missions and rural inebriate colonies also provided institutional intervention for chronic alcoholism. This rescue work with chronic or late-stage alcoholics was later institutionalized within the programs of the Salvation Army (White 2004).

Abstinence-based mutual-aid societies organized by and for those with alcohol problems originated in two cultural contexts: first within Native American tribes in the eighteenth century and then within Euro-American communities in the mid-nineteenth century (White 2003). The earliest recovery mutual-aid societies grew out of Native American religious and cultural revitalization movements during the 1730s. These societies continued to remain active and influential well into the nineteenth century. Among the more prominent leaders were Wangomend, the Delaware Prophet (Papoonan, Neolin), the Kickapoo Prophet (Kenekuk), the Shawnee Prophet (Tenskwatawa), and Handsome Lake (Ganioda'yo) (White 2004).

Similarly, by the 1830s, and some one hundred years before the founding of Alcoholics Anonymous, Anglo American alcoholics began seeking abstinence and recovery within local temperance societies. However, it took the Washingtonian Movement of 1840 to motivate large numbers of Anglo American alcoholics into joining sobriety-based mutual-aid societies. The Washingtonians rapidly grew to an organization of more than 400,000 members, but then collapsed.

Many of its former members dispersed into more underground organizations via the creation of sobriety-based Fraternal Temperance societies. Eventually, the Fraternal Temperance societies disintegrated over political conflict or deviation from their initial mission to help the still-suffering alcoholic, and were replaced by the Ribbon Reform clubs and other local sobriety-based fellowships such as the Drunkard's Club in New York City. Within the network of inebriate homes, asylums, and addiction cure institutes emerged additional alcoholic mutual-aid societies (White 2004).

## Professional and Medical Approaches to Nineteenth-Century Alcohol Problems

Inebriate homes were introduced during the 1830s out of the belief, among some temperance societies, that alcoholics needed more than to sign pledges and attend meetings to achieve and sustain abstinence. The new viewpoint believed recovery from alcoholism was a process of moral reformation and immersion in sober fellowship. The inebriate homes utilized short, voluntary stays followed by affiliation with local recovery support groups (White 2004).

The medically directed inebriate asylum was another institution created during the mid-nineteenth century. It arose from the need for specialized medical facilities for chronic alcoholics. Many of the clients in these institutions were legally coerced by multiyear legal commitments. These facilities combined physical and psychological treatment with drug therapies, hydrotherapy, and hypnotherapy. In 1864, the first of these facilities—the New York State Inebriate Asylum—opened under the leadership of Dr. Joseph Edward Turner (White 2004), a prominent advocate of a disease concept of inebriety (White 2000a).

The inebriate homes and asylums began to face competition from private, for-profit addiction cure institutes, the most famous being the Keeley Institute. There was also competition from the patent medicine industry, which bottled and sold home remedies and cures for alcohol, tobacco, and drug habits. Some of these products originated from the addiction cure institutes. The widespread use of these addiction cures continued until an exposé in 1905 revealed that most of these products contained high doses of morphine, cocaine, alcohol, or cannabis (White 2004).

An increasingly vast network of inebriate homes and asylums, private addiction treatment institutes, and patent medicines that cured addiction became established between 1850 and 1900. In 1870, directors of several inebriate homes and asylums met in New York City to create the first professional association for addiction treatment providers called the American Association for the Cure of Inebriety.

In 1876, the Association published the first journal specializing in addictions called the *Quarterly Journal of Inebriety* (White 2004). This journal published hundreds of articles that shared the theme of alcohol addiction as a disease. Joined by a growing number of medical textbooks on inebriety, the journal advocated for a disease concept of addiction (White 2000a).

The 1870 Bylaws of the American Association for the Study and Cure of Inebriety include the following:

1.  Intemperance is a disease.
2.  It is curable in the same sense that other diseases are.
3.  Its primary cause is a constitutional susceptibility to the alcoholic impression.
4.  This constitutional tendency may be either inherited or acquired (White 2000a).

Eventually, the urban hospital assumed an increasing level of responsibility for the care of the chronic inebriate. In 1879, Bellevue Hospital in New York City opened an inebriate ward. The number of alcoholic patients admitted for care increased from 4,190 in 1895 to more than 11,000 in 1910. Almost all of these institutions treated addictions to all drugs including alcohol (White 2004).

Following is a discussion of some of the more noteworthy "medical" approaches to the treatment of alcoholism.

### The Keeley Cure

The Keeley Institute was an organization for the treatment of opiate and alcohol addiction by Leslie Keeley, a Civil War surgeon who announced his cure in 1879 with his famed slogan, "Drunkenness is a disease and I can cure it." His secret injections of gold chloride became known as the Gold Cure. Keeley's cure was touted as being made from "double chloride of gold," but in truth actually contained atropine, strychnine, arsenic, cinchona, and glycerin.

Patients admitted to his institutes were tapered from alcohol or opiates, received periodic injections, ingested a small amount of Keeley's formula every two hours, and followed a regimen of healthful diet, fresh air, exercise, and adequate sleep. Patients were required to pay $160 up front and stay for thirty-one days. It is unknown how many of the 400,000 Keeley graduates remained abstinent from opiates or alcohol (Blair Historic Preservation Alliance 2008; "Medicine: Keeley Cure" 1939). It is also unknown how many died of his cure.

Through his practice, Dr. Keeley eventually amassed a fortune of more than $1 million. However, by 1900 the approach was largely discredited. The Keeley Cure, however, did have some initial success. At one time more than 200 treatment centers existed. Keeley Institute patients who recovered from their addiction were honored as graduates and urged to promote the treatment that had helped them. Patients were also encouraged to involve themselves in what would now be referred to as group therapy, a factor that likely contributed to the success of those who remained abstinent.

Despite the view that Keeley's Gold Cure was merely a successful example of nineteenth-century quackery, Dr. Keeley made an important contribution to the field of addiction treatment. He was one of the first to widely treat addiction as a medical problem (Blair Historic Preservation Alliance 2008). The Keeley Institute was also significant because, although it predated modern treatment programs by seventy years, several elements common to contemporary treatment were used, such as use of the group process for support; an emphasis on a holistic approach addressing diet, exercise, and sleep; and the one-month residential stay.

### Morphine in Late Nineteenth to Early Twentieth Century

Legitimate medical use of opiates emerged in the late nineteenth century as a substitute treatment for alcoholism. Although morphine was well known for its addiction potential, it was viewed as a dramatic improvement over the effects of alcoholic drinking (Black 1889). Many physicians converted alcoholics to morphine users, and in some parts of the country this practice did not die out among older physicians until the late 1930s or early 1940s.

In 1928, Dr. Lawrence Kolb, Assistant Surgeon General of the United States Public Health Service, pointed out the advantages of opiate substitution therapy. "More than any other unstable group," Dr. Kolb wrote, "drunkards are likely to be benefited in their social relations by becoming addicts. When they give up alcohol and start using opium [i.e., morphine or other opiates], they are able to secure the effect for which they are striving without becoming drunk or violent" (Kolb 1962).

### LSD Research in the 1950s–1960s

Following its discovery in 1943, the hallucinogenic drug LSD (d-lysergic acid diethylamide) was introduced to medical and behavioral research in the late 1940s (Dyck 2005). Treatment of alcoholism was considered one of the most promising areas of investigation involving LSD. The initial rationale for its use was to replicate some of the experiences of a delirium tremens (DT) to facilitate the alcoholic hitting bottom. However, when it was observed that LSD had the potential to induce a profound transformative experience similar to a religious conversion, its use and purpose was revised (Mangini 1998).

Early enthusiasm over the initial positive results gave way to skepticism when researchers attempted to isolate the drug effect from the set and setting, often by blindfolding or restraining and isolating subjects given the drug. The environment in which the subject experienced the drug effect was eventually recognized as an important factor in the outcome (Dyck 2005).

In 1962, the first controlled trial involving LSD and alcoholism was published. It compared subjects who received group therapy, individual therapy from a psychiatrist, or LSD at the end of a hospital stay. The study followed patients for six to eighteen months, and reported that 38 of the 58 patients treated with LSD remained abstinent during the follow-up period. This was a remarkable finding when compared with those who received only group therapy (7 of 38 remained abstinent) and individual therapy (4 of 35 remained abstinent) (Dyck 2005; Jensen 1962). However, all research involving LSD was halted in the mid-1960s when the drug became illegal.

## Origin and History of the Disease
## Concept of Alcoholism

Three key issues helped usher in the birth of a disease concept of alcoholism in America. The first was the emergence of alcohol problems resulting in a breakdown of community norms that had long contained drunkenness in colonial America; the second was the changing patterns of consumption from fermented beverages to distilled spirits; and the third was the nearly threefold increase in alcohol consumption between 1790 and 1830 (White 2000a).

Dr. Benjamin Rush was the first to articulate a disease concept of chronic drunkenness and call for the creation of special institutions for the care of the inebriate (White 2007a). In 1784, Rush described the progressive nature and medical consequences of chronic drunkenness. He suggested the condition was a medical instead of a moral problem and argued that physicians had the responsibility of caring for persons with this disorder (White 2004). The changing perception of chronic drunkenness was also strongly influenced by the Reverend Lyman Beecher, who in 1825 characterized intemperance as an accelerating disease. He described in detail the early stages of alcoholism and argued that complete long-term abstinence was the only viable approach to prevention and cure (White 2004).

These two highly influential figures, Rush and Beecher, along with other prominent physicians and social reformers, helped to redefine drunkenness as a medical problem during the transition from the eighteenth to the nineteenth century. These leaders encouraged physicians to treat inebriety within specialized institutions for the alcoholic. At this time, the core elements of an addiction disease concept were identified and described as

- a hereditary predisposition;
- drug toxicity;

- morbid appetite (craving);
- pharmacological tolerance and progression;
- loss of control of substance intake; and
- the pathophysiology of chronic alcohol, opiate, or cocaine consumption (White 2001b; White 2004).

Although the term *alcoholism* was coined in 1849 by Swedish physician Magnus Huss, the preferred term of this era was *inebriety,* whose meaning was analogous to the term *addiction.* Medical textbooks included chapters on alcohol inebriety, opium inebriety, cocaine inebriety, and inebriety from coffee and tea. The widespread use of the term *alcoholism* did not actually occur until the early twentieth century (White 2007b; White 2004).

During the 1870s and 1880s, the disease concept of inebriety or alcoholism formed the foundation of the movement to treat the disease medically and scientifically. The movement advocated for specialized institutions where inebriates could be treated.

However, support for a disease concept of alcoholism among professionals caring for the inebriate was not unanimous. In 1874, Dr. Robert Harris mounted perhaps the most fully articulated opposition to the disease concept, stating that drunkenness should be viewed as a habit, sin, or crime that cannot be cured in a hospital but can be reformed. The chronic drunk was also viewed as a victim of the promotion or marketing of alcoholic beverages (White 2000a).

In summary, nonmedical concepts of alcohol and other drug addiction competed for prominence with the disease concept. They espoused that

- addiction originated in the person and was a reflection of vice and sin;
- addiction resided in the product (alcohol, opium, or cocaine); and
- addiction was caused by aggressive alcohol and other drug promotion by distilleries and breweries, saloons, and physicians and pharmacists.

Each of these views produced radically different solutions to address the source of the addiction problem. The disease concept as a purely medical concept soon fell out of favor at the end of the nineteenth century along with the collapse of the treatment infrastructure (White 2000a).

## The Collapse of Specialized Treatment for Alcohol Problems in the Early Twentieth Century

The collapse of America's first addiction treatment infrastructure was due to multiple factors, including

- the exposure of ethical abuses related to business and clinical practices,
- ideological differences within the field,
- the lack of scientific validation of treatment effectiveness,
- the departure through aging and death of leaders in the field,
- economic downturns that impacted philanthropic and government support, and
- cultural pessimism over whether permanent recovery from alcohol and drug problems could ever be achieved (White 2004).

As a result, the nineteenth-century mutual-aid societies had collapsed in tandem with the inebriate homes and asylums (White 2004).

Eventually, the care of alcoholics and addicts shifted to penal institutions and large public hospitals, and to psychiatry. The prevailing belief in psychiatry during this time was that excessive alcohol or other drug use was not a primary disease but the superficial symptom of a deeper psychological problem. It could be treated if the hidden subconscious forces that drove excessive alcohol or other drug use were confronted during psychotherapy (White 2000a).

The reluctant assumption of responsibility by psychiatry for the care of alcoholics and drug addicts led to a new push to find more humane and effective treatments. These included the founding of the Emmanuel Clinic model. Its early efforts included using recovered alcoholics as lay therapists, treating affluent alcoholics and addicts in private hospitals and clinics, and starting a model for outpatient treatment in Connecticut and Georgia.

There was also a dark side to the involvement of psychiatry in the treatment of addiction. It stemmed from alcoholics and addicts being subjected to the same treatments and policies currently in vogue with mentally ill patients. These included forced sterilization and legal commitment in the early twentieth century, prefrontal lobotomies, and chemical and electroconvulsive therapies (White 2000a). When admitted or sentenced to the aging state mental hospitals or the rural inebriate penal colonies, alcoholics and addicts were also subjected to the worst abuses of these institutions.

The obvious disregard for the well-being of alcoholics and addicts was evidenced by some of the medical procedures they were subjected to, such as serum therapy (a procedure involving blistering the skin, withdrawing the serum from the blisters, and then re-injecting it as an alleged aid in withdrawal) and the use of bromide therapy to aid detoxification, which had a high mortality rate.

Much of the modern antimedication bias that lingers among some members in the addiction treatment field and older members of AA today stems from the past abusive and barbaric practices during this period under the guise of medicine (White 2004).

Among the very few enlightened resources available to alcoholics and addicts during the early twentieth century was the beginning of a new generation of private hospitals that started with the Charles B. Towns Hospital in New York City and an outpatient clinic in Boston that arose from the Emmanuel Church. This clinic employed a unique program of lay therapy that was the precursor to modern addiction counseling. The Emmanuel Clinic also organized its own self-help program, the Jacoby Club, for patients who had completed its program (White 2004).

The Jacoby Club was founded in 1910 as a club for alcoholic men, and sought to combine religion, psychology, and medicine in the treatment of alcoholism. This absence of mutual-aid resources changed in 1935 when the meeting of two alcoholics, Bill Wilson and Dr. Robert Smith, reaching out for mutual support, marked the founding of Alcoholics Anonymous (AA) (White 2003).

## The History of Alcoholics Anonymous

Alcoholics Anonymous (AA) was established in 1935 in response to pervasive alcohol problems during a time when resources were scarce (Trice
and Staudenmeier 1989). AA offered unconditional support and practical
advice to help its members stop drinking. The message of forgiveness and
understanding given by people who themselves had been actively dependent on alcohol helped alleviate shame and guilt associated with alcoholism (Kurtz 1981).

Self-help organizations tend to internalize the broader cultural and societal themes into which they are born, and AA's birth in 1935 and many of
its core concepts (e.g., powerlessness, unmanageability, hope, and service)
were rooted in the economic and spiritual crash of the Great Depression
of the 1930s. AA historian Ernest Kurtz (1991) has suggested that the
unique program of recovery of AA could only have sprung from the circumstances of the Depression era. AA also arrived in the wake of the repeal of Prohibition and a century-long, culturally divisive debate between
wet and dry political opponents.

### Conception of AA

In 1926, Rowland Hazard, a Yale graduate and prominent Rhode Island
businessman, was treated for alcoholism by the renowned psychoanalyst
Carl Jung (Bluhm 2006). Following a relapse in 1927, Hazard requested
further treatment from Jung. Jung communicated to Hazard that he could
no longer treat him because Hazard had already received the best care psychiatry and medicine had to offer. Jung also told Hazard that any hope for
future recovery would have to be found elsewhere. He said that some alcoholics had found relief from their insatiable appetite for alcohol through a
powerful spiritual or religious experience, and he suggested that Hazard
seek out such an experience.

This recommendation led to Hazard's subsequent involvement with
the Christian evangelical Oxford Group. Achieving sobriety within the
Oxford Group, Rowland Hazard began carrying his message of hope and
sobriety to other alcoholics. In November 1934, Hazard carried this mes-

sage to Ebby Thacher. On the verge of being sentenced to Windsor Prison, Thacher was instead released to Hazard's custody.

In late November 1934, the newly sobered Thacher carried that same message of hope to his longtime friend Bill Wilson. Thacher's visits did not produce an immediate effect, but instead began an internal dialogue that triggered a crisis in Wilson's drinking and served as a catalyst for the subsequent events that eventually led to the founding of AA (*Pass It On* 1984, 115; White and Kurtz 2008).

The chain of interaction among Jung, Hazard, Thacher, and Wilson mark the earliest moments in the founding of AA. Jung acknowledged the limitations of professional assistance in treating alcoholism, and believed in the legitimacy to the transformative power of spiritual experience. The Hazard–Thacher–Wilson connections established the kinship of common suffering (one alcoholic sharing with another alcoholic) as the basic unit of interaction in the yet-to-be-born organization of AA (Alcoholics Anonymous World Services, Inc., 1957; White and Kurtz 2008).

Following Ebby Thacher's visits, Bill Wilson's drinking reached another critical point on December 11, 1934, when he was rehospitalized for detoxification at the Charles B. Towns Hospital in New York City. At age thirty-nine, Wilson had had his last drink. Although a confirmed agnostic, a few days later during a belladonna-facilitated detoxification,[2] Wilson underwent a profound spiritual experience in the aftermath of a deepening depression. Later, questioning whether he was losing his sanity, Wilson consulted his physician, Dr. William Silkworth. Silkworth, known in AA folklore as "the little doctor who loved drunks," framed the event as a potential conversion experience (White and Kurtz 2008) much like the one Carl Jung spoke of.

---

2. The belladonna detoxification (or Belladonna Cure) was a regimen given to newly admitted alcoholics to Towns Hospital who showed signs of DTs or severe alcohol withdrawal. Within the first twelve hours, the patient was sedated with a combination of chloral hydrate, morphine, paraldehyde, mercury, and strychnine, followed by repeated administration of belladonna (*Atropa belladonna*, deadly nightshade) and henbane (*Hyoscyamus niger*) over the next two days. Both plant-derived products produce delirium, hallucinations, light sensitivity, confusion, and dry mouth (Pittman 1988).

Following Thacher's lead, Wilson joined the Oxford Group, a Christian movement popular among wealthy mainstream Protestants. Headed by an ex-YMCA missionary named Frank Buchman, the Oxford Group combined religion with pop psychology to emphasize that all people can achieve happiness through moral improvement. To help reach this goal, the organization's members met in private homes to study devotional literature and share their inner thoughts and experiences (Koerner 2010).

In the months following his discharge, Bill Wilson went on a crusade to sober up the alcoholics at the Towns Hospital and Calvary mission by describing his spiritual experience, but he was met with indifference (White and Kurtz 2008).

In May 1935 during an extended business trip to Akron, Ohio, Wilson began attending Oxford Group meetings at the home of a local industrialist. It was through the group that he obtained the name of surgeon and closet alcoholic Robert Smith, who was also an Oxford member. Demoralized at the end of a failed business trip, Wilson found himself in the lobby of the Mayflower Hotel fearing that he might take a drink and destroy his hard-earned sobriety. He sensed that he needed to find another alcoholic with whom he could talk in order to maintain his sobriety. Rather than reach out to a professional, he made contact through a series of phone calls with Robert Smith (Alcoholics Anonymous 1956).

Their growing friendship, mutual support, and vision of helping other alcoholics marked the formal ignition of AA as a social movement. The date of Dr. Bob Smith's last drink in June of 1935 is celebrated as AA's founding date. Soon after that last drink, Bill Wilson and Dr. Bob Smith began the search for AA number three. The mutual discovery that Bill Wilson and Dr. Bob Smith could achieve together what they were unable to do alone became the foundation of the soon-to-emerge AA program (Koerner 2010; White and Kurtz 2008).

### The Growth of AA, 1936–1950

In its earliest days, AA existed within the confines of the Oxford Group. By late 1936, fledgling groups of recovering alcoholics were meeting within the larger framework of the Oxford Group in Akron, Ohio, and the New

York City area, offering special meetings for members who wished to end their dependence on alcohol. However, Wilson and his followers left the Oxford Group in large part because Wilson dreamed of creating a truly mass movement instead of one that catered to the elites that Buchman targeted (Koerner 2010; White and Kurtz 2008). Although Wilson and Smith left the Oxford Group, this movement greatly influenced the structure, practices, and ideology of AA (Bufe 1998).

Bill Wilson stayed sober and immersed himself in growing the AA movement. But soon a crisis unfolded over the poverty in which he and his wife Lois were living. Charles B. Towns, owner of the Towns Hospital where Wilson had repeatedly been treated, offered Wilson paid employment at the hospital as a "lay alcoholism therapist." The decision by Wilson to turn down the offer was actually forced by his fellow recovering alcoholics who were concerned over the potential harm to the fledgling organization with Wilson becoming employed and affiliated with the hospital (White and Kurtz 2008).

During the mid to late 1930s, Wilson began drafting what would become the book *Alcoholics Anonymous*. When published, the book was referred to as the Big Book because the printers of the book were instructed to use the thickest paper available for the first edition so that it would seem worth the price to the generally financially strapped alcoholics to whom it was targeted (Kurtz and White 2003).

The core of AA principles is found in chapter five of the Big Book, entitled "How It Works." Wilson formulated the Twelve Steps in 1939, and it is speculated that he decided on twelve because of the twelve apostles. Formulating these Steps, Wilson was strongly influenced by the precepts of the Oxford Group and by psychologist William James and his classic work *The Varieties of Religious Experience,* which Wilson read shortly after his spiritual experience at Towns Hospital (Koerner 2010).

The initial publication of the Big Book was barely noticed. Attempts at publicity, such as the mass mailing of postcards to physicians, failed to generate sales. However, the media attention that was about to unfold began to increase public awareness of AA, and sales of the Big Book slowly increased (Kurtz and White 2003). AA experienced local and national membership surges in the 1940s that were largely generated by media coverage.

Most prominent of these were the September 1939 article on AA in *Liberty Magazine,* a 1939 series in the *Cleveland Plain Dealer,* and newspaper sports-page coverage of the spring 1940 announcement that the Cleveland Indians star catcher had joined AA. This early visibility was followed by a *Saturday Evening Post* article in March 1941, considered the most important single piece of media coverage that contributed to the growth of AA. Its membership grew from 2,000 members to 8,000 members in that year alone (White and Kurtz 2008).

In June 1944, publication of AA's unofficial but significant periodical, *The AA Grapevine,* initially began as a means of keeping in touch with AA members in the Armed Forces during World War II. During the postwar era, the magazine began to serve the purpose of offering a forum in which the variety of AA and recovery experiences could be presented and discussed. Over the first decade of its existence, the fellowship of AA grew from two members to 12,986 members and 556 AA groups.

The Twelve Traditions of AA were first disseminated during the first international convention of AA, held in Cleveland, Ohio, in 1950. They represented the general guidelines that were meant to preserve the organizational integrity of AA. In 1950, AA membership exceeded 96,000 and local groups numbered more than 3,500 (White and Kurtz 2008).

Not all of Bill Wilson's ideas to grow the organization were met with great acceptance. According to the New York State Office of Alcoholism and Substance Abuse Services, in 1940 Bill Wilson brought two African American men to an AA meeting in New York City and was sharply criticized by some attendees for his attempt at racial integration (New York State OASAS 2011).

### Early Outcomes

In the earlier days of AA, many alcoholics who desired sobriety required hospital-based detoxification due to the severity of their addiction. Those who could make the trip to Akron, Ohio, were put under the care of Dr. Bob Smith, but many could not travel to Akron. Hospitals were still reluctant to admit alcoholics because they did not pay their bills. Sponsorship in AA actually began by another man who promised to pay the detoxification hospital bill if a new AA recruit failed to do so. Eventually the AA sponsor would assume a much more comprehensive role in the sobriety of the new member (Kurtz and White 2003).

During the first few years of AA, several physicians in Philadelphia began keeping track of patients they knew who either attempted to get sober or had obtained sobriety in AA. In 1937, Dr. Silkworth and Bill Wilson concurred that AA was unlikely to work for around half of those who tried it; however, the data gathered in Philadelphia suggested a more positive result with roughly 50% achieving abstinence during their initial ninety days of involvement. Another 25% eventually achieved sobriety in AA after a period of relapse. The final 25% appeared to be beyond the help of AA. They also observed that those who made it were persons who had come to realize they needed AA, were highly motivated, and "really tried" to get it (Kurtz and White 2003).

## AA Hits Its Stride, 1951–1970

The early 1950s were marked by two developments that strengthened the growing momentum of AA. The first was the large-scale social acceptance of AA in the United States. The second was the publication of the book *Twelve Steps and Twelve Traditions,* written by Bill Wilson. This book guided and shaped the understanding of the spiritual concepts of AA among many members in the 1950s and the decades to come.

The Eisenhower decade of the 1950s proved to be an ideal backdrop for the widespread acceptance of the spiritual rather than religious program of AA. Among the many events reflecting cultural acceptance of AA included AA winning the 1951 Lasker Award. (The Lasker Awards, administered by the Lasker Foundation, have been awarded annually since 1946 to living persons who have made major contributions to medical science or who have performed public service on behalf of medicine. The awards are sometimes referred to as America's Nobel Prizes.)

The congratulatory telegram sent to AA by President Dwight Eisenhower on its twentieth-year Coming of Age convention in 1955, and the regular recommendations given to the readers of advice columnists Ann Landers and Dear Abby, also contributed to a more widespread cultural acceptance of AA. In addition, the movies *Smash-Up* and *The Lost Weekend,* followed by *Days of Wine and Roses,* reflected a cultural awareness of alcoholism by their very creation. In 1967, the American Medical Association stated that AA involvement remained the most effective means of treating alcoholism (Menninger quoted in Alcoholics Anonymous World Services, Inc., n.d.).

As the 1960s progressed, AA cofounder Bill Wilson suffered an increasing decline in his health largely due to emphysema, which resulted from his smoking. At the time of his death in Miami Beach on January 24, 1971, there were more than 16,000 local AA groups and more than 310,000 members. Few organizations led for so long by a charismatic leader survive his or her demise. But Alcoholics Anonymous was an exception, due to the decentralized autonomous structure mandated by the Twelve Traditions (Kurtz and White 2003).

## AA During the Era of Treatment Expansion, 1970–1990

From the start, AA groups carried their experience, strength, and hope to alcoholics residing in local missions, general and psychiatric hospitals, prisons, halfway houses, sanatoriums, and various "drying out" facilities. During the middle decades of the twentieth century, individual AA members created sober sanctuaries (AA farms, AA retreats, Twelve Step houses) in communities where institutional support for recovery was deficient. AA members were also heavily represented in the leadership of newly forming alcoholism councils whose mission was to advocate the establishment of alcoholism information and referral centers, detoxification facilities, and rehabilitation programs. In the culmination of these efforts, the passage of the 1970 Comprehensive Alcoholism Prevention and Treatment Act launched the modern alcoholism treatment field by infusing federal funding into alcoholism treatment facilities. The number of treatment facilities in the U.S. rocketed from 200 in 1970 to 4,200 in 1980, and to more than 9,000 in 1990 (Kurtz and White 2003).

The majority of these emerging treatment facilities used the AA Twelve Step model, especially among programs that replicated the Minnesota

Model. Many AA members became employed as alcoholism counselors, nurses, physicians, and administrators in the growing treatment field. Concern was voiced during the mid-1970s by some professionals over the undue influence of AA on the alcoholism treatment field. However, AA was dramatically influenced by the treatment field during this period as well, most obviously by fueling the huge growth in AA membership. Between 1970 and 1980, AA membership grew from 311,450 to 907,575, with the number of local AA groups increasing from 16,459 to 42,105. By 1990, AA had further increased to 2,047,469 members in 93,914 groups. The Twelve Steps of AA were also adapted to an increasingly vast number of problems and conditions, and the concepts of addiction and recovery were applied to other processes in addition to substances. Recovery became something of a cultural phenomenon (Kurtz and White 2003).

As a growing percentage of AA members entered AA while in treatment or were coerced to attend through the criminal justice system, concern within AA was raised over the prospect of the infusion of a secular, pop-psychology influence that would displace the language and elements of the classic Alcoholics Anonymous insight and approach. The fellowship responded by reasserting the importance of the Twelve Traditions, and releasing new literature and guidelines distinguishing and defining the differences between AA and treatment. There also emerged within AA a fundamentalist movement to recapture the spiritual practices of the earlier days of the organization (Kurtz and White 2003).

### Criticism of AA

Public criticism of AA was first observed with a 1964 magazine article by psychologist Arthur Cain, in which he argued that AA had become anti-science, dogmatic, and cult-like (Kurtz 1979). This laid the groundwork for subsequent attacks over the following decades. Such criticisms were usually part of a broader attack on the disease concept (erroneously attributed to AA) and of alcoholism treatment. Some of the critics advocated alternate organizations to AA, most notably the secular recovery approaches of Women for Sobriety, Secular Organization for Sobriety, Rational Recovery, and Moderation Management. By the mid-1980s, an extremist faction of critics aggregated into something resembling a countermovement with their own circuit speakers, publishing genre, and websites with names such as AA Kills, AA Deprogramming, and Recovery Liberation.

Despite the diversity of sources generating criticism of AA, five common themes pervaded their attacks. They were

- AA was ineffective or lacked scientific proof of effectiveness,
- AA helped only some types of alcoholics and may harm others,
- the religious ideas and language of AA discouraged many alcoholics from seeking help,
- AA was just a substitute dependence, and
- AA impeded the scientific advancement of alcoholism treatment (Kurtz and White 2003).

Just in the past decade, many of these arguments have been debunked by the quality and quantity of scientific research on AA.

## Birth of Modern Alcoholism Treatment, Mid-Twentieth Century

Substance abuse treatment programs evolved to meet the needs of patients who were not successful at establishing recovery solely through Twelve Step meetings (Brigham 2003). The birth and expansion of modern community-based treatment programs for alcohol and drug dependence was facilitated by five concepts that greatly influenced public opinion and legislative policy:

1. Alcoholism is a disease.
2. The alcoholic is a sick person.
3. The alcoholic can be helped.
4. The alcoholic is worth helping.
5. Alcoholism is our number four public health problem, and our public responsibility (Mann 1944; White 2004).

During the 1940s and 1950s several institutions pioneered new approaches to alcohol-related problems. Their collective efforts, including those of Alcoholics Anonymous and its professional friends who restored optimism that long-term sobriety could be achieved, were termed the Modern Alcoholism Movement (White 2004). Some of them include the following:

- The Research Council on Problems of Alcohol promised a new scientific approach to the prevention and management of alcohol problems.
- The Yale Center of Studies on Alcohol conducted alcoholism research, educated professionals, established an outpatient clinic model, and promoted occupational programs for alcoholism.
- The National Committee for Education on Alcoholism, founded by Mrs. Marty Mann in 1944, waged a relentless public education campaign about alcoholism and encouraged local communities to establish detoxification and treatment facilities. Mrs. Mann, referred to as the First Lady of Alcoholics Anonymous, was perhaps the single most influential figure in this advocacy movement that laid the foundation for modern addiction treatment (White and Schulstad 2009).

The success of the Modern Alcoholism Movement in changing the public perception of alcoholism is shown by the percentage of U.S. citizens who viewed alcoholism as an illness, which increased from 6% in 1947 to 66% in 1967, and by the number of new professional organizations studying alcoholism (White 2004).

## The Minnesota Model

By the time the thirteen-year reign of prohibition ended in 1933, most alcoholics were detoxified and institutionalized with the chronically mentally ill in the locked wards of state psychiatric hospitals. Conditions were often poor, and the custodial system of care typically resulted in revolving-door cycles of admission, detoxification, release, relapse, and readmission (Slaymaker and Sheehan 2008).

The model that most represents the archetype of modern alcoholism treatment emerged from the synergy of three programs in Minnesota: Pioneer House (1948), Hazelden (1949), and Willmar State Hospital (1950). This model, termed the Minnesota Model, drew heavily on the experience of AA members in its conceptualization of alcoholism (White 2000a). As articulated by its early proponents—Dr. Nelson Bradley, Dr. Dan Anderson, Reverend John Keller, and Reverend Gordon Grimm—the Minnesota Model defined alcoholism as a primary, progressive disease that could not be cured but could be arrested with lifelong abstinence. These proponents also emphasized the importance of treating the alcoholic and addict patients with dignity and respect, the importance of a mutually supportive treatment environment, utilization of a multidisciplinary treatment team and a full continuum of services, and integration of the Twelve Steps and social support of AA during and following treatment (White 2003).

The Minnesota Model blended AA concepts and philosophy with professional approaches, such as group and individual counseling. The addition of the alcoholism counselors, many of whom were recovering AA members, was a key ingredient in aligning a closely identified professional with the alcoholic to foster integration of Twelve Step principles and practices in everyday life. The psychiatric services, heavily influenced by psychoanalysis, that had been the prevailing mode of therapy were abandoned in favor of an emphasis on patient education, therapeutic group process, peer interaction, and the development of lifelong support systems through AA (Slaymaker and Sheehan 2008).

### Hazelden

Hazelden was conceived in an era when alcoholics languished in the "drunk tanks" of city and county jails, and in the back wards of aging state psychiatric hospitals. Few resources were available for any alcoholic, rich or poor. The Hazelden treatment center opened in Center City, Minnesota, following extended discussions about the need for an alcoholism treatment facility for priests and business executives. Initial financial support came from the Catholic Diocese and contributions from local businesses. The first residents experienced a formal program with very simple directives:

make your bed, conduct yourself as a gentleman, attend the daily lectures on the Twelve Steps of AA, and talk with one another (White 2003).

Hazelden was able to grow and evolve due in large part to the financial resources of Emmet, Patrick, and Lawrence Butler, whose combined largesse sustained Hazelden through its early years. Patrick himself had been a Hazelden patient in 1949. During the 1950s, Hazelden, as well as Pioneer House and Willmar State Hospital, exerted an enormous influence on the evolution of addiction treatment that continued through the second half of the twentieth century (White 2003).

The 1950s also marked the beginning of AA's profound and widespread influence on alcoholism treatment as the Minnesota Model was replicated nationally and worldwide over the next several decades. To avoid the potential for a mistaken impression of affiliation between AA and professional alcoholism treatment, AA discouraged the use of its name in the names of institution or professional titles used by treatment centers (Alcoholics Anonymous, n. d.; White and Kurtz 2008).

## Expansion of Treatment and Then Backlash

In the U.S., modern treatment approaches received a considerable boost from substantial growth in AA membership. The impetus for treating alcohol dependence as a disease rather than a moral problem grew out of the AA philosophy that individuals were not responsible for becoming dependent upon alcohol, but were responsible to do something about it once it developed (Trice and Staudenmeier 1989).

During the 1960s, alcoholism services grew through federal funding from the National Institute of Mental Health (NIMH) and the Office of Economic Opportunity. In 1970, the decades-long campaign of the Modern Alcoholism Movement culminated in the passage of the Comprehensive Alcoholism Prevention and Treatment Act. This legislative milestone (often termed the Hughes Act for its champion, Senator Harold Hughes of Iowa) created the National Institute on Alcohol Abuse and Alcoholism (NIAAA) to lead a federal, state, and local partnership to build, staff, operate, and evaluate community-based alcoholism treatment programs across the U.S. The number of alcoholism programs in the U.S. jumped astonishingly from a few hundred in 1970 to more than 4,200 programs by 1980 (White 2004).

It appeared then that many of the goals of the Modern Alcoholism Movement were being achieved. The movement had extended its influence into major cultural institutions that included the media, law, medicine, religion, education, business, and labor. There was growing professional and public acceptance of alcoholism as a disease. The country had established national institutes that funded and advocated medical research on addiction and public health approaches to alcohol and other drug-related problems. The disease concept was also applied to a wide spectrum of other drugs and behaviors as recovery became something of a cultural phenomenon. There was also an explosion in the growth of treatment programs based on the disease concept (White 2000a), spurred in large part by the decision of many insurance companies to begin offering alcoholism treatment benefits (White 2004).

However, during the very peak of the expansion in treatment services and facilities, a backlash began to develop. It came in two forms. The first was a financial response against the treatment industry. The prototypical twenty-eight-day inpatient treatment programs that had been the standard of care were hardest hit (White 2004). The dominance of managed care and of aggressively managed behavioral health care by the end of the 1980s led to the severely curtailed reimbursement for chemical dependency services. Insurance providers only paid then for what was deemed medically necessary. This resulted in third-party payment for three to six days of treatment instead of twenty-eight days (John Curtiss, pers. comm.), leading to a massive number of closures of chemical dependency treatment programs from the period of 1988 to 1993.

The surviving hospitals and clinics that continued to offer chemical dependency services often had to shift their emphasis from inpatient to outpatient services, or to the identification and treatment of co-occurring psychiatric and behavioral disorders in order to receive insurance reimbursement (John Curtiss, pers. comm.; White 2004). The net result has been a dramatic reduction in the availability and accessibility of chemical dependency services as the number of persons needing help continues to climb (John Curtiss, pers. comm.).

The second backlash was ideological, and came in the form of philosophical and scientific attacks on the disease concept and the treatment programs based on it. Some of the more prominent examples include *Heavy Drinking: The Myth of Alcoholism as a Disease* (Fingarette 1989), *The Diseasing of America* (Peele 1989), *The Myth of Addiction* (Davies 1992), and *Addiction Is a Choice* (Schaler 2000). The twentieth century ended without popular or professional consensus or a resolution strategy on the nature of alcohol and other drug problems (White 2000b; White 2001a).

In response to the intense attacks on the disease basis of addiction, the National Institute on Drug Abuse (NIDA) began a decade-long research and public education campaign to re-educate the public about the nature of addiction. The first manifestation of this campaign was the 1997 article by Dr. Alan Leshner, then director of NIDA, published in one of the world's leading scientific journals entitled "Addiction is a Brain Disease, and It Matters" (Leshner 1997). Adding momentum to the "addiction is a brain disease" campaign was a 2005 special issue of *Nature* entitled "Focus on the Neurobiology of Addiction" (2005), in which a distinguished group of scientists assembled the latest evidence that addiction at its most fundamental essence is a neurobiological disorder.

Two years later in 2007, NIDA director Dr. Nora Volkov presented the historic lecture "The Neurobiology of Free Will," at the American Psychiatric Association's annual conference. This lecture revealed a maturing in the understanding of addiction as a brain disease, and contained the most complex and comprehensive description to date of how continued alcohol and other drug use selectively and progressively alters multiple brain regions to result in substance use eclipsing all other familial and social needs of the individual (White 2007b).

The media—with Bill Moyers's 1998 PBS special, *Moyers on Addiction: Close to Home*; the 2007 HBO special *Addiction: Why Can't They Just Stop?*; and *Time Magazine*'s July 16, 2007, cover story "How We Get Addicted"— has also been instrumental in transmitting these scientific findings to the public (White 2007b).

Although many recovery advocates have celebrated these scientific discoveries, some have made the point that emphasizing the chronic brain disease aspect is unlikely to reduce the stigma surrounding alcoholism and drug addiction unless it is accompanied by two companion communications: (1) With abstinence and proper care, addiction-induced brain impairments reverse themselves, and (2) millions of individuals have achieved long-term recovery and are leading healthy, meaningful, and productive lives. Including these additional messages is important because the public may construe the term *chronic* as meaning "forever" and "hopeless" (White 2007b).

# The Demographics of
# Alcohol Abuse and Alcoholism

Many different terms have been used by professionals, patients, and the media to describe drinking patterns and alcohol problems. Therefore, a useful place to begin our discussion of alcohol and alcoholism is to clarify the terms and definitions that the reader will frequently encounter in reading this book.

## Definitions of Drinking Patterns

Many people think that since whiskey is stronger, with a higher alcohol content than beer or wine, then drinking either of these wouldn't be as intoxicating as drinking hard liquor. So, instead they may drink three or four beers and believe they aren't as intoxicated as if they just had the same number of shots of whiskey.

To clarify this and for the purpose of consistency, alcohol researchers and public health officials have created the concept of a *standard drink*. A standard drink takes into account the different concentrations of alcohol in different beverages and is defined by the following (NIAAA 2008):

<u>Standard drink</u>: one standard drink equals
- 12 ounces of beer or wine cooler
- 8–9 ounces of malt liquor
- 5 ounces of table wine
- 3–4 ounces of fortified wine
- 2–3 ounces of cordial, liqueur, or aperitif
- 1.5 ounces (one shot) of brandy
- 1.5 ounces (one shot) of 80-proof distilled spirits

*Moderate alcohol use* is defined as up to two drinks per day for men and one drink per day for women and older persons. For most adults, drinking alcohol at this level causes few if any problems (NIAAA 2007a). Drinking becomes excessive, and is termed high-risk or hazardous drinking, when it causes or elevates the risk for alcohol-related problems or complicates the management of other health problems.

*High-risk* or *hazardous drinking* for men is more than four standard drinks in a day (or more than fourteen per week), and for women is more than three drinks in a day (or more than seven per week). Epidemiologic research has found this level of alcohol use to significantly heighten the risk for alcohol-related problems (Dawson, Grant, and Li 2005).

*Heavy drinking* is defined as five or more drinks in a day at least once a week for males, and four or more for females (NIAAA 2007a).

*Binge drinking* is defined as drinking five or more drinks on the same occasion (SAMHSA 2008a).

Explore or encourage your clients to explore the following NIAAA website for more information about "How Much Is Too Much?" drinking: http://rethinkingdrinking.niaaa.nih.gov/WhatCountsDrink/HowMuchIsTooMuch.asp.

# Definitions of Alcohol Problems

### Alcohol Abuse

The American Psychiatric Association (APA 2000) defines alcohol abuse as "a maladaptive pattern of alcohol use, leading to clinically significant impairment or distress as manifested by one or more behaviorally based criteria within a twelve-month period." These criteria all involve the continued use of alcohol despite consequences from drinking, which include failure to fulfill major role obligations at work, school, or home; situations where drinking is physically hazardous; legal problems; or social or interpersonal problems.

### Alcohol Dependence

Alcohol dependence is the term now used to describe alcoholism. The criteria that defines alcohol dependence is also used to diagnose core symptoms of dependence syndromes to all other drugs of abuse.

Alcohol and other drug dependence is defined by the American Society of Addiction Medicine (ASAM) as a primary, chronic, neurobiological disease, with genetic, psychosocial, and environmental factors influencing the development and manifestations. People with a substance addiction exhibit behaviors that include being unable to control their substance use, compulsive substance use, continued substance use despite harm, and urges and cravings for the substance (Ling, Wesson, and Smith 2005).

The American Psychiatric Association (APA 2000) defines alcohol dependence in the *Diagnostic and Statistical Manual of Mental Disorders (DSM-IV-TR)* as a maladaptive pattern of alcohol use leading to clinically significant impairment or distress, which is manifested by three or more behaviorally based criteria within a twelve-month period. These criteria include

1. tolerance, defined by either the need to dramatically increase alcohol use to achieve the desired effect, or a markedly diminished effect from the same level of continued alcohol use;

2.  withdrawal, as manifested by either an alcohol withdrawal syndrome or drinking to avoid alcohol withdrawal;

3.  alcohol often being used in larger amounts or over a longer period than intended;

4.  a persistent desire or unsuccessful attempts to cut down or control the use of alcohol;

5.  considerable time spent in activities necessary to obtain alcohol, use alcohol, or recover from the effects of alcohol;

6.  important social, occupational, or recreational activities given up or reduced because of alcohol use;

7.  alcohol use continuing despite knowledge of having a persistent physical or psychological problem caused or worsened by alcohol (e.g., continued drinking despite awareness that alcohol use makes an ulcer worse).

### Alcohol Use Disorders

The term *alcohol use disorders* refers to either alcohol abuse or alcohol dependence.

### Alcoholism

The authors define *alcoholism* the same as *alcohol dependence*. Both terms will be used in this book interchangeably.

### Substance Dependence

The authors use the term *substance dependence* to combine both alcohol and other drug dependence.

# Other Definitions

## Psychosocial Therapy

This is a broad term that means any psychological-based therapy delivered to individuals or groups that addresses the thinking, behavioral, relationship, or family problems of the alcoholic.

## Comorbid or Co-occurring

These terms refer to two or more conditions occurring at the same time. A person with both alcohol dependence and bipolar disorder (or another mental health disorder) is said to have comorbid alcohol dependence and bipolar disorder. Sometimes the term *co-occurring disorders* is referred to as *dual disorders* or *dual diagnosis*.

# Current Alcohol Use in the U.S.

According to the World Health Organization (WHO 2004), alcohol is consumed by roughly two billion people worldwide, of whom 76.3 million have an alcohol use disorder.

Alcohol is the most widely used drug in the U.S., with roughly 104 million current users in the last year. Of persons aged 12 and older in the U.S., 51.39% have used alcohol in the past month, and 23.28% have binged (five or more drinks per occasion) on alcohol in the past month (SAMHSA 2008a). Table 2.1 shows the rates of past-year alcohol use disorders (alcohol abuse and dependence) that were found in the U.S. in 2006 (adapted from OAS 2006).

Table 2.1

## Past-Year Rates of Alcohol Use Disorders
## in Demographic Subgroups

| Demographic subgroup | Percent (%) |
| --- | --- |
| *Age (12 and older)* | |
| 12–17 | 5.9 |
| 18–25 | 17.4 |
| 26–34 | 11.1 |
| 35–49 | 7.5 |
| 50 and older | 3.0 |
| *Gender (age 12 and older)* | |
| Males | 10.6 |
| Females | 4.9 |
| *Race (age 12 and older)* | |
| American Indian/Alaska Native | 14.0 |
| Hispanic | 8.2 |
| Caucasian | 7.9 |
| African American | 6.5 |
| Asian | 4.3 |
| *Marital status (age 18 and older)* | |
| Never married | 16.0 |
| Divorced or separated | 10.0 |
| Married | 4.6 |
| Widowed | 1.3 |

An interesting comparison between alcohol and other drugs involves looking at the percentage of persons who try each substance at least once *and* who develop an addiction to the same substance at some point in their lives (Anthony, Warner, and Kessler 1994; Chen and Anthony 2004; Hughes, Helzer, and Lindberg 2006):

Table 2.2

Lifetime Rates of Addiction among Persons Who Use
Specific Substances One or More Times

| Substance | Percent (%) of people who become addicted |
|---|---|
| Nicotine | 32 |
| Heroin | 23 |
| Crack | 20 |
| Powdered cocaine | 17 |
| *Alcohol* | *15* |
| Stimulants other than cocaine | 11 |
| Cannabis | 9 |
| Sedatives | 9 |
| Prescription opiates | 9 |
| Psychedelics | 5 |
| Inhalants | 4 |

Note the highest percentage of addiction among all the drugs: nicotine. Why do you think that is? Perhaps your own investigation into this matter might prove especially meaningful.

Changes in alcohol use between 1991–1992 and 2001–2002 have been found. Persons meeting the criteria for alcohol abuse increased, but those meeting criteria for alcohol dependence decreased (Grant, Dawson, et al. 2004).

## Per Capita Use of Alcohol by Country, Ranking of U.S.

This table shows the per capita recorded alcohol consumption (in liters of pure alcohol) among adults who are 15 years of age or older. (One liter equals 33.32 ounces.) Data is for the year 2003.

Table 2.3

### Per Capita Recorded Alcohol Consumption

| Country | Liters of pure alcohol |
|---|---|
| Turkey | 1.4 |
| Kenya | 1.5 |
| Israel | 2.5 |
| Cuba | 2.3 |
| China | 5.2 |
| Norway | 5.5 |
| Sweden | 6.0 |
| Japan | 7.6 |
| Canada | 7.8 |
| *USA* | *8.6* |
| Italy | 8.0 |
| United Kingdom | 11.8 |
| Russian Federation | 10.3 |
| Germany | 12.0 |
| Ireland | 13.7 |

*(Excerpted from WHO 2008)*

## Drinking Patterns in the U.S.

The following table provides an overall summary of the drinking patterns among the U.S. drinking population (ages 18 and older). As mentioned on page 42, the established safe limit for the number of drinks on any day is no more than four for men or three for women and in a typical week no more than fourteen for men or seven for women (NIAAA 2007a):

Table 2.4

### Frequency of Drinking Patterns among Adults in the U.S.

| Drinking pattern | How common | Frequency of alcohol use disorders with this pattern |
|---|---|---|
| Never exceed the daily or weekly limits | 72% | Fewer than 1 in 100 |
| Exceed only the daily limit (More than 8 out of 10 in this group exceed the daily limit *less than once a week*) | 16% | 1 in 5 |
| Exceed both daily and weekly limits (8 out of 10 in this group exceed the daily limit *once a week or more*) | 10% | 1 in 2 |

Between 1993 and 2001, the average yearly number of binge-drinking episodes per person increased from 6.3 to 7.4, a 17% increase. Men accounted for 81% of binge-drinking episodes. Although rates of binge-drinking episodes were highest in persons aged 18 to 25 years, 69% of binge-drinking episodes occurred in persons aged 26 years or older. Overall, 47% of binge-drinking episodes occurred among otherwise moderate (i.e., nonheavy) drinkers, and 73% of all binge drinkers were moderate drinkers. Most significantly, binge drinkers were fourteen times more likely to drive while impaired by alcohol compared with nonbinge drinkers (Naimi et al. 2003).

Heavy drinking contributes to illnesses in each of the top three causes of death: heart disease, cancer, and stroke. The Centers for Disease Control and Prevention (CDC) ranks alcohol as the third-leading cause of preventable death in the United States (Mokdad et al. 2004).

As demonstrated in table 2.4, three out of ten U.S. adults engage in at-risk drinking patterns and would benefit from counseling or a referral for a detailed assessment. The CDC also links excessive alcohol use, such as heavy drinking and binge drinking, to immediate health risks that endanger the drinker and those around him or her. These include traffic fatalities, unintentional firearm injuries, domestic violence and child abuse, unsafe sexual behaviors, sexual assault, miscarriage and stillbirth, and birth defects (RSA 2009; NIAAA 2008).

## Drinking Patterns in Persons under 18 Years (Underage Drinkers)

Currently, there are an estimated 10.8 million underage drinkers in the U.S. According to the 2005 Monitoring the Future (MTF) Survey, three-fourths of twelfth graders, more than two-thirds of tenth graders, and about two in every five eighth graders drank alcohol in their lifetimes. Forty-five percent of twelfth graders, 34% of tenth graders, and 17% of eighth graders had used alcohol in the previous month, which is more than cigarettes and marijuana combined. Young drinkers tend to drink heavily when they do drink. The MTF data found that 1% of eighth graders, 22% of tenth graders, and 29% of twelfth graders binge-drank (five or more drinks) within the past two weeks (Johnston et al. 2008).

Another survey underscored how common binge drinking is for young drinkers. According to the results of the 2003 National Youth Risk Behavior Survey, 44.9% of high school students reported drinking alcohol during the past thirty days (28.8% binge drank and 16.1% drank alcohol but did not binge drink) (Miller et al. 2007). Although girls had higher rates of current nonbinge drinking, the actual rates of binge drinking were similar among boys and girls. The rates of binge drinking were found to increase with age and school grade.

Also found was that teens who drank heavily when they drank suffered more problems and engaged in more high-risk behavior than nondrinkers and nonbinge drinkers. Students who binge drank were more likely to report poor school performance, ride with an intoxicated driver, be currently sexually active, smoke tobacco, be a victim of dating violence, attempt suicide, and use illicit drugs. A strong association was found between the frequency of binge drinking and the prevalence of other high-risk behaviors (Miller et al. 2007).

A national survey provided information on how adolescent drinkers obtain alcohol (SAMHSA 2008b). More than 40% of underage drinkers (persons aged 12 to 20 who drank in the past thirty days) reported obtaining alcohol from adults at no cost (SAMHSA 2008b). The same survey also found that more than 6% of underage drinkers were given alcohol by their parents in the past month, and that the younger the drinker, the more likely they obtained alcohol from a parent, guardian, or other family member.

Underage drinking is also common in the military. According to the most recent (2005) U.S. Department of Defense Survey, 62.3% of underage military members drank at least once a year. The same survey found that 21% of active duty military personnel aged 20 and younger reported heavy alcohol use—defined as drinking five or more drinks per typical drinking occasion—within the past thirty days (Bray and Hourani 2007).

## Drinking Patterns in College Students

Persons in their late teens and early twenties are the most likely to drink heavily. In 2001–2002, about 70% of young adults, or about 19 million people, reported drinking in the previous year (Chen, Dufour, and Yi 2004). Among college students, 4 out of 5 drink alcohol, including almost 60% of students aged 18 to 20. Roughly 2 of every 5 college students of all ages reported binge drinking at least once in the past two weeks. However, colleges vary widely in the binge-drinking rates of their students, ranging from 1% to more than 70%. The consequences of excessive and underage drinking affect virtually all college campuses, college communities, and college students, whether they are younger or older than the minimum legal drinking age and whether or not they drink (NIAAA 2006).

Excessive alcohol use among members of the Greek system on college campuses has long been a concern of the academic community. Numerous studies on the drinking patterns of fraternity and sorority members (Greeks) have shown that Greeks drink more frequently and more heavily, show more alcohol dependence symptoms, are more likely to initiate and continue abusive alcohol use patterns, and are more likely to experience alcohol-related problems than are nonaffiliated students (non-Greeks). Although it is well established that affiliation with the Greek system on college campuses is related to problematic levels of college alcohol use, one study found that alcohol use patterns among Greek members was no longer different from their non-Greek counterparts three years after college (Sher, Bartholow, and Nanda 2001).

## Special Populations and Alcohol Use

Racial and ethnic differences in alcohol use disorders have been observed in the U.S. Native Americans have the highest rates of alcohol dependence (Lamarine 1988; May and Moran 1995; Frank, Moore, and Ames 2000), and alcohol dependence is more frequent in non-African American races (Grant and Dawson 2006). Alcohol use in African Americans rises in their late twenties, a period when Hispanic and Caucasian use lessens (Fothergill and Ensminger 2006). African Americans suffer worse consequences than white Americans, such as loss of control, binge drinking, and health and interpersonal problems (Fothergill and Ensminger 2006), and African Americans are more likely than Caucasians to need treatment for alcohol and other drug abuse (Fothergill and Ensminger 2006).

In the U.S., the overall prevalence of alcohol abuse and dependence in 2001–2002 was more common among males and younger persons. Alcohol abuse was more prevalent among Caucasians than among African Americans, Asians, and Hispanics. The prevalence of alcohol dependence was higher in Caucasians, Native Americans, and Hispanics than Asians. In the ten-year period between 1991–1992 and 2001–2002, alcohol abuse increased while alcohol dependence declined in the U.S. Increases in alcohol abuse were observed among males, females, and young African American and Hispanic minorities, while the rates of alcohol dependence rose among males, young African American females, and Asian males (Grant, Dawson, et al. 2004).

Studying the rates of alcohol use disorders among persons from different racial and ethnic backgrounds can be challenging. For example, drinking rates are very different among Hispanics of Mexican, Puerto Rican, and Cuban origin. Similar differences exist among Asian Americans from various ethnic backgrounds and among members of the different Native American tribes (Caetano, Clark, and Tam 1998).

### Native Americans

The high prevalence of alcohol use and its related problems among American Indians may stem from a variety of factors, ranging from the influence of the past European colonizers to current social and cultural factors (Beauvais 1998).

### African Americans

Although more African Americans than Caucasians abstain from drinking, similar levels of frequent heavy drinking are found in both groups (Jones-Webb 1998).

### Hispanics

Patterns of alcohol use among Hispanics in the United States vary considerably. These differences between Hispanic groups in drinking patterns may be related to variations in the culture of origin, the result of the individual ethnic group's merging into mainstream culture, or a combination of both factors (Randolph et al. 1998).

### Asian/Pacific Islander

People of Asian and Pacific Islander (API) descent generally have lower rates of alcohol use and alcoholism than do other groups, although large variations in drinking behaviors are found between different API subgroups.

Drinking and heavy-drinking rates are much higher among Japanese-Americans than among Chinese-Americans. Also, many Southeast Asian immigrants are at particularly high risk for heavy drinking, especially those who left their homelands during or after the Vietnam War. Among this group, heavy alcohol use may result from war and refugee-related psychological problems and trauma (Makimoto 1998).

### Women

Sixty percent of women in the U.S. have at least one drink a year. Among women who drink, 13% have more than seven drinks per week (NIAAA 2008).

Men have traditionally consumed more alcohol than women, but over the past thirty years, women (especially teens and college students) have steadily been narrowing this gap in consumption. During the 1950s only 6% of college women drank one or more times a week (Straus and Bacon 1953); in 2001, nearly 17% reported drinking ten or more times in the past month (Wechsler et al. 2002). In 1986, the frequency of binge drinking among men was 24% higher than women; in 1997 this dropped to 16% (O'Malley and Johnston 2002; LaBrie et al. 2009).

A national survey found that roughly 18% of women have had an alcohol or other drug problem (abuse or dependence) during their lives, with the highest rates occurring between the ages of 21 and 34. However, older women may have hidden problems, with one report finding that 25.6 million American women over the age of 60 abuse substances such as alcohol, prescription drugs, and cigarettes, resulting in $30 billion in health care expenses (Hazelden Jan. 1999).

### Active Military and Veterans

The prevalence of heavy drinking is higher among active military members (16.1%) than among civilians of comparable age and gender (12.9%). About one in four Marines (25.4%) and Army soldiers (24.5%) engages in heavy drinking. This high prevalence of heavy drinking has raised the concern over combat readiness. Also, members of the Army have shown an increase in heavy drinking from 2002 to 2005. These patterns of alcohol use are often acquired in the military and persist into civilian life, and are associated with the high rate of alcohol-related medical problems among Armed Forces veterans (RSA 2009).

Veterans with combat experience may be at elevated risk of developing alcohol use disorders. The effects of combat exposure on subsequent alcohol use have been shown to persist for over a decade after extremely stressful exposure. Branchey, Davis, and Lieber (1984) found that close to 60% of a group of combat veterans drank heavily at the time of their study, versus 25% of a group of noncombat veterans from the Vietnam and Korean War eras.

A study examined the relationship between specific combat experiences and alcohol use among Iraqi war veterans three to four months after they returned from deployment. Soldiers who had higher rates of exposure to the threat of death or injury were significantly more likely to exhibit an alcohol use disorder, while solders exposed to atrocities had the highest rates of alcohol use disorders and alcohol-related behavioral problems (Wilk et al. 2010). Among Iraq and Afghanistan war veterans receiving care from the Department of Veterans Affairs between 2001 and 2005, roughly 20% were diagnosed with an alcohol or substance use disorder (Seal et al. 2007).

Veterans exposed to wartime violence are also at risk of developing a variety of behavioral and emotional problems such as post-traumatic stress disorder (PTSD). Many veterans with PTSD abuse alcohol or other substances in an attempt to lessen the distress of the PTSD symptoms. Among Vietnam-era veterans seeking treatment for PTSD a decade after the war, 60–80% had a concurrent diagnosis of substance abuse, alcohol abuse, or alcohol dependence (Keane et al. 1988).

Veterans who took part in war crimes evaluated six to fifteen years after the Vietnam War reported more stress symptoms and greater use of heroin and marijuana than did other veterans. The ability or inability of the solders to dehumanize the victims afterwards contributed to the subsequent emotional response to the experience (Yager, Laufer, and Gallops 1984). A study of the longitudinal course of PTSD and alcohol/substance abuse among Vietnam combat veterans found that the onset of symptoms typically occurred at the time of exposure to combat trauma, and rapidly increased in the first few years after combat. With the passage of more time, symptom severity transitioned into a chronic and unremitting course.

Hyperarousal symptoms such as always feeling on guard and feeling easily startled developed first, followed by avoidant symptoms and finally the intrusive symptoms such as flashbacks. The onset of alcohol and substance abuse typically coincided with the onset of PTSD symptoms, and increased alcohol and substance use paralleled the increase in symptom severity. Overall, patients reported that alcohol, marijuana, heroin, and benzodiazepines (Valium, Ativan, Xanax) lessened PTSD symptoms, while cocaine worsened the hyperarousal symptoms. Sadly, the results of the study did not find a relationship between treatment interventions and the ability to interrupt the natural course of the PTSD and substance abuse (Bremner et al. 1996).

However, not all studies have found a strong association between combat experience and risk of alcohol use disorders. Among Vietnam-era veterans, military service in a war zone was found to have only a modest long-term effect on alcohol drinking patterns (Goldberg et al. 1990).

### The Elderly

Although alcohol use tends to decline through adulthood (SAMHSA 1999), a large proportion of older adults continue or begin to drink heavily. In community samples (Mirand and Welte 1996), the prevalence rates of problem drinking among older adults range from 0.9 to 9% with rates up to 24% found among older medical and psychiatric patients (Moore et al. 1999; Patterson and Jeste 1999; Blow et al. 2000; Friedmann et al. 1999; Ganry et al. 2000). Similar to younger adults, older adult males had higher prevalence rates than females (Hazelden Dec. 2001).

Prevalence rates of alcohol or drug dependence among the elderly may be underestimated because of difficulties with detection and proper assessment. Assessment often focuses on social, legal, and occupational consequences of drinking, which may not apply to older adults. In addition, the commonly used diagnostic criteria of substance dependence do not readily apply to older adults (Hazelden Dec. 2001).

## Comorbid (Co-occurring or Dual) Conditions

An estimated 1.1% of persons in the U.S. have a comorbid alcohol and other drug use disorder (Arias and Kranzler 2008), making the simultaneous use of alcohol and other drugs a major public health concern. The interaction of a concurrent alcohol and other drug abuse or dependence can lead to dangerous consequences, such as overdose or death (Martin 2008).

### Alcoholism and Psychiatric Disorders

Alcohol dependence can precede, co-occur with, or result from many psychiatric conditions, including mood disorders (such as major depression), anxiety disorders, psychotic disorders, eating disorders (such as bulimia), and personality disorders (such as antisocial personality disorder). Psychological factors may contribute to problem drinking, including the need for relief from anxiety or depression, unresolved relationship conflict, and interpersonal loss.

Genetic factors can increase the risk of both alcohol and other drug abuse or dependence. Some of these factors also increase the risk of various psychiatric disorders that are characterized by impulsive or disinhibited behavior (i.e., externalizing disorders) such as antisocial personality disorder, attention-deficit/hyperactivity disorder (ADHD), and conduct disorder (Dick and Agrawal 2008).

Epidemiological studies have found that among persons with alcohol dependence, 15.15% and 17.75% also met criteria for a depressive disorder or anxiety disorder, respectively (Grant, Stinson, et al. 2006; Grant, Stinson, et al. 2004).

Personality disorders (PDs), such as antisocial disorders, are common among alcoholics. Among individuals with a current alcohol use disorder, 28.6% have a PD, and 16.4% of persons with a PD have a current alcohol use disorder. Overall, alcohol use disorders are most strongly associated with antisocial, histrionic, and dependent PDs. The association between obsessive-compulsive, histrionic, schizoid, and antisocial PDs and specific alcohol and other drug use disorders is higher among women than men (Grant, Stinson, et al. 2006; Grant, Stinson, et al. 2004). Alcoholics are twenty-one times more likely to have a diagnosis of antisocial personality disorder than are nonalcoholics (Regier et al. 1990), and PDs (especially antisocial PD) are more common among alcoholics with early age of onset of problem drinking, heavier alcohol use, and a more severe course of alcohol dependence (Bottlender, Preuss, and Soyka 2006).

Alcohol use disorders are very common among people with schizophrenia. Several biological and psychosocial factors may contribute to this comorbidity. Schizophrenic patients with alcohol use disorder are more likely to have social, legal, and medical problems compared with nonproblem drinking schizophrenic patients. Alcohol use disorders also complicate the course and treatment of schizophrenia (Drake and Mueser 2002).

Alcoholism and bipolar disorder often co-occur, and the presence of alcoholism worsens the course and prognosis of bipolar disorder and makes it more difficult to treat. Although it is unclear why these conditions co-occur, researchers have proposed that one disorder may contribute to the development of the other. Genetic risk factors common to both disorders may also play a role (Sonne and Brady 2002).

People suffering from social anxiety and social phobia disorder have an excessive and irrational fear that they will do something embarrassing in social situations or display obvious symptoms of anxiety such as blushing or sweating that will lead to humiliation. People with social anxiety also have a higher incidence of alcohol use disorders compared with the general population, possibly due to their attempts to manage the interpersonal anxiety (Book and Randall 2002).

Alcohol use disorders also frequently co-occur with behavioral disorders such as compulsive gambling and eating disorders (Grant, Kushner, and Kim 2002; Grilo, Sinha, and O'Malley 2002).

### Comorbid Conditions with Adolescent Alcohol Use Disorders

Several factors contribute to adolescent alcohol and other drug use, including psychological, psychiatric, environmental, and peer and family influences. Psychological risk factors include personality characteristics such as novelty seeking or aggressiveness, low self-esteem, and exposure to stressful and traumatic life events. Co-occurring psychiatric disorders include depression, anxiety disorders, conduct disorder, and attention-deficit/hyperactivity disorder (Deas and Thomas 2002).

Attention-deficit/hyperactivity disorder (ADHD) is a childhood mental disorder characterized by inattention, impulsivity, and hyperactivity, and may contribute to alcohol-related problems in adolescence and adulthood. ADHD is highly associated with the early onset of drinking and progression to abuse or dependence. The presence of ADHD in persons with alcohol abuse or dependence has important treatment implications because treatment approaches must take into consideration their deficits in attention and impulse control (Smith, Molina, and Pelham 2002; Molina and Pelham 2003).

Children with antisocial behavior and related mental disorders such as conduct disorder and oppositional defiant disorder are more likely to develop alcohol problems during adolescence. This may be due to a common origin of both disorders; both antisocial behavior and alcohol use disorders may result from common genetic or environmental influences coupled with poor impulse control in the person. Programs aimed at reducing antisocial and impulsive behavior during childhood may prevent the future development of alcohol problems (Clark, Vanukov, and Cornelius 2002).

## Risk Factors for Alcohol Abuse and Dependence

The regulation of all behavior, including drinking behavior, is influenced by the interaction of genes, brain transmitter chemicals, and environmental influences (Schuessler 2004). The development of alcohol dependence is also determined by multiple factors, including genetic makeup, familial influence, environmental experience, and the interaction of these factors.

### Genetics

The role of a genetic influence in the development of alcoholism has been confirmed by several investigations. These include a fourfold risk of alcohol dependence in relatives of alcoholics. Identical twins of alcohol-dependent subjects carry a higher risk for alcoholism than do fraternal twins or full siblings. And adopted children of alcoholics have the same fourfold increased risk for this disorder as do offspring raised by their alcohol-dependent parent (Goodwin et al. 1974; Cotton 1979; Prescott and Kendler 1999). Studies have confirmed that identical twins, who share the same genes, are about twice as likely as fraternal twins, who share an average of 50% of their genes, to resemble each other in terms of developing an alcohol use disorder (NIAAA 2003).

Many genes play a role in shaping alcoholism risk. Some of these genes direct the production of proteins involved in the signaling process between neurons (brain cells), while other genes encode the enzymes that metabolize (break down) alcohol (NIAAA 2004). One well-studied relationship between genes and alcoholism involves variations in the liver enzymes that metabolize alcohol. Persons with this genetic variation accumulate greater amounts of the toxic alcohol metabolic product acetaldehyde, causing the symptoms of flushing, nausea, and rapid heartbeat.

Genes associated with flushing are more common among Asian populations than other ethnic groups, and the rates of excessive alcohol use are correspondingly lower in these Asian groups (Luczak et al. 2001; Suwaki et al. 2001; Fromme et al. 2004).

Persons vary greatly in their response to stress. These individual differences are also genetically influenced and help shape susceptibility to psychiatric illness, including alcoholism. Research suggests that genes affecting the activity of the neurotransmitters (brain chemicals) serotonin and GABA (gamma-aminobutyric acid) may play a role in alcoholism risk by influencing response to alcohol or vulnerability to stress (NIAAA 2003).

Although the offspring of alcoholics are four times more likely to develop alcoholism than children of nonalcoholics (Gilbertson, Prather, and Nixon 2008), and 40 to 60% of the risk for alcoholism is genetically determined, genes alone do not preordain that someone will be alcoholic. The development of alcohol dependence is a complex problem largely involving the interaction between genetic and environmental factors (Hazelden Aug. 2001).

### Early Environment

In general, exposure to stressors early in life and the cumulative effect of chronic stress exposure result in long-lasting neuroendocrine, physiological, behavioral, and psychological changes. These changes negatively affect the development of brain systems involved in learning, motivation, and the capacity to handle stress.

There is also evidence that the greater the number of stressors an individual is exposed to, the higher the risk of developing addiction (Sinha 2008).

### Deficient Infant Caregiving

Considerable brain development occurs during the first two years of life, and this developmental process is very susceptible to adverse influences from the environment. A chaotic, unstable caregiving environment during infancy may create an overreactive stress response system, resulting in subsequent impairments in the ability to regulate emotions, motivation-reward, and impulse control that constitute a vulnerability to development of an addictive disorder (Kalinichev, Easterling, and Holtzman 2003; Pryce and Feldon 2003; Goodman 2009).

Researchers have found that children who were adopted from deprived institutional settings before age three and a half display marked degrees of inattention and overactivity at six and eleven years of age, as well as deficits in the executive functions of planning, inhibition, set-shifting (ability to change behavior in response to change in the environment), working memory, generativity (concern for others), and action monitoring (capacity to evaluate correctness of response to a current situation) (Goodman 2009).

These executive function deficits were most severe in children who had experienced more than six months of institutional maternal deprivation (Colvert et al. 2008; Stevens et al. 2008). While deficient infant caregiving has been associated with many neurobiological abnormalities, the most widely reported are hypersensitivity of the stress response systems (Caldji, Diorio, and Meaney 2000; Holmes et al. 2005; Aisa et al. 2008; Ladd et al. 2004; Plotsky et al. 2005; Goodman 2009).

### Childhood Stress and Trauma

Substantial evidence has linked adverse childhood experiences and later development of substance use disorders. A study of female identical twins where one twin, but not the other, had experienced childhood sexual abuse, found the twins exposed to sexual abuse had a substantially increased risk for alcoholism and other drug addictions (Kendler et al. 2000). Researchers following substantiated cases of child abuse and neglect into young adulthood have verified the causal role played by childhood victimization in the development of alcohol abuse (Schuck and Widom 2001). Childhood sexual abuse also increases the overall risk for the development of numerous psychiatric disorders (Fergusson and Mullen 1999; Bulik, Prescott, and Kendler 2001; Goodman 2009).

Children who have been sexually or physically abused manifest either abnormally elevated or abnormally flat cortisol (a stress hormone) levels in response to stress, and childhood abuse may initially sensitize the stress response system, creating a heightened vulnerability to stress during childhood and increasing the risk for stress-related disorders. Changes in the brain from childhood abuse may include the abnormally excessive release of the stress hormone called corticotropin-releasing hormone during stress (Fries et al. 2005; Goodman 2009). Also, the greater the duration of childhood physical abuse, the more likely the person is to later develop an alcohol or other drug addiction (Lo and Cheng 2007).

Together, these processes enhance the risk of developing an addictive disorder by facilitating the atrophy, or shrinkage, of two brain regions called the hippocampus and cortex.

The resultant reduction of brain cell and brain circuit integrity in these two brain regions worsens the ability to modulate or inhibit stress or fear responses that are generated by other brain regions, and the ability to block or slow the release of other stress hormones (de Geus et al. 2007). These stress-induced processes may degrade executive functioning, impair the ability to regulate one's emotions, and increase the risk of problems with impulse control.

Studies have also found that the chronic stress of neglectful or abusive parental care during childhood results in a major stress response system in the body (the hypothalamic-pituitary-adrenal axis, or HPA) that is hypersensitive to psychosocial stressors and a midbrain that produces an exaggerated response to triggers of dopamine release. Both of these conditions are highly conducive to the development of addictive disorders (Pruessner et al. 2004; Goodman 2009).

We currently don't know whether alterations in brain chemistry observed in chronic addicts are caused by environmental factors such as physical or sexual abuse which came before the substance abuse, or by the long-term alcohol or other drug use itself (Cleck and Blendy 2008).

### Psychosocial Environment

Many people drink in response to stress, and this drinking can increase when stress becomes chronic (Walter et al. 2005). People are more likely to consume alcohol in response to stress when other means of coping are absent, when alcohol is available, and when the person believes that alcohol will relieve stress. Many factors influence whether and to what extent a person will drink for stress relief, including genetic factors, the individual's pre-stress drinking pattern, the intensity and type of stressor, the sense of control over the stressor, and the presence or lack of social support (Tsigos and Chrousos 1995).

The physiological response to stress, and the perception of what is stressful, is influenced by genetic factors and by the early caregiving environment. Exposure to severe or chronic stress in childhood can increase the vulnerability to alcohol problems by permanently altering the stress responses that are mediated by HPA axis activity and locus coeruleus (brain region involved in mediating the emotional and physiological response to stress) function. Abnormal activity and function in these two brain networks in turn alters the response to alcohol (De Bellis 2002; Pohorecky 1991).

Although a direct relationship between stress, drinking behavior, and the development of alcoholism has not been established, the connection is considerably stronger in persons who are already alcoholic. Relapse in abstinent alcoholics can be triggered by personally threatening, severe, or chronic stress, although the likelihood of relapse is reduced by sufficient coping skills, self-efficacy, and social support (Brown et al. 1995).

The beliefs and attitudes (expectancies) that people harbor toward alcohol can influence how they drink. People are motivated to drink alcohol, sometimes to excess, by social influences, social norms, and social contexts. The perception of social reward through cultivating and maintaining a certain image, and the assumed avoidance of social rejection, can serve as powerful motivators to drink (NIAAA 2000). Experience with the pharmacologic effects of alcohol and vicarious learning from parents, peers, and media portrayals of drinking can result in the development of expectancies regarding the effects of drinking. These expectancies can then influence the decision to consume alcohol.

Expectancies about drinking are typically formed much earlier in life than the first drinking experience and can predict future drinking behavior. For instance, young teenagers who believe that alcohol makes it easier to socialize will later drink significantly more than their peers who did not share this belief. Expectancies and the immediate effects of alcohol are mutually reinforcing, and some researchers believe that expectancy bridges the gap between the pleasurable effects of alcohol and the decision to drink in a given situation (NIAAA 2000; Smith et al. 1995).

The impact of the social environment is also seen in women who drink, or drink more than they normally would, to fulfill what they believe are the expectations of others such as peers or boyfriends. A study showed that female college students overestimate the amount of alcohol that males want their female friends, dating partners, and sexual partners to consume, and that this misperception affects females' drinking behavior (LaBrie et al. 2009).

A large percentage of women mistakenly believe that males want them to drink to risky levels, defined as five or more drinks, especially in the context of female friends and sexual partners. Also found was that women drink more than they otherwise would in order to make themselves appear attractive and desirable in the pursuit of intimate relationships and attention from male peers (LaBrie et al. 2009).

### The Influence of Family

In addition to the genes passed on from parent to child, and the direct effects of childhood abuse or neglect, other factors encountered in the family environment can increase the risk of developing an alcohol problem when the following are present:

- an alcoholic parent who is depressed or has other psychological problems,
- abuse of alcohol or other drugs by both parents,

- severe parental alcohol abuse, or
- family conflicts that escalate to aggression or violence (NIAAA 2007b).

Although a positive family history of alcoholism is a risk factor for alcoholism, and the risk of alcohol dependence is three to four times greater among the first-degree relatives of persons with alcohol dependence, *most* children of alcoholics do not become problem drinkers (APA 2000).

### Cultural Influences

Traditional cultural expectations of alcohol use provide specific, often gender-based norms that designate approval or disapproval over specific drinking behaviors (Bussey and Bandura 1999). For instance, traditional Mexican gender-based cultural expectations communicate a message of community disapproval of alcohol use by Mexican women while communicating an acceptance of it among men. This cultural expectation creates great differences in the rates of alcohol use by Mexican men relative to Mexican women, which is much greater than the differences between white American men and women (Castro and Coe 2007).

### Gene-Environment Interaction

Zucker et al. (1996) described a pattern of influence for the development of alcoholism, which includes the following genetic, psychological, and environmental factors:

1. A heightened genetic vulnerability for alcoholism (genetic)

2. A temperament that results in relationship problems and conflict (psychological)

3. A child-rearing environment that may encourage problem alcohol use (environmental)

4. A family structure with conflict within its boundaries (environmental and psychological)

Research involving children of alcoholics (COAs) has found protective and risk factors in the development of alcoholism. Parenting approach plays an important role. Parenting influences can be placed into two categories:

- Alcohol-specific
- Nonalcohol-specific

*Alcohol-specific* parenting influences include the modeling of parental drinking behavior and thinking positively about alcohol and its anticipated effect (alcohol expectancies). These influences probably affect COAs more strongly than children of nonalcoholics.

In contrast, *nonalcohol-specific* influences, such as parent–child interactions that favor aggressive, antisocial behavior, or parents with psychological disorders, similarly increase the risk for alcohol problems in children of both alcoholics and nonalcoholics (Jacob and Johnson 1997).

Further research on COAs has found differences between sons of alcoholics (SOAs) and sons of nonalcoholics (non-SOAs). These differences may increase the risk in SOAs of developing alcohol problems. For example, SOAs are likely to react to stressful stimuli more intensely than do non-SOAs and to exhibit physiological responses, such as increased heart rate, that are associated with heightened tension and anxiety. Following alcohol use, SOAs' reactions to both stressful and nonstressful stimuli are substantially reduced compared with non-SOAs. SOAs also tend to have a more heightened reward experience and less impairment from alcohol than non-SOAs, both of which predict future alcohol problems (Finn and Justus 1997).

## CHAPTER 3

# Societal Impact of Alcohol Use
# and Dependence

The abuse of alcohol is linked to many harmful consequences, not only for the drinker, but also for his or her family and friends. In addition, the community and society where the drinker lives and works incur consequences. Some of the social harms commonly associated with drinking include crime, accidents and injuries, illness, disease and death, and disrupted school and work performance and productivity (Gmel and Rehm 2003).

## Social Impact

When someone experiences alcohol problems, the negative effects of drinking exert a toll not only on the drinker, but also on his or her partner and other family members (McCrady and Hay 1987). About one child in every four (28.6%) in the U.S. is exposed to alcohol abuse or dependence in the family (Grant 2000). The widely documented association between alcohol use and interpersonal violence clearly demonstrates how alcohol use negatively impacts the family (Roberts, Roberts, and Leonard 1999). Family problems that are likely to co-occur with alcohol problems include the following (Brennan, Moos, and Kelly 1994):

- Violence
- Marital conflict
- Infidelity
- Jealousy
- Economic insecurity
- Divorce
- Fetal alcohol effects

Drinking problems may negatively alter marital and family functioning, but there is also evidence that they can increase as a consequence of marital and family problems (Magura and Shapiro 1988). Heavy drinking and alcohol abuse is also associated with unemployment, and can likewise result in economic consequences for the individual and emotional strain on the family. Heavy drinking can lead to financial hardship and poverty through a number of means, including lowered wages due to missed work and poor job performance, lost employment opportunities, increased medical expenses for illness and accidents, legal cost of alcohol-related offenses, and reduced loan eligibility (WHO 2004).

## Public Health, Morbidity, and Mortality

Alcohol use contributes to a wide range of negative health consequences to the drinker and those in proximity to the drinker, such as his or her friends and/or colleagues at work. Some of these consequences occur during intoxication, while others are the result of chronic alcohol abuse (Rehm et al. 1996).

### Ranking of Alcohol in Causes of Disease and Death

The leading causes of death in 2000 were

- tobacco (435,000 deaths, or 18.1% of all U.S. deaths),
- poor diet and physical inactivity (365,000 deaths; 15.2%), and
- *alcohol* consumption (85,000 deaths; 3.5%) (Mokdad et al. 2004).

Other specific causes of death were microbial agents (75,000), toxic agents (55,000), motor vehicle accidents (43,000), incidents involving firearms (29,000), sexual behaviors (20,000), and illicit drug use (17,000) (Mokdad et al. 2004).

## Impact of Underage Drinking

Injury is the leading cause of death among young people in the U.S., and alcohol is the leading contributor to injury deaths. In the U.S., an estimated 5,000 persons under age 21 die each year from injuries caused by drinking (USDHHS 2007). These include

- motor vehicle crashes (about 1,900 deaths),
- homicides (about 1,600 deaths), and
- suicides (about 300 deaths).

## Impact of College Drinking

Alcohol use among college students aged 18–24 results in a wide range of injuries and criminal conduct (Hingson et al. 2005):

- Deaths: An estimated 1,700 college students die each year from alcohol-related unintentional injuries, including motor vehicle accidents; roughly half of these students were under age 21.
- Injuries: An estimated 599,000 students are unintentionally injured under the influence of alcohol every year.
- Assaults: It is estimated that more than 696,000 students are assaulted by another student who is under the influence of alcohol each year, including 430,000 by a college student under age 21.
- Sexual Assault: An estimated 97,000 students between the ages of 18 and 24 are victims of alcohol-related sexual assault or date rape each year, with about half being students under 21.
- Unsafe Sex: It is estimated that more than 400,000 college students had unprotected sex as a result of drinking, and more than 100,000 students each year report having been too intoxicated to know if they consented to having sex.

- Academic Problems: An estimated 25% of college students report academic consequences from alcohol use, including missing class, falling behind, doing poorly on exams or papers, and receiving lower grades.
- Vandalism: Roughly 11% of college student drinkers report that they have damaged property while intoxicated.

## Accidents and Injuries

Unintentional injury is the leading cause of death in the U.S. among those under 44 years of age. More than 100,000 Americans die annually as a result of accidental injuries, nearly half of which are from motor vehicle crashes, and the remainder from falls, burns, poisonings, and drownings, among other causes. Unintentional injury accounts for an even higher rate of morbidity, with the rate of serious injury estimated to be more than 300 times the mortality rate (Vyrostek, Annest, and Ryan 2004), and it is estimated that more than 70 million Americans annually require medical treatment for nonfatal unintentional injuries. Intentional injuries, those resulting from violence-related events (homicides and assaults) and from suicide (attempted and completed), also account for substantial proportions of fatalities and those requiring medical intervention.

A substantial amount of literature exists on the association of alcohol and injury. Longitudinal studies in the general population have found injuries to be more common among those who are alcohol dependent and heavy drinkers than among others (Anda, Williamson, and Remington 1988; Klatsky, Friedman, and Siegelaub 1981). Other data supporting the alcohol-injury link have come from a variety of sources including reports of trauma histories among alcoholics, case series reports from hospital and coroner records, and epidemiologic studies, many of which have been conducted in hospital emergency rooms (ERs) (Cherpitel et al. 2009; reviewed in Cherpitel 1993, 2007; Roizen 1989; Romelsjö 1995).

While alcohol is known to be associated with injury, its association with severity of injury has been an issue of ongoing debate, and the literature suggests mixed findings (Li et al. 1997). Alcohol may be significantly associated with increased risk of serious injury, possibly due to other factors that are associated with alcohol use, such as speeding, not wearing seat belts or helmets, and other risk-taking behaviors. On the other hand, alcohol intoxication itself can bias injury severity scores upward (Waller 1988), and those more severely injured are also more likely to reach the ER sooner, and consequently more likely to have a positive (and higher) blood alcohol concentration (BAC) than those less severely injured who arrive later.

More attention has been paid to fatal accidents compared to nonfatal accidents, and among nonfatal accidents, motor vehicular crashes have received the most attention.

### Alcohol Involvement by Location and Cause of Injury

*Motor Vehicle Accidents*

**Automobiles.** Car crashes are the leading cause of death from injury and the greatest single cause of all deaths for those between the ages of 15 and 34. Almost 50% of these fatalities are believed to be alcohol-related and alcohol's involvement is even greater for drivers involved in single-vehicle nighttime fatal crashes. The risk of a fatal crash is estimated to be from 3 to 15 times greater for those with a blood alcohol concentration (BAC) of 0.10 g/dL or above compared to a nondrinking driver (Roizen 1982).

Alcohol is less frequently present in nonfatal than in fatal crashes, and it is estimated that about 25–35% of those injured drivers requiring ER care have a BAC of 0.10 or greater. One study found that accident-involved drivers were six times more likely to have positive BACs than site-controlled nonaccident drivers (Borkenstein et al. 1964), and the likelihood of an accident risk increased with increasing BACs (Hurst, Harte, and Frith 1994).

**Motorcycles.** Motorcyclists are at an even greater risk of death than automobile occupants, with up to 50% of fatally injured motorcyclists having a BAC of 0.10 or greater (Romelsjö 1995).

**Pedestrians.** Pedestrians killed or injured by motor vehicles also have been found more likely to have been drinking than those not involved in such accidents (Romelsjö 1995). Estimates of 31–44% of fatally injured pedestrians have been found to be drinking at the time of the accident, with 14% of fatal pedestrian accidents involving an intoxicated driver compared to 24% involving an intoxicated pedestrian.

**Aviation.** Flying skills have been found to be impaired at BACs as low as 0.025, and a BAC of 0.015 or greater was found in 18–43% of deceased pilots (Romelsjö 1995; Ryan and Mohler 1979).

*Home Accidents*

Among all nonfatal injuries occurring in the home, an estimated 22–30% involve alcohol, with 10% having BACs above 0.10. Coroner data suggest that alcohol consumption immediately before a fatal accident occurs more often in deaths from falls and fires than in motor vehicle deaths.

**Falls.** Falls are the most common cause of nonfatal injuries in the U.S. (accounting for more than 60%) and the second-leading cause of fatal accidents. The risk of a fall is directly related to impairment of balance. Several studies have found that individuals with BACs above 0.10 are at increased risk of swaying on the Romberg test, which measures the ability to stand upright (Hingson and Howland 1993). Alcohol's involvement in fatal falls has been found to range from 21% to 77%, and in nonfatal falls from 17% to 57%. Risk is likely even higher for the elderly who may already have balance impairment due to neurological processes or side effects of certain medications, coupled with a lower tolerance to alcohol when they do drink.

**Fires and Burns.** Fires and burns are the fourth-leading cause of accidental death in the U.S. Alcohol involvement has been estimated in 12–83% of these fatalities (with a median value of 46%) and up to 50% among nonfatal burn injuries (with a median value of 17%) (Hingson and Howland 1993). It has been estimated that about 50% of burn fatalities were intoxicated and that alcohol exposure is most frequent among victims of fires caused by cigarettes.

### Recreational Accidents

**Drownings.** Drownings rank as the third-leading cause of accidental death in the U.S. for those aged 5 to 44, and the fourth-leading cause across all age groups (Howland et al. 1995). Estimates of alcohol involvement have ranged from 30% to 54% (with an average of 38%) in drowning fatalities and 35% in those coming close to drowning. Alcohol is associated with physiological and cognitive effects which may contribute to drowning, including dilation of the blood vessels leading to hypothermia in cold water and an increased possibility of caloric labyrinthitis, an inner-ear disturbance which may cause the person suddenly immersed in cold water to become disoriented and swim down rather than up, as well as retard laryngospasm when water is aspirated.

One survey found 36% of the males and 11% of the females reported drinking at the last recreational occasion on or near the water, and nearly a third of the males reported at least four drinks at that occasion (Howland and Hingson 1990).

**Bicycle Injuries.** Bicycling is the leading cause of recreational injuries, resulting in more than 500,000 ER visits, 20,000 hospitalizations, and 1,000 deaths annually in the U.S. (Li et al. 1996). Among those fatally injured, 32% were found to be BAC positive and 23% had BACs of .10 or above (Li and Baker 1994). A comparison of fatal bicycle injuries with nonfatal injuries found fatal injuries more likely to have positive BACs (30% vs. 16%) and to have BACs of .10 and above (22% vs. 13%) (Li et al. 1996).

**Snowmobiles and Mopeds.** Forty percent of snowmobile injuries have been found to involve alcohol (Smith and Kraus 1988), along with 30% of moped injuries (Roizen 1989).

**Hypothermia and Frostbite.** Alcohol has been found to greatly increase the risk of hypothermia and frostbite. Among exposure-related fatalities, 63% were found to be BAC positive with 48% at 0.15 or higher (Luke and Levy 1982), while 53% of frostbite patients have been found to be alcohol positive (Urschel 1990).

*Occupational Injuries*

Alcohol's involvement in work-related accidents varies greatly by type of industry. The proportion of those positive for blood alcohol is considerably lower than for other kinds of injuries, regardless of workplace. This is particularly true in the U.S. where drinking on the job is not a widespread regular activity. An estimated 15% of work-related fatalities have been found to be alcohol positive, with a range of 1–16% for nonfatal injuries (Roizen 1989; Stallones and Kraus 1993).

*Intentional Injuries*

**Violence-Related Injuries.** Alcohol has been found to be more prevalent in violence-related injuries (homicide, assault, domestic violence, robbery) than in those from unintentional causes. High proportions of both victims and perpetrators were found to be alcohol positive at the time of the event. Alcohol is thought to facilitate aggressive behaviors on the part of the perpetrator, as well as induce cognitive impairment related to normal judgment and decision making on the part of the victim. Among homicides, more than half involved alcohol by either the offender or the victim (Collins and Messerschmidt 1993). In a review of ER studies, between 22% and 70% of violent-related injuries were BAC positive compared to a range of 7–22% for nonviolence-related injuries attending the same ERs during the same period of time (Cherpitel 2007).

**Suicide.** A review of suicides found a range of 10–69% for completed suicides (with an average of 33%) and a range of 10–73% for attempted suicides (Cherpitel, Borges, and Wilcox 2004). About 20% of suicide victims have been identified as alcohol dependent, and are at increased risk of suicide compared to those in the general population. The suicide risk among alcoholics is estimated to be almost twice as high as for nonalcoholics and 60 to 120 times higher than for other nonpsychiatrically ill in the general population (Roy 1993).

## Mechanisms Linking Alcohol to Injury

A number of factors in combination (one of which is alcohol) link alcohol consumption to injury with various time relationships to one another and to the outcome of injury (Romelsjö 1995). Alcohol consumption, together with other contributory causes, provides a sufficient cause for injury.

### Drinking during the Event

Alcohol consumption is known to diminish motor coordination and balance and/or increase reaction time and impair attention, perception, and judgment regarding behavior, all of which may potentiate the likelihood of both intentional and unintentional injury occurrence. A *dose-response relationship* is also presumed; that is, the more alcohol consumed, the greater the likelihood of injury occurrence. Reviews of fatal vehicular crashes have found risk increases exponentially with increasing BAC (Hurst 1973; Perrine, Peck, and Fell 1989), and a summary of U.S. findings show a dose-response relationship, with a BAC of 0.8%, 1.0%, 1.5%, and 2.0% associated with a twofold, sevenfold, tenfold, and twentyfold increased risk, respectively, for a road traffic accident (Brismar and Bergman 1998).

A Finnish ER study found a dose-response relationship between BAC and the likelihood of injury from falls, with those with BACs between 0.06 and 0.10 three times more likely to be injured than those with nondetectable blood alcohol; while those with BACs between 0.10 and 0.15 were ten times more likely, and those with BACs above 0.15 were sixty times more likely to have suffered a fall injury (Honkanen et al. 1983).

The influence of hangover may also be linked to injury, but it has received little attention. A case-control study of those incurring ski injuries found drinking at least twelve hours prior to injury increased the risk for a skiing accident, but no association was found for drinking in closer proximity to the event, suggesting injury may have been due to the residual alcohol effect including fatigue (Cherpitel, Meyers, and Perrine 1998).

### Usual Drinking Patterns

While the amount of drinking on any particular occasion is an important risk factor in the occurrence of injuries, the pattern of usual drinking may also play a part in risk of injury. Injured patients, generally, have been found more likely to report frequent, heavy, and problem drinking compared to both non-injured patients and those in the general population from which they come (Borges et al. 1998; Cherpitel 1995).

A study of crash-involved drivers, however, found more frequent drinkers to be at lower risk than less frequent drinkers at all BAC levels (Hurst, Harte, and Frith 1994). Other analysis of cross-sectional data of drinking and driving in the U.S. found the highest risk of injury was associated with those who only occasionally drank heavily but who drank more than their usual amounts at the time of the event (Gruenewald, Mitchell, and Treno 1996; Treno and Holder 1997), suggesting heavy episodic drinking may be more strongly related to injury than usual volume of drinking.

Although heavy drinkers are at highest risk of injury, usually light drinkers may account for more alcohol-related injuries because they are more numerous and are more liable to the effects of heavy drinking occasions (Gmel et al. 2001). Data from a Swiss ER study found risk of injury increased with volume of drinking, heavy episodic drinking, and drinking in the twenty-four hours prior to injury (Gmel et al. 2006).

At the same level of alcohol use in the twenty-four hours prior to injury, however, high-volume drinkers were at a lower risk of injury than low-volume drinkers, suggesting that while all groups of drinkers were at increased risk of alcohol-related injury, those who usually drank little but on occasion drank heavily were at greater risk (Gmel et al. 2006).

### Alcohol Use Disorders

The literature on the role of alcohol use disorders (alcohol dependence and alcohol abuse), as opposed to unwise drinking in injury occurrence, suggests that those with dependence or abuse may be at a greater risk of both fatal and nonfatal injuries than those who drink prior to an accident.

Those with alcohol use disorders are significantly more likely to be drinking and to be drinking heavily prior to an accident than others. Among fatalities from all injury causes, they have been found to be more than twice as likely as other drinkers to have a BAC at 0.10 and above (Haberman and Baden 1974). The risk of accidental death has been estimated to be from three to sixteen times greater for dependent drinkers than for other drinkers (Haberman and Baden 1974). Dependent drinkers have also been found to experience higher rates of both fatal and nonfatal accidents even when sober.

Studies conducted in hospital ERs have reported mixed findings regarding alcohol use disorders (AUDs) and injury. However, these studies have used varying measures of AUDs, so prevalence rates across studies are not comparable (Cherpitel 2007). Additionally, some of these studies based prevalence rates on both drinkers and nondrinkers, which would provide lower prevalence rates since nondrinkers would not be expected to report symptoms of AUDs.

These data, then, raise the question as to whether chronic use and abuse of alcohol are more closely linked to injury occurrence than acute use of alcohol (drinking in the injury event). While the association of drinking during the injury may be attributed to a number of known physiological phenomena as described earlier, including diminished coordination and balance, less is known about the role and mechanism of usual alcohol consumption in injury occurrence or the interaction of acute and chronic use.

It is possible that prolonged use of alcohol over time may provide a protective effect for injury occurrence if an individual has developed a level of tolerance that allows him or her to engage in certain activities while drinking, which could result in injury at lower levels of consumption for a less experienced drinker. On the other hand, chronic alcohol abuse has long-term physiological and neurological effects that may increase the risk of accidents, as well as recovery from injury (impairing liver function, which compromises the immune system, predisposing the alcoholic to bacterial infections).

## Medical and Health Conditions Associated with Short-Term Alcohol Use

Alcohol use affects practically every organ in the human body. More than sixty disease conditions have been linked to the use of alcohol. This association between alcohol and health problems is primarily dependent on the quantity and pattern of alcohol use and by the presence of alcohol dependence (WHO 2004). Some of the more common medical consequences from alcohol use are described below and on pages 79–80.

### Hangover

Hangover is experienced by approximately 75% of persons who drink alcohol (Harburg et al. 1993), and consists of headache, malaise, diarrhea, nausea, fatigue, tremulousness, and anorexia the day following drinking. Hangover can have sufficient severity to disrupt the performance of daily tasks and responsibilities (Wiese, Shlipak, and Browner 2000).

The amount of alcohol typically sufficient to produce hangover in an average adult is five to six drinks for an 80-kg (approximately 176 pounds) male and three to five drinks for a 60-kg (approximately 132 pounds) woman (Wiese, Shiplak, and Browner 2000). Hangover symptoms peak twelve to fourteen hours after drinking ends (Ylikahri et al. 1976).

Alcohol hangover impairs the cognitive functioning in healthy adults, resulting in decreased functioning in visual, memory, and intellectual processing (Kim et al. 2003). Memory retrieval has also been found to be impaired by alcohol hangover (Verster et al. 2003). Social drinkers tested forty-eight hours after heavy drinking have shown impairments in tasks involving memory recall, recognition, and psychomotor performance (McKinney and Coyle 2004). Concern has been raised over the lingering negative effects of drinking on cognition, especially in persons such as pilots involved in mentally complex tasks when the awareness of impairment is likely to be absent (Yesavage and Leirer 1986).

### Blackouts

During a drinking episode, certain types of memory can be impaired. Some drinkers experience a partial or complete inability to recall events that occurred during drinking. Termed *blackouts,* these memory disruptions are caused by the blocked transfer of short-term memory into long-term storage for later retrieval.

Interestingly, immediate memory (memory of events and conversation topics in the past thirty to ninety seconds) and long-term memory of facts, events, and procedures are not affected by alcohol intoxication. Blackouts are strongly associated with a rapid rise in BAC, so that a person rapidly ingesting four drinks is more likely to experience a blackout than a person slowly drinking seven drinks.

Women are more susceptible to blackouts and undergo a slower recovery from cognitive impairment than men.

Different brain functions are impaired by alcohol at different rates and levels of BAC. For example, memory impairment usually occurs before motor skills and coordination become impaired. This can result in the drinker having little or no recall of events from the previous night, which may cause the drinker to falsely conclude that he or she must have appeared severely intoxicated even though the person appeared relatively normal to others.

Because immediate and long-term memory recall is intact, and since short-term memory may become disrupted *before* motor coordination, persons in a blackout are capable of participating in conversation and operating vehicles. There are even reports of highly complex activities being performed by persons in the middle of a blackout, such as surgery and piloting an aircraft (Rose and Grant 2010).

### Trauma, Burns, and Recovery from Injury

By increasing both the likelihood and severity of injury, alcohol plays a significant role in trauma. Alcohol abusers are more likely than nondrinkers to be involved in a trauma event. They are also more likely to be hurt seriously. Also, an estimated 27% of all trauma patients treated in emergency departments and hospitals are candidates for an intervention on their drinking (Gentilello et al. 2005; RSA 2009).

Recovery from trauma and injury can be hampered by alcohol use. Alcohol use can alter the natural inflammatory response and immune function, which is worsened in cases of existing or concurrent injury. Chronic heavy drinking also depresses estrogen levels, which eliminates estrogen's beneficial effects on the immune system and weakens a woman's ability to fight infections and tumors. This negative effect may be compounded by an alcohol-induced elevation in steroidal hormones, known as *glucocorticoids,* which suppress immune responses in both men and women (Kovacs and Messingham 2002; RSA 2009).

### Alcohol Overdose or Poisoning

From 1996 to 1998, the average number of deaths directly caused by alcohol poisoning was 317 a year, with an additional 1,076 deaths caused by alcohol as a contributing factor (Yoon et al. 2003).

## Medical and Health Conditions Associated with Chronic Alcohol Abuse

### Nutrient Deficiency

Chronic alcohol abuse can lead to depletion of important nutrients. Epidemiological data have found vitamin B1 (thiamine) deficiencies in 30% to 80% of alcoholics; folate deficiencies in 60% to 80%; B6 (pyridoxine) deficiencies in 50%; and B2 (riboflavin) deficiencies in 17% of alcoholics (Cook and Thomson 1997). Pyridoxal 5'-phosphate (the biologically active coenzyme of vitamin B6) is often deficient in alcoholics (Stickel et al. 2003). Compared with 2% in a control population, 46% of chronic alcoholics admitted to an ER displayed abnormalities suggestive of a thiamine deficiency (Hell, Six, and Salkeld 1976). These B vitamins are involved in many physiologic processes, including glucose metabolism, lipid metabolism, amino acid production, and synthesis of glucose-derived neurotransmitters (Stickel et al. 2003).

### Liver Disease

Alcoholic liver disease (ALD) includes three conditions: fatty liver, alcoholic hepatitis, and cirrhosis. ALD, and cirrhosis in particular, has long been considered one of the most frequent and devastating conditions caused by alcoholism, and is one of the leading causes of alcohol-related death (Mann, Smart, and Govoni 2003).

Some of the ways that heavy alcohol use promotes ALD include the impaired absorption of nutrients, such as protein and vitamin A; the impaired metabolism of lipids by alcohol; and the toxic byproducts of alcohol itself (Lieber 2003).

Hepatitis C virus (HCV) is particularly common among alcoholics. Infection with HCV is a common cause of liver disease, including cirrhosis, and of cirrhosis-related death in the U.S. The high incidence of HCV among alcoholics is due to

- the immune system dysfunction and chronic liver inflammation from heavy alcohol consumption,
- exposure to infection with certain viruses and bacteria, and
- high-risk behaviors such as sharing needles and unsafe sex (Lieber 2001).

Chronic alcohol consumption also interferes with treatment for HCV by promoting liver disease; by reducing the effectiveness of interferon-alpha, a drug commonly used to treat HCV infection; and by disrupting the patient's ability to follow the medication regimen (Lieber 2001).

**Brain Dysfunction**

Alcoholism can affect the brain and behavior in a variety of ways, ranging from simple "slips" in memory to permanent and devastating conditions requiring the need for permanent custodial care. The risk of alcohol-induced brain damage and neurobehavioral deficits varies from person to person and is influenced by age, gender, drinking history, and nutrition (Oscar-Berman and Marinkovic 2003).

The breakdown of carbohydrates in brain cells is largely reliant on the B-vitamin thiamine; without thiamine, cells cannot produce vital brain chemicals such as neurotransmitters and other molecules that are necessary for building proteins and DNA.

Up to 80% of alcoholics have a thiamine deficiency, and serious brain disorders, including Wernicke-Korsakoff syndrome, result from the long-term alcohol-induced disruption in dietary thiamine intake, thiamine absorption from the gastrointestinal tract, or impaired use of thiamine by the cells (Martin, Singleton, and Hiller-Sturmhöfel 2003).

Persistent ALD can also lead to the buildup of toxic ammonia and manganese in the blood and brain, leading to hepatic encephalopathy—a serious and potentially fatal brain disorder characterized by severe cognitive deficits, psychiatric symptoms, and motor disturbances (Butterworth 2003). Also, certain brain areas are often smaller in volume in people with an alcoholism history than in nonalcoholic subjects. Some examples of the brain damage that may occur from chronic alcoholism are

- brain shrinkage,
- the disruption of fibers that carry information between brain cells, and
- the impairment of associated cognitive and motor functions (Rosenbloom, Sullivan, and Pfefferbaum 2003).

### Birth Defects

Children born to drinking mothers represent a distinct subgroup of children of alcoholics because they were directly exposed to the toxic effect of alcohol as a fetus (Maier and West 2001). Exposure of the growing fetus to alcohol can have a potentially catastrophic effect on the development of many normal behaviors, including motor and sensory skills, social skills, and learning abilities that lasts a lifetime (RSA 2009).

Data from the CDC indicate that 12% of pregnant women drink alcohol. Roughly one in one hundred babies is born with a fetal alcohol spectrum disorder, ranging in severity from minor cognitive and behavior abnormalities all the way to full-blown fetal alcohol syndrome (FAS) (RSA 2009). The magnitude of harm to the fetus is dependent on the amount and pattern of maternal alcohol use during pregnancy and during the various stages of fetal development; a binge-like pattern of drinking may produce greater and more persistent deficits, such as reduced brain growth, than continuous alcohol use (Maier and West 2001). In addition to prenatal alcohol exposure producing lasting changes in brain anatomy, impaired cognitive and behavioral function, and low IQ (Chen et al. 2003), other effects can include stunted physical growth, abnormal facial features, and central nervous system deficits (Mattson, Schoenfeld, and Riley 2001; Larkby and Day 1997).

The term *executive functioning* refers to the cognitive functions involved in anticipating, planning, and executing behavior, and also the ability not to act on impulse and to delay gratification. These functions are grouped into cognition-based and emotion-related executive functions.

They are particularly impaired in people who were exposed to alcohol *in utero*. These deficits in executive function are believed to account for many of the behavioral problems seen in alcohol-exposed children and adults, such as difficulty in understanding the social consequences of behavior. Impairment in this group of functions is believed to originate from alcohol-induced abnormalities in specific brain structures, and abnormalities in the connections between these brain regions (Kodituwakku, Kalberg, and May 2001). It is now believed that there is no amount of alcohol that is considered safe during any stage of pregnancy (RSA 2009).

### Cancer

Chronic alcohol abuse is associated with an increased risk of several types of cancer. Cancers that are most strongly linked with alcohol use include cancers of the oral cavity, pharynx, esophagus, and larynx. Alcohol modestly increases the risk of developing stomach, colon, rectum, liver, breast, and ovarian cancers. Most importantly, drinking four or more drinks per day significantly increases the risk of developing any type of cancer. However, alcohol use alone does not appear to cause cancer, but may instead act as a co-carcinogen—a substance that promotes or accelerates cancer when taken with other cancer-causing substances such as cigarettes (Bagnardi et al. 2001).

### Endocrine Dysfunction

Heavy alcohol use can delay puberty in girls by suppressing the normal growth of the ovaries by disrupting the hormones that control ovarian function. Alcohol also can disrupt important endocrine functions, which can result in delayed puberty and poorly coordinated development of the reproductive system (Dees, Srivastava, and Hiney 2001). Alcohol use is also associated with low testosterone and altered levels of other reproductive hormones in males (Emanuele and Emanuele 2001).

### Cardiovascular Disease

Consumption of more than three drinks per day has a direct toxic effect on the heart. Heavy drinking, particularly over time, can damage the heart and lead to high blood pressure, alcoholic cardiomyopathy, congestive heart failure, and hemorrhagic stroke. Heavy drinking also impairs fat metabolism and raises triglyceride levels (RSA 2009).

## Beneficial Health Effects of Alcohol

Many studies suggest that moderate drinking (no more than two drinks per day for men and one drink per day for women) helps protect against heart disease by raising HDL (good) cholesterol and reducing plaque buildup in the arteries. Alcohol also has a mild anticoagulant effect, which keeps blood platelets from clumping together to form clots. Both actions can reduce the risk of heart attack, but the exact mechanism remains unclear (WHO 2004). Genetic factors (e.g., differences in the enzymes that break down alcohol in the body) can modify the positive effect that alcohol has on coronary heart disease (Mukamal and Rimm 2001). There is also some evidence that moderate alcohol use may offer some protection against developing diabetes and gallstones (WHO 2004).

## Criminal Justice Impact of Alcohol Use

### Overall Contribution to Crime

Although the stereotype of a criminal offender is often that of a drug addict, alcohol use is actually the major problem. More arrestees over the age of 21 report recent alcohol use than test positive for drugs (Hazelden Mar. 2002). Alcohol use is powerfully associated with criminal behavior. The Bureau of Justice reports that 36% of all offenders under jurisdiction of the criminal justice system reported being under the influence of alcohol at the time of their offense. This accounts for approximately one and a half million convictions annually (Greenfield 1998). When broken down by type of offense, state prisoners reported that alcohol was used at the time of offense in

- 41.7% of violent crimes,
- 34.5% of property offenses,
- 27.4% of drug offenses, and
- 43.2% of public-order offenses (Mumola 1999; Hazelden Dec. 2000).

### Violence and Violent Crime

An association between alcohol use and all forms of violence has been known for a long time. The amount of alcohol consumed directly influences the severity of violent behavior (WHO 2004). The types of violence linked with alcohol use include personal violence such as suicide; interpersonal violence such as assault, rape, homicide, and domestic abuse; and group violence such as disorderly and riotous acts at sporting events (Gordis 2001).

Persons with antisocial personality disorder (ASPD), a psychiatric condition characterized by a long-term pattern of violent behavior and disregard for other people's rights, may be especially prone to alcohol-induced aggression. However, persons without an ASPD diagnosis can also become more aggressive under the influence of alcohol, especially if they show aggressive tendencies while sober (Moeller and Dougherty 2001).

Alcohol increases the risk of aggressive behavior through several mechanisms. Alcohol may interact with the brain chemicals serotonin and GABA to reduce fear and anxiety over the social, physical, or legal consequences of one's actions. Alcohol also affects cognitive functioning by impairing problem solving in conflict situations, and by making it more likely the drinker will overreact with an excessively emotional response in conflict. Alcohol use can also intensify the concern among males of demonstrating personal power (WHO 2004).

### Sexual Assault

Approximately half of all sexual assaults involve alcohol use by the perpetrator, the victim, or both. Although perpetrator and victim know each other in at least 80% of sexual assaults, alcohol-involved sexual assaults often occur among strangers or persons who barely know each other. Certain beliefs surrounding alcohol's effects, attitudes regarding women and alcohol use, and high levels of alcohol consumption may heighten the risk of sexual assault by men. In addition, alcohol can interfere with the accurate interpretation of subtle nonverbal cues indicating a sexual interest or lack thereof in both the victim and the perpetrator (Abbey et al. 2001).

## Domestic Violence

Domestic violence is defined as the intentional use of force by one family member or partner to control another. A strong correlation exists between alcohol use and physical violence in marital or partner relationships. Domestic violence is a significant public health issue in the U.S.—one in six couples experience a physical assault each year (O'Farrell, Van Hutton, and Murphy 1999), and one-fourth to one-half of those who commit domestic violence also have substance abuse problems (Fazzone, Holton, and Reed 1997). While alcohol and/or other drug use does not cause or explain domestic violence, the importance of its association cannot be overlooked (Hazelden Nov. 2000).

### Prevalence

Domestic violence is the most common cause of nonfatal injury to women. It represents a substantial threat to women for both injury and death. For instance,

- 22% of all women receive an injury of some type resulting from domestic violence,
- 30% of female trauma patients have been victims of domestic violence, and
- 33% of women who are victims of homicide die as a result of violence committed by a spouse or partner (Kyriacou et al. 1999).

Perpetrators are not easily categorized when multiple factors are involved, such as experiencing violence while growing up, the need for control and power, and intimacy and dependency issues (Fazzone, Holton, and Reed 1997). Severe physical assaults occur in 8–13% of marriages and reoccur in two-thirds of these marriages (Hazelden Nov. 2000; Fazzone, Holton, and Reed 1997). Figures are not available on the prevalence of male victims of domestic abuse and violence.

### Strong Correlation

A strong correlation exists between alcohol use and domestic violence. In one study where newlyweds were interviewed one year after marriage, researchers found a strong association between alcohol use and escalating severity of domestic violence (Leonard and Quigley 1999).

- *In cases of verbal abuse,* 3–10% of the husbands were using alcohol.
- *In cases of mild physical abuse* (defined as throwing something, pushing, grabbing, shoving, or slapping), 11–27% of the husbands were using alcohol.
- *In cases of severe physical aggression* (defined as being kicked, hit with a fist, hit with an object, beaten up), 38–43% of the husbands were drinking.

These researchers followed the couples into the third year of their marriage and found that the violence present in the first year predicted violence in the third year. The relationship between drinking and violence of husbands and wives was complex. The most violence occurred in marriages where the husband was a heavy drinker and the wife was not (Hazelden Nov. 2000; Quigley and Leonard 2000).

Violence appears to be more closely associated with alcohol than with other drug use.

In one study of women who were injured intentionally, 52% reported that their partners were using alcohol just before the assault while 15% said their partners used drugs prior to the assault (Kyriacou et al. 1999). In general, women's drinking does not seem to predict whether a woman is a victim of marital violence (Kyriacou et al. 1999; Leonard and Quigley 1999). But even though there appears to be a strong correlation between alcohol and other drug use and domestic violence, two factors remain unexplained.

First, we do not know the direction of the correlation between alcohol and domestic violence. Abuse of alcohol or other drugs may cause domestic violence, or domestic violence may cause alcohol or other drug abuse, or an entirely different factor may cause both.

And second, a large proportion of domestic violence (i.e., probably at least 50%) is *not* associated with alcohol use. Alcohol may increase the distortion of power and control, which is believed to be the main determinant of conflict in intimate relationships, and lead to violence (Kyriacou et al. 1999). Some researchers have theorized there are different types of male perpetrators of domestic violence: (1) antisocial types who are generally violent, both inside and outside the home; (2) controlling, perfectionistic, or domineering men whose violence mainly occurs in the home; and (3) men with attachment and abandonment issues, who vacillate between being calculatingly violent and desperately needy and remorseful (Hazelden Nov. 2000; Fazzone, Holton, and Reed 1997). Little information is available on the types of female perpetrators of domestic violence.

## Youth Crime, Violence, and Alcohol

According to a National Household Survey on Drug Abuse (NHSDA), adolescents who used alcohol in the previous month before the survey were significantly more likely to have behaved violently in the previous year (Greenblatt 2000). Youth aged 12–17 were divided into groups based on their alcohol use patterns in the past month: heavy drinkers (drank five or more drinks per occasion on five or more days), binge drinkers (five or more drinks on one to five occasions), light drinkers (one to four drinks on any occasion), and nondrinkers. Heavy drinkers were much more likely than binge or light drinkers to report destroying property and threatening or assaulting others. Nondrinkers were the least likely to engage in these behaviors (Hazelden Jan. 2002).

The levels of alcohol use were also associated with the severity of criminal behavior. Heavy- and binge-drinking youth were significantly more likely to report shoplifting, drunken driving, drug trafficking, and having been arrested or booked for legal violations at least once in their lifetimes compared to nondrinking peers. The NHSDA report also found significant differences among drinking groups in terms of violence directed toward the self. Heavy- and binge-drinking youth were twice as likely to think about killing themselves and three times more likely to try to hurt or kill themselves compared to nondrinking peers.

Violent behavior appears to be both a risk factor for and a consequence of alcohol and other drug abuse in this population. Aggression and impulsivity in young children is predictive of later chemical abuse in adolescence (Berman et al. 1993; Caspi et al. 1996). Conversely, studies have shown that substance use decreases inhibitions and self-control, which, in turn, increase the likelihood of violent behavior (Hazelden Jan. 2002).

# DWI Policy and Practices

Driving while intoxicated (DWI) is one of the most common criminal behaviors engaged in during drinking, and many DWI offenders continue to drive while intoxicated after their first arrest (Voas and Fisher 2001).

In 2001–2002, 23.4 million, or 11.3%, of American adults aged 18 and older reported they had drank and driven one or more times. Younger drivers; men; Native Americans; people who were widowed, separated, divorced, or never married; and those with a post–high school education were more likely to drink and drive (Voas and Fisher 2001).

## Changing Perception of the DWI (DUI) Offender

During the mid-twentieth century, both the American public and health care professionals viewed the DWI offender as an otherwise law-abiding social drinker who made an isolated error in judgment that could be remedied through a brief educational intervention. The real problem, according to the viewpoint of the time, was the small percentage of alcoholic repeat DUI offenders (Vingilis 1983). This "needle in the hay-stack" view of the high-risk DUI offender went on to be challenged by judicial activists (Kramer 1986) and researchers (Crancer 1986) as being based on the false assumption of the social-drinking DWI offender. Further studies of DUI offenders have revealed the following information (White and Gasperin 2007):

- Between 40% and 70% of first-time DUI offenders have already been convicted of alcohol- or drug-related criminal offenses (Taxman and Piquero 1998; Chang and Lapham 1996; Kochis 1997).

- A driver would have to operate a vehicle while impaired between 200 and 2,000 times to statistically generate one arrest (Voas and Hause 1987; Beitel, Sharp, and Glauz 2000).

- Most alcohol-impaired drivers treated in hospital emergency departments are not arrested and prosecuted for the intoxicated driving that led to their injuries (Soderstrom et al. 2001).

- The proportion of social drinkers within the DUI arrest pool has been reduced by the cumulative exposure to successful media-based DUI educational campaigns (NHTSA 1997; Yi, Williams, and Dufour 2002).

- More than 80% of DUI offenders have a significant alcohol and/ or other drug problem (Lapham et al. 2001; Brinkmann et al. 2002).

Thus, it is now believed that collectively DUI offenders are drinkers who are developing or have developed a serious alcohol problem. There is also growing awareness that a subgroup of hardcore drinking drivers poses the most serious and sustained threat to public safety (White and Gasperin 2007).

# Impact of Alcohol Use on Special Populations

## Binge Drinking in Teens and Young Adults

Binge drinking (five or more drinks per occasion) is a very common drinking pattern among young drinkers. Underage drinking in persons aged 12 to 20 years contributes to the three leading causes of death (unintentional injury, homicide, and suicide) in that age bracket, and most of the adverse health problems from underage drinking stem from binge drinking and the resulting state of intoxication. Students who binge drink are more likely than nondrinkers and drinkers who do not binge to perform poorly in school, and to be involved in other health risk behaviors such as riding with an intoxicated driver, being sexually active, using tobacco and illicit drugs, being a victim of dating violence, or attempting suicide. A direct relationship has been found between the frequency of binge drinking and the frequency of these other health risk behaviors (Miller et al. 2007).

One of the complications from underage drinking is the potentially harmful impact on normal development. As children mature, they achieve key developmental milestones such as changing the way they interact with parents and peers, starting school and progressing through different grade levels and school settings, undergoing puberty, gaining greater independence, and taking on more responsibilities. The immediate, short-term, and long-term negative effects of alcohol vary with developmental periods. In persons aged 15 years and younger, the negative effects of alcohol can include disrupted school attendance, impaired concentration, relationship harm with parents and peers, and the potential for altered brain function and/or other aspects of development.

The negative effects of alcohol use in this age bracket can have future consequences in such areas as work, adult relationships, health, and overall well-being (Masten et al. 2005). Chronic alcohol abuse during adolescence is associated with cognitive deficits and alterations in brain activity and structure (Tapert and Schweinsburg 2005; De Bellis et al. 2000). However, it is unknown whether these deficits came before the drinking and contributed to the alcohol use, or if they are the result of alcohol use (Hill 2004). Also unknown is the degree to which these deficits resolve with abstinence (Dahl 2004; Dahl and Hariri 2004).

## Women and Alcohol Problems

Alcohol use disorders produce different physiological, psychological, and social consequences in women than in men.

### *Physiological Factors*

Heavy drinking among women is associated with increased rates of breast cancer (Smith-Warner et al. 1998). Women are often more susceptible to alcohol-related medical disorders than are men. For example, alcoholic women develop cirrhosis (Gavaler 1982), cardiomyopathy (Urbano-Marquez et al. 1995), and brain impairment (Mann et al. 1992) at the same rate, or sooner than, their male counterparts despite lower lifetime levels of alcohol consumption.

This accelerated development of physical problems is consistent with other research that shows that overall the course of the disease of alcoholism seems to develop somewhat more rapidly among women than men, though the progression of symptoms is quite similar (Schuckit et al. 1995). This phenomenon is known as a "telescoping effect," where the time from first heavy drinking to first treatment or other major problems is shortened (Hazelden Jan. 1999).

Why do women have unique health risks associated with heavy alcohol use? Women may have reduced levels of the gastric enzyme that metabolizes alcohol, resulting in proportionately higher BAC. In addition, alcohol may increase estrogen-related hormones, such as estradiol. Complicating matters, these two systems may be interrelated, creating synergistic effects (Erikkson et al. 1996). Women who are pregnant and use substances face additional problems. Fetal alcohol syndrome (FAS) is a serious *teratogenic* (a teratogen is a substance that causes birth defects) alcohol-related problem, and is one of the leading causes of mental retardation (Welsh 1994; Hazelden Jan. 1999).

*Psychological Factors*

Women with alcohol and other drug problems generally have a more complex mental health picture than do men. Common psychological problems among women in treatment include depression, anxiety, eating disorders (Sinha et al. 1996; Walters and Kendler 1995), borderline personality disorder, suicide attempts, post-traumatic stress disorder (PTSD), and histories of physical and/or sexual abuse (Wilsnack et al. 1997; Windle et al. 1995). Rates of these disorders are at least twice as high among alcohol- and drug-addicted women as women from the general populations (Regier et al. 1990). Despite the presence of these disorders, women's treatment outcomes are generally comparable or better than men's. It may be that the psychopathology is greater, but the severity of the substance abuse is less (Pettinati et al. 1997), or it may be that women more readily engage in the treatment process (Gil-Rivas, Fiorentine, and Anglin 1996; Hazelden Jan. 1999).

Research suggests that women who experience problems in their intimate relationships tend to drink more than other women. Heavy drinking is also more common among women who have never married, are living unmarried with a partner, or are divorced, separated, or widowed. The effect of divorce on a woman's later drinking may depend on her drinking pattern during the marriage. Women are also more likely to drink excessively if their husbands are heavy drinkers (NIAAA 2008).

Alcohol use is a significant risk factor for sexual assault and other consequences. A woman's odds of experiencing sexual aggression are three to nine times higher on days when alcohol has been consumed (Parks and Fals-Stewart 2004), and more than 65% of women involved in a sexual assault were drinking at the time (Frintner and Rubinson 1993; LaBrie et al. 2009).

*Social Factors*

Women with alcohol or other drug use problems battle ingrained stigma and stereotyping from society at large. The resulting stigma serves to victimize substance-abusing women and becomes a treatment barrier. Screening instruments may miss some of the unique features of women's early developing alcohol and drug problems, such as unsafe sexual behavior, breakdown in child care routines, and neglect of personal appearance (Ames et al. 1996; Hazelden Jan. 1999).

Many women may seek help at mental health or medical clinics, or are placed in correctional settings where alcohol or other drug problems may be missed. One study found women in relationships with substance-dependent men were heavy users of alcohol, cocaine, or marijuana and were twice as likely as other women to marry men with drinking problems (Windle et al. 1995; Hazelden Jan. 1999).

## Economic Cost of Alcohol Problems

The economic cost of alcohol abuse and alcoholism was estimated to be $184.6 billion in 1998 (Harwood 2000). When this figure is adjusted for the 2007 dollar value, the total economic cost becomes $234.8 billion (Thavorncharoensap et al. 2009).

This estimate represented a 25% increase from the $148 billion comprehensive estimate for 1992 (Harwood 2000). By comparison, estimates of the total overall cost of the abuse of other substances, including health- and crime-related costs and lost productivity, are $181 billion for illicit drugs (which includes the abuse of prescribed drugs as well as illegal drugs) (ONDCP 2004) and $168 billion for tobacco (CDC 2005).

Table 3.1 breaks down the components of the total cost incurred by alcohol (Harwood 2000).

Table 3.1

## Contributing Factors to the Total Economic Cost of Alcohol Problems

| Cost component | Cost estimates ($ in millions) | | Average % change, per year, 1992–1998 |
|---|---|---|---|
| | 1992 | 1998 | |
| Specialty alcohol services (treatment, prevention, research) | 5,573 | 7,466 | 5.0 |
| Medical consequences (except FAS)[1] | 11,205 | 15,963 | 6.1 |
| Medical consequences of FAS | 2,042 | 2,909 | 6.1 |
| Lost future earnings due to premature deaths | 31,327 | 36,499 | 2.6 |
| Lost earnings due to alcohol-related illness | 68,219 | 86,368 | 4.0 |
| Lost earnings due to FAS | 960 | 1,253 | 4.0 |
| Lost earnings due to crime (victims and prisoners) | 6,461 | 10,085 | 7.7 |
| Auto crashes, fires, violent crime, property crime, criminal justice cost | 22,204 | 24,093 | 1.4 |
| Total | 148,021 | 184,636 | 3.8 |

1. *FAS: fetal alcohol syndrome*

Of the total economic cost incurred by alcohol use in the U.S.,

- 15% stems from the cost of medical consequences and alcohol treatment;
- more than 70% is due to reduced, lost, and forgone earnings; and
- the rest is due to the cost of lost worker productivity, accidents, violence, and premature death (RSA 2009).

Of the $134 billion in productivity losses that alcohol use costs American business, 65.3% is caused by alcohol-related illness and absence from work, 27.2% is due to premature death, and 7.5% is due to crime. People who are alcohol dependent use twice as much sick time as non-problem drinkers, are five times more likely to file a worker's compensation claim, and are the cause of most of the injuries to themselves or others while on the job (Mangione, Howland, and Lee 1998; SAMHSA 2004; Hazelden Sept. 2002; SAMHSA 1998; RSA 2009).

Other economic costs incurred by alcohol use include the following (Hazelden Sept. 1998):

- Children of alcoholics are hospitalized more often and stay longer than other children (Children of Alcoholics Foundation 1990).
- Twenty percent of the total national health expenditure for hospital care is spent on alcohol-related illness (NIAAA 1990).
- In 1990, more than one million arrests were made for drug offenses and more than three million for alcohol offenses (Institute for Health Policy 1993).
- Elderly people are hospitalized for alcohol-related problems at the same rate as for myocardial infarction, at considerable cost to Medicare (Adams et al. 1993).

The total economic impact of costs incurred from acute intoxication and chronic use are considerable. Table 3.2 summarizes the total economic cost of alcohol use, by country.

Table 3.2

## Percent of GDP [Gross Domestic Product]

| Country | Total cost in 2007 U.S. dollars, in millions | Total cost as % of GDP | Cost per capita, in 2007 U.S. dollars |
|---|---|---|---|
| Australia | 6,818.6 | 1.09 | 359.8 |
| Canada | 13,406.3 | 1.24 | 428.04 |
| France | 22,376 | 1.44 | 384.40 |
| Germany | 30,847.15 | 1.24 | 373.77 |
| Japan | 62,461.8 | 3.15 | 511.85 |
| The Netherlands | 3,314.22 | 0.6 | 206.49 |
| New Zealand | 930.69–3,542.74 | 1.43–5.44 | 265.9–1,012.21 |
| Portugal | 853.64 | 0.45 | 85.53 |
| Sweden | 2,390–3,441 | 0.88–1.27 | 267.38–384.89 |
| South Korea | 24,913.7 | 2.76 | 530.08 |
| Thailand | 9,767.7 | 1.98 | 149.63 |
| *United States* | *234,854.2* | *2.11* | *850.86* |

(Adapted from Thavorncharoensap et al. 2009)

# The Science of Alcohol and Alcoholism

In 2000, the American Psychiatric Association (APA) published the re-vised criteria used in the diagnosis of alcohol dependence. According to this criteria, the single most defining aspect of alcohol dependence is the power of the relationship with alcohol: *The stronger the relationship, the more likely the person will continue problematic drinking despite internal and external consequences.*

Psychological dependence, where the person believes alcohol is neces-sary to get through daily activities, alleviate stress, and cope with prob-lems, is a symptom of alcohol addiction. Tolerance and withdrawal are often present, but they alone are not sufficient for a diagnosis of alcohol dependence. Alcohol dependence is diagnosed behaviorally by these signs and symptoms:

- the presence of cravings for alcohol;
- preoccupation with drinking;
- sneaking and concealing the use of alcohol;
- loss of ability to control drinking; and
- continued drinking despite physical, psychological, social, occupational, or legal consequences (APA 2000).

Valdez and Koob (2004) state that physical withdrawal alone should not be used as a barometer of alcohol dependence because physical withdrawal is usually not the most powerful motivator for seeking alcohol. Instead, a separate component of withdrawal, consisting of the emotional or psychological component of withdrawal manifested as anxiety or depressed mood, is critical in the development of dependence.

This negative psychological state is called *motivational withdrawal* (Valdez and Koob 2004). In 2008, Kalivas and O'Brien concluded that the essential elements of dependence are the persistent and recurrent seeking and use of alcohol at the expense of the pursuit of normal rewards (Kalivas and O'Brien 2008). Also in 2008, Angres and Bettinardi-Angres stated that although the disease of alcohol or drug addiction represents a diversity of people, the end result is the same: compulsive behavior in the face of negative consequences.

This pattern of behavior is complicated by the presence of denial, a complex defense mechanism that typically accompanies addictive disease. Addiction is said to be the one disease where the affected individual is convinced he or she really doesn't have it. Denial is reinforced both by the powerful reward of the alcohol or drug addiction, and by the deficits in learning, motivation, memory, and decision making that accompany the development of addiction (Angres and Bettinardi-Angres 2008).

## Alcohol Dependence Is a Chronic Disease and Illness

The question of whether alcoholism is a disease has been debated for decades, if not centuries. The answer is vitally important to researchers, medical practitioners, and treatment providers, as well as to those who suffer from addiction and their family members. This is especially the case in light of absurd proclamations that alcoholism is a behavior choice and not a disease, that it represents a failure of willpower and a reflection of a maladapted and warped character formation, and therefore merits the assignment of judgment and blame. Of course the normal nondependent use of alcohol is a choice; it is alcohol *dependence* for which the designation of disease is appropriate.

History reveals many examples of illnesses for which the afflicted were held personally responsible until science and medicine were able to provide abundant proof that a biological disease process was responsible and not the weak will of the patients. Such illnesses have included leprosy, seizure disorders, cancer, and major depression. If addiction were really a choice, people would simply quit after the consequences exceeded the perceived benefits (Halpern 2002).

Addiction scientists have produced substantial evidence supporting the viewpoint that alcohol dependence is a chronic disease. Many aspects of alcohol dependence are similar to those of other recognized chronic illnesses, such as type 2 diabetes, diseases, and high blood pressure (McLellan et al. 2000). Alcohol dependence is fundamentally similar to other chronic diseases on several key dimensions:

- **Identifiable signs and symptoms:** The *Diagnostic and Statistical Manual (DSM-IV-TR)* of the American Psychiatric Association (APA 2000) describes the symptoms of alcohol dependence, which are based on research evidence and expert consensus. The diagnosis of alcohol dependence is established when several of these symptoms are present. Likewise, diabetes and hypertension are diagnosed through an established set of symptoms, signs, and laboratory findings (Lewis 1994; Hazelden Aug. 1998).

- **Biological basis:** Neuroscience has made enormous contributions in the understanding of alcoholism as a chronic brain disease. Scientists have identified changes that occur in brain functioning and brain structure that correspond with the progression from regular drinking to alcohol abuse, alcohol dependence, and chronic alcoholism. These changes in brain function and structure are also believed to account for the behavioral signs and symptoms that define alcohol dependence, including loss of control over drinking and the inability to stop drinking, preoccupation over alcohol, craving, and continued use despite consequences. Some of these changes do not revert back to normal when the person stops drinking. The alcohol-dependent person remains at risk of relapse for years and even decades after drinking has ceased, and a long-term and varied pattern of relapse and remission is observed in many alcoholics.

- **Genetic heritability:** Similar to many chronic diseases, a genetic contribution plays a prominent role in many cases of alcoholism. Response to the effects of alcohol is complex, and some persons experience, for example, intense euphoria and a sense of well-being, or a marked reduction in stress or anxiety. Many of the individual responses to alcohol that increase the risk of alcoholism are genetically determined. Researchers study family members to understand the role of genetics in disease. They have found a fourfold risk of alcohol dependence in relatives of alcoholics, higher rates among identical twins than in fraternal twins or full siblings, and the same fourfold increased risk of alcoholism among adopted children of alcoholics as with children raised by their alcohol-dependent parent (Goodwin et al. 1974; Cotton 1979; Prescott and Kendler 1999). Persons vary greatly in their responses to stress. These individual differences are also genetically influenced and help shape susceptibility to psychiatric illness, including alcoholism. Although the children of alcoholics are four times more likely to develop alcoholism than children of nonalcoholics (Gilbertson, Prather, and Nixon 2008), and 40 to 60 percent of the risk for alcoholism is genetically determined, genes alone do not preordain that someone will become alcoholic. As with other chronic diseases, the development of alcohol dependence largely involves the interaction between genetic and environmental factors (Hazelden Aug. 2001).

- **Effective treatment:** Also consistent with alcohol dependence as a chronic disease is a recent paradigm change in how best to treat alcoholism. The conventional treatment model for decades has been twenty-eight to thirty days in a service- and staff-intensive residential or inpatient care, combined with brief "follow-up" or "aftercare" with the expectation of sustained recovery or even "cure" (White, Boyle, and Loveland 2003). The poor patient outcomes and high costs with this approach are increasingly viewed as reflecting the shortcomings of a treatment approach appropriate for an acute illness but inadequate for a chronic disease. This acute care model of alcoholism and drug addiction treatment was challenged in 1983 by George Vaillant with results from a long-term study of alcoholism and recovery. He concluded that alcoholism cannot be effectively treated with a single episode of "acute care" treatment, and that repeated relapses following multiple episodes of acute treatment do not mean that the particular patient is untreatable (Vaillant 1983; White, Boyle, and Loveland 2003). Subsequent researchers have made compelling arguments that alcohol and drug dependence are often chronic and relapsing in nature (Simpson et al. 1986), have much in common with other chronic relapsing diseases such as diabetes and hypertension (O'Brien and McLellan 1996), and that approaches used in managing chronic disease should be adapted for the treatment of alcohol and drug dependence (Lewis 1994; McLellan et al. 2000; White, Boyle, and Loveland 2003).

- **Role of personal responsibility:** The concept of alcoholism as a chronic disease is not incompatible with personal responsibility. With alcoholism and drug addiction, the concept of personal responsibility is most relevant in relation to the motivation and capacity for self-care and "self-management" following treatment. As is the case with other chronic diseases such as diabetes and high blood pressure, self-care is often the determinant in preventing disease recurrence or relapse. Capacity for self-care of one's recovery can include regular and long-term involvement in Alcoholics Anonymous, establishing meaningful connections with other persons in recovery, and breaking ties with former addicted companions. However, as with the self-care in other chronic diseases, these can be undermined by factors such as an unstable, unsupportive, or stressful living or family environment; chronic unemployment; homelessness; addiction to multiple substances; or active psychiatric illness.

- **Other similarities:** Alcohol dependence shares the following additional characteristics with other chronic disease:
  - a pattern of onset that may be sudden or gradual;
  - a prolonged course that varies from person to person in intensity and pattern; and
  - the risk of profound pathophysiology, disability, and premature death (White and McLellan 2008).

## Social Use and Abuse of Alcohol (i.e., Nondependent Use) Is Not an Illness

Not all persons who experience alcohol problems inevitably progress to alcohol dependence. Some young persons experience alcohol use problems that are developmental and are outgrown in the successful transition from adolescence into adulthood. Others develop an alcohol use problem when experiencing difficult life events such as the death of a loved one, divorce, or job loss. Their problem is often resolved with time, emotional support, brief professional intervention, or peer-based intervention by others in recovery (Burman 1997; Granfield and Cloud 1999; Bien, Miller, and Tonigan 1993; Bernstein et al. 2005). Similarly, many persons will experience a period of high blood pressure that essentially resolves through lifestyle change, weight loss, and increased physical activity without developing chronic hypertension (White and McLellan 2008).

Although most adults have used alcohol, and some have abused alcohol, the recreational use of alcohol and alcohol abuse is obviously not considered an illness. Many persons drink heavily without developing an alcohol dependency syndrome. Only alcohol dependence is characterized by profound changes in the structure and function of key brain regions. These biological changes are what drives the symptoms of alcohol dependence, and are viewed as hallmarks of the disease of alcoholism. None of the patterns of nondependent drinking are associated with these profound and lasting changes to the brain.

## Other Considerations Regarding Alcohol Dependence as a Chronic Illness

Relapse is not inevitable, and not all persons suffering from alcohol dependence require multiple treatments to achieve stable, long-term recovery. Even among those who relapse following treatment, families, friends, and employers should not abandon hope that recovery is possible. Community studies of recovery from alcoholism report long-term recovery rates of 50% and higher (Dawson et al. 2005).

Viewing alcohol dependence as a chronic illness does not reduce or absolve the alcohol-dependent person of personal responsibility, any less than persons with diabetes or hypertension are absolved of the responsibility for continuous self-care because their condition is a recognized disease (White and McLellan 2008).

Comparing alcoholism with other chronic illnesses can arouse strong negative feelings. To some people, discussing alcohol dependence as a disease appears to communicate what they think is an inappropriate "medicalization" of addiction. Some believe that calling addiction a disease contributes to the denial of personal responsibility and creates a built-in excuse for treatment failure. Individuals with alcohol dependence who have achieved sobriety may also resent the idea that they have a continuing chronic illness (White and McLellan 2008). Therefore, care must be taken in how the chronic nature of addictive disease is communicated to the public, clients, family members, referral sources, and those working on the front lines of addiction treatment (White and McLellan 2008).

When we view alcohol dependence as a chronic illness, it helps explain the frequent and high rates of relapse following the completion of treatment. An important implication of alcohol and other drug dependence as a chronic illness relates to its treatment approach. Treatment of alcohol dependence is currently delivered in a manner more appropriate for *acute* illnesses, and there is growing belief that treatment of these patients should adapt the *chronic* care medical monitoring strategies currently used in the treatment of other chronic illnesses (McLellan et al. 2000; White and McLellan 2008).

> *Note:*
>
> *Alcohol dependence shares many of the characteristics that define chronic diseases such as hypertension, asthma, and type 2 diabetes. These include an established set of signs and symptoms, a biological basis, a genetic component, the contributing role of behavior choices, treatment response, and high rates of relapse that are influenced by poor patient self-care and self-management. People with social or heavy nondependent alcohol use are not considered to have a disease. It is only alcohol dependence that has a disease basis, and this is because the symptoms and behavior are the direct reflection of abnormalities in brain structure and function. As with type 2 diabetes and high blood pressure, having the disease of alcohol dependence does not reduce or free the alcoholic of personal responsibility for managing the illness. Relapse following treatment for alcoholism is not inevitable, and if a relapse does occur, those close to the patient should remain hopeful that long-term recovery can still be achieved.*

## Alcohol Pharmacology and the Biology of Alcoholism

To understand how alcohol dependence is a brain disease, we must first understand the changes that occur in the brain as a drinker progresses from social drinking to alcohol abuse and ultimately to dependence (Cruz et al. 2008).

Alcohol and other drugs of abuse affect the brain in three major ways. They

1. immediately alter perceptions or emotions;
2. lay the stage for dependence in persons with heavy and frequent use by producing symptoms of tolerance, withdrawal,

and other changes such as alterations in important interconnected brain pathways that control motivational processes
such as arousal, reward, and stress; and

3. result in neurological damage with chronic addiction
(Hazelden July 2001).

All substances with addiction potential have strikingly similar effects
on many of the same networks of brain cells and brain regions (Iacono,
Malone, and McGue 2008). Even behavioral addictions—such as sex, gambling, and food (especially sweets) addiction—are driven by many of the
same core brain processes that underlie alcohol and other drug addiction
(Goodman 2008).

Neuroscience studies the relationship between brain function and behavior, which makes it an ideal discipline to study the biological basis of
addiction. Neuroscientists have contributed enormously to our understanding of how the thoughts, feelings, and behaviors associated with addiction are actually a reflection of the changes in the structure and function
of key brain regions (Winger et al. 2005).

**The Basics**

The human brain is made of billions of nerve cells, which are called *neurons.* Every thought, feeling, behavior, sensation, perception, and effect
from alcohol or other drug that a person experiences is the result of a
"conversation" between neurons. Neurons "talk" to other neurons, and
these conversations take place when information passes between neurons
in the form of a chemical message, called a *neurotransmission.* The molecule that makes up the chemical message passed between neurons is called
a *neurotransmitter.*

When a neurotransmitter is released from one neuron, it travels across
the small space between neurons called the *synapse,* to bind to an adjacent neuron that has a receptor for the specific type of neurotransmitter. Neurotransmitters bind to these receptors to either stimulate (excite)
or slow (inhibit) the activity of the receiving neuron (Clapp, Bhave, and
Hoffman 2008; Schuessler 2004).

Until recently, efforts to pinpoint the biological origin of addiction focused on isolated brain regions. The *nucleus accumbens,* a brain region with a high concentration of neurons that contain receptors for the neurotransmitter dopamine (simply termed *dopamine receptors*), was identified as the source of the euphoria and high produced by alcohol and other drugs. Therefore, the nucleus accumbens was believed to be the location where addiction developed (Dackis and Gold 1985).

Recent advances in brain science have produced a much broader and more complex understanding. We now understand that it is not a single brain region but multiple brain regions and neuron pathways that are involved in the addiction process.

Neural circuits or pathways are large and often widespread. The networks perform the brain's essential functions, such as storing information, regulating basic body functions, and directing behavior. Neuron pathways link and coordinate communication between different brain regions. It is now believed that addiction develops from alterations to these neuron pathways within the mesolimbic dopamine system (MDS).

The MDS is a good example of how neuron pathways harness different brain regions so that together they can perform complex brain functions. The MDS neuron pathway connects brain regions that control

1. bodily functions (the brain stem and peripheral nervous system);
2. emotion (the limbic system, including the amygdala) with brain regions involved in thinking, planning, and decision making (the prefrontal cortex); and
3. reward/reinforcement (nucleus accumbens).

These different brain regions within the MDS relay information back and forth, using the neurotransmitter dopamine, the endogenous opioids, and several other neurotransmitters (Angres and Bettinardi-Angres 2008; Gonzales, Job, and Doyon 2004).

One of the essential functions of the MDS is to serve as a reward pathway. The MDS serves to motivate the behavior that is essential for survival, such as eating, loving, and reproducing. MDS releases dopamine and other neurotransmitters to produce pleasure that rewards these pro-survival behaviors. The same release of dopamine is achieved with alcohol and other drugs, but the effect is much more intense than what can be achieved by natural rewards (Comings and Blum 2000). All five classes of commonly abused drugs (stimulants, opiates, alcohol, cannabis, and nicotine) activate the MDS to produce euphoria and the high. Differences in the extent of MDS activation partially explain the differences in abuse liability among the various recreational drugs and alcohol (Pierce and Kumaresan 2006).

*Note:*

*Brain cells or neurons are the most basic components of the brain. Neurons form extended networks with other neurons, called* neuron pathways. *These pathways link different parts of the brain together to perform the complex functions of the brain and body. Neurons communicate with adjacent neurons by using chemicals called* neurotransmitters. *These neurotransmitters either excite or slow the activity of the receiving neuron. One of the neuron pathways that is fundamental in the development of alcohol dependence is called the* mesolimbic dopamine system, *or MDS.*

*Any behavior is likely to be repeated when it is associated with the experience of pleasure. And one of the normal functions of the MDS is to produce pleasure when a person has sex, eats (especially sweets), or engages in other behavior that is conducive to survival. This pleasurable effect is caused by the temporary increase within the MDS of the neurotransmitter dopamine. Alcohol and drugs of abuse also stimulate dopamine release in the MDS. The intensity of the pleasurable effect from drugs is much greater than what can be achieved through natural rewards. The MDS is referred to as the* reward pathway.

## The Initial Effects of Alcohol

Alcohol and all other drugs of abuse have an immediate effect on neuro-transmitters and the molecules that carry messages from one brain cell to another. Although every cell in the brain is affected by alcohol, dopamine is believed to be the primary neurotransmitter responsible for the pleasurable effect of alcohol. Dopamine is associated with feelings of well-being and euphoria.

Within the MDS, earlier called the reward pathway, alcohol causes dopamine cells in the *ventral tegmental area* to release dopamine into the prefrontal cortex, amygdala, and nucleus accumbens. Although dopamine is released in the MDS when we engage in pleasurable and rewarding activities such as eating (especially sweets) or sex (Blum et al. 2000), MDS dopamine release may be three to five times higher in response to alcohol (Di Chiara and Imperato 1988; Wise 2002). This is an important point.

As you can see, alcohol causes a release of dopamine and ensuing euphoria and high that is vastly greater and more intense than what any non-drug experience can deliver. Although nondrug experiences can produce some of the same feelings of euphoria, the dopamine response to nondrug experiences diminishes with successive exposures. In contrast, alcohol delivers the same powerful rewarding effect with every use (at least before addiction develops) (Kalivas and O'Brien 2008).

The highly pleasurable dopamine effect produced by alcohol is referred to as the positive reinforcing effect because it motivates the person to repeat the behavior. In other words, the behavior of drinking alcohol is reinforced through pleasure (Kalivas and Volkow 2005). This process of striving to recapture the euphoria from previous drinking experiences actually describes a learning effect that is based on reward, and reveals that dopamine release is a key event in the process of learned behaviors (Clapp, Bhave, and Hoffman 2008).

Other brain chemicals besides dopamine also contribute to the pleasurable effects of alcohol. A second neurotransmitter called *serotonin* also plays an important role in alcohol response. Individuals with dysfunctional serotonin activity may be more prone to developing alcoholism (Heinz et al. 2001; Hazelden July 2001).

Alcohol enhances the activity of the inhibitory neurotransmitter GABA (gamma-aminobutyric acid) and curtails the activity of the excitatory neurotransmitter glutamate. These two actions produce the sedating effect of alcohol (NIAAA 2004). Alcohol also activates the release of endogenous (produced within the body/brain) opioids, which contribute to the pleasurable effects of drinking (Kalivas and O'Brien 2008).

During the initial stage of alcohol use, changes in brain chemistry begin to occur that affect the normal balance of neurotransmitters, the receptors these neurotransmitters interact with, and various other molecules. Although these early changes are short-lived and are based on the initial effects of alcohol in the brain, repeated exposure of the brain to alcohol eventually creates longer-lasting changes in neuron and neurotransmitter function (Clapp, Bhave, and Hoffman 2008).

*Note:*

*When a person drinks, changes occur in the activity of several neurotransmitters, which account for the short-term effects of alcohol. Alcohol stimulates the release of dopamine in the MDS, or the pleasure pathway, to produce the mood-altering effect of euphoria and high. Alcohol also (1) increases the release of serotonin and the endogenous (produced within the body/brain) opioids, (2) increases the activity of GABA, and (3) decreases the activity of glutamate. The combined effect of alcohol on GABA and glutamate produces the well-known sedating effect of alcohol.*

## The Transition to Alcohol Dependence

Relatively short-lived changes in brain chemistry and brain function are thought to initially occur at the onset of alcohol dependence. Continued heavy and persistent alcohol use transforms these short-term changes into lasting changes by the functioning of several neuron pathways (Nestler 2005). Problem drinking progresses to alcohol dependence at different rates in different people. Some drinkers rapidly progress to very heavy, loss-of-control drinking within a short period of time; for other drinkers this escalation may take several decades.

Before the development of addiction, alcohol use is regarded as voluntary, while alcohol use after the onset of addiction is considered compulsive. For example, before the development of addiction, a parent may have to make a choice between helping a child with homework or drinking a glass of wine in the evening. At this stage the drinker will usually make the socially appropriate choice. With the development of alcohol dependence, the drinker may make a deliberate choice to drink and to neglect his or her obligations or responsibilities.

Using the same example, the dependent drinker may encounter other people, places, or things associated with alcohol use (environmental cues) that conflict with his or her wish to help the child with homework that evening. As a result, the parent may begin experiencing steadily increasing levels of anxiety, irritability, and feelings of unease since his or her last drink. Contact with environmental cues and increasing distress since the last drink can both intensify and trigger the overwhelming urge to drink.

The urge itself activates a powerful goal-directed drive to seek and consume alcohol. The intensity of this impulse to drink, and the inability to control the impulse (i.e., to not drink) directly stems not from a lack of will or moral judgment but from substantial neural changes beginning to occur to the structure and function of the brain (Leshner 1997).

Addiction to alcohol represents at its most basic level a dramatic and persistent change in brain structure and function. With the development of alcohol addiction come the establishment and strengthening of new memory pathways. These new pathways contribute to the distortions in thinking and behavior seen in alcoholics. These pathways are accompanied by the weakening of the brain process involved in planning, impulse control, and judgment. In time, the impulse to drink simply overwhelms the progressive loss of ability to resist (Kalivas and O'Brien 2008). It is this compulsive craving to drink alcohol—and the intensity of the craving that overwhelms all other motivations, such as feeling responsible to help the child with homework—that is the root cause of the enormous health and social problems created by alcoholism (Leshner 2001).

### Earlier Theories of How Alcohol Addiction Developed

Earlier theories of addiction focused on the pleasurable effect or reward of drinking alcohol or using other drugs. Dependence was thought to stem solely from the intense and recurrent drive to experience the reward sensation (Wise 1980); in other words, addiction was driven by the positive reinforcement induced by the alcohol or other drug (Gill, Amit, and Koe 1988). Researchers also observed that alcohol or other drug dependence often resulted in unpleasant psychological and physical effects if the person stopped abruptly.

As a result, the addicted person often resumed drinking as a means to avoid the distressing symptoms of withdrawal (that is, negative reinforcement or behavior motivated to avoid or reduce an unpleasant experience or state). The positive and negative reinforcement theories provided some insight into the development and maintenance of alcohol and other drug dependence, but the theories were unable to fully account for many aspects, such as relapse after prolonged abstinence.

Current neuroscience discovery goes further by showing that addiction is a series of persistent changes in brain structure and function from prolonged heavy alcohol use that explains the nature of addiction, and the tendency to relapse even when abstinence has been achieved (Feltenstein and See 2008).

### Many Alcohol Abusers Do Not Develop Alcohol Dependence

Although the risk factors for developing alcohol addiction have been identified, the exact mechanism by which some heavy drinkers progress to alcohol dependence while others do not has yet to be discovered. However, an important point is that many heavy drinkers do not develop alcohol dependence. Some actually abuse alcohol for decades without developing alcohol addiction (Vaillant 2003).

Individuals differ substantially in how easily and quickly they become addicted; these individual differences are the result of a combination of environmental and genetic factors (Leshner 2001). Also, many people who abuse alcohol or other drugs as teenagers or young adults either quit or moderate their use as they get older, a process referred to as "maturing out" (Chen and Kandel 1995). The process of maturing out may occur in tandem with major positive life events such as marriage, family, or career. This process is explained by a rewarding event or opportunity (positive reinforcer) that enters into the life of the drinker and is incompatible with alcohol use. At this point, the reinforcing properties of the alcohol or other drug, relative to those of the competing reinforcers (marriage, family, or career), diminish to the point where addictive alcohol or other drug abuse is no longer behaviorally sustainable.

People who do not mature out of heavy alcohol or other drug use may not have access to these alternative positive reinforcers, may not seek them out, or may find the reinforcement from alcohol or other drugs superior to these nonsubstance experiences (Winger et al. 2005). However, alcohol abuse in the absence of alternative reinforcers, or even heavy alcohol use in preference of other normally rewarding activities, does not in itself indicate alcohol dependence.

### Brain Regions That Mediate the Process of Alcohol Dependence

During the development of alcohol dependence, neuron pathways are reorganized to establish the behaviors that are characteristic of addiction (Kalivas and Volkow 2005). The MDS, or reward pathway, is believed to be the primary brain location in the development of alcohol dependence. The role played by components of the MDS in the process of alcohol dependence involve the following three brain regions:

1. *The nucleus accumbens/central nucleus of the amygdala:* This is a structure in the forebrain involved in the rewarding effects of alcohol that promote the binge intoxication stage of addiction. This system contains the reward neurotransmitter dopamine and the endogenous opioids that are released when alcohol is consumed to produce euphoria and high (Koob 2006). Another important function of this system is the regulation of emotional states (Hyytia and Koob 1995).

2. *The extended amygdala:* Persistent alcohol abuse activates what are referred to as brain stress pathways. The amygdala is involved in the memory of emotionally powerful events and experiences, and contains the brain stress systems involving the neurotransmitters CRF and NPY (neuropeptide Y). CRF controls the hormonal, sympathetic, and behavioral responses to stress, and is believed to mediate the motivational withdrawal (described below) and negative emotional state that develops with alcohol dependence (Koob and Volkow 2010).

3. *The medial prefrontal cortex:* This region regulates the executive functions that are degraded with alcohol dependence, and also plays a key role in relapse (Koob 2006). The prefrontal cortex is involved in decision making, judgment, and planning (executive function). In a normal nonaddicted person, the prefrontal cortex suppresses the impulse to act on an anticipated reward when the behavior is judged as socially inappropriate or detrimental to a larger, long-term goal.

Examples of the medial prefrontal cortex in action include a person turning down an invitation to get drunk on a work night, or deciding not to pursue a sexual encounter with a co-worker or subordinate. The changes in the prefrontal cortex during the development of addiction have been described as an acceleration of "go" signals (to get drunk) and the impairment of "stop" signals (not on a work night), which contribute to uncontrolled alcohol use despite severe consequences (Clay, Allen, and Parran 2008).

All three of these brain regions linked by the MDS are involved in the activation and modulation of behavior. The nucleus accumbens and extended amygdala are involved in reward-motivated and fear-motivated behavior. The prefrontal cortex is involved in control over the behavioral response to the input from these other two brain regions (Kalivas and Volkow 2005).

Returning to the earlier example, the opportunity for a sexual encounter with an attractive subordinate at work may be intensely enticing to the normal nonaddicted person. However, the impulse to pursue the sexual encounter will not be acted on because activity in the normal, nonimpaired prefrontal cortex weighs the potential negative social and long-term consequences of the behavior against the short-term gratification. The person concludes the risks far outweigh the reward (Kalivas and Volkow 2005). Not so with an alcoholic.

The various processes and pathways that contribute to the development of addiction are very complex and sometimes overlapping. Another way to look at this process is to isolate some of the behavioral aspects of alcohol dependence and to identify the brain regions where these symptoms originate (Koob and Volkow 2010):

- Binge drinking and intoxication: ventral tegmental area, ventral striatum
- Motivational withdrawal and negative emotional states: extended amygdala
- Craving for alcohol: orbitofrontal cortex-dorsal striatum, prefontal cortex, basolateral amygdala, hippocampus, insula
- Disrupted control over inhibitions: cingulate gyrus, dorsolateral prefrontal cortex, inferior frontal cortices

### Changes in Brain Pathways Involved in Alcohol Reinforcement (i.e., Changes in the Motivation That Drives Alcohol Use)

As described earlier, alcohol or other drug dependence is much more likely to occur when adverse life experiences, genetics, or their combination alter brain function in such a way that predisposes the person to addiction.

For instance, during extreme stress such as emotional trauma or childhood neglect by one's parent, the brain releases powerful stress hormones that over time can alter brain function to result in an abnormally intense sensitivity. It can result in a diminished capacity to delay gratification and an increased risk of impulsive behaviors.

In this case, the brain reward system also becomes sensitized so that a more powerful and intense experience of euphoria and pleasure may occur from the use of substances and behaviors that trigger and release dopamine in the MDS. The same chronic release of stress hormones can also result in a persistent negative emotional state of irritability, sadness, anxiety, distress, and poor affect regulation (the ability to calm oneself when emotionally upset, to control one's thought response to an unsettling event, and to control emotion-based behavior). This can make the use of substances that calm or numb the emotional distress much more enticing (Goodman 2009).

Thus, the exact mechanism by which alcohol dependence develops in some but not most drinkers is unknown. However, persons with a heightened sensitivity to the pleasurable mood-altering effects and to the reduction in distressing emotions with alcohol use are most susceptible to developing alcohol dependence. Although these persons may possess altered brain reward pathways that came before their alcohol use, persistent alcohol abuse over time further alters these reward pathways to result in profound and lasting changes in the brain pathways involved in motivation. Some of these pathways mediate reward, while others mediate stress. These changes are the basis of the development of sensitization, tolerance, withdrawal, and dependence, and are described on the next pages.

### Positive Reinforcement

*Positive reinforcement* describes behavior that is driven or motivated by the desire to achieve a pleasant or exhilarating state like euphoria. The positive reinforcing effects of alcohol are important factors that motivate the continued drinking before the onset of alcohol dependence (Gilpin and Koob 2008). However, the onset and progression of alcohol dependence is accompanied by impaired function of brain reward systems, including MDS dopamine and opioid function that produces the mood-altering euphoria with drinking. This loss of function in brain systems that produce reward and reinforcement occurs in tandem with the progressive activation of brain stress systems (Gilpin and Koob 2008).

### Negative Reinforcement

*Negative reinforcement* describes behavior that is motivated or driven by the desire to reduce or remove an unpleasant state. With the development of alcohol dependence, an unpleasant emotional state begins to emerge during abstinence from alcohol that consists of dysphoria, anxiety, and irritability, and is distinct from the actual physical withdrawal from alcohol (described later). This negative emotional state is termed *motivational withdrawal,* and persons who have become alcohol dependent may drink to prevent or reduce the anxiety and distress they experience when they are not drinking (Gilpin and Koob 2008).

There are two factors that contribute to the development of negative reinforcement during alcohol dependence. The first involves the loss of normal MDS function. Impaired dopamine function in this system creates dysphoria (a state of dissatisfaction, unhappiness, and emotional distress). It is accompanied by impaired serotonin function that contributes to dysphoria, and decreased GABA activity that contributes to anxiety and irritability (Koob 2006). The second factor involves the recruitment of brain stress systems in the extended amygdala (CRF and NPY), which contribute to the negative emotional state (dysphoria, anxiety, and irritability) that drives compulsive alcohol use (Koob 2006).

Negative reinforcement often develops and intensifies during the course of addiction. However, some people, especially those who have experienced childhood trauma or severe and chronic stress, are more vulnerable to the powerfully rewarding and motivating effects of negative reinforcement. Such persons are very likely to possess impaired affect regulation and to experience painful and overwhelming emotions and emotional instability. If they find that alcohol provides temporary emotional relief, a powerful negative reinforcement is activated (Goodman 2008).

### Neuroadaptation

*Neuroadaptation* is a term that describes the process by which the brain adapts to the constant presence of alcohol in order to keep performing the normal brain functions (NIAAA 2009). The function and activity of key neurotransmitters is altered with neuroadaptation, and several processes that occur during neuroadaptation serve to increase the compulsion to drink. These processes include

- *sensitization,* in which heightened sensitivity to alcohol causes the desire for alcohol to escalate into a pathological craving;
- *tolerance,* which describes the diminished response to alcohol and the need to drink greater amounts to achieve the desired effect; and
- *physical withdrawal* (described in chapter 5), which is the process that can occur when the alcohol-dependent person abruptly stops drinking (Koob 2003; Gilpin and Koob 2008; NIAAA 2009).

As mentioned earlier, an important effect of alcohol on neurotransmitter function is to reduce the activity of excitatory glutamate, and to increase the activity of inhibitory GABA. Now, an alcoholic doesn't drink with that intention in mind, but the chronic stimulation of GABA and suppression of glutamate with chronic alcohol exposure cause the brain to attempt to regain a normal state by cranking up the activity of glutamate receptors (Vengeliene et al. 2008). As a result, intoxication begins to feel normal for a person dependent on alcohol.

When a drinker passes out or falls asleep, and alcohol use is abruptly stopped, this heightened glutamate receptor activity creates a state termed *hyper-excitability,* which is believed to account for many of the symptoms of physical alcohol withdrawal or hangover such as agitation, anxiety, insomnia, and potentially seizures or convulsions (Pulvirenti and Diana 2001; Gilpin and Koob 2008).

Three distinct types of alcohol craving have been identified below. Each type of craving is associated with a different stage in the development of alcohol dependence, and is a reflection of corresponding disruptions in different neurotransmitter systems and brain regions (Clapp, Bhave, and Hoffman 2008):

- *Craving for reward,* stemming from alterations in dopamine and/or brain opioid systems that diminish the positive reinforcing effects of alcohol (Clapp, Bhave, and Hoffman 2008).

- *Craving for relief* from emotional distress or anxiety: Adaptations within the amygdala stress systems help increase the anxiety and emotional distress that compels the drinker to escalate alcohol use. The craving to drink is motivated by the intense desire for relief from anxiety and distress, or negative reinforcement (Clapp, Bhave, and Hoffman 2008).
- *Obsessional craving.* This is the loss of control over alcohol-related thoughts as they intrude into the person's normal thinking process. This type of craving is believed to result from alcohol-induced deficits in serotonin function (Addolorato et al. 2005). Obsessive craving, when accompanied by loss of control and compulsive alcohol use, may also reflect enduring changes in glutamate signaling pathways in the limbic and motor systems (Clapp, Bhave, and Hoffman 2008).

## Completion of the Transition to Alcohol Dependence

The transition to alcohol dependence is believed to occur in a sequence.

The first system to become altered is the MDS, followed by the ventral striatum, dorsal striatum, and orbitofrontal cortex, and eventually the prefrontal cortex, cingulate gyrus, and extended amygdala (Koob and Volkow 2010). The final significant brain alteration with alcohol dependence involves the development of a signaling pathway from the prefrontal cortex to the nucleus accumbens that transmits glutamate. This development has profound behavioral consequences.

It greatly diminishes the capacity of the drinker to respond to non-alcohol rewards; substantially decreases the ability to deliberate, plan, control impulses, and use judgment over the use of alcohol; and creates a hyper-response to people, places, and things associated with drinking, which intensifies the behavior directed toward obtaining and using alcohol (Kalivas and Volkow 2005).

The resultant state is termed *impaired behavioral inhibition,* which means that the person is much more likely to act on the urge for short-term reward or reinforcement (positive, negative, or both) despite longer-term consequences. An important point is that impaired behavioral inhibition is usually present in addicted persons to some degree before they develop an addiction, which also serves to heighten the risk for addiction (Goodman 2008).

The development of this excitatory glutamate pathway contributes to the two hallmarks of alcoholism: loss of control over alcohol use and continued drinking despite harmful consequences (Clapp, Bhave, and Hoffman 2008; Angres and Bettinardi-Angres 2008). Persons with the symptom of loss of control may not necessarily lose control of their alcohol use every time they drink, but instead, their attempts to control their drinking have often failed (Goodman 2008).

*Note:*

*The progression to alcohol dependence is accompanied by profound changes in several brain regions and neuron pathways, which produce the symptoms and behavior changes that define alcoholism. During the development of alcohol dependence, the MDS reward pathway becomes impaired so that pleasurable effects from alcohol are diminished. This loss of function in the MDS pathway, and the growth and activation of other neuron pathways that produce emotional distress, result in the drinker experiencing anxiety, irritability, or depression during dry periods. The drinker is now compelled to resume drinking in order to avoid this unpleasant state, and to compulsively pursue the pleasurable effects of alcohol, which have become more difficult to recapture.*

*As the drive to consume alcohol intensifies, nondrinking activities and pursuits lose the ability to produce reward. Eventually, the motivation to drink overrides all other competing drives and motivations, leading to the abandonment of activities and pursuits that were formerly enjoyable and rewarding, such as family involvement, career, and hobbies.*

*With the increasing intensity in the urge to drink comes an increasing inability to control or put the brakes on this urge. This is due to loss in function of the prefrontal cortex, and accounts for such behaviors as drinking to intoxication when the drinker initially only intended to have one or two drinks. In addition, drinking despite predictably severe social, occupational, or legal consequences is another sign of dependence. To summarize it another way: continued drinking is positively reinforced and abstinence is negatively reinforced (Gorski 2001).*

## Chronic Alcohol Dependence

By the time the alcohol-dependent person has reached this stage, obtaining and consuming alcohol influences behavior to the point where the need for alcohol dominates the motivational hierarchy (Bozarth 1990). In other words, the need to drink eclipses all other obligations, relationships, and activities.

As described above, this progressively greater orientation of behavior toward alcohol use and the progressive loss of reward and reinforcement from nonalcohol experiences are the direct results of the profound changes in the brain motivational circuitry (Kalivas and O'Brien 2008). Alcohol has become the only potent reinforcer, and perhaps the only reinforcer at all, relative to competing rewards, such as family involvement and hobbies in the life of the alcoholic (Winger et al. 2005). Essentially, alcohol has "hijacked" the brain motivation and reinforcement pathways (Lubman, Yucel, and Pantelis 2004). These profound alterations in brain pathways can persist long after alcohol use has stopped (Kalivas and O'Brien 2008).

This loss of interest in previously gratifying and rewarding relationships, obligations, and leisure activities can result in child neglect and abandonment, the disintegration of marriages and business partnerships, and professional irresponsibility and misconduct. It is not surprising that the behavior and conduct of persons in this stage of addiction can resemble elements of psychiatric disorders such as antisocial personality disorder (ASPD) or narcissistic personality disorder (NPD). The overlap in behavior is considerable.

ASPD is characterized, in part, by a chronic pattern of failure to meet important financial and family obligations, employment instability and the abandonment of multiple jobs, impulsivity, pursuit of illegal activities and occupations, little regard for the truth, and the absence of guilt or remorse. NPD is characterized, in part, by a chronic pattern of extreme self-centeredness and the inability to experience empathy for others (APA 2000).

However, while the symptoms of ASPD and NPD typically emerge during adolescence to early adulthood and remain stable throughout adulthood, persons with chronic alcohol or other drug dependence, in the absence of a pre-existing personality disorder, are usually able to regain the ability to fulfill their financial and family obligations when they have stopped drinking. Then, they can re-enter into meaningful relationships that do not revolve around alcohol use and find enjoyment from nondrinking activities and pursuits. And unlike persons with ASPD and NPD, individuals who have stopped drinking are often intensely remorseful over the suffering endured by others as a consequence of their addiction.

For others, the capacity to experience pleasure or reward from ordinary nondrinking, or nondrug experiences remains grossly impaired. A powerful drive to alter one's distressing emotional state may persist long after alcohol or other drug use has stopped and physical withdrawal ended. Such persons may begin the compulsive pursuit of activities that are not otherwise harmful and that provide a degree of symptom relief. These in some cases may be physical in nature and include running, martial arts, or yoga. Although these activities may be labeled as substitute addictions, they serve a positive purpose of introducing new, indirect substance reward that is sustainable, and in doing so can help the transition from active drinking to ongoing abstinence.

However, in other cases the intense drive to alter one's feeling[s ? emo]tional state unfolds destructively with the development of a sex[ual or] gambling addiction. They are often driven by the same dynamics as alcohol and other drug dependence:

- the desire to experience mood alteration through intense (if fleeting) euphoria and well-being,
- the intense desire to reduce or eliminate emotional distress,

- chronic feelings of emptiness or low self-esteem, and
- the inability to control or moderate the behavior despite consequences.

These shared dynamics are the reflection of a common underlying biological and psychological basis (Goodman 2008; Goodman 2009).

### Neurodegeneration

Chronic ingestion of high doses of alcohol can lead to profound changes in the structure, growth, and survival of neurons. Researchers have found substantially reduced volumes of many brain structures in alcoholics, particularly the prefrontal cortex and cerebellum, although this is at least partially reversed with prolonged abstinence. As described above, deficits in the prefrontal cortex can affect motivational circuits and impair the ability to control impulsive behavior, further contributing to alcoholic drinking (Jentsch and Taylor 1999). Alcohol dependent persons also possess smaller amygdala volumes than nondependent individuals, which is associated with risk of alcohol relapse (Wrase et al. 2008; Gilpin and Koob 2008).

### Relapse to Alcohol Use during Abstinence

The cardinal behavioral feature of alcohol addiction is the persistent vulnerability to relapse after physical withdrawal from alcohol has ended. This risk of relapse persists even after years of abstinence, and arises from an intense desire for alcohol and a diminished capacity to control that desire (Kalivas and Volkow 2005; Wolffgramm and Heyne 1995). Intense alcohol cravings, even after years of abstinence, can be provoked by emotional distress; exposure to people, places, or things (cues) associated with drinking; or changes in mood (Vengeliene et al. 2008). As mentioned earlier, alcohol addiction is caused, in part, by a learning process involving the lasting memories of powerful alcohol experiences, and in this context, relapse occurring from cue exposure may be understood as a response to learned behavior (Kauer and Malenka 2007).

The brain of addicted persons is altered and responds very differently to stress than the brains of nonaddicted persons in ways that increase relapse risk (Cleck and Blendy 2008). Studies examining the well-established relationship between stress and relapse have found that exposure to stress activates brain reward pathways, possibly explaining why craving for alcohol or other drugs is triggered when recovering alcoholics and addicts are under stress (Sinha et al. 2000; Cleck and Blendy 2008).

Researchers have found that relapse occurring from exposure to people, places, or things associated with drinking may be mediated by the endogenous opioid system. These findings have important implications for the development of pharmacological therapies to prevent relapse in alcoholics (Gilpin and Koob 2008).

The summary of a scientific conference addressing the interactions between stress, craving for alcohol or other drugs, and relapse during abstinence was published (Breese et al. 2005). Some of the key findings included

- exposure to stressful life events is an important risk factor for relapse in abstinent alcoholics;
- stress exposure in abstinent alcoholics increases alcohol craving and susceptibility to relapse after treatment completion;
- alcohol craving triggered by stress can be amplified by other risk factors, such as exposure to people, places, and things connected with drinking, and by the disruption of brain stress-regulatory systems stemming from chronic alcohol abuse;
- the cumulative adaptive changes from chronic alcohol abuse can interact with stress to increase the severity of physical and motivational withdrawal symptoms;
- the behavioral and physiological changes that contribute to relapse extend well beyond the period of physical withdrawal from alcohol, and this vulnerability to relapse is associated with a heightened sensitivity to stress;
- stress and alcohol-related environmental triggers can interact to increase relapse risk.

The results presented at this conference provide the rationale for the support of research efforts to reduce stress-induced alcohol craving through pharmacological or psychosocial interventions. They also underscore the powerful effect of people, places, and things associated with alcohol use on increasing the risk of relapse.

### Summary of the Biological Basis of Relapse Vulnerability

Several factors related to altered brain chemistry and function contribute to the high risk of relapse among alcoholics trying to remain sober. Alcoholism can alter normal dopamine and serotonin function, especially within the MDS, and enhance stress pathways to increase the release of CRF. These effects may persist well into abstinence, leading to difficulties in experiencing pleasure from nonalcohol activities and the emergence of a restless irritability, anxiety, mood instability, and feelings of emptiness. Other factors that contribute to relapse risk include the conditioning process that has occurred throughout active alcohol addiction.

Conditioning refers to the deeply ingrained learning and memory process where people, places, and things (environmental cues) become strongly associated with alcohol use and intoxication. A poor stress tolerance, where stress can emotionally overwhelm the abstinent alcoholic, is another factor that reflects the altered brain chemistry with alcoholism. Abstinent alcoholics can experience intense urges to drink when under high levels of stress. Poor stress tolerance can also interact with exposure to environmental cues to overwhelm the ability of the alcoholic to resist drinking (Goodman 2008; Weiss et al. 2001).

In conclusion, several factors contribute to the very high risk of relapse in the recovering alcoholic. These include biological changes in the brain; the behavioral choices made by the alcoholic in recovery, such as whether or not to avoid old drinking associates and environments; and the degree (or lack of) self-care, such as involvement in a recovery program like AA.

*Note:*

*The profound changes in the brain that occur during alcohol dependence can persist long after drinking has stopped and physical withdrawal has ended. These persistent alterations account for the vulnerability to relapse even years after the alcoholic has quit drinking. This vulnerability is ex-*

*plained by the impaired ability to experience pleasure and reward from nondrinking experiences, ongoing emotional distress, and reduced capacity to resist acting on impulses and urges. The impulse to drink can be triggered by contact with people, places, or things that were associated with drinking experiences, and stress can also trigger the urge to drink, increasing the risk of relapse.*

## Neurotoxic Effects of Alcohol on Cognitive Function

Alcohol can damage brain cells by impacting the structure, function, and production (i.e., neurogenesis) of neurons, ultimately resulting in cognitive impairment (Crews 2008).

Alcoholism is the second-leading cause of dementia, after Alzheimer's disease (Eckardt and Martin 1986). Wernicke-Korsakoff's syndrome (commonly known as "wet brain") is a type of dementia associated with long-term alcohol use and the malnutrition that often accompanies alcoholism. This syndrome is characterized by the inability to learn new information. Often, the person with Wernicke-Korsakoff's syndrome will make up or create scenarios to fill in the missing information (Beeder and Millman 1997). In addition to eroding cognitive function, chronic alcohol dependence may produce personality changes. Damage to the frontal lobe of the brain, for example, reduces impulse control, which can result in impulsive or violent behavior (NIAAA 2000; Hazelden July 2001).

Brain impairment from chronic alcoholism may reveal itself in the following areas:

- *Working memory:* Temporarily retaining numbers or facts for use in the immediate future, e.g., for balancing a checkbook or considering several options. While new information may be learned, it may take more review and repetition than it normally would.

- *Executive functioning:* These are the higher-level cognitive functions involving attention, planning, abstract reasoning, problem solving, judgment, and sensitivity to the consequences of one's behavior.

- *Visuospatial perception:* The ability to grasp new and complex information visually; recognition and recall of visual images; the skills to learn new routes through buildings, or to solve a puzzle (Hazelden Nov. 2006).

Brain science has recently provided us with a greater understanding of how alcoholism can result in deficits in cognitive function:

1. *Structural changes:* Magnetic resonance imaging (MRI) studies consistently show shrinkage of the brain among alcoholics, with both gray matter (nerve cells) and white matter (transmission routes) losing volume, especially in the prefrontal region (Ende et al. 2005; Sullivan and Pfefferbaum 2005). This loss of brain mass is associated with age and the quantity of alcohol consumed (Spaminato et al. 2005).

2. *Neurotoxicity:* Alcohol causes new nerve cells to die. Throughout life (though more slowly as we age) new brain cells are normally created in a process known as neurogenesis; alcohol, however, interferes with neurogenesis (Herrera et al. 2003).

3. *Circuitry:* The degradation of the neural circuitry, or nerve transmission, may be responsible for cognitive deficits, resulting in what is called processing inefficiency. As the brain reorganizes how it processes information during active alcohol dependence, it compensates for deficits and uses higher-level functions for lower-level tasks. This means the brain needs to work harder to perform the same functions (Fama, Pfefferbaum, and Sullivan 2004; Sullivan and Pfefferbaum 2005).

Some people may be more susceptible to alcohol's effects. Women generally experience the negative physical consequences of alcoholism sooner than men, given the same number of years of drinking. This phenomenon, known as telescoping, accounts for earlier onset of liver and heart damage among alcoholic women, and is very likely to occur in the brain as well (Mann et al. 1992; Mann et al. 2005). Adolescents may be especially vulnerable to the neurotoxic effects of alcohol because their brain is still active and developing (Barron et al. 2005; Goldstein and Volkow 2002; Hazelden Nov. 2006).

*Note:*

*Alcohol dependence is associated with damage to brain cells, brain regions, and neuron pathways, resulting in persistent problems in thinking and memory function for some persons. The specific functions most likely to be impaired from chronic alcohol use include short-term memory; judgment, planning, and anticipating the consequences of one's actions; and the learning and recall of visual information.*

## Cognitive Impairment and Recovery

Between 50% and 80% of individuals with alcohol use disorders experience some degree of neurocognitive impairment. There has been a persistent belief among clinicians that neurocognitive impairment plays an important role in determining treatment outcome (Bates, Bowden, and Barry 2002).

For most people, the brain heals itself given abstinence and time. Abstinent alcoholics show improvements in cognitive function within a few months of their last drink (Nixon and Crews 2004). Brain imaging (MRI scans) has shown increases in brain volume during abstinence as gray and white matter increase.

Neuropsychological tests reflect improvements in functioning in abstinence that correspond to normalization of brain structure (Rosenbloom, Pfefferbaum, and Sullivan 2004). Neurogenesis begins to resume, and is associated with increases in positive mood and the ability to learn. In turn, recovery tasks become easier and the resulting abstinence makes continued cognitive improvement possible, creating a spiral of continued progress (Crews et al. 2005).

These positive changes take place over a variable timeline. Some improvements occur within the first month of recovery and shortly thereafter, particularly in short-term memory and visuospatial tasks (Sullivan et al. 2000). Interestingly, patients with a diagnosis of antisocial personality disorder have a slower rate of recovery in deficits involving executive functioning. Age alone is not a factor in the rate of cognitive recovery, and persons of all ages who quit substance abuse are capable of some degree of short-term cognitive recovery (Bates et al. 2005). While some gains come early in recovery, other subtle cognitive improvements in executive control functioning may take several years. As one group of researchers concluded after reviewing longitudinal results, ". . . the message emerging from these studies is clear: Abstinence contributes to recovery, and longer abstinence contributes to greater recovery . . ." (Rosenbloom, Pfefferbaum, and Sullivan 2004).

Persons with substantial cognitive impairment do not have a worse chance for recovery. One MRI study found that those with the greatest impairment showed, with abstinence, improvement (Sullivan et al. 2000), reflecting not only the obvious greater room for improvement but also the resiliency of the brain. Also, the extent of cognitive impairment does not predict treatment success. However, motivation may be a critical component, and the relatively simple strategies of using support systems and avoiding alcohol-related situations may be the most important tools in early recovery. The Twelve Step approach may be especially helpful because of the repetition and social network it provides, and because it reinforces breaking complex tasks into smaller ones (Hazelden Nov. 2006).

*Note:*

*Impairments in memory, learning, and thinking that are caused by alcohol dependence are in most cases reversed if the drinker remains abstinent. Recovery in cognitive function occurs at different rates in different people, and some areas of function recover more rapidly than other areas. Contrary to popular belief, persons with more extensive cognitive impairment do not have a worse chance for successful recovery from their addiction. One of the reasons for this is that motivation is a crucial element of success in treatment and recovery.*

## Subtypes of Alcoholics

Earlier in this chapter we looked at the brain process that forms the basis of the development as well as the progression of alcohol dependence. We also saw how these changes in the brain account for the symptoms of alcohol dependence that are described by the *DSM-IV-TR,* which include loss of control over drinking, continued drinking despite consequences, preoccupation with alcohol use, tolerance, physical withdrawal, and the foregoing of important social and recreational activities in favor of alcohol use (APA 2000). Although core symptoms representing alcohol dependence are generally agreed upon, not all persons with a serious drinking problem exhibit the same pattern of symptoms.

Alcoholism is a complex disease with a development that is influenced by genetic, environmental, psychological, and behavioral factors. For more than sixty years, researchers and clinicians have recognized distinct differences in the pattern of symptoms that manifest among alcoholic patients. This recognition resulted in efforts to classify alcoholics into meaningful subgroups in the belief that identifying subtypes of alcoholic patients could increase the effectiveness of treatment selection, treatment outcome prediction, and prediction of the future disease course (Pombo et al. 2008; Moss, Chen, and Yi 2007).

The history of modern alcoholic subtyping systems actually began with the Big Book of Alcoholics Anonymous, first published in 1939. On page 31 there is reference to the moderate drinker, the problem drinker, and the "real alcoholic" (Alcoholics Anonymous 1939). This unscientific observation was the catalyst for the first scientific investigations into various types of problem drinking. E. M. Jellinek began the scientific investigation of alcoholism in the late 1930s, and devised a classification system consisting of what he termed "species" of alcoholism primarily influenced by responses to a questionnaire from the Alcoholics Anonymous newsletter called the *Grapevine* (Fingarette 1989). The following are brief descriptions of the species identified by Jellinek (Jellinek 1960).

### Alpha Alcoholism

Alpha alcoholism is marked by a purely psychological dependence on alcohol, but without loss of control or the inability to abstain. There is a powerful reliance on alcohol to self-medicate stress and life problems, but progression is not inevitable. Jellinek notes that other writers may refer to this species as problem drinkers.

### Beta Alcoholism

Beta alcoholism is identified by medical problems resulting from alcohol use, such as cirrhosis or gastritis, in the absence of psychological or physical dependence. It is more likely to occur in persons from cultures with widespread heavy drinking and inadequate diet.

### Gamma Alcoholism

This species exhibits tolerance to alcohol, physiological changes leading to withdrawal symptoms, and loss of control over drinking; undergoes a progression from psychological to physical dependence; and experiences the most devastating physical and social consequences. According to Jellinek this is the most common species in the U.S. and in AA.

### Delta Alcoholism

Very similar to the gamma variety, delta alcoholism exhibits psychological and physical dependence but without loss of control, and persons are likely to suffer from withdrawal when abstaining for even brief periods.

### Epsilon Alcoholism

This species has not been studied in depth, but it is fundamentally different from other species. Jellinek called this *periodic alcoholism* as it is characterized by binge drinking.

### Recently Identified Alcoholism Subtypes

A study of Swedish adoptees and their biological and adoptive parents resulted in identifying two distinct alcoholism subtypes, Type I and Type II. These two subtypes differ by the age of onset of alcoholism, the relative contributions of genetic and environmental factors, gender and personality traits, and whether co-occurring psychiatric disorders (such as antisocial personality disorder) are present (Cloninger, Sigvardsson, and Bohman 1996).

C. Robert Cloninger, M.D., identified Type I alcoholism as characterized by later onset of dependence (25 years or older), few sociopathic features, drinking that is motivated by the desire for stress and anxiety relief, and fewer alcohol-related problems and childhood risk factors. Type II alcoholism was characterized by early age of onset, character pathology with antisocial and impulsive features, childhood risk factors, and more severe alcohol-related problems (Kenna, McGeary, and Swift 2004). Further research revealed three traits that most readily identified type: harm avoidance, reward dependence, and novelty (thrill) seeking. Different brain systems are believed to underlie these traits, an example being dopamine involvement in the trait of novelty seeking (Cloninger 1987).

The following table highlights the differences between Cloninger Type I and Type II alcoholics (Henderson 2000).

Table 4.1

Traits That Distinguish the Cloninger Alcoholism Subtypes

|  | Type I | Type II |
| --- | --- | --- |
| Onset of alcoholism | after age twenty-five | before age twenty-five |
| Fighting, arrests | infrequent | frequent |
| Feelings of guilt, apprehension | frequent | infrequent |
| Novelty-seeking behavior | infrequent | frequent |
| Introversion | frequent | infrequent |
| Alcoholic parent | mother | father |
| Drinking pattern | episodic | continuous |
| Effect of milieu | significant | insignificant |

The Lesch typology integrates biological, social, and psychological factors in one classification (Lesch et al. 1990; Lesch and Walter 1996) and identifies four subtypes:

- Type 1 (model of allergy) are patients with heavy alcohol withdrawal symptoms who tend to use alcohol to reduce or eliminate withdrawal symptoms.

- Type 2 (model of anxiety or conflict) are patients who use alcohol to self-medicate anxiety and stress.
- Type 3 patients have an underlying mood disorder and use alcohol as an antidepressant (Kiefer and Barocka 1999).
- Type 4 patients (alcohol as adaptation) show pre-alcohol brain dysfunction, behavioral disorders, and a high social burden (Hillemacher and Bleich 2008).

Perhaps the most-studied alcoholism typology is that of Babor et al. (1992). Relative to type A alcoholics, type Bs are characterized by greater severity, earlier onset, stronger family history of alcoholism, more childhood risk factors such as conduct disorder, and greater frequency of co-occurring psychiatric and substance use disorders (Bogenschutz, Tonigan, and Pettinati 2009).

Several of the typologies share common features, such as the Cloninger and Babor systems. The most widely recognized subtyping of alcoholics separates alcoholics who have a later onset of problem drinking and less severe alcohol dependence and alcohol-related problems from alcoholics with an early age of onset of problem drinking, a strong family history of alcoholism problems, pre-existing disorders such as conduct disorder, and severe alcohol dependence and alcohol-related problems. The age of onset of problem drinking and disease progression are also partially determined by genetics (Babor and Caetano 2006).

The recognition of these differences in disease pattern has been critically important in the discovery of differences between subgroups of alcoholics in treatment response, reflecting the genetic differences between these subgroups (O'Brien 2005). Several types of medications that act on brain serotonin systems have been found to be helpful in some subtypes and not in others. The two FDA-approved medications, acamprosate and naltrexone, are more effective in certain subtypes of alcoholics than in others (Pombo and Lesch 2009).

The different subtypes in Lesch's typology have corresponding differences in neurobiology that may have practical implications for clinicians. One of these is related to differences in how glutamate transmission is regulated by the NMDA (N-methyl-D-aspartate) receptor, which has important implications for treatment response to acamprosate and naltrexone (Hillemacher and Bleich 2008). This approach to studying how medication response is influenced by genetic makeup is referred to as *pharmacogenetics* or *pharmacogenomics*, and is further described below (Hillemacher and Bleich 2008).

*Note:*

*For many decades, workers in the field of alcoholism have noticed pronounced differences among their patients in the patterns of alcohol use, co-occurring problems, and family histories. These observations led to efforts to identify distinct subgroups of alcoholics in order to better match alcoholism subtype with treatment and to optimize outcome and improve the prediction of disease course. More recently, researchers have used their understanding of the genetics of alcoholism, the role of environmental factors, and the interaction of genetics with environment to identify and define several subtypes of alcoholism. Although several classification schemes have been published, two subtypes have been consistently identified. The two differ by*

- *the age of onset;*
- *the severity of the alcohol addiction;*
- *the extent of alcoholism and psychiatric illness in the biological family; and*
- *the presence or absence of character and personality traits such as impulsive or antisocial traits, thrill seeking, anxiety and stress, and harm avoidance.*

*These differences between subtypes are believed to reflect differences in the underlying neurobiology. Numerous studies have found important differences in how subtypes of alcoholics respond to treatment.*

## Brain Science on the Frontier of Treatment Development

Alcoholism, like other addictions, is a brain disorder. Research has shown that genes help shape how an individual experiences alcohol—how intoxicating, pleasant, or sedating it is—and helps influence how susceptible the drinker is to developing an alcohol problem. Research has also shown that alcohol dependence causes long-term—and perhaps permanent—changes in the way the brain responds to alcohol. These parallel insights from neuroscience research are paving the way for new medications that will improve alcoholism treatment and relapse prevention (NIAAA 2004).

Based on neuroscience research, scientists are developing medications that could potentially target both the acute response to alcohol and the adaptation of the brain to constant alcohol exposure (neuroadaptation) that occurs with alcohol dependence. Potential medications may target specific receptor types, the series of chemical reactions set off by receptor activation, or the production of critical protein enzymes involved in these processes within the brain cells. To use these strategies effectively and safely, however, researchers must first understand in detail where and how alcohol produces its effects (NIAAA 2004).

The age of initial use and regular use of alcohol, and the age of onset of alcohol dependence, are influenced by environmental and genetic factors, as are the adaptive changes in the brain that occur with chronic alcohol exposure. It is likely that differences between alcoholics in the brain process of adaptation will be found in the near future, and that this discovery will further help researchers understand the differences in response to medication treatment (Spanagel and Kiefer 2008).

Enormous ground has been covered by neuroscience in explaining the development of addiction, and in describing how the persistent changes in brain structure and function continue to place the recovering alcoholic at risk of relapse long after abstinence has been achieved. Many prominent researchers in the field of alcoholism and addiction are also looking to neuroscience to address key issues related to recovery from alcohol and other drug addiction. It will be this focus on the neurobiology of recovery that represents the new frontier of addiction research. Among the questions that remain to be answered by neuroscience include the following (White 2007):

- What is the degree to which neurobiology influences the ability or inability to recover from addiction?
- To what extent can long-term recovery reverse addiction-related brain pathology?
- What is the time frame over which such pathologies are reversed?
- What is the role played by pharmacological adjuncts, social support, and other services in extending and speeding this brain recovery process?
- Is the extent and time frame of neurobiological recovery influenced by the age of onset of use, duration of addiction, problem severity and complexity, age of onset of recovery, gender, genetic load for addiction, or developmental trauma?

*Note:*

*Neuroscience has contributed enormously to a greater understanding of many aspects of alcoholism. These include the vulnerability to developing alcohol addiction, how changes in brain structure and function influence the change in behavior as one's drinking progresses into alcohol dependence, and how these changes in brain structure and function persist into abstinence to heighten relapse risk. This information is now being used to develop interventions that more accurately target the functional abnormalities in brain chemicals and neuron pathways. However, many questions remain unanswered and will be the focus of ongoing future investigation by neuroscientists and addiction researchers. Especially important areas for future research include the process of recovery from addiction, restoration of normal brain function, and factors that influence the ability or inability to achieve recovery from addiction.*

CHAPTER 5

# Alcohol Withdrawal and Its Management

An alcoholic is likely to experience the symptoms of alcohol withdrawal when he or she suddenly stops drinking. Although symptoms of alcohol withdrawal have been recognized since ancient times, even today alcohol withdrawal remains under-recognized and undertreated. The signs and symptoms of acute alcohol withdrawal can begin as early as six hours after the initial decline from peak intoxication (even when the patient still has significant blood alcohol concentrations) and include the following: (CSAT 2006; Trevisan et al. 1998):

- Restlessness, irritability, anxiety, agitation
- Anorexia (lack of appetite), nausea, vomiting
- Tremor, elevated heart rate, increased blood pressure
- Insomnia, nightmares
- Poor concentration, impaired memory and judgment
- Increased sensitivity to sound, light, and tactile sensations
- Hallucinations that can be auditory, visual, or touch-related (tactile)
- Paranoia or delusions of being persecuted

- Grand mal seizures (a severe, abnormal electrical discharge in major brain regions that may cause loss of consciousness, brief cessation of breathing, and muscle rigidity followed by muscle jerking and then confusion)
- Hyperthermia (high fever)
- Delirium with disorientation, fluctuating level of consciousness

## Acute Alcohol Withdrawal, Delirium Tremens, and Their Treatment

Mild alcohol withdrawal generally consists of anxiety, irritability, difficulty sleeping, and decreased appetite. Severe alcohol withdrawal, occurring in roughly 10% of patients, consists of trembling hands and arms, sweating, elevated pulse and blood pressure, heightened sensitivity to noise and light, and brief periods of hallucinations.

Seizures and full-blown delirium tremens (DTs) reflect the most extreme forms of acute and severe alcohol withdrawal. DTs are fatal in as many as 25% of patients who experience them. Since alcohol withdrawal is potentially deadly, patients may require admission to an intensive care unit for severe or complicated alcohol withdrawal (CSAT 2006; Trevisan et al. 1998).

The course of alcohol withdrawal varies from patient to patient. Symptoms usually start within a few hours of the last drink. DTs sometimes follow after one to three days and may last two to ten days, and consist of an altered awareness of one's surroundings, disorientation, poor short-term memory, disrupted sleep–wake cycle, and hallucinations (NIAAA 2005). The severity of alcohol withdrawal may be influenced by the quantity of alcohol consumed before withdrawal, the severity of the last withdrawal episodes, and the number of previously treated or untreated withdrawal episodes. The severity of alcohol withdrawal can be intensified by older age; poor health and nutritional status; the presence of co-existing medical or psychiatric disorders; and the use of prescription, over-the-counter, or herbal medications (CSAT 2006).

A class of drugs known as the benzodiazepines has been the medication of choice in managing alcohol withdrawal for decades, and remains so today. The favored drugs from this class are diazepam (Valium), chlordiazepoxide (Librium), lorazepam (Ativan), and oxazepam (Serax). Early recognition of alcohol withdrawal and rapid administration of a suitable benzodiazepine will usually prevent a progression in symptom severity. Generally, patients with severe withdrawal require 20 mg of diazepam or 100 mg of chlordiazepoxide every two to three hours until improvement or sedation prevails (CSAT 2006). Other medications have been used to manage alcohol withdrawal, including antiseizure drugs, beta-blockers, alpha-adrenergic agonists, and antipsychotic drugs. However, these agents are either incompletely effective or have not been sufficiently evaluated (CSAT 2006). An approach called symptoms-triggered withdrawal therapy involves the rating of signs and symptoms by medical personnel, and then administering benzodiazepines only when the signs and symptoms reach a particular threshold score (CSAT 2006).

Alcohol withdrawal must be treated aggressively because the severity of alcohol withdrawal is progressive and life-threatening. Death or permanent disability can result from delirium tremens or seizures without adequate medical care. Patients who have experienced seizures and delirium tremens during withdrawal are likely to experience even more severe alcohol withdrawal in the future, and there is evidence that some patients become less and less responsive to medication during subsequent alcohol withdrawal episodes (CSAT 2006).

## Post-acute Alcohol Withdrawal

Post-acute alcohol withdrawal (PAW), also called protracted abstinence syndrome and protracted withdrawal, are symptoms of alcohol withdrawal that extend beyond the period of acute alcohol withdrawal (Satel et al. 1993).

The symptoms of PAW can include the following (CSAT 2010):

- Cognitive impairment, including difficulty concentrating, impairment in abstract reasoning, rigid repetitive thinking

- Memory impairment, including short-term memory problems, difficulty in remembering significant events, difficulty learning new information
- Emotional overreaction, irritability, mood instability
- Sleep disturbances
- Fatigue
- Hypersensitivity to stress
- Emotional numbness, difficulty in experiencing pleasure

The intensity and time frame of PAW varies; some will experience few if any symptoms of PAW following acute alcohol withdrawal, while others may experience symptoms for several months (CSAT 2010).

Several factors are believed to contribute to PAW. For some recently sober persons, anxiety and depression may be the result of single or multiple drinking-related crises such as job termination, divorce, or legal problems that occurred before they became sober.

For others, problems with mood and emotion can reflect a psychiatric condition such as depression that has become unmasked during abstinence. Significant problems with memory and cognitive function may reflect the neurotoxic effects of chronic alcoholism or brain trauma that may have occurred during intoxication.

But perhaps for most persons, the symptoms of PAW stem from the long-lasting changes to the brain from chronic alcohol abuse, such as the process of neuroadaptation described previously. In this case, the brain attempts to compensate for the sedating effects of alcohol by cranking up the release of excitatory neurotransmitters such as glutamate, which are suppressed by alcohol. When alcohol is withdrawn from the system, this compensation process may take some time to revert back to normal, resulting in the continued release of excessive amounts of stimulating brain chemicals that produce agitation, insomnia, anxiety, and restlessness (CSAT 2010; Martinotti et al. 2008; Pozzi et al. 2008).

A very interesting aspect of PAW is the observation by workers in the field of alcoholism and by the original authors of the text used by Alcoholics Anonymous (*Alcoholics Anonymous* 1976). They believed that active engagement in a recovery program such as AA can lessen PAW, and that the symptoms of PAW can re-emerge in recovering alcoholics who discontinue their participation in a recovery program. The book *Alcoholics Anonymous* (the Big Book) describes the alcoholic as in a restless, irritable, and discontented state before a relapse (*Alcoholics Anonymous* 1976). Although disengagement from a recovery program as the *cause* of re-emergent PAW has not yet been validated (or disproven) by scientific investigation, the *association* between the two has received wide enough observation to be incorporated into the Gorski and Miller model of relapse prevention (Gorski and Miller 1986).

An important point is that although the distress some persons experience during PAW may result in relapse, the risk of relapse persists long after the resolution of PAW (Heilig et al. 2010).

Before we begin a discussion of specific therapy approaches in chapter six that help alcoholics achieve sobriety, a couple of questions related to alcoholism treatment in general need to be addressed.

### Should Abstinence Be the Goal for Alcohol-Dependent Patients?

With a drinker who has progressed into an alcohol-dependency syndrome, the goal of abstinence is logical, achievable, and, in the end, easier than attempting to moderate the drinking. There are other compelling reasons for abstinence as a treatment goal. Persons with multiple substance dependencies increase the risk of relapsing to another drug, such as cocaine, if they resume drinking (Owen and Marlatt 2001).

The concept of teaching alcohol-dependent patients to control their drinking reached the pinnacle of enthusiasm a couple of decades ago with Linda and Mark Sobell's 1970s study that involved training alcohol-dependent patients to control and moderate their drinking (Sobell and Sobell 1976). This study was famous worldwide for years—until their patients were followed up at the ten-year mark and found to have fared no better than controls (Pendery, Maltzman, and West 1982). These long-term results served to discredit controlled drinking as a viable treatment option for alcohol-dependent drinkers (Vaillant 2005).

### How Can the Twelve Steps or Psychological Therapy Help Treat a Biological Brain Disease?

Current neuroscience research has shown that alcohol dependence is a brain disease characterized by dramatic and persistent changes in brain structure and function that are responsible for producing the various behavioral symptoms of alcoholism.

A natural question to ask at this point is, "How can a biological brain disease be successfully treated with Twelve Steps or psychosocial interventions?" Or in other words, how can a biological disease be treated by a nonbiological therapy?

As we know, sensations, perceptions, emotions, psychological experiences and problems, and psychiatric disorders are mediated by biochemical events in the brain (Seidel 2005). Likewise, life experiences and events, especially ones involving trauma, can produce substantial and even permanent changes in the biochemical functioning of specific brain regions and interconnected pathways of neurons. Childhood abuse, for example, is a risk factor for developing alcoholism because the extreme stress can create lasting alterations in brain systems that regulate the ability to manage emotional stress.

The brain is now viewed as an open system that is influenced by, and interacts with, the environment. Brain cells continue to grow and the neural circuitry that integrates various parts of the brain remains active throughout life. This adaptive aspect of the brain is referred to as *neuroplasticity,* which also means that early deficits in brain functioning can be changed with new experiences and new learning, and changing old memories with new information.

Also, "emotionally meaningful experience" helps create new neuron connections, suggesting that new learning may not be possible without emotion. Research has also found that a significant close relationship later in adulthood with an intimate partner or a therapist can reduce impaired development and psychological deficiencies, and that such transformative relationships actually alter the structure and function of the brain in a positive, more healthy direction (Kranzberg 2000/2001; Allen 1999; Rolfe 2000).

A growing body of research is establishing that the positive effects of psychotherapy are dependent on long-term positive changes in pathological brain patterns. These studies have used imaging tests, typically PET (positron emission tomography) or fMRI (functional magnetic resonance imaging) to scan the brains of patients with major depression, obsessive-compulsive disorder, and other psychiatric conditions before, during, and after the successful completion of psychotherapy. Most of these studies have employed cognitive-behavioral therapy, behavioral therapy, interpersonal therapy, or psychodynamic psychotherapy as the form of psychotherapy. These studies have identified changes that occur as progress is made in therapy and distressing symptoms lessen or resolve (Etkin et al. 2005). Psychotherapy facilitates therapeutic change through biological mechanisms, and symptom reduction is directly related to underlying changes in brain function (Seidel 2005). It should be stressed that psychosocial therapy has a very complex effect on neurobiology that defies simple explanations (Schuessler 2003).

Some of the mechanisms involved in the positive change in brain structure and function associated with psychotherapy include the alteration of memory processing, reducing the overactivation of brain stress systems, normalizing the metabolic activity in key brain regions such as the prefrontal cortex, improving the regulation of specific neurotransmitter function, modifying brain circuits involved in negative emotions and fear, and altering activity in the thyroid axis stress response system (Porto et al. 2009; Frewen, Dozois, and Lanius 2008; Centonze et al. 2005; Liggan and Kay 1999).

Fundamental changes in brain biology are now regarded as the basis for the lasting positive changes in behavior, thinking, or emotions resulting from successful involvement in psychological therapy (Bogerts 1996). Very little is known of the neurobiological changes that result from sudden transformative spiritual experience, or whether a profound spiritual experience might be the result of a sudden and dramatic or quantum change in brain chemistry. William Miller, the creator of Motivational Interviewing, co-authored a book called *Quantum Change: When Epiphanies and Sudden Insights Transform Ordinary Lives* that explores this issue. AA involvement is the most effective approach for achieving durable sobriety from alcohol dependence. Folk wisdom in AA states that its Steps and principles are the basis of its spiritual program. However, many psychosocial factors have been identified as "active ingredients" in AA, and in addition to spiritual factors, these psychosocial factors have been confirmed as playing a significant role in helping members of AA achieve and maintain sobriety.

Thus, it seems reasonable to assume that some of the positive changes in brain structure and function that result from psychotherapy are also likely to occur with long-term regular AA involvement. These positive changes in brain function account for at least some of the improvements in thinking, mood, behavior, feelings of serenity and well-being, and ability to achieve sobriety that develops over time with AA involvement.

*Note:*

*Alcohol dependence is a disease with symptoms and behaviors caused by the altered function of brain chemicals and networks of brain cells. This biological basis may lead a person to ask how talk therapy such as Twelve Step participation or psychological treatment can help the alcoholic achieve abstinence. Neuroscientists have begun answering this question with brain imaging technologies that have identified specific brain changes that occur as patients undergo psychotherapy for psychiatric conditions. As will be discussed later, psychological factors play an essential role in the process by which alcoholics recover through AA involvement. Because research is now showing how psychological therapy alters and normalizes abnormal brain function in persons with psychiatric conditions, it seems reasonable to assume that many of the psychological factors that contribute to the benefits of AA involvement also produce positive brain changes. At this time there is very little information on how spiritual experiences or spiritual factors produce positive changes in brain biology that promote abstinence. This would be a fascinating and very useful area for future research.*

## CHAPTER 6

# Twelve Step and Other Self-Help Therapies

In the U.S., roughly eighteen million persons are in need of treatment for alcohol dependence every year, but only about one million receive any treatment (Kranzler et al. 2006). Because of this, self-help groups provide a vital resource for the alcoholic who is seeking support for abstinence. Self-help groups are nonprofessional organizations that are peer-operated by persons who share the same addictive disorder. Self-help groups are free (Humphreys et al. 2004), and members can attend them indefinitely if they wish. This is an important point in light of the emerging view that alcohol and drug addiction is best treated as a chronic illness that entails a long-term, low-intensity management approach that is similar to diabetes and high blood pressure (hypertension) (WSASHO 2003).

Some key facts about alcoholism self-help groups in the U.S. include the following:

- They are the most frequently accessed resource for alcohol problems.
- AA is much larger and more available than non-Twelve Step organizations.

- Alternative self-help groups exist both for individuals desiring a different approach to the traditional Twelve Step model and for persons with co-occurring psychiatric illness and alcoholism (WSASHO 2003).

The growth of AA has also spawned a larger self-help movement. The Twelve Steps of AA have been adapted for those addicted to other substances (Narcotics Anonymous, Cocaine Anonymous), for family members and spouses or partners (Al-Anon, Alateen, Ala-Tot), for other compulsive behaviors (Gamblers Anonymous, Sex Addicts Anonymous, Overeaters Anonymous), for child abusers (Parents Anonymous), and even for persons who grew up in a dysfunctional family (Adult Children of Alcoholics, Adult Children of Dysfunctional Families) (Kurtz 1991).

## Alcoholics Anonymous

Alcoholics Anonymous (AA) is an abstinence-based support and self-improvement program that is based on the Twelve Step model of recovery. AA is widely considered the most successful treatment for alcoholism, and has helped hundreds of thousands of alcoholics achieve and maintain sobriety (McGee 2000). The Twelve Step model emphasizes acceptance of addiction as a chronic progressive disease that can be arrested through abstinence but not cured. Additional elements of the AA model include spiritual growth, personal responsibility, and helping other alcoholics. By inducing a shift in the consciousness of the alcoholic, AA offers a holistic solution. AA is also a resource for emotional support (Humphreys et al. 2004), and is perhaps more accurately classified as a mutual-help organization (Kranzler et al. 2006). AA is widely available, and in AA there are no dues or fees. AA is guided by a tradition to be fully self-supporting. Many AA meetings and members are willing to work with treatment centers and medical professionals.

A sizable number of adults in the U.S. have had at least some contact with AA. A study from 1990 found that 13.3% of the adult U.S. population reported attending one or more Twelve Step meetings of any kind (Room and

Greenfield 1993), while a more recent study estimated that 3 to 3.5% of adults have attended at least one AA meeting (Kaskutas et al. 2008). An estimated 80% to 90% of abstinence-based treatment programs are built—to a greater or lesser degree—around the Twelve Step model (Forman, Humphreys, and Tonigan 2003).

Referral to AA following treatment is also very widespread. Among substance abuse treatment programs in Veterans Administration Medical Centers, 79% referred clients to AA upon discharge (Humphreys, Huebsch, et al. 1999). Almost 80% of adults who seek help for alcohol dependence participate in AA (Dawson et al. 2006). Most persons receiving formal substance abuse treatment attend AA, even if only for a limited time, and for many people AA is the first and only point of contact for receiving help for their alcohol problem (Tonigan 2007). Thus, AA is a widely used resource for alcoholics attempting to get sober.

## Demographics of AA: Who Shows Up and Who Stays

AA membership is informal. The only requirement for membership is a desire to stop drinking (i.e., the person may still be drinking), and membership is achieved simply by expressing this desire. Membership records are not kept. A key principle for Twelve Step groups is anonymity, which allows members to attend meetings without fear that their addiction or what they discuss in the meeting will be revealed to anyone outside the group. There are no dues or fees for AA membership. AA groups are self-supporting through their own contributions.

A report of the General Service Office of AA, dated January 1, 2010, produced the membership figures shown in table 6.1 (Alcoholics Anonymous 2010):

Table 6.1

## AA Membership by Individuals and Groups

| Description | Number of members |
| --- | --- |
| AA groups in the U.S. | 56,694 |
| AA members in the U.S. | 1,264,716 |
| AA groups in Canada | 4,887 |
| AA members in Canada | 94,163 |
| AA groups outside U.S./Canada | 52,600 |
| AA members outside U.S./Canada | 704,266 |
| AA groups in U.S./Canada correctional facilities | 1,589 |
| AA members in U.S./Canada correctional facilities | 39,731 |
| Lone members | 157 |
| Internationalist groups | 3 |
| Total members | 2,103,033 |
| Total groups | 115,773 |

### The Most Recent AA Membership Survey Results

AA conducts a membership survey every three years. The most recent survey is from 2007 and was based on the responses by more than 8,000 AA members in the U.S. and Canada. The survey was due to be conducted again in 2010, but due to an oversight, the request for approval was left off the Agenda for the 2010 General Service Conference (Nancy B. 2010). The *Alcoholics Anonymous 2007 Membership Survey* pamphlet and current 2011 demographic data are available online at www.aa.org.

## AA Attendance Is Not the Same as AA Involvement, and the Difference Matters

Historically, mere attendance of AA meetings was regarded as the sole and sufficient measure of AA involvement, and attendance was also viewed as sufficient to obtain the benefits of sobriety and improved emotional health (Emrick et al. 1993; Tonigan, Toscova, and Miller 1996). A perspective of AA affiliation has recently emerged (Tonigan, Connors, and Miller 1996; Humphreys, Kaskutas, and Weisner 1998; Tonigan, Miller, and Vick 2000) that has allowed researchers to more precisely measure the outcome of AA affiliation based on the different levels of engagement and commitment to AA. Research consensus is that the level of involvement in AA has a much more powerful effect on the achievement of abstinence and other benefits than the number of meetings attended.

Another important finding is the long-term beneficial effect of the level of AA participation; the extent of involvement at three years strongly predicts involvement at ten years. The different elements that make up AA involvement included practicing the principles of the AA program, involvement in the fellowship of AA, and attendance at AA meetings (Westphal, Worth, and Tonigan 2003). A pattern of AA affiliation has been observed among many persons who are successfully staying sober; initially, attendance of meetings is higher, but over time attendance declines while involvement remains steady or increases (Owen et al. 2003).

### Research on AA Affiliation and Drop-Out

The different patterns of AA participation are important to study in order to (1) identify AA-related behaviors that are associated with positive outcome, and to (2) understand why and under what circumstances people choose to discontinue their AA involvement.

An examination of AA membership surveys, U.S. population surveys, and longitudinal treatment data have found stable female and minority representation in AA over time. Disengagement from AA did not appear to necessarily translate into loss of abstinence among those with initial high levels of AA involvement, but long-term abstinence was more likely among those with continued AA involvement (Kaskutas et al. 2008).

Despite the narrow demographic origin of AA as a program founded by white, male, Protestant, middle-class Americans, AA has been shown to be equally attractive to clients from a wide range of ethnic and cultural backgrounds. Results from the Project MATCH treatment study suggest that AA affiliation patterns may vary among persons from different ethnic backgrounds. For example, although the AA attendance rates of Hispanics and African Americans were lower than those of whites, Hispanics demonstrated higher levels of commitment to AA despite lower attendance than did whites. Most importantly in the Project MATCH study, both AA attendance and AA involvement were associated with improved abstinence regardless of racial or ethnic background (Tonigan, Connors, and Miller 1998).

Evidence shows that persons considered members of special populations (women, adolescents, the elderly, persons from different racial and ethnic groups, and people with disabilities) do not experience undue problems with AA affiliation (Timko 2008). This may be due to the intentional design of the Twelve Step program to be broad and open to divergent interpretations, and that AA's ideological flexibility allows wide application across diverse special populations holding different beliefs and values. However, people are more likely to join and benefit from groups that are composed of members with similar characteristics and who have goals and values that are consistent with their own (Mankowski, Humphreys, and Moos 2001; Timko 2008).

Although Twelve Step groups are an important resource for managing alcohol and other drug problems, their efficacy in patients with a history of physical or sexual abuse is unknown. Schneider, Burnette, and Timko (2008) observed that physical or sexual abuse history was actually associated with greater attendance and involvement in Twelve Step groups and found that the extent of participation in these groups predicted abstinence at one year, regardless of abuse history.

Dually diagnosed individuals (those with alcohol or other drug dependence and a co-occurring psychiatric condition) attend Twelve Step programs at rates comparable to the nondually diagnosed, although specific diagnoses may have some effect on attendance. The benefits of Twelve Step attendance do not appear to be markedly different for those with psychiatric disorders. Although specialized Twelve Step programs such as Dual Recovery Anonymous, Dual Diagnosis Anonymous, and Double Trouble in Recovery may have benefits for the dually diagnosed above and beyond those of AA, it is also likely that all three organizations possess a common mechanism that facilitates sobriety and emotional health (Bogenschutz 2007).

A study that followed persons with impaired executive functioning (problems with decision making, impulse control, planning, and organization) in their first six months of sobriety found similar outcomes between participants with and without impaired executive functioning, although persons with neurological damage are likely to use different means of working the AA program to compensate for their deficits (Morgenstern and Bates 1999).

AA affiliation was found to be unaffected by differences in alcoholism subtype, suggesting that AA participation appeals equally to type A and type B alcoholics (Bogenschutz, Tonigan, and Miller 2006).

Anecdotes from Minneapolis/Saint Paul AA members suggest an income disparity between those who attend AA only after completing treatment and those who attend AA without having gone through formal treatment. Persons with fewer financial resources appear to use AA as a primary resource more often than those in the middle or upper classes. This was observed by the difference in proportion of members who have not had treatment between inner city and suburban AA clubs (Willenbring and Rose 1993).

**Atheists and Agnostics**

The well-documented problem of high dropout rates among new AA members may be related to alienation over the spiritual/religious emphasis (Zemore 2008). Further exploration of this potential obstacle is vitally important, since persons who drop out of AA cannot obtain the benefits of AA involvement.

To examine the process by which atheists and agnostics enter and affiliate with AA, Tonigan, Miller, and Schermer (2002) tracked 1,526 alco-holics during and after outpatient treatment. Atheist and agnostic clients attended AA significantly less often than clients who described themselves as spiritual or religious. However, AA attendance was significantly associ-ated with improved abstinence regardless of God belief. No differences in abstinence were found between atheist and agnostic clients compared with spiritual and religious clients.

The researchers concluded that although God belief appears relatively unimportant in obtaining the benefits of AA, atheist and agnostic clients are less likely to initiate and sustain their AA attendance relative to spiri-tual and religious clients. This reluctance among atheists and agnostics to become involved with AA should be recognized by clinicians and counsel-ors. They should be sensitive to this issue but still encourage these clients to affiliate with AA since they obtain the same positive outcomes as religious and spiritually oriented clients. Therapists need to understand the positive outcomes with atheist and agnostic AA members, because research has shown that therapists are much less likely to refer problem drinkers to AA who identify themselves as atheists (Winzelberg and Humphreys 1999).

### AA Attendance by Drug-Dependent Persons

Another very important aspect related to the background characteris-tics of persons who affiliate with AA involves the large numbers of drug-dependent persons who choose to attend AA in conjunction with or to the exclusion of Narcotics Anonymous (NA) and other drug-oriented Twelve Step programs. In the past, some AA meetings strictly enforced the singleness of purpose principle (limit sharing only to alcohol and alcohol-related problems) and banned the sharing of other drug experi-ences. Today, most, if not all, AA meetings are flexible and meet the needs of their group members, whether or not they also use drugs. Reasons for affiliating with AA among persons with drug addiction histories may have less to do with the need to identify with persons whose addiction involved the same substance and more to do with the desire to connect with other persons in recovery who share similar demographic characteristics such as race, gender, or social class (Laudet 2008).

# Components of AA

Just as individual members are encouraged to achieve sobriety by working the Twelve Steps, AA is guided in its structure and function by the Twelve Traditions, originally developed by Bill Wilson and the early members of AA to preserve the unique nature of AA while allowing for an independent and thriving recovery organization (Alcoholics Anonymous 1952).

## Structure and Organization

Some examples of guidance by the Twelve Traditions include the following, the Second Tradition: "For our group purpose, there is but one ultimate authority—a loving God as He may express Himself in our group conscience. Our leaders are but trusted servants; they do not govern." AA does not have a leader running the organization or making decisions for the membership. In addition, the Seventh and Eighth Traditions state that each AA group shall be "fully self-supporting, declining outside contributions" and shall "remain forever nonprofessional" (Laudet 2008; Alcoholics Anonymous 2010).

AA has a General Service Board made up of alcoholic and nonalcoholic trustees. Whenever a decision on movement-wide policy is needed, the Board turns to the General Service Conference, a body that includes the trustees and non-trustee directors, AA staff, and delegates who represent AA members. The General Service Board takes care of its administrative duties through two operating corporations (Alcoholics Anonymous 2010): (1) AA World Services, Inc., based in New York City, where 85 employees maintain contact information for AA groups in the community, in treatment centers, and correctional facilities; respond to inquiries from the media and the public; and prepare, publish, and distribute conference-approved AA literature; and (2) the AA Grapevine, Inc., which publishes the *Grapevine,* the monthly international periodical of AA with a current circulation of 120,000. Each corporation is overseen by a board of AA members who are trustees, non-trustee directors, and management of the respective corporation.

## The Twelve Step Program

The organization of AA has its roots in the Oxford Group, a religious movement that operated informally through small discussion groups, where an emphasis was placed on confession, honesty, frank discussion of emotional difficulties, unselfishness, and praying to God as personally conceived. Both cofounders of AA had been involved in the Oxford Group and for a short time worked within its framework (Trice 1959).

The program of AA is described in the basic texts of AA: the books *Alcoholics Anonymous* (usually referred to as the Big Book) and *Twelve Steps and Twelve Traditions* (sometimes referred to as the Twelve by Twelve). Such great care is taken to preserve the original message and language (Kurtz 1979) of AA that the principal texts of both volumes are reprinted but not revised.

Admitting powerlessness over alcohol and living a life based on spiritual principles are the foundation of the Twelve Step program of AA. The program encourages members to refrain from drinking alcohol one day at a time, to look to a power greater than themselves for strength (termed a Higher Power), and to embrace spiritual values and practices as suggested in the Twelve Steps. The concept and definition of Higher Power is left entirely to each individual. Some common interpretations or representations of the Higher Power include the AA meeting itself, a sponsor, the God of an organized religion, or simply an external force or the energy of the Universe (Laudet 2008).

In fact, one of the most bitterly debated points in the development of the Twelve Steps related to spiritual references. Atheist and agnostic members adamantly challenged the concept of God, and other members objected to doctrinal implications. Ultimately, the common agreement was on the phrase "a Power greater than ourselves" and "God, *as we understood Him*." Thus, the Twelve Steps rest on a broad spiritual base that allows members to use virtually any conception of a Higher Power (Trice 1959).

The suggested program for recovery includes attending AA meetings, reading the AA literature such as the Big Book, having between-meeting contact with other AA members, working the Steps, working with a sponsor, sponsoring other members, and performing service work (the Twelfth Step), which can include making coffee and setting up chairs at meetings; serving as secretary, chair, or treasurer of a meeting; bringing AA meetings to hospitals and jails; or carrying the message to active alcoholics.

The Twelve Step program has been described as "a simple program for complicated people." The deceptively simple and suggested prescription for sobriety, and mental and spiritual well-being, is referred to as "the AA six pack": Don't drink or use no matter what, go to meetings, ask for help, get a sponsor, find a home group, and get active. Thus, while relying on a Higher Power, AA members are also encouraged to take responsibility for their recovery by working the program and "doing the footwork" (Laudet 2008).

### The Fellowship of AA

The fellowship of AA refers to the informal social contacts made through attending AA meetings and becoming socially involved with other AA members (Kurtz 1979). Twelve Step groups have been described as social worlds (Humphreys, Mankowski, et al. 1999); an important part of Twelve Step fellowships is what happens among members outside of meetings, such as coffee after the meeting and regular telephone contacts.

Local AA groups often sponsor dances, parties, and picnics. Families of members who attend such events together are often themselves members of Al-Anon. Individual members get together to eat lunch or drink coffee, or meet after work to bowl, fish, play cards, or go to movies. These informal contacts between members extend the relationships developed at the formal meetings. The core of this network of interpersonal relations is a shared effort to remain sober (Trice 1959).

### The Spiritual Framework of AA

AA and its Twelve Step program provide a spiritual framework for recovery from addiction. The premise of spirituality as a pathway out of active addiction is based on the understanding that people are born with an inner void that craves to be filled with meaning. Of course, alcoholics know well that this void can be artificially and temporarily filled with alcohol and drug intoxication, and that only more authentic and lasting frameworks of meaning can displace the craving for intoxication (White and Kurtz 2006).

Spiritual programs of recovery such as AA focus on defects of character such as self-centeredness, selfishness, dishonesty, resentment, anger, and preoccupation with power and control as the root of addiction, and provide a means of reaching both into oneself (through a fearless and searching moral inventory; developing the traits of honesty, humility, and tolerance) and outside oneself (reliance on a Higher Power; prayer; sharing one's experience, strength, and hope; making amends; service work; and involvement in the fellowship of AA) to resolve these character defects (Miller and Kurtz 1994; Green, Fullilove, and Fullilove 1998; White and Kurtz 2006).

## Therapeutic Processes (the "Active Ingredients") within AA

The AA experience is made up of many concepts and activities, and identifying the specific aspects of AA that play the greatest role in facilitating sobriety has become the focus of intense research interest (White and Kurtz 2006).

AA co-founder Bill Wilson stated in a 1944 presentation to the Medical Society of the State of New York (B. Wilson 1944) that AA is a synthesis of elements of medicine, psychiatry, religion, and the personal experience of its early members. He also stated that several of the core AA principles borrowed from medicine and religion are in agreement with each other, and include the following (B. Wilson 1944, 27–28; W. G. Wilson 1944):

1. *Medicine says:* The alcoholic needs a personality change.

   *Religion says:* The alcoholic needs a change of heart, a spiritual awakening.

2. *Medicine says:* The patient ought to be analyzed and should make a full and honest mental catharsis.

*Religion says:* The alcoholic should make examination of the "conscience" and a confession—or a moral inventory and a frank discussion.

3. *Medicine says:* Serious "personality defects" must be eliminated through accurate self-knowledge and realistic readjustment to life.

   *Religion says:* Character defects (sins) can be eliminated by acquiring more honesty, humility, unselfishness, tolerance, generosity, love, etc.

4. *Medicine says:* The alcoholic neurotic retreats from life, is a picture of anxiety and abnormal self-concern; he withdraws from the "herd."

   *Religion says:* The alcoholic's basic trouble is self-centeredness. Filled with fear and self-seeking, he has forgotten the "Brotherhood of Man."

5. *Medicine says:* The alcoholic must find "a new compelling interest in life," must "get back in the herd." Should find an interesting occupation, should join clubs, social activities, political parties, or discover hobbies to take the place of alcohol.

   *Religion says:* The alcoholic should learn "the expulsive power of a new affection," love of serving man, of serving God. He must "lose his life to find it," he should join a church, and there find self-forgetfulness in service. For "faith without works is dead."

In this same 1944 presentation, Wilson condenses the meaning of the Twelve Steps into the following (B. Wilson 1944, 29):

1. Admission of alcoholism

2. Personality analysis and catharsis

3. Adjustment of personal relations

4. Dependence upon some Higher Power

5. Working with other alcoholics

Wilson goes on to state that the initial aim of AA is to induce a crisis in the alcoholic by using the experience of hitting bottom to help the alcoholic reach the conclusion that he or she is an alcoholic and cannot recover without help. Under these conditions, the alcoholic is very likely to accept, and even embrace, the spiritual implications of the AA program.

Essential elements of recovery are symbolized by the acronym HOW, which means

- **H**onesty (with self and others),
- **O**pen-mindedness (to explore new ways of thinking and behaving), and
- **W**illingness (to acquire new behaviors and thought patterns).

Honesty about one's addiction is observed at AA meetings where members introduce themselves with: "My name is X, and I'm an alcoholic." This is done to counteract denial, which is considered the hallmark of addiction, "the disease that tells you that you don't have the disease" (Laudet 2008).

Fully aware of the self-willed rebellious nature of the alcoholic, the AA founders presented the Twelve Step program of recovery as a suggestion rather than a directive that must be adhered to (Laudet 2008).

Witbrodt and Kaskutas (2005) have developed a set of guidelines to assist professionals in helping their clients prioritize which element of the AA program to practice at specific stages of sobriety. In early sobriety, clients should be encouraged to commit to meeting attendance, obtain an AA sponsor, and form a social network that encourages sobriety such as the kind that AA can provide. Early involvement in service work also has a definite sobriety-enhancing effect.

### Spiritual Processes

The spiritual principles deeply embedded in the Twelve Steps are regarded by AA members as the key vehicle for attitude and behavior change in recovery (Sandoz 1999). One of the core principles of AA is that alcohol abuse is incompatible with spirituality. The essence of the AA program is not actually the disease model with which it is often confused, but the understanding that an alcoholic's best, if not only, hope for sobriety is through recognizing, appealing to, accepting help from, and directing his or her life toward a transcendent Higher Power, which is referred to as God in AA's Twelve Steps (Miller and Kurtz 1994).

The Twelve Steps are worked not just once, but rather as an ongoing lifelong program for living and transformation. Sobriety is understood in a spiritual context and involves far more than mere abstinence. It is taken for granted within AA that one can remain dry but not truly be sober, the latter having to do with a spiritual maturity that involves acceptance, humility, and serenity, with the former being a state where the underlying character defects remain unaddressed and active (Borkman 2008). It is, in AA's understanding, spirituality that finally and reliably drives out the possessive grip of addiction. Although AA meetings vary in many ways, one of the more reliable consistencies across groups is the presence of this emphasis on spirituality as the foundation for recovery (Miller 1998).

The concept of a Higher Power is the spiritual aspect most associated with AA. For many members of AA, this Higher Power is the God of a particular religious practice. However, the AA literature is not dogmatic on this issue and is clear on the importance of the Higher Power being any transcendent being or source that can serve in this capacity. The only parameter that applies to a Higher Power is that it is greater than and external to the individual, or conversely, that the AA member not be his or her own Higher Power. It was with much foresight that the founders of AA allowed for a broad and inclusive definition of God and/or Higher Power. For many persons in AA, the AA group, their AA sponsor, and the community of AA members with whom they have made an emotional connection form the basis of a Higher Power or power greater than themselves (Connors, Walitzer, and Tonigan 2008).

What exactly is spirituality and how is it defined? Spirituality, unlike religion, is difficult to define and describe, in part because spirituality has many dimensions. Several dimensions of spirituality have been suggested, and include (Miller 1998):

- overt *behavior,* such as religious and spiritual practices;
- *belief,* as it relates to a deity, the interrelatedness of living beings, soul or spirit, or life beyond material existence; and
- *experience,* such as mystical and conversion experiences, serenity, and oneness.

Bill Wilson, who authored the first edition of *Alcoholics Anonymous* in 1939, described the effect of a spiritual experience as a reformation of one's attitude toward one's life and other people (Alcoholics Anonymous 1976, 25) and described the two types of spiritual conversion processes which the recovering alcoholic may experience. The first type from the term *spiritual experience* suggests a sudden, spectacular, and profound phenomenon that is considered to be rare.

The second type is termed a *spiritual awakening* and is a slower, more gradual process considered to be much more common among recovering alcoholics in AA. Wilson also cites William James's description of a spiritual awakening as an educational process, in that spiritual growth is slow and gradual and based on learning experiences rather than dramatic, sudden transformation as described by William Miller in *Quantum Change* (Miller and C'de Baca 2001). Regardless of the type of spiritual process, the result is a personality change sufficient to bring about the recovery from alcoholism (Sandoz 1999).

Tiebout (1961) described this process of spiritual conversion among AA members as hitting bottom, followed by the maintenance of humility, surrender, and ego deflation. He also stated that the effect of both the sudden and the slow educational variety of spiritual experience produces a psychic change sufficient for recovery from alcoholism. Brown and Peterson (1987; 1990) described a change in the value system accompanied by the ability to handle life stress without resorting to alcohol or other drug use. This process includes working a Twelve Step program of recovery, which transforms one's value system.

Other authors have linked the spiritual practices of AA members with enhanced life meaning and sobriety, and that practicing the Twelve Steps in all affairs in one's life actually represents that basis of recovery in AA

(Carroll 1993). Others have described the process of recovery as moving beyond an attitude of selfishness into the service of helping others by changing one's attitudes and actions through the Twelve Steps (Gilbert 1991), while others have described the completion of specific Steps as a barometer in measuring spiritual health (Veach and Chappel 1992).

Connors, Walitzer, and Tonigan (2008) described the primary spiritual practices of AA as the activities associated with the Twelve Steps, such as practicing prayer and meditation (Step Eleven); identifying one's character defects and admitting the results of a personal inventory "to God, to ourselves, and to another human being" (Steps Four, Five, and Ten); and the willingness to make amends to persons harmed in the past (Steps Eight and Nine). Also identified was the development of personal relationships characterized by the expression of feelings, honest communication, admitting when one is wrong, treating others as one would like to be treated, forgiving others as quickly as possible, and listening to others even when not agreeing with them (Brown and Peterson 1991).

The final Step of AA reflects the expectation that working and practicing all Twelve Steps will result in a spiritual awakening. Although there are many definitions of *spiritual awakening,* the most frequently used descriptions of spiritual progress among AA members include humility, serenity, gratitude, hope, and forgiveness (Connors, Walitzer, and Tonigan 2008).

**Psychosocial Processes**

Several top addiction researchers have concluded that success in AA is partially explained by its incorporation of sophisticated forms of biopsychosocial therapy. For example, many persons who enter AA have difficulties with what is termed self-regulation (the ability to keep emotions from becoming overwhelming and to limit behavior to within a socially acceptable range). The character defects that AA addresses are personality and character traits that make interdependence—the ability to experience and express feelings and emotions—and self-care problematic and difficult.

AA encourages its members to confront these defects by effectively advocating surrender and acceptance of a Higher Power, and by challenging self-centeredness. AA also employs several of the tools used in group therapy—such as insistence on openness and honesty, emotional support, and sharing of experiences and mutual concerns—that address the vulnerabilities in self-governance and problems in regulating emotions and self-care (Khantzian and Mack 1989). After achieving sobriety in AA, a member cannot simply rest on his or her laurels but must actively engage in changing negative past behavior.

The process by which the Twelve Steps of AA facilitate change has also been described as one of cognitive restructuring. Treatment programs often use a Twelve Step approach to assist patients in developing a command of recovery slogans, which are then used to assist in problem solving and to address thinking errors. The cognitive restructuring process of the Twelve Steps describes its effect in helping the recovering alcoholic in learning to recognize and change unhealthy thoughts and attitudes (Steigerwald and Stone 1999). Others have concluded that the effectiveness of AA may be due to the use of four factors widely known to be effective in relapse prevention in addictions: external supervision, substitute dependency, new caring relationships, and enhancement of spirituality (Vaillant 2005).

The prominent alcoholism researcher Rudolf Moos (2008) reviewed an extensive body of research to identify the social processes within AA that account for the favorable outcomes among many members. He identified and described four theories that likely account for these effective outcomes:

### Social Control Theory

Social control theory states that strong connections with family, friends, work, religion, and other aspects of traditional society motivate individuals to engage in responsible behavior and refrain from substance abuse and other destructive pursuits. Because these connections with others embody the elements of monitoring, supervision, and direction toward acceptable goals and pursuits, persons are more likely to engage in alcohol or other drug abuse, or other undesirable behavior, when these social bonds are weak or absent (Hirschi 1969).

### Social Learning Theory

Social learning theory states that alcohol and other drug use is influenced by the attitudes and behaviors of the adults and peers who serve as role models for an individual. This modeling effect begins with observing and imitating the thinking and behavior that surrounds the use of substances, continues with social reinforcement and the expectation of positive effects from substance use, and culminates in the use and abuse of alcohol or other drugs (Maisto, Carey, and Bradizza 1999).

### Behavioral Economics or Behavioral Choice Theory

Behavioral economics or behavioral choice theory addresses the protective factor from substance abuse played by activities that provide alternative rewards. This theory states that substance abuse is less likely to occur when a person has access to alternate rewards such as education, work, religion, and social/recreational pursuits (Bickel and Vuchinich 2000).

### Stress and Coping Theory

Stress and coping theory states that stressful life circumstances that originate from family members and friends, work, and financial or other problems lead to distress and alienation and ultimately to substance abuse, especially in impulsive persons who lack self-confidence and healthy coping skills and who avoid facing their problems. For these persons, substance use is a form of avoidance coping that involves self-medication to reduce alienation and depression, which can reinforce substance use (Kaplan 1996).

Moos (2008) identifies the elements of AA involvement that are consistent with the four social processes described above and on page 164:

- *Social control theory:* AA groups provide support, goal direction, and structure by encouraging positive social values and the importance of re-establishing and maintaining the connections with family, friends, work, and religion.

- *Social learning/stress and coping theories:* AA groups emphasize the importance of identifying with sober persons who are
  working a good program of recovery, and bolster the members'
  self-efficacy and coping skills.
- *Behavioral economics:* AA members are encouraged to participate in rewarding alcohol- and other drug-free pursuits, such as
  social activities and helping others with alcohol problems.

Moos concludes that the combination of all four of these factors enhances the motivation for recovery, improves self-efficacy to resist substance use, and provides effective coping skills.

### Sponsors and Sponsorship in AA

During the initial weeks and months of AA attendance, new members are
encouraged to attend ninety meetings in ninety days, and to find a sponsor. A sponsor is someone who has had more time in the AA program
and who can offer guidance and support to the newcomer. Sponsorship is
seen as an offshoot of the Twelfth Step of AA, with helping others viewed
as a way to help oneself. Sponsors are advised to offer what they can that
the newcomer needs, including help with detoxification, transportation,
companionship, encouragement, and hope. They are cautioned to avoid
giving too much advice or trying to force sobriety upon the newcomer.
Similarly, newcomers are urged to ask someone to sponsor them (Doe
1955; Alcoholics Anonymous 1975).

Helping other alcoholics is the embodiment of the "helper therapy"
principle (Riessman 1965), where helping others benefits the helper, not
just the recipient. Carrying the AA message of recovery to other alcoholics
is viewed as enriching the recovery of the AA member through participation in a spiritual activity and by moving beyond one's self-centeredness
to be concerned for the other person (Borkman 2008).

Anecdotal evidence from AA members suggests that the sponsor plays
a crucial role in the way that AA functions. Often, it is the presence of an
AA sponsor that is instrumental in helping the new AA member make it
through the difficult period of early sobriety, or if a relapse does occur, to

help the person get back on the right track. Sheeren (1988), in a study of the relationship between relapse and involvement in AA, found that persons who relapsed were much less likely to be involved with an AA sponsor. Another study (Zemore and Kaskutas 2004) found that involvement in Twelve Step activities such as sponsoring newer AA members was strongly linked with total abstinence.

# Empirical Studies of AA

Historically, AA has been a notoriously difficult organization to study for several reasons, including the decentralized structure and emphasis on anonymity (Mattson and Allen 1991). However, the past ten to fifteen years has witnessed a literal explosion of scientific studies involving AA that are not only abundant but very high in quality. The collective information provided by these studies has profoundly increased the level of understanding of the outcomes associated with AA and the processes that contribute to these outcomes (Tonigan 2008).

## Process Research on AA

Because of the overwhelming data supporting the overall effectiveness of AA in promoting sobriety, the focus of research has now shifted to identifying and describing the processes within AA that contribute to its effectiveness, such as spirituality and psychosocial factors.

### Spirituality

A core belief in AA is that spiritual development is fundamental in achieving sustained abstinence. However, research findings have been modest at best in terms of establishing a direct link between spirituality and abstinence. One of the reasons for this modest relationship has to do with the types of study design used in the published research. Although many of these studies have found a strong association between spirituality and enduring sobriety, determining a causal relationship between spirituality and long-term sobriety has been more difficult to establish. Other long-term studies that have measured level of spirituality at one point in time and drinking or abstinence at a second point in time have only found a modest effect (Tonigan 2007).

However, it is very likely that spirituality produces a very important indirect effect on the achievement of sobriety. In this case, spiritual practices are associated with activity involving elements of the AA program, which in turn play a significant role in the achievement of abstinence. Thus, although the level of spiritual *beliefs* (measured by questionnaire) has only shown a modest effect on the achievement of abstinence, the level of spiritual *practices* significantly and positively influences successful abstinence (Tonigan 2007). Other findings that are related to spirituality and abstinence include the following (Tonigan 2007; Tonigan 2003):

- Alcoholism severity predicts later AA attendance.
- Atheists are less likely to attend AA, but once engaged in AA they obtain the same benefits as members believing in God before joining.
- Belief in God before joining AA does not offer an advantage in AA-related outcomes.
- The spiritual principles of AA appear to be endorsed in all AA meetings regardless of other differences.
- Spiritual or religious beliefs and practices typically increase among AA members over time.

The rate of dropout among persons who attend AA is high, with some estimates ranging as high as 80%. Interventions that facilitate initial increases in spirituality have been found to increase the rates of AA affiliation, which, in turn, improves abstinence rates (Tonigan 2003). And contrary to popular belief, many atheists and agnostics attend and benefit from AA (Winzelberg and Humphreys 1999).

### Psychosocial Factors

Involvement in AA increases the motivation and commitment to abstinence, increases the use of active coping skills, increases social support for sobriety, and improves self-efficacy (the confidence to reduce and stop drinking). All four of these factors significantly contribute to the effectiveness of AA (Morgenstern et al. 1997; Hazelden Dec. 2004)

A study of 914 AA participants that specifically examined the impact of self-efficacy on drinking outcomes (Connors, Tonigan, and Miller 2001) found that AA participation improved abstinence rates seven to twelve months after treatment. Self-efficacy was found to mediate this effect, in that AA participation improved self-efficacy levels, which in turn increased the abstinence rate. This effect persisted into the end of the third year following treatment (Owen et al. 2003; Hazelden Dec. 2004).

Other theories of AA success include the replacement of the drinking social network with a sober peer group, and the learning of healthy coping skills similar to those gained from psychotherapy involvement (Humphreys, Mankowski, et al. 1999). A study of 2,337 male patients seeking treatment who had no previous AA experience supports the contribution of active coping skills and changes in social support networks to positive outcome in AA, in that AA participation resulted in greater use of active coping responses, improved quality of friendships, and support from friends to remain abstinent. All three of these factors were associated with reductions in substance use (Humphreys, Mankowski, et al. 1999; Hazelden Dec. 2004).

Additional evidence confirming the vital role of social support within AA comes from Bond, Kaskutas, and Weisner (2003), who followed 655 people for three years after treatment. They found the impact of AA on drinking outcome was strongly influenced by the number of social contacts who supported and encouraged abstinence from alcohol. Another study found that AA participation one year after treatment had a positive impact on lifestyle change, which included ending relationships with using friends and making new friends in recovery. These lifestyle changes, in turn, positively affected abstinence rates (Owen et al. 2003; Hazelden Dec. 2004).

### Outcome Research

There is now an abundant body of research with outcomes on AA. For instance, there is research on drinking outcomes, the interactive effect and outcomes between AA and treatment, combining AA attendance with professional counseling, the effect of sobriety on health care costs and the quality of life, outcomes on those whose attendance was coerced (such as mandated clients in criminal justice), and outcomes on attendance by other special populations (such as women).

### Drinking Outcomes

There is a remarkable consistency in the association between participation in AA and other Twelve Step groups and improved drinking and other drug use outcomes. These outcomes apply to persons with alcohol use disorders, drug use disorders, or co-occurring alcohol or other drug use disorders and psychiatric disorders, and to women, youth, and older adults (Moos 2008).

A recent summary of the entire body of published research on AA concluded that a causal relationship has been established between AA involvement and abstinence from drinking. Evidence supporting this conclusion includes the following: (1) the degree of effect (an effect much greater than chance would predict); (2) dose-response effect (greater AA involvement and longer duration of AA involvement equals greater likelihood of abstinence); (3) consistent effect (the same effect is demonstrated by several studies); (4) temporally accurate effects (controls for hindsight bias); and (5) plausibility (makes rational sense) (Kaskutas 2009).

Overall, abstinence rates are twice as high among those who attend AA. Those with higher levels of AA attendance are related to higher rates of abstinence, and this relationship has been found among many different demographic groups and follow-up periods. A person's prior AA attendance is predictive of subsequent abstinence, and the mechanisms of action predicted by theories of behavior change (which were described earlier) are present in AA (Kaskutas 2009). With few exceptions, AA-focused studies have shown that commitment to and the practice of the AA program is a stronger predictor of long-term abstinence than the mere number of AA meetings attended (Tonigan 2008).

Perhaps the first data on the drinking outcomes of alcoholics attending AA comes from Bill Wilson (1958). In a 1958 lecture to the New York

City Medical Society on Alcoholism, Wilson stated that among those who wrote their stories for the first edition of the AA Big Book (Alcoholics Anonymous 1939), 75% eventually achieved sobriety and that "only 25% died or went mad." He also stated that many members who eventually achieved sobriety went through numerous tentative or fleeting contacts with AA followed by drop-out and relapse before they re-entered AA with a higher level of commitment.

Another consistent finding in studies of AA is what is called a *dose-response effect*. This term is borrowed from medicine, and refers to the extent of association between a higher dose or a more frequent administration of a medication and a corresponding reduction or elimination of symptoms. Longer AA participation is associated with better abstinence and self-efficacy outcomes. Persons participating in AA for twenty-seven weeks or more in their first year, and in years two and three after treatment, had better abstinence rates sixteen years into the study follow-up than did individuals who did not participate in AA (Moos and Moos 2006).

Some of the contribution of treatment to drinking outcomes reflected participation in AA, while the contribution from AA was independent of the contribution from treatment. The results from this study underscore the importance of extended engagement in AA (Moos and Moos 2006). It was also found that attendance in AA for more than fifty-two weeks over a five-year period was associated with higher abstinence rates than attendance of less than fifty-two weeks over a five-year period. Part of the association between AA attendance and improvements in social functioning were related to AA participation. For some individuals, involvement in a circle of sober friends represents a turning point that enables them to address their problems, build healthy coping skills, and establish supportive social resources (Moos and Moos 2006).

An analysis of the body of published research on AA arrived at the following conclusions (WSASHO 2003):

1. Longitudinal studies (where participants are followed over an extended period) have linked AA involvement with

abstinence, improved social functioning, and greater self-efficacy, and show that participation is more helpful when members engage in other group activities in addition to attending meetings.

2. AA involvement significantly reduces health care use and costs, thus removing a significant burden from the health care system.

3. Self-help groups are best viewed as a form of continuing care rather than as a substitute for acute care treatment services such as detoxification or hospital-based treatment.

4. Randomized trials with coerced populations (such as persons convicted of DWI) suggest that AA combined with professional treatment is superior to AA alone.

A positive relationship between AA attendance and psychological health was found in an analysis of seventy-four published studies (Tonigan, Toscova, and Miller 1996; Hazelden Dec. 2004).

In a study of 2,319 male alcohol-dependent veterans one and two years following treatment, AA participation predicted improved rates of abstinence, with the effect on abstinence unrelated to patient motivation or the severity of their alcoholism (McKellar, Stewart, and Humphreys 2003; Hazelden Dec. 2004).

Patients who involve themselves in the AA program with such activities as reading the AA literature, participating as sponsors, and applying the Twelve Steps to their daily life are more likely to remain abstinent than persons who do not engage in these activities (Humphreys et al. 2004). Between 40 and 70% of patients admitted to alcoholism treatment centers based on the Twelve Steps have already tried and dropped out of Twelve Step programs. Although enrolling these patients in treatment using the same approach that appears to not have previously worked may seem illogical, researchers have found that in general, the shortcomings of earlier engagements in Twelve Step programs among these persons is due to low levels of commitment or engagement. Thus, the challenge for treatment providers is to find effective ways to get these patients engaged and committed to AA participation after they leave treatment (Forman, Humphreys, and Tonigan 2003).

### Interactive Effect and Outcomes between AA and Treatment

Several studies have compared the effectiveness of treatment plus AA involvement versus treatment alone or AA involvement alone. The following conclusions have been found:

1. Treatment combined with AA participation resulted in better initial outcomes than treatment alone (Timko et al. 2000). Persons attending treatment with AA had significantly higher rates of abstinence than those who attended treatment alone at one- and three-year follow-ups (Hazelden Dec. 2004).

2. Higher levels of AA involvement during the first year after treatment were predictive of better long-term outcomes (McKellar, Stewart, and Humphreys 2003; Moos and Moos 2004).

3. AA involvement is positively related to improved psycho-social and drinking outcomes. In the early 1990s, Emrick et al. (1993) conducted an analysis of 107 studies and found a positive correlation between AA involvement and substance use outcome when professional treatment and AA were combined (Hazelden Dec. 2004).

4. Fiorentine and Hillhouse (2000) reported that patients who attended at least one Twelve Step meeting per week remained in treatment longer, were more likely to complete treatment, and were more likely to be abstinent after treatment. These findings suggest that patients benefit from attending weekly AA meetings during the time they are in treatment.

5. Interestingly, the mere presence of an onsite AA group in an outpatient treatment setting enhances nearly threefold the rate of Twelve Step participation during treatment as well

as nearly six times the rate of continuous abstinence from substance use one year after treatment ends. This represents a cost-free strategy that significantly enhances patient outcomes and that is easily implemented through a local AA hospital and institution committee for any treatment program that requests it (Laudet, Stanick, and Sands 2007).

6. Because approaches that integrate formal treatment with AA result in better outcomes, AA and other self-help groups should not be used as a substitute for treatment. Instead, AA can be thought of as a low-intensity aftercare that stabilizes the progress made in treatment and facilitates further growth (Humphreys et al. 2004).

### AA Attendance Combined with Professional Counseling

Persons attending AA may need to seek professional help for a variety of reasons. The most recent AA membership survey estimated that 63% of members seek counseling for emotional, medical, and spiritual problems, and that 86% of these members report that such counseling was important for their recovery (Alcoholics Anonymous 2008).

Given the frequent and recurrent nature of relapse among alcoholics, formal alcohol treatment may also occur during the course of AA involvement. Obtaining outside help from professionals when needed is likely to improve long-term outcomes. One study that followed persons for ten years after they left treatment concluded that commitment to, and the practice of, AA-prescribed behaviors at ten-year follow-up was predicted by both prior AA participation and professional counseling. This is explained by the fact that previous AA participation, seeking the help of professional counselors, and current AA participation are enmeshed and mutually reinforcing processes (Tonigan and Connors 2003).

### Health Care Costs

Patients involved in AA are more likely to be abstinent one year after treatment, are less likely to utilize treatment services, and incur significantly fewer health care costs than patients not attending AA (Humphreys and Moos 2001; Humphreys and Moos 1996).

### Quality of Life

Persons who develop alcohol or other drug dependence often report that they sought help because they became "sick and tired of being sick and tired." Improvement in the quality of life (QOL) has been an overlooked aspect of treatment outcome and recovery from alcohol and other drug dependence, and may play a vital role in sustaining abstinence (Laudet, Becker, and White 2009). Research shows that this desire for an improved quality of life may become a reality for many.

To study stress and QOL as a function of length of sobriety, 353 recovering persons in New York City were evaluated. Social support, spirituality, life meaning, religiousness, and Twelve Step involvement significantly buffered the participants from stress and also enhanced their QOL. Stress levels significantly decreased as time in recovery increased, and life satisfaction was also found to increase over time. General social support and recovery support, spirituality, life meaning, and Twelve Step attendance significantly enhanced the QOL and recovery, and were significantly and positively associated with sober time, suggesting that social support, spirituality, religious/spiritual activities, and life meaning increase over time (Laudet, Morgen, and White 2006).

The finding that QOL increases and that stress decreases as sobriety progresses can give hope for a better future to persons in early recovery who are struggling to stay sober and to move forward one day at a time. While there is already overwhelming empirical evidence that Twelve Step involvement is effective in helping members achieve abstinence, these findings suggest the benefits of AA involvement extend to life satisfaction. The importance of social and recovery support in buffering stress and enhancing QOL also underscores the need for recovering persons to establish a social network of other recovering persons who can provide encouragement, acceptance, and a sense of belonging (Laudet, Morgen, and White 2006).

To study the transformative effect of AA involvement (Zemansky 2005), a study of 164 AA members (100 of whom had been sober ten or more years) was conducted. Several positive associations were found, including a relationship between AA involvement and gratitude, between using an AA sponsor and spirituality, and between working all Twelve Steps and having a greater sense of meaning and purpose in life. The AA members in this survey scored significantly higher on measures of optimism, gratitude, spirituality, and subjective well-being than did reference groups of normal nonclinical adults. These results provide measurable evidence of a positive transformation that occurs within AA.

Other benefits from AA involvement include increased self-efficacy, improved social support, decreased levels of anxiety and depression, and improved coping skills (Humphreys 2003).

### Coerced AA Attendance

Trials randomizing coerced patients, such as those convicted of DWI, to either AA alone or treatment plus AA suggest better drinking outcomes and retention with treatment plus AA (Walsh et al. 1991; Brandsma, Maultby, and Welsh 1980).

### Women

Women have consistently made up roughly one-third of AA membership (Timko 2008). Research on previously untreated problem drinkers has found that women generally function at a lower level and experience greater stress and problems related to resources and ability to cope. Interestingly, when compared with men who had similar levels of impaired functioning, stress, and alcohol-related problems at treatment entry, women have been found to have better resources, coping skills, and abstinence rates than men did at one- and eight-year follow-ups. Longer durations of treatment and AA attendance were associated with greater use of approach coping (directly confronting the problem) and less use of drinking to cope during the first year following treatment. A longer duration of AA participation during the eight years of follow-up was also associated with increases in the resources of friends and adaptive coping skills (Timko, Finney, and Moos 2005).

*Population-Based Studies*

Several studies have examined the positive effects of AA on large populations. The impact of alcohol consumption and AA membership rates on homicide and suicide rates in Ontario between 1968 and 1991 were examined by Mann et al. (2006a; 2006b). For the total population and for males, homicide rates were significantly and positively related to total alcohol consumption, and negatively related to AA membership rates. Total alcohol consumption was also significantly and positively related to total and female suicide rates, and AA membership rates were negatively associated with total and female suicide rates. The authors conclude that the beneficial effects of AA involvement are observable even at the population level.

Research on the relationship between cirrhosis mortality rates, alcohol consumption, and AA membership rates in Ontario between 1968 and 1989 (Mann et al. 2005) found that higher levels of AA membership were associated with lower rates of mortality from cirrhosis. These results were consistent with those of a similar study published in 1993 (Smart and Mann) that examined the relationship between treatment and AA membership, and recent declines in the hospitalization and death from cirrhosis in Ontario from 1975 to 1986 and in the U.S. from 1979 to 1987. They found that increased treatment levels and AA membership accounted for all of the reductions in cirrhosis deaths and hospital admissions in Ontario, and all of the deaths and about 40% of the hospital admissions in the U.S.

# Clinician Facilitation of AA Attendance and Involvement

Dropout and sporadic attendance of AA are much more common than regular, longer-term involvement, and only 25–30% of those who initially attend AA continue for an extended period (Pettinati et al. 1982). Many persons initially comply with the recommendation for frequent meeting attendance during early recovery, but most do not remain engaged in the program over time (Caldwell and Cutter 1998). AA attendance is also much less likely to happen if not initiated during treatment (Owen et al. 2003).

Researchers have found that perhaps the most effective way to increase the rates of affiliation and long-term involvement in AA is to ensure that alcoholic patients are introduced to AA and initially attend AA while they are still in treatment (Owen et al. 2003). Many persons in early recovery may initially attend AA meetings with the intention of using AA in their recovery, but may be unable to accept or put to use various aspects of the AA program or fellowship. Professional assistance can play a key role in helping such persons who experience difficulty in understanding or embracing elements of AA.

Beyond establishing the commitment to abstinence, professionals may need to help individuals overcome barriers to emotional intimacy, develop social and communication skills, and define and explore spiritual aspects of life. Such activities can serve both counseling goals and the connection with AA (Caldwell and Cutter 1998). Gay, lesbian, bisexual, and transgender (GLBT) clients are especially likely to benefit from such an approach, since they may mistakenly assume that AA is a religious program due to the references to a Higher Power and God in the Twelve Step model, and choose to avoid AA since many religious institutions denounce or condemn homosexuality (SCCMHA 2007).

In general, professionals who work with alcoholic clients should do everything they can to help their clients come away with a positive feeling about AA. This can include preparing clients realistically for what (and whom) they will encounter in AA, explaining the nature of the support, and helping them know how to ask for that support. Several Twelve Step facilitation approaches are now available for the purpose of successfully bridging the transition into successful AA affiliation. These include the group format MAAEZ intervention (Kaskutas et al. 2009), the individual format TSF intervention from Project MATCH (Nowinski, Baker, and Carroll 1992), and the Intensive Referral approach (Timko and Debenedetti 2007; Kaskutas et al. 2009).

The MAAEZ intervention (Kaskutas et al. 2009) is an approach that aims to overcome resistance to Twelve Step group involvement through several means. These include changing the participants' attitude toward the members who attend AA, NA, or Cocaine Anonymous (CA); addressing the perceived social desirability of AA, NA, or CA involvement; and increasing participants' ability to control and manage their Twelve Step meeting experiences, choice of people they affiliate with, and interpretation of the Twelve Step philosophy.

MAAEZ consists of six weekly ninety-minute sessions delivered in a group format by counselors who are currently involved in AA, NA, or CA. The main points of each session, take-home messages, and homework assignments are outlined on a two-sided sheet given to participants. Two MAAEZ sessions are conducted weekly: the introductory session (for new clients and clients who have completed the core sessions), and one of the four core sessions (for continuing clients) (Kaskutas et al. 2009).

During the introductory session, new clients discuss their previous AA, NA, or CA experience. After completing the four core sessions, clients return to the introductory session as graduates so that they can experience the benefits of assisting others (Zemore 2007; Zemore and Kaskutas 2004; Zemore, Kaskutas, and Ammon 2004).

The focus of the four core MAAEZ sessions are "Spirituality," "Principles Not Personalities," "Sponsorship," and "Living Sober." "Spirituality" provides a broad range of spirituality definitions, many of which do not include religious references, followed by a homework assignment to talk to someone with more sobriety than the client after a meeting. "Principles Not Personalities" addresses myths about AA, different types of meetings, and meeting etiquette. The homework assignment for this session is to ask a fellow attendee at an AA meeting for his or her phone number and to speak with that person before the next MAAEZ session. "Sponsorship" describes the sponsor function and guidelines for sponsor selection, and includes role-playing to practice asking for a sponsor and to overcome rejection. The homework assignment is to get a temporary sponsor. In "Living Sober," tools for staying sober are addressed and include relapse triggers, service work, and avoiding "slippery" people, places, and things. The homework assignment for this session is to socialize with someone in AA with more sobriety than the client (Kaskutas et al. 2009).

Research has found that MAAEZ participation has resulted in higher overall abstinence rates, and higher abstinence rates in important subgroups such as unmarried persons; those with more severe psychiatric problems; atheists, agnostics, and persons unsure of their religious beliefs; clients with previous treatment experience; and those with more prior AA exposure. Abstinence rates increased significantly with each additional MAAEZ session. MAAEZ represents an evidence-based intervention that is easily implemented in existing treatment programs (Kaskutas et al. 2009).

## Other Self-Help and Twelve Step Recovery Groups

AA's sole ownership of alcoholism self-help was challenged in the mid-1970s and the 1980s with the emergence of new alcoholism self-help organizations with a secular or dual-diagnosis focus (White 2003).

### Secular Recovery Support Groups

Secular recovery support groups (with their founding dates) include Women for Sobriety (WFS, 1975), Secular Sobriety Groups (later renamed Secular Organization for Sobriety—Save Our Selves) (SOS, 1985), Rational Recovery (RR, 1986), Men for Sobriety (MFS, 1988), Moderation Management (MM, 1994), SMART Recovery (1994), and LifeRing Secular Recovery (LSR, 1999) (White 2003).

Groups with a secular orientation differ from AA on several dimensions, including

- meeting locations in homes and religiously neutral sites;
- lack of reference to religious deities;
- discouragement of labels, such as *alcoholic* and *addict*;
- emphasis on personal empowerment and self-reliance;
- openness to crosstalk during meetings (direct feedback and advice between members);
- absence of formal sponsorship;

- endorsement of the concept of complete recovery and time-limited involvement (rather than indefinite participation); and
- use of nonrecovering volunteer professionals to facilitate and speak at meetings (White and Nicolaus 2005; White, Kurtz, and Sanders 2006).

Another fundamental difference is that while spiritual-based recovery programs such as AA emphasize wisdom (emphasis on experience, search for meaning, freedom rooted in the acceptance of limitation, self-transcendence by connection to a greater whole, strength flowing from limitation), secular recovery programs emphasize knowledge (emphasis on scientific evidence, an assertion of control, self-mastery through knowledge of self and knowledge of one's problem, and strength from personal competence) (White and Kurtz 2006). Little research has been conducted on the effectiveness of these programs (WSASHO 2003; Humphreys et al. 2004).

A few of the more widely attended secular self-help groups for persons who desire abstinence from alcohol problems are described below:

### Secular Organization for Sobriety (SOS)

Secular Organization for Sobriety (SOS) emphasizes rational scientific knowledge over spiritual orientation and growth, and believes that abstinence can be achieved through support from the group and by making sobriety a priority (Humphreys et al. 2004; WSASHO 2003). The therapeutic processes, along with the organizational principles and language of SOS, are very similar to those of AA, and SOS encourages honest sharing, association with other recovering alcoholics, and a focused "Sobriety Priority" of not drinking "no matter what." Although the exact means used to achieve sobriety are largely left up to the individual to decide, members are encouraged to use the experience of those SOS members who have attained sobriety (Kelly and Yeterian 2008).

### SMART Recovery

SMART Recovery is a program based on cognitive-behavioral theory that views alcoholism as a maladaptive behavior instead of a disease. The objective of SMART Recovery is for members to utilize scientifically validated cognitive-behavioral techniques to enhance their motivation to abstain, ability to cope with cravings, capacity to identify and change irrational thinking, and judgment to balance immediate gratification and enduring satisfactions (Humphreys et al. 2004; WSASHO 2003). SMART Recovery meetings have a cognitive-behavioral educational orientation and include open discussions. The appropriate use of prescribed medications and the use of psychological treatments are explicitly advocated. SMART Recovery draws on evidence-based practices and "evolves as scientific knowledge evolves" (Kelly and Yeterian 2008).

### Women for Sobriety

Women for Sobriety (WFS) uses a positive, feminist approach to help female alcoholics recover through a program that emphasizes the importance of all-female groups to facilitate self-discovery, improve self-esteem, and foster emotional and spiritual growth (Humphreys et al. 2004; WSASHO 2003). A survey of 600 members of WFS (Kaskutas 1994) found the following reasons for attending WFS: support and nurturance (54%), a safe environment (26%), sharing about women's issues (42%), its positive emphasis (38%), and focus on self-esteem (39%). Among those surveyed, women who did not attend AA identified the following reasons: feeling as though they never fit in at AA (20%), finding AA too negative (18%), disliking the "drunkalogs" and their focus on the past (14%), and feeling that AA is geared to men's needs (15%).

### Rational Recovery

Rational Recovery (RR) was founded in 1986 by former alcoholic Jack Trimpey, a licensed clinical social worker practicing in California. RR claims to have made self-help groups for alcoholics seeking abstinence obsolete through a technique called the addictive voice recognition technique

(AVRT). RR is not technically a self-help group but is well known, and once consisted of an extensive recovery group network that offered a cognitive-behavioral self-help approach along with an undeveloped version of AVRT. The organization split into RR and SMART Recovery (see page 182) following internal conflict, and RR now operates solely through the Internet, by mail, and through literature. The goal of RR is abstinence, which is achievable by recognizing and confronting the internal addictive voice. Thus, RR espouses an explicitly cognitive approach similar to the rational emotive therapy developed by Albert Ellis (Kelly and Yeterian 2008).

## Recovery Support Groups for Dual-Diagnosed Persons

Although AA has special meetings intended for members with a co-occurring psychiatric illness, other fellowships have emerged that specifically address the needs of persons in dual recovery, most notably Double Trouble in Recovery, Dual Recovery Anonymous, and Dual Diagnosis Anonymous. These groups provide members with an opportunity to discuss both substance abuse and mental health issues, including the use of medications, in an accepting and psychologically safe environment (Laudet 2008; Hazelden 1993).

### *Double Trouble in Recovery (DTR)*

DTR was formed in New York State in 1989 and currently has more than 200 groups that meet in fourteen states, with the largest number in New York and growing memberships in Georgia, Colorado, New Mexico, and New Jersey. New DTR groups are started by consumers and professionals. DTR developed as a grassroots initiative and functions today with minimal involvement from the professional community. Groups meet in psychosocial clubs; supportive mental health residential programs; day-treatment programs for mental health, substance abuse, and dual diagnosis; and hospital inpatient units and community-based organizations. All DTR groups are led by recovering individuals (Vogel et al. 1998).

DTR meetings follow a traditional Twelve Step format, including group member introductions, a speaker sharing his or her experience, and group discussion and sharing by all attendees. Meetings typically last sixty to ninety minutes (NREPP 2007). The DTR program uses the same Twelve Steps as does AA, with modifications made only to Steps One and Twelve (www.doubletroubleinrecovery.org):

> Step One: We admitted we were powerless over mental disorders and substance abuse—that our lives had become unmanageable.
>
> Step Twelve: Having had a spiritual awakening as the result of these Steps, we tried to carry this message to other dually diagnosed people, and to practice these principles in all our affairs.

A member survey found that the primary problem substances among DTR members were cocaine and alcohol, with the most prevalent psychiatric diagnoses being schizophrenia (43%), bipolar disorder (25%), and unipolar (major) depression (26%) (Laudet et al. 2000; Laudet 2008). A study that examined the impact of DTR involvement on substance use, adherence to psychiatric medication, and attendance of conventional Twelve Step meetings followed persons who participated in DTR for six months, and compared their outcomes with a similar group of persons who did not participate in DTR. The researchers found that DTR participants reported fewer days of alcohol or other drug use during the past ninety days, and at a six-month follow-up had better psychiatric medication adherence and more frequent traditional Twelve Step attendance than non-DTR participants (Magura et al. 2008).

### Dual Recovery Anonymous (DRA)

DRA was formed in 1989 in Kansas City, and in 1993 the Hazelden Foundation began distributing DRA educational recovery material, which greatly contributed to the growth of the organization (Laudet 2008). DRA currently holds meetings in most states in the U.S. as well as Canada, Australia, New Zealand, India, and Iceland (Laudet 2008), and new meetings are in the start-up process in Mexico, the Philippines, England, Scotland, Ireland, Wales, Spain, and the Slovak Republic (www.draonline.org).

DRA is a Twelve Step self-help program that is based on the principles of the Twelve Steps and the experiences of men and women in recovery with a dual diagnosis. The DRA program assists its members in recovery from both chemical dependency and emotional or psychiatric illness by focusing on relapse prevention and actively improving the quality of life. By providing a community of mutual support, members learn to avoid the risks that lead back to alcohol and other drug use, and to reduce the symptoms of emotional or psychiatric illness (www.draonline.org).

DRA defines its criteria for membership in the Second Tradition, which states that "DRA has two requirements for membership: a desire to stop using alcohol and other intoxicating drugs, and a desire to manage our emotional or psychiatric illness in a healthy and constructive way." This leaves the option of joining to the individual if after reading the Second Tradition, the person feels he or she meets both requirements (www .draonline.org).

Similar to DTR, the DRA program uses the same Twelve Steps as does AA, with modifications made only to Steps One and Twelve (www .draonline.org):

> Step One: We admitted we were powerless over our dual illness of chemical dependency and emotional or psychiatric illness— that our lives had become unmanageable.

> Step Twelve: Having had a spiritual awakening as a result of these Steps, we tried to carry this message to others who experience dual disorders and to practice these principles in all our affairs.

### Dual Diagnosis Anonymous (DDA)

Dual Diagnosis Anonymous (DDA) was conceived in 1996 in Southern California from the awareness that many people suffering from addiction to alcohol or other drugs also suffer from some form of major mental illness, and vice versa. Concurrent substance abuse and mental illness is referred to as dual diagnosis. DDA states that addressing both conditions is essential, rather than focusing on one or the other. For persons who are dually diagnosed, DDA believes it essential to go beyond the social model recovery philosophy that tends to claim that successful substance abuse treatment results in a cessation of mental illness symptoms, and to likewise go beyond the medical model clinical philosophy that claims successful treatment of mental illness necessarily leads to a cessation of substance abuse. In essence, DDA offers a support group with a philosophical platform that blends the social model of recovery with the clinical philosophy of the medical model, and emphasizes the Twelve Steps of Recovery (DDA 1996).

In addition to a philosophy tailored for persons who are dually diagnosed, DDA provides a supportive accepting environment for persons whose mental illness symptoms may result in the perception of symptomatic differences between alcoholics and addicts and the dual diagnoses at conventional Twelve Step meetings. DDA recognized issues encountered by dually diagnosed alcoholics and addicts that present obstacles to traditional Twelve Step program attendance, such as symptom-driven disruptive behaviors during meetings, feelings of alienation, heightened levels of fear, anxiety and/or paranoia in group settings, and stigmatization of psychotropic medication use among some traditional Twelve Step members, and seeks to provide an alternative support group (DDA 1996).

### THE TWELVE STEPS OF DDA
### (BASED ON THE TWELVE STEPS OF AA)

1. We admitted we were powerless over our dual diagnosis, and that our lives had become unmanageable.

2. Came to believe that a Power greater than ourselves could restore us to sanity.

3. Made a decision to turn our will and our lives over to the care of God, as we understood Him.

4. Made a searching and fearless moral inventory of ourselves.

5. Admitted to God, to ourselves, and to another human being the exact nature of our wrongs.

6.  Were entirely ready to have God remove all these defects of character.

7.  Humbly asked Him to remove our shortcomings.

8.  Made a list of all persons we had harmed, and became willing to make amends to them all.

9.  Made direct amends to such people wherever possible, except when to do so would injure them or others.

10. Continued to take personal inventory and when we were wrong promptly admitted it.

11. Sought through prayer and meditation to improve our conscious contact with God as we understood Him, praying only for knowledge of His will for us and the power to carry that out.

12. Having had a spiritual awakening as the result of these steps, we tried to carry this message to others who still suffer from the effects of dual diagnosis, and to practice these principles in all our affairs.

### THE (ADDITIONAL) FIVE STEPS OF DDA

1.  We admitted that we had a mental illness, in addition to our substance abuse, and we accepted our dual diagnosis.

2.  We became willing to accept help for both of these diseases.

3.  We have understood the importance of medication, clinical interventions and therapies, and we have accepted the need for sobriety from alcohol and abstinence from all non-prescribed drugs in our program.

4.  We came to believe that when our own efforts were combined with the help of others in the fellowship of DDA, and God, as we understood Him, we would develop healthy drug and alcohol free life styles.

5. We continued to follow the DDA Recovery Program of the Twelve Steps plus Five and we maintained healthy drug and alcohol free lifestyles, and helped others.

### How DDA Meetings Work

Meetings of DDA are very much like traditional Twelve Step meetings. Although there is no formal leader during meetings, DDA has found it helpful and encourages the presence of an experienced DDA member or trained professional who understands Twelve Step programs and can gently redirect the meeting if necessary to keep it focused and on track (DDA 1996).

### Self-Help Group Membership in the U.S.

Addiction professionals and representatives of alternative recovery self-help groups ask, sometimes resentfully, why AA represents the standard by which all other recovery support programs are measured. AA has attained this status by virtue of its size (measured by total membership and number of groups), the scope of its international dispersion, the range of its adaptation to address other problems, its influence on professionally directed addiction treatment, the quantity and increasing quality of AA-related scientific research, and AA's growing visibility as a cultural institution. AA has also earned this status by its longevity and survival, raising the question of why AA survived and thrived when its predecessors collapsed or were diverted from their recovery-focused missions (White 2010).

Table 6.2 shows an estimate of attendance at self-help groups in the U.S., with AA at the top in numbers.

Table 6.2

### Estimated Alcoholism Self-Help Group Membership in the U.S.

| Twelve Step programs | |
|---|---|
| Alcoholics Anonymous[1] | 1,264,716 |
| Al-Anon Family Groups | 200,000 |
| Oxford House[2] | 9,000 |
| Dual Diagnosis Anonymous | 700 |
| Other self-help programs | |
| Adult Children of Alcoholics[3] | 40,000 |
| Secular Organization for Sobriety | 3,000 |
| Double Trouble in Recovery | 3,000 |
| SMART Recovery | 2,000 |
| Women for Sobriety | 1,500 |

*(Humphreys et al. 2004 except where noted)*

1. *AA General Service Office estimate, 2010.*
2. *Oxford House is a nationwide network of drug and alcohol-free peer-run residential homes.*
3. *Adult Children of Alcoholics is a support group for persons raised in an alcoholic home; the goal is not abstinence.*

## Moderation Management: Who It Is and Is *Not* Intended For

Moderation Management (MM) is the only self-help organization to offer its members the goal of achieving moderate drinking, which the organization defines as not more than three drinks per day or nine drinks per week for women, and not more than four drinks per day or fourteen drinks per week for men (Kelly and Yeterian 2008).

Founded in 1993, MM operates under the premise that problem drinking, unlike alcohol dependence, is a learned behavioral habit that can be modified and controlled (WSASHO 2003). The rationale for MM is that an organization with the explicit goal of moderate drinking would attract nondependent problem drinkers who were not interested in abstinence-only programs such as AA or professionally operated Twelve Step treatment programs. MM generated controversy during the 1990s over the wrongful perception that it was attempting to teach alcoholics how to control their drinking (Humphreys 2003).

A survey of 177 MM members was performed to help researchers understand the background of persons who join MM (Humphreys and Klaw 2001). Overall, MM attracted women, younger drinkers, and nondependent problem drinkers. Roughly 15% of the survey respondents indicated moderate to severe alcohol dependence. Thus, the majority of MM members have low-severity alcohol problems, high social stability, and little interest in abstinence-oriented interventions.

Despite a minority of MM members for whom MM offers an insufficient intervention, MM offers a valuable service for the following reasons: (1) some alcohol-dependent persons change their drinking goals from moderation to abstinence after becoming engaged in a supportive setting; (2) most MM members would not seek help for their drinking in abstinence-oriented programs; (3) there are many times more nondependent drinkers with alcohol problems than there are drinkers who are alcohol dependent, and these nondependent drinkers underuse existing resources to seek help for their problem drinking (Humphreys 2003). An optimal development in the future of MM would be to implement a more stringent set of norms and procedures for recognizing and advising participants whose alcohol problems are too severe for MM to address (Humphreys 2003).

## Twelve Step Facilitation and Project MATCH

Twelve Step facilitation (TSF) is a formalized treatment approach composed of elements of AA and Twelve Step programs that can be offered on an inpatient or outpatient basis (Galanter 2006). The goal of TSF is to introduce and involve patients in AA, the rationale being that Twelve Step–based treatment and involvement are as effective as more heavily researched psychosocial approaches, and that changes in health care reimbursement in the U.S. have reduced access to treatment, treatment duration, and treatment intensity (Longabaugh et al. 2005; Humphreys 1999). TSF involves patients with the first five Steps of AA, promotes AA attendance and involvement, and teaches the AA concept of alcoholism.

It was long observed and understood that no single treatment approach worked best for all alcoholic patients, and that different treatment approaches might be more effective for certain types of patients (Institute of Medicine 1990; Del Boca and Mattson 1994). The concept of patient matching refers to selecting the most effective treatment for a particular type of patient, and the National Institute on Alcohol Abuse and Alcoholism initiated a study, Project MATCH, to investigate the optimal treatment matching of alcoholic patients. Project MATCH was designed as a large-scale, multi-site, scientifically rigorous study, the results of which were projected to have important implications for clinical practice (Project MATCH Research Group 1993; Hazelden June 2010).

Project MATCH randomly assigned 952 outpatients and 774 aftercare patients to one of three treatment approaches and followed these patients over several years. The three treatment approaches were

1. cognitive-behavioral therapy (CBT),

2. Twelve Step facilitation (TSF), and

3. motivational enhancement therapy (MET).

Overall, clients with more severe alcohol problems did better at a three-year follow-up than clients with lower severity. Patients with higher anger levels had better outcomes with MET than with the other two therapies. At months 37–39 another match appeared: clients who had a social network that supported their drinking before they received treatment had better outcomes with TSF than MET, partially because of the higher AA involvement of TSF clients (Project MATCH Research Group 1998; Hazelden June 2010).

One year after treatment, patients in all three treatment groups reported significant reductions in drinking. Differences across treatment groups were not significant, although TSF showed a slight advantage (Project MATCH Research Group 1997). Three years after treatment, however, a significant difference emerged between the three treatment groups. Patients receiving the Twelve Step–based TSF had significantly higher abstinence rates than those in the other two treatment approaches, with 36% of TSF clients remaining abstinent versus 27% of MET and 24% of CBT clients (Project MATCH Research Group 1998).

Project MATCH remains the largest behavioral intervention trial conducted on alcoholism. The overall implication of Project MATCH findings is that all three treatment approaches are effective in the treatment of alcoholism: TSF, CBT, and MET (Project MATCH Research Group 1997). The fact that few patient-treatment matches resulted in modestly improved treatment outcomes suggests that a major overhaul of current treatment approaches based on patient characteristics is unnecessary (Hazelden June 2010).

Since AA dropout rate is high, a sub-study of Project MATCH explored what types of patients were more likely to continue their involvement with AA. The researchers found that greater alcohol problem severity predicted greater AA attendance, and opposite to prediction, clients with less severe alcohol impairment were more than twice as likely to discontinue AA attendance after treatment. They concluded that when sustained AA attendance is desired, evaluating the severity of pretreatment alcohol problems may be useful for identifying potential AA dropout after TSF treatment (Tonigan, Bogenschutz, and Miller 2006).

# Professional Treatment of Alcoholism

**N**ew advances in the understanding of the brain biology of alcohol dependence has revolutionized the field of addiction science. These advances have led to the identification of several brain chemical systems that are vital in causing and maintaining alcoholism (Volpicelli 2001). Different brain transmitter systems are believed to underlie the various behavioral components of alcohol dependence such as craving, preoccupation with, and obsession with drinking; the motivation to drink; and loss of control. The idea behind pharmacotherapy for alcoholism is to manipulate these brain chemical systems in such a way as to reduce the symptoms that increase the risk of relapse, or if relapse occurs, to minimize relapse severity by blocking the pleasurable effects of alcohol.

There is nothing inherent in the Twelve Step philosophy that contradicts the use of medications (as long as they are free of abuse liability) for the purpose of achieving or maintaining abstinence, or for the treatment of psychiatric conditions or disorders. An interesting side note to history occurred during the 1960s, when one of the pioneers of the use of methadone maintenance to treat heroin addiction, Dr. Vincent Dole, served as a trustee of Alcoholics Anonymous and became friends with Bill Wilson. Dole recalled a conversation he had with Bill Wilson (Dole 1991), in which

Wilson expressed his concern over alcoholics who could not achieve sobriety despite repeated attempts through AA:

> At the last trustee meeting (of AA) that we (Vincent Dole and Bill Wilson) both attended, he (Bill Wilson) spoke to me of his deep concern for the alcoholics who are not reached by AA, and for those who enter and drop out and never return. Always the good shepherd, he was thinking about the many lost sheep who are lost in the dark world of alcoholism. He suggested that in my future research I should look for an analogue of methadone, a medication that would relieve the alcoholic's sometimes irresistible craving and enable him to progress in AA toward social and emotional recovery, following the Twelve Steps.

This anecdote indicates that the founder of AA was open to and encouraging of the concept of developing a medication that could be used by alcoholics struggling to achieve sobriety, that would bridge the gap from very early abstinence to stable integration and recovery in AA by blocking alcohol cravings and the obsession to drink.

## Medications Are Never Intended as Sole Treatment

Occasionally, sensational headlines in the media exclaiming "A Pill to Cure Alcoholism" (*U.S. News and World Report* 2008) grab the attention of the public and generate controversy and misunderstanding over the intent of medication use for alcoholism. Concerns are often voiced over whether pharmaceutical companies are trying to make AA obsolete.

Such concern is understandable but completely unwarranted. Drug therapy for alcoholism is never intended to replace Twelve Step or psychosocial therapy involvement. Instead, medications are used with persons in early sobriety, usually in treatment, to complement the other treatment approaches and help the alcoholic achieve treatment objectives sooner.

The goal of medication is to reduce the intensity of the ongoing cravings for alcohol and reduce the frequency of relapse and the amount of alcohol consumed if a relapse occurs. In this way, medication use actually increases the ability of the patient to remain engaged in Twelve Step involvement and/or therapy during the critical early period of sobriety when relapse is most likely (Weiss and Kueppenbender 2006).

An additional point is that none of the medications that are either approved by the FDA or that are used "off-label" to treat alcohol dependence have abuse potential. Also, the FDA approves medications to be used in alcohol dependence only with the strictly worded stipulation that these medications are not intended as sole therapy for alcoholism, and must only be prescribed to patients who are receiving psychosocial therapy (NASADAD 2001).

And finally, numerous trials have found an interactive effect between pharmacotherapy and psychosocial therapy, in that the combination of the two produces better results than either one used alone (O'Malley et al. 1992; Anton et al. 1999). This makes sense, because the benefits of pharmacotherapy for alcoholism are only attainable with persistent patient compliance and motivation, both of which can be addressed through professional interventions that enhance patient motivation for sobriety and medication compliance (Volpicelli 2001).

## FDA-Approved Medications and Pharmacological Interventions for Alcohol Dependence

A number of FDA-approved medications have been tested to serve as pharmacological intervention for alcohol dependence. Below and on the pages that follow, a list of them appears.

### Disulfiram (Antabuse)

Disulfiram was approved by the FDA in 1951 as a treatment of alcoholism. Disulfiram acts by creating a toxic reaction when alcohol is consumed, which is achieved through interference with the normal breakdown of alcohol in the liver. Disulfiram blocks the initial breakdown product of alcohol to increase its concentration, and it is this buildup that causes the extremely unpleasant reaction when alcohol is ingested (West et al. 1999). Disulfiram is referred to as aversion therapy because of the aversive state that follows drinking, which often includes a throbbing headache, nausea, vomiting, tachycardia (racing heart), hypotension, respiratory depression, and cardiovascular collapse in severe cases (Parantainen 1983).

Disulfiram can reduce drinking by inducing a fear of a toxic reaction; however, there is no evidence of abstinence enhancement, and patient compliance is essential for drinking reduction. Patients taking disulfiram must also avoid taking over-the-counter drugs that contain alcohol (some contain as much as 40%) (West et al. 1999). This now-obsolete approach to pharmacotherapy for alcoholism has been replaced by an emphasis on drugs that target the brain chemical systems involved in alcoholism.

### Naltrexone (ReVia)

Naltrexone is an opioid receptor blocker that is FDA approved for the treatment of alcohol dependence. Naltrexone may reduce drinking frequency, amount of alcohol consumed, and the relapse rate, and appears to blunt the emotional response to alcohol. Studies enrolling both alcohol-dependent and social drinkers have found that naltrexone reduced the euphoria from alcohol (Volpicelli et al. 1995). Instead, drinkers felt sluggish instead of stimulated from drinking (Swift and Pettinati 2005). They drank less often and consumed less alcohol when they did drink regardless of their racial, ethnic, and economic differences and the varying levels of behavioral treatments received (Volpicelli et al. 1992; O'Malley et al. 1992).

Other studies have found that patients who returned to drinking refrained for a longer period of time and delayed their first episode of heavy drinking when naltrexone was taken; they also drank less often and were less likely to relapse to heavy drinking (O'Malley et. al. 1995; NASADAD 2001). Side effects may include nausea, dizziness, and headache. Some patients benefit from naltrexone, but its efficacy has only been demonstrated as an adjunct to psychosocial therapy.

A long-acting formulation of naltrexone (Vivitrex) has been approved for use in the U.S. This extended-release version, which releases the drug over the course of a month from a single injection, was developed in an effort to minimize the risk of poor compliance and fluctuating blood levels that can occur with the oral version of naltrexone. Compared with a placebo (an inactive sugar pill), patients receiving long-acting naltrexone have demonstrated significant reductions in heavy drinking. In addition, patients entering therapy with the goal of abstinence, as well as patients who intended to reduce but not to quit drinking, equally benefited from this drug (Garbutt et al. 2005).

### Acamprosate (Campral)

Acamprosate is another drug that is FDA approved for the treatment of alcohol dependence, and has been available in Europe since 1989, where it has been used to treat alcohol dependence in many countries (Mason and Goodman 1997).

Unlike other pharmacotherapies used with alcoholism, acamprosate acts on the brain to restore the disrupted neurochemistry that is the consequence of alcohol dependence. Acamprosate appears to act by regulating NMDA (N-methyl-D-aspartate) and GABA (gamma-aminobutyric acid) pathways in the brain, which restore the normal activity of glutamate signaling that is altered by chronic alcohol abuse (Mason and Heyser 2010b, 2010a).

As discussed in a previous section, chronic alcohol abuse forces several brain chemical systems to dramatically alter their function as they attempt to adapt to the constant alcohol presence. When alcohol is withdrawn, the altered function persists in the absence of alcohol. This disruption, as it occurs in the two brain chemical systems of NMDA and GABA, contribute to the ongoing craving, insomnia, anxiety, and restlessness for alcohol that are experienced by some alcoholics in early sobriety. Acamprosate is not used to treat acute alcohol withdrawal, but instead acts to normalize NMDA function and thus reduces craving and many of the symptoms associated with post-acute withdrawal from alcohol (SAMHSA 2005).

Research involving alcohol-dependent patients has found that acamprosate increases the rates of total abstinence and the percent of days abstinent, and delays the amount of time to an initial relapse (Kranzler and Gage 2008). Higher doses of acamprosate significantly increase the proportion of patients who remained abstinent for six and twelve months, and significantly reduced alcohol cravings during the first three months of sobriety (Paille et al. 1995).

There is no evidence that acamprosate interacts with alcohol, alcohol-based medications, or medications used to treat mental illness such as antidepressants (Durbin, Hulot, and Chabac 1996). And since acamprosate is not significantly metabolized in the liver, patients with liver disease can safely take the drug (Wilde and Wagstaff 1997; NASADAD 2001). Possible side effects include diarrhea, dizziness, and itching (West et al. 1999).

### Naltrexone and Acamprosate Combination Therapy

A potentially promising approach to the treatment of alcoholism involves combining naltrexone and acamprosate. However, the results of this combination have been mixed. One trial found this combination more effective than a placebo and acamprosate alone, but not significantly better than naltrexone alone in preventing relapse (Kranzler et al. 2006), while another study failed to find any added benefit from combining the drugs compared with using each drug alone (Anton et al. 2006).

### Other Issues with FDA-Approved Medications

The effectiveness of medications for alcoholism is highly dependent on patient compliance, which is often poor in alcoholic patients. The extended-release form of naltrexone promises to minimize compliance issues, and advances in drug delivery approaches such as injectable and extended-release versions may improve patient outcomes (Swift 2007).

It is likely that the effectiveness of drug therapies will improve through greater knowledge of the disease of alcohol dependence, reliable identification of treatment-responsive patients, identifying the predictors of medication response, and approaches that improve medication adherence (Garbutt 2009).

# Medications Used Off-Label for Alcohol Dependence (Drugs Already Approved for Other Conditions)

Alcohol use, and intense cravings for alcohol, releases opioid molecules in the brain, which in turn cause dopamine release. Drugs that block these opioid receptors, including naltrexone, were first investigated to see if blocking this effect would reduce drinking and the craving to drink (Krahn 2009). In addition, the findings that severe alcoholics exhibited lower serotonin levels than nonalcoholics, and that deficient serotonin was associated with impulsive behavior, anxiety, and stress, led researchers to investigate a wide variety of drugs acting on brain serotonin systems for the treatment of alcoholism (Kenna, McGeary, and Swift 2004). The two receptors are discussed below.

### Drugs Acting on Opioid Receptors

Nalmefene is an opiate blocker that is similar in structure and action to naltrexone, but has the advantage of being easier on the liver to metabolize (NIAAA 2000). In a twelve-week study of alcohol-dependent patients, those given nalmefene were 2.4 times less likely to relapse to heavy drinking than patients who received a placebo. Patients had high medication compliance rates and experienced no adverse side effects (Mason et al. 1999). This drug may serve as a good alternative to naltrexone in patients who do not respond to or are intolerant of naltrexone (NASADAD 2001).

### Drugs Acting on Serotonin Receptors

Alcoholics who consume large quantities of alcohol exhibit lower serotonin levels relative to nonalcoholics. Impulsive use of alcohol is associated with low serotonin levels. Deficient serotonin is associated with anxiety and some alcoholics drink to self-medicate their anxiety and stress. Alcohol can stimulate serotonin release in the brain, leading researchers to investigate drugs that act on serotonin as a treatment of alcoholism (Kenna, McGeary, and Swift 2004).

Studies using SSRIs (selective serotonin reuptake inhibitors) in nondepressed alcoholics have produced inconsistent results. Even in depressed alcoholics, antidepressants in general have not led to significant reductions in alcohol use. Buspirone hydrochloride (Buspar) is a serotonin 1A partial agonist (binds to and activates a receptor, but less than to a full agonist) that is FDA approved for the treatment of generalized anxiety disorder. When controlling for pretreatment anxiety, buspirone was found no more effective than a placebo in reducing drinking in alcoholic patients. Ritanserin, another drug acting on serotonin, failed to demonstrate effectiveness in relapse prevention in alcohol dependence (Kenna 2010).

On the other hand, promising results have been published on drinking outcomes in alcohol-dependent patients given ondansetron (Zofran), a serotonin-3 receptor antagonist (binds to and blocks the activity of a receptor) (Kenna 2010). The most responsive patients to ondansetron have been type B alcoholics (those with early-onset alcoholism), who have been found to drink significantly less alcohol when given modest doses of ondansetron. This early-onset subtype of alcoholism is believed to be mediated by greater serotonin dysfunction, explaining the much greater treatment response (Kenna, McGeary, and Swift 2004).

### Anticonvulsant Agents

Several drugs originally developed to treat seizures act, in part, by increasing the amount of GABA in the brain, with some drugs in this class also reducing the amount of glutamate. This pharmacological action was thought to have the potential of reducing the symptoms of ongoing protracted or motivational withdrawal experienced by many alcoholics in earlier recovery (Krahn 2009).

Several antiseizure drugs have been studied as possible therapeutic agents in the treatment of alcoholism. These agents have a common mechanism of action (modulation of NMDA and enhancement of GABA neurotransmission), which, in addition to their mood-stabilizing properties when used in the treatment of bipolar disorder, have made them attractive targets of investigation in alcoholism (Croissant et al. 2006).

Topiramate is an anticonvulsant drug that is also FDA approved for the treatment of migraine headaches, and is the most widely used anticonvulsant in the treatment of alcohol dependence (De Sousa 2010). Topiramate in clinical trials has demonstrated safety and effectiveness in decreasing craving and withdrawal symptoms, reducing the number of drinks per day and total days of alcohol consumption, reducing liver enzyme markers of heavy drinking (Kranzler et al. 2006; Johnson et al. 2007), and increasing the quality of life of alcohol-dependent patients. While the manufacturer of topiramate will not pursue FDA approval for alcohol dependence, the drug will soon be available as a generic drug, making it more affordable for a greater proportion of the public (Kenna et al. 2009).

Oxcarbazepine is a derivative of the antiseizure drug carbamazepine that offers the advantage of being eliminated by the kidneys instead of being metabolized by the liver. A small pilot study comparing oxcarbazepine to acamprosate found comparable efficacy on several measures related to drinking outcome, which included the amount of time to first relapse and drinks per drinking day. Although the study was not large enough to detect significant differences, preliminary safety and efficacy data on this drug merit larger, more definitive trials in the future (Croissant et al. 2006).

The effectiveness of gabapentin (Neurontin) in reducing symptoms of post-acute alcohol withdrawal was examined by Mason et al. (2009). The researchers found that compared with alcohol-dependent participants who received a placebo, those who received gabapentin showed substantial improvements in sleep quality and significant reductions in craving strength, intent to drink, craving intensity triggered by alcohol-related cues, and emotional disturbance. Side effects were minor and short-lived. Although additional research needs to confirm these results, gabapentin seems to be helpful for alcoholics in early recovery who experience ongoing problems with sleep difficulties, irritability, and craving for alcohol.

The results of baclofen treatment of alcohol dependence have been mixed, with two studies showing reductions in withdrawal-related anxiety, alcohol craving, and improved abstinence, while another study found no advantage (Leggio, Garbutt, and Addolorato 2010).

### Varenicline (Chantix)

Several factors suggested that Varenicline, an FDA-approved drug for nicotine addiction, may be helpful in treating alcoholism. These include high rates of co-occurring alcohol and nicotine dependence, the finding that nicotine increases alcohol intake, and that drugs that block (antagonize) nicotine receptors reduce alcohol ingestion (Chatterjee and Bartlett 2010). Varenicline (Chantix) was evaluated in twenty heavy nondependent drinkers who were also daily smokers (McKee et al. 2009). The researchers found that varenicline significantly reduced the pleasurable effects of alcohol, craving for alcohol, and alcohol ingestion; was well-tolerated; and did not adversely interact with alcohol. They concluded that varenicline should be further investigated as a potential treatment for alcohol use disorders.

### Neuroleptics

Because brain dopamine systems are believed to play an important role in alcohol dependence, drugs that alter dopamine function, such as aripiprazole, may have the potential to reduce craving and relapse.

Aripiprazole is a third-generation atypical (class of drugs developed to treat the same conditions as first-generation antipsychotic drugs but with fewer side effects) antipsychotic drug that has shown some positive, but inconsistent, results in alcoholic patients. Aripiprazole may be especially helpful for alcoholics with intense craving and problems with impulsivity (Vergne and Anton 2010).

## Experimental Drugs (Drugs Being Investigated but Not Yet Approved for Any Condition)

### Endocannabinoid Receptor Antagonists (blockers)

Research in animals has suggested that a specific type of receptor, cannabinoid CB(1), plays a role in influencing alcohol-related behaviors, and that blocking the activity of this receptor might have beneficial effects in alcoholics.

Although initially promising in preclinical trials, all research involving cannabinoid CB(1) receptor antagonists such as rimonabant has been halted due to the occurrence of adverse psychiatric symptoms in some participants (Maccioni, Colombo, and Carai 2010).

### Corticotropin-Releasing Hormone Receptor 1 (CRFI) Antagonists

The findings that elevated brain levels of CRF are associated with an exaggerated response to stress, and that the brain overproduces CRF during alcohol dependence and into abstinence, has led researchers to identify a drug that can block CRF.

As described in the previous section, alcohol dependence induces long-term neuroadaptation resulting in a persistent negative emotional state, which in turn perpetuates alcohol use for symptom relief. A key mechanism in this process involves the progressive increase in CRF signaling (hormone produced in response to stress) within the amygdala (brain region involved in the processing and memory of intense emotional experiences). Early results with drugs that block CRF have shown reductions in excessive emotionality, alcohol use, and stress-induced relapse, making the CRF system an enticing target for drug development in the treatment of alcoholism (Heilig and Koob 2007).

Agents that block CRF are available, but are not able to penetrate the blood–brain barrier, limiting their effectiveness. However, small molecules that approximate the effects of CRF blocking agents are able to reach the brain CRF system, and considerable research effort is being made to develop these compounds (Richardson et al. 2008).

### Ayahuasca

The long-term study by scientists of native tribes living in the Amazon Basin in South America revealed a pattern of diminished alcohol use over time among natives ingesting ayahuasca.

Derived from plant sources, ayahuasca is a hallucinogenic beverage used by native tribes in the Amazon Basin for medicinal and sacramental purposes. The active compounds in ayahuasca are DMT (N,N-dimethyl-tryptamine) and b-carboline alkaloids. Long-term indigenous users have been the subject of intensive scientific observation. Many of the Amazonian inhabitants studied had lengthy histories of alcoholism, drug addiction, domestic violence, and other maladaptive behaviors that vanished with repeated long-term ayahuasca use. These findings, coupled with the observation that long-term use of this compound results in stable modulation of brain serotonin systems via increased serotonin transporter density, has stimulated interest in this substance as an alcoholism treatment (McKenna 2004). Although the data collected so far from native South American users is fascinating, formidable regulatory obstacles exist in the U.S. before clinical trials can be implemented.

### Acetyl-L-carnitine

Reducing relapse is a major focus of alcoholism researchers. Craving for alcohol and negative emotional states greatly contribute to relapse, and Martinotti et al. (2010) evaluated the potential of the nutritional supplement acetyl-L-carnitine (ALC) to reduce alcohol cravings among detoxified alcohol-dependent patients who were troubled by the inability to experience pleasure (termed anhedonia). Anhedonia is believed to reflect abnormal function of brain dopamine systems. The researchers found that compared with a placebo, patients given ALC remained abstinent longer, experienced fewer cravings for alcohol, and had greater reductions in anhedonia. The same group of scientists performed a subsequent trial where they compared the effects of ALC at 1 or 3 grams per day (given intravenously the first ten days, then orally the next eighty days) with a placebo for ninety days in detoxified alcohol-dependent patients with prominent symptoms of anhedonia and sadness. Intravenous ALC accelerated the reduction in anhedonia, with no further reductions occurring in the oral phase of the trial. The group given a placebo experienced a modest decline in anhedonia over the first thirty days of the trial, and then a plateau. Patients receiving both doses of ALC experienced significant reductions in anhedonia and sadness compared with those receiving a placebo. Furthermore, ALC was free of side effects (Martinotti et al. 2011).

### N-acetyl cysteine

Dysfunction in brain glutamate systems has been linked to alcohol and other drug dependence and to behavioral addictions. N-acetyl cysteine is an anti-oxidant amino acid that reduces the release of glutamate and helps restore normal glutamate activity to the nucleus accumbens, which is believed to account for its effectiveness in reducing or blocking compulsive behaviors (Grant, Odlaug, and Kim 2009).

N-acetyl cysteine has been found to be effective in the treatment of several impulse-control disorders and addictions, including pathological gambling (Grant, Kim, and Odlaug 2007), compulsive hair pulling (trichotillomania) (Grant, Odlaug, and Kim 2009), compulsive skin picking (Grant, unpublished data), compulsive grooming (Odlaug and Grant 2007), and cocaine dependence (LaRowe et al. 2007; Mardikian et al. 2007).

Although research on N-acetyl cysteine treatment of alcohol dependence has not yet been published, a study evaluating the effectiveness of N-acetyl cysteine in reducing craving and alcohol use in alcoholic-dependent men was just completed, and the results should be published sometime in 2011 (www.clinicaltrials.gov). Additionally, Jon Grant and colleagues at the University of Minnesota believe that combining naltrexone with N-acetyl cysteine may offer a greater reduction in drinking urges than either agent alone, since they act on different brain pathways that may complement each other (Grant, Odlaug, and Kim 2010). N-acetylcysteine is available in health-food stores, is very inexpensive, and has very few side effects (Grant, Odlaug, and Kim 2009).

## Medical Device Treatment

As discussed earlier, the symptoms and the persistent vulnerability to relapse in alcohol dependence are the result of alterations that occur in entire brain neuron pathways. A new generation of medical device therapies has been developed to treat severe cases of neurological and psychiatric disorders that have failed to respond to conventional treatment (Ressler and Mayberg 2007).

These devices use what is called *neurostimulation* as the mode of intervention. Neurostimulation involves the precise targeted delivery of energy into key areas of the brain, with the goal of stimulating dormant or underactive neuron pathways and structures, or slowing neuron pathways and structures that are overactive, to produce measurable change in regional brain activity, behavior, and symptoms. Various forms of neurostimulation therapy have been successful in treating severe cases of Parkinson's disease, obsessive-compulsive disorder, severe major depression, and seizure disorders (Berlim, Neto, and Turecki 2009), and are now being investigated as a therapy for alcohol dependence.

### Deep Brain Stimulation

The process of deep brain stimulation (DBS) involves neurosurgery to implant stimulating electrodes inside the brain that target a specific brain region, and is similar in concept to that of a heart pacemaker.

A case report was published (Kuhn et al. 2007) that described DBS treatment of a patient with a severe anxiety disorder that remained unresponsive to numerous treatments. The patient was also chronically alcohol dependent. The anxiety disorder was the intended therapeutic target, and DBS of the nucleus accumbens did not lead to meaningful reductions in anxiety symptoms. However, an unexpected effect was a rapid and dramatic reduction in alcohol use that persisted one year later, with the patient describing an almost complete absence of the desire to drink during the year of DBS treatment. Liver functions, which were severely abnormal before DBS, became normal after the first year of treatment.

Another report of the effects of DBS used to treat alcoholism found that cravings for alcohol and alcohol consumption were greatly reduced in three long-term, treatment-refractory alcohol-dependent individuals who underwent DBS of the nucleus accumbens; two were abstinent, and a third had markedly reduced drinking occurrences after one year (Heinze et al. 2009; Müller et al. 2009). Although these results are very compelling, DBS is associated with the potential of severe complications, and the small number of patients and brief follow-up periods reported in the published research do not yet provide the basis for broader use of DBS with severe alcohol dependence (Carter and Hall 2011).

### Transcranial Magnetic Stimulation

Transcranial magnetic stimulation, or TMS, is a method of brain stimulation in which magnetic fields are used to induce electric currents in the cerebral cortex to stimulate the release of neurotransmitters. Treatment involves the delivery of a magnetic pulse to the brain through a hand-held stimulating coil applied directly to the head of the patient (Berlim, Neto, and Turecki 2009). The potential of TMS to reduce cravings was studied in a group of forty-five alcohol-dependent patients, who received either active or sham TMS over a region of the brain thought to play a key role in the perpetuation of alcohol addiction (the right dorsolateral pre-frontal cortex). By evaluating the participants throughout the first thirty days following TMS, the authors found that active TMS produced a significant anticraving effect, and concluded that TMS combined with anticraving medication may offer an effective strategy to reduce craving and relapse in early sobriety (Mishra et al. 2010).

## Insomnia in Early Recovery

Insomnia causes difficulty in falling or staying asleep, and is a problem experienced by many persons in recovery, especially during the initial weeks and months. Insomnia not only robs people of a much-needed full night of sleep, but it is associated with irritability, depressed mood, and an increased risk of relapse. The only drugs effective for short-term treatment of insomnia—Restoril, Halcyon, and Ambien—are likely to be abused by persons with a history of alcohol or other drug dependence and are thus unsafe to use in early recovery. Other medications used for insomnia, such as melatonin and trazodone, are ineffective in recovering alcoholics with serious and persistent insomnia (Mahowald, pers. comm.; Krahn 2009).

However, several recent studies have found that very low doses of an older antidepressant, Doxepin, are very effective in treating insomnia. The effective insomnia dose is a fraction of the dose used to treat depression, and doses of 3 mg and 6 mg before bed have substantially improved the duration and quality of sleep, without residual sedation the next day (Krystal et al. 2010; Roth et al. 2010; Weber et al. 2010).

Studies lasting twelve weeks found no evidence of tolerance, rebound insomnia, or discontinuation symptoms when the medication Doxepin was stopped (Owen 2009). Doxepin is free of risk for persons in recovery from addiction and may represent a breakthrough in the safe and effective management of insomnia (Mahowald, pers. comm.).

*Note:*

*Pharmacological-based therapies for alcohol dependence are used as a supplement to Twelve Step involvement or psychosocial therapy, and are used to target specific symptoms of alcoholism that make it difficult for the person to achieve or maintain abstinence. Several drugs have been shown to be helpful in reducing the overpowering urge to drink. A couple of drugs have also shown the ability to limit the severity of relapse, if drinking is resumed, by removing some of the pleasurable effects of alcohol. Other drugs may be helpful in reducing the anxiety, agitation, irritability, and insomnia that are often encountered in early sobriety. None of the drugs used in treating alcohol dependence have a risk of being abused themselves, and their effectiveness is highly dependent on patient adherence. These drugs are not used as stand-alone treatment. There is nearly universal recognition that medications will never substitute or replace AA involvement or psychological therapy.*

### Pharmacogenetics—Matching Pharmacotherapy to Patient

Pharmacogenetics (also referred to as pharmacogenomics) refers to the study of how genetic makeup influences the response to medications (Centre for Genetics Education 2007). Pharmacogenetics in alcoholism treatment begins with identifying the alcoholism subtype (see page 131) of a patient. Since alcoholism subtypes have a genetic basis, patients within each subtype share similar fundamental characteristics with other patients of the same subtype, including the response to medications. Thus, pharmacogenetics involves the matching of a patient with the most compatible treatment approach based on what is known of the genetic makeup of the patient (Leggio et al. 2009). A growing body of research is validating the effectiveness of this subtype-treatment matching approach (Bogenschutz, Tonigan, and Pettinati 2009).

In the past decade, scientists have become much more sophisticated in understanding why certain medications work for some alcoholic patients and not for others. What they are finding is that certain subtypes of alcoholics—those who share common genetic features with other members of the subtype—are substantially more likely to respond to naltrexone and other medications than other subtypes (O'Brien 2005). As discussed on page 134, relative to type A alcoholics, type B alcoholics are characterized by greater alcoholism severity, earlier onset of problem drinking and disease progression, more prominent family history of alcoholism, childhood risk factors such as conduct disorder, and greater frequency of co-occurring psychiatric and substance use disorders. Type B alcoholics have been found to substantially benefit from naltrexone therapy, while the beneficial effects of naltrexone have been very minimal in type A alcoholics (Bogenschutz, Tonigan, and Pettinati 2009).

In addition to studies on naltrexone response, additional evidence supports the type-A-versus-type-B distinction (Babor et al. 1992) in determining the strength of response to other pharmacologic treatments for alcoholism. Researchers have repeatedly found that early-onset type B alcoholics have substantially better responses to ondansetron than do later-onset type A alcoholics (Roache et al. 2008).

Different medication response between type A and type B alcoholics has also been demonstrated with quetiapine, with type B alcoholics showing substantially reduced drinking and reduced craving for alcohol, and type A alcoholics obtaining no significant benefit in drinking reduction (Kampman et al. 2007). A study compared the response to olanzapine between two different groups of alcoholics—those with a specific genetic variation and those without it. During the twelve-week study, participants with the genetic variation experienced reductions in craving and alcohol use, which was not found in the comparison group (Hutchison et al. 2006).

*Note:*

*Pharmacogenomics refers to the process by which alcoholic patients of a given genetic subtype are matched with the optimum treatment. Advances in the understanding of how genetic variations influence the response to treatment have allowed researchers to more accurately treat alcoholics, and treatment response has been found to differ substantially between subtypes of alcoholics.*

# Psychosocial Therapies

Cognitive, cognitive-behavioral, and behavioral therapies—which make up the mainstay of psychosocial therapies for alcohol dependence—originated in the early 1970s with the emergence of social learning theory. Later in that decade, the first studies were published that showed improved drinking outcomes. Cognitive and behavioral therapies were introduced to alcoholism treatment because they were believed to offer an advantage over Twelve Step approaches by addressing not only the drinking but also the cognitive and behavioral coping-skill deficits observed in alcoholic patients (Morgenstern and Longabaugh 2000).

Traditionally, many alcoholism treatment providers have been recovering alcoholics themselves. With little formal training or familiarity with research-grounded treatment approaches, their counseling approaches were based on what worked for them. Addiction researchers believed that psychosocial treatments such as cognitive and behavioral therapy had the potential to improve patient outcomes compared with the Twelve Step approaches offered by most treatment centers. Unlike the Twelve Step model, they were empirically validated (Marinelli-Casey, Domier, and Rawson 2002). However, this controversy was at least partially resolved by the results of Project MATCH (see page 211). In addition, the large amount of scientific support of AA effectiveness has only been recently published.

The Twelve Step approach and psychosocial treatments are often compatible. For example, a cognitive-behavioral therapist does little that an AA sponsor would be likely to object to. Other than word choice, there is little difference between advising a recovering person to beware of people, places, or things that may be "slippery places" and telling a patient to avoid relapse "cues and triggers" (Forman, Humphreys, and Tonigan 2003).

## Cognitive-Behavioral Therapy

Cognitive-behavioral therapy (CBT) integrates behavioral theory, cognitive social learning theory, and cognitive therapy, and is primarily derived from social learning theory, which views excessive drinking as functionally connected to problems and situations in the person's life. CBT views alcohol dependence as a maladaptive way of coping. Since coping-skill deficits are presumed to underlie problem drinking, CBT is also referred to as Coping Skills training (McCaul and Petry 2003).

CBT is concerned with both the triggers and consequences of drinking, with the primary focus on helping the client acquire new intra- and inter-personal skills that reduce relapse risk, maintain abstinence, and promote self-efficacy (Kadden 2001). The core elements of CBT include

- functional analysis, which identifies the precursors and consequences of drinking behavior;
- coping skills training; and
- relapse prevention, which identifies high-risk relapse situations and how to cope with them, addresses the thought process surrounding relapse, and builds self-efficacy (Longabaugh and Morgenstern 1999).

CBT can serve either as primary therapy or as an adjunct to other therapies or a Twelve Step program, and has been shown to be helpful in assisting clients to deal more effectively with feelings, situations, and behaviors related to problem drinking. CBT can be used at any point during the treatment process when exploration of inaccurate or self-defeating thinking is needed (Humphreys 1999; AHCPR 1999).

CBT is the most widely studied psychosocial therapy for alcoholism, and has been consistently ranked as one of the most effective psychosocial therapies with this population (Kadden 2001). CBT has been consistently found to be superior to minimal or no treatment, but the results are inconsistent when compared with other active treatments using random assignment.

In the definitive Project MATCH (the landmark study that compared the drinking outcomes of alcoholics assigned to CBT, motivational enhancement therapy, or Twelve Step facilitation), CBT was no more effective than motivational enhancement therapy (discussed on pages 218–219) or Twelve Step facilitation therapy when drinking was evaluated one year after treatment completion (Project MATCH Research Group 1997b, 1997a), although CBT may result in delayed positive effects that emerge after formal completion of treatment (McCaul and Petry 2003).

CBT may be more effective than group therapy for clients with significant sociopathy, psychopathology, and drinking urges. Other clients more likely to benefit from CBT include those with an external locus of control and higher anxiety levels (Longabaugh and Morgenstern 1999).

*Note:*

*CBT is more effective than no treatment and is similar to other psychosocial therapies in reducing drinking. CBT may be most helpful in clients with anxiety and other psychiatric conditions.*

### Relapse Prevention

Relapse Prevention (RP) is a variant of CBT/coping skills training that contains elements of several treatment approaches to provide training of specific coping skills to help identify and prevent high-risk situations associated with relapse (Witkiewitz and Marlatt 2004). The RP approach was developed by analyzing the thoughts, feelings, and events that took place before relapse in seventy male alcoholics following inpatient treatment (Marlatt and Gordon 1985). An intriguing aspect of RP involves the analysis of apparently irrelevant decisions, defined as decisions made by the alcoholic patient without the awareness of placing his or her sobriety at risk. An example might involve a patient taking a shortcut that involves walking past his or her favorite bar (Witkiewitz and Marlatt 2004).

RP can be used as a stand-alone treatment or as an aftercare program to sustain gains achieved during the initial treatment. Coping skills training is the cornerstone of RP, which teaches clients the following strategies (NREPP 2008):

- Understand relapse as a process
- Identify and cope effectively with high-risk situations such as negative emotional states, interpersonal conflict, and social pressure
- Cope with urges and cravings

- Implement damage control procedures during a lapse to minimize negative consequences
- Stay engaged in treatment even after a relapse
- Learn how to create a more balanced lifestyle

Coping skills training strategies include both cognitive and behavioral techniques. Cognitive techniques provide clients with ways to reframe the habit-changing process as a learning experience with errors and setbacks expected as mastery develops. Behavioral techniques include the use of lifestyle modifications such as meditation, exercise, and spiritual practices to strengthen a client's overall coping capacity (NREPP 2008).

The research yields mixed results on RP, with this approach being found more effective than minimal or no treatment and comparable to alternative treatments such as interpersonal therapy or supportive therapy (Witkiewitz and Marlatt 2004). There is some evidence that RP is more helpful in increasing psychosocial functioning than in decreasing substance use, and that RP can help sustain abstinence following completion of a formal treatment program, although this effect diminishes over time (Kadden 2001).

Negative emotions are identified by the RP approach as a primary relapse precursor, although it is unclear whether the negative emotions are the cause of relapse or a symptom of lifestyle dysfunction. However, this finding has been consistent enough to warrant the inclusion of skills training for coping with negative emotions in several modalities of psychosocial therapy for alcoholism.

Other refinements have involved addressing patient trait and personality factors, social and interpersonal factors, environmental factors, and past events as potential relapse triggers (Cooney et al. 1997; Monti and Rohsenow 1999).

*Note:*

*RP is comparable to other psychosocial therapies in reducing drinking. The particular focus on negative emotions as a relapse risk is particularly useful, and has been incorporated into other therapy approaches.*

## Behavioral Therapies

Behavioral therapies for alcoholism are based on the premise that alcohol use is a conditioned (learned) behavior reinforced by the positive effects of alcohol, and that this same learning process can be used to change the behavior (Monti and Rohsenow 1999). Therefore, to decrease alcohol use, reinforcement from alcohol is decreased while reinforcement from alternate sources is increased.

Treatment entails a behavioral assessment and functional analysis to establish how and when drinking occurs and what learning-based interventions to use, and to provide opportunities to practice the new behavior in real-world situations (Kadden 2001). Behavioral therapy approaches depart from CBT through the emphasis on external triggers and consequences that impact behavior, with limited emphasis on the internal process of thoughts and attitudes (Kadden 2001). In contrast, cognitive-behavioral approaches focus on the thoughts and feelings that precipitate, maintain, or change behavior, although behavioral approaches are used to promote behavior change (Litt et al. 2003). Behavioral therapy may not be suitable for patients with severe maladaptive beliefs and attitudes, for whom a cognitive-based approach is more appropriate. Following are discussions of major behavioral therapies.

### Cue Exposure Therapy

Cue exposure therapy (CET) is based on the principle that neutral stimuli preceding drinking can become paired with drinking, and in time evoke conditioned responses that can trigger drinking. CET aims to help the alcoholic cope with urges and other reactions directly induced by the sight and smell of alcohol through systematic exposure, with the goal of extinguishing the triggered responses and encouraging the patient to substitute behavior consistent with recovery to the presence of these cues (Rohsenow, Monti, and Abrams 1995).

The research on CET is mixed, in part because alcohol-related cue exposure has not been found to be as powerful a trigger as predicted. Additionally, efforts to increase the impact of cue exposure procedures have been inconsistent, and there is a lack of agreement on which elicited cue responses are the best predictors of subsequent drinking (Kadden 2001). Research has shown that recipients of CET have reported fewer urges to drink in simulated high-risk situations and an increased use of alternative coping responses at one-year follow-up (McCaul and Petry 2003). Other studies have reported that CET reduced drinking severity but did not reduce the frequency of alcohol relapse (Kadden 2001). CET has successfully been used with naltrexone to reduce drinking urges, total drinking days, and drinks per drinking day (McCaul and Petry 2003). Issues that have complicated the clinical application of CET include spontaneous recovery, stimulus generalizability, and rapid reinstatement of conditioned responses (Kadden 2001).

### Contingency Management

In contrast to CET, where the focus is on drinking precursors, contingency management (CM) is concerned with events that follow drinking. CM is grounded in operant conditioning theory, which states that drinking is maintained by reinforcing physiological and social effects (AHCPR 1999). CM strives to weaken or eliminate the reinforcement of drinking by encouraging alternate, desired behaviors, often through the use of *tokens* (surrogate currency that can "purchase" desired items) or *vouchers* (a piece of paper that can be exchanged for goods and services), and through withholding reinforcement or enacting punishment for undesired behavior (Kadden 2001; Higgins and Petry 1999).

An issue in using CM approaches with alcoholics is the difficulty in verifying the occurrence of the behavior (in this case abstinence) before rewarding it. Alcohol use cannot be detected more than twelve hours following consumption by serum, blood, or breath analysis. Another issue with CM approaches is the tendency toward relapse after the discontinuation of reward contingencies (Higgins and Petry 1999). However, CM is a feasible approach with alcoholic patients. Variable and fixed-ratio reinforcement schedules have gained client acceptance and are more cost-effective. A more effective use of CM involves shifting from vouchers to rewards in the community as the client prepares to leave treatment (Higgins et al. 1994).

A variant of CM is the Community Reinforcement Approach (CRA).

Although based on operant conditioning theory, CRA borrows from social skills training, behavioral marital therapy, behavior contracting, stress management training, and social/recreational counseling. Disulfiram has also been used as a component of CRA (Miller, Meyers, and Hiller-Sturmhofel 1999).

In CRA, the patient's environment is rearranged by the therapist with the goal of making drinking less reinforcing than abstinence. In addition to vouchers and tokens for goods and services, reinforcers competing with drinking can also include recreational activities and a reorganization of the daily life of the drinker (McCaul and Petry 2003). Although assembling and managing community resources can be an imposing barrier to implementing CRA, several well-designed studies have shown that the social and lifestyle changes enacted by CRA can translate into improved drinking outcomes, more consistent employment, and greater social stability compared to standard treatment (Miller, Meyers, and Hiller-Sturmhofel 1999).

### Behavioral Marital/Family Therapy

Behavioral marital therapy (BMT) is based on social learning theory and the family systems model, and is the most widely studied marital therapy in alcoholism treatment. BMT is most helpful in clients whose families contribute to or enable substance abuse, and assumes a reciprocal relationship between relationship functioning and alcohol use. The focus of BMT is on improving communication, problem solving, interactional behavior, and social support (McCaul and Petry 2003).

Areas where BMT is most useful include addressing expectations of change within the family, encouraging new client behavior, education on how the family system works, eliciting family member strengths, examining the meaning of substance abuse within the family (AHCPR 1999), and reinforcing abstinence. Relapse prevention is also a component of BMT. A variation is to individually treat the spouse or partner of the alcoholic to motivate the drinker to accept treatment (O'Farrell and Fals-Stewart 2001).

BMT is based on the assumptions that

1. intimate partners can reward abstinence, and

2. reducing relationship distress lowers the risk of relapse.

The program components include a recovery or sobriety contract between the partners and therapist, activities and assignments designed to increase positive feelings, shared activities and constructive communication, and relapse prevention planning (NREPP 2008).

Compared with individual therapy, BMT is associated with improved relationship functioning and decreased alcohol consumption in several studies with eighteen- to twenty-four-month follow-ups, as well as reduced domestic violence and reduced treatment attrition (O'Farrell, Choquette, and Cutter 1998). The most dramatic reductions in husband-on-wife violence have occurred in couples where the husband remained abstinent. Additionally, BMT is more cost-effective than individual or group therapy in that it has been shown to reduce hospital and jail costs incurred by the alcoholic, and BMT is associated with reductions in emotional problems in the children of the couple (O'Farrell and Fals-Stewart 2003).

A shortened version of BMT, Brief Relationship Therapy, produced drinking outcomes and couples adjustment comparable to BMT at twelve-month follow-up (Fals-Stewart et al. 2005). An obvious limitation of BMT is the necessity for a cooperative spouse or partner, and most research on BMT has employed homogenous populations with little psychiatric comorbidity.

Nonetheless, BMT has consistently demonstrated treatment-specific effects such as reduction in family problems (McCaul and Petry 2003). Despite supportive empirical validation indicating the important role of behavioral therapy involving the spouse or partner and the alcoholic, BMT has not been widely implemented because of the complexity of addressing the psychopathology in two individuals, whose interactions may be destructive and chaotic (Kadden 2001).

Note:

*The effectiveness of behavioral therapies in reducing drinking is mixed. While cue exposure therapy and contingency management may lead to short-lived reductions in drinking, CRA can facilitate reduced drinking and improved vocational and social functioning; while BMT can reduce alcohol use and domestic violence over an extended period.*

## Motivational-Enhancement Interventions

Motivational-enhancement interventions are based on the Transtheoretical Stages of Change Theory (Prochaska, DiClemente, and Norcross 1992), which states that clients pass through a series of stages of thought, planning, and action in the process of behavior change.

The stages of readiness to change are the following:

- *Precontemplation:* The patient is ambivalent about change, not concerned with substance abuse or changing behavior.
- *Contemplation of change:* There is intention of change in the future.
- *Preparation:* There is intention of change in the near future, with some concrete steps taken in this direction.
- *Action:* Patient has made observable behavior changes, which may not last if earlier stages are not addressed.
- *Maintenance:* The behavior changes have persisted for several months.
- *Termination:* The behavior changes are long-term and stable, relapse is unlikely (DiClemente, Bellino, and Neavins 1999).

*Motivational interviewing (MI)* is a goal-directed, client-centered counseling approach intended to facilitate behavioral change by helping clients to explore and resolve ambivalence. The assumption in MI is that ambivalent attitudes or lack of resolve is the primary obstacle to behavioral change, so that the examination and resolution of ambivalence becomes the key goal. MI has been applied to a wide range of problem behaviors related to alcohol and substance abuse as well as health promotion, medical treatment adherence, and mental health issues. Although many variations in technique exist, the MI counseling style generally includes the following elements (NREPP 2007):

- Establishing rapport with the client and listening reflectively
- Asking open-ended questions to explore the client's own motivations for change

- Affirming the client's change-related statements and efforts
- Eliciting recognition of the gap between current behavior and desired life goals
- Asking permission before providing information or advice
- Responding to resistance without direct confrontation
- Encouraging the client's self-efficacy for change
- Developing an action plan to which the client is willing to commit

Adaptations of the MI counseling approach include a brief intervention for college-age youth visiting hospital emergency rooms after an alcohol-related event; a brief intervention for adult patients with histories of heavy drinking presenting to primary medical care settings for routine care; and a brief intervention for cocaine and heroin users presenting to urban walk-in medical clinics. Community-based substance abuse treatment clinics have also incorporated the MI style approach for the intake process to improve treatment retention (NREPP 2007).

Motivational enhancement therapy (MET) is an adaptation of MI that includes one or more client feedback sessions in which normative feedback is presented and discussed in an explicitly nonconfrontational manner. MET uses an empathic but directive approach in which the therapist provides feedback intended to strengthen and consolidate the client's commitment to change and promote a sense of self-efficacy. MET aims to elicit intrinsic motivation to change substance abuse behavior by resolving client ambivalence, evoking self-motivational statements and commitment to change, and rolling with resistance (responding in a neutral way to the client's resistance to change rather than contradicting or correcting the client) (NREPP 2007).

Motivational enhancement interventions are not a form of psychosocial therapy per se, but instead are used to resolve client ambivalence, promote commitment to change, and set goals. The goal of motivational enhancement interventions is to improve treatment retention, treatment outcome, and client willingness to address the substance use problem.

## Brief Interventions

Unlike traditional alcoholism treatment, which focuses on helping people who are alcohol dependent to achieve abstinence, brief interventions—or short, one-on-one counseling sessions—are ideally suited for people who drink in ways that are harmful or risky but who have not developed alcohol dependence. Also unlike traditional alcoholism treatment, brief interventions can be delivered in a matter of minutes and require minimal follow-up (NIAAA 2005).

The goals of brief interventions are also different from alcoholism treatment. Brief interventions generally strive to moderate a person's alcohol use to sensible levels and to eliminate hazardous drinking practices such as binge drinking, although abstinence may be encouraged if appropriate. Research also shows that problems associated with drinking begin at much lower levels of alcohol use than previously thought, making brief interventions a potentially useful approach for people engaged in a variety of problem drinking behaviors (Moyer and Finney 2004/2005).

Thus, the rationale for reducing drinking or changing patterns of alcohol use is explained through data demonstrating a reduction in negative outcomes (medical problems, injuries, domestic violence, motor vehicle crashes, arrests, or damage to a developing fetus) for nondependent drinkers (NIAAA 2005).

Brief interventions typically consist of one to four short counseling sessions with a trained interventionist such as a physician, psychologist, or social worker. Persons who receive brief interventions while being treated for other conditions have consistently shown greater reductions in alcohol use than comparable groups not receiving an intervention. People seeking treatment specifically for alcohol abuse appear to reduce their alcohol use about the same amount whether receiving one to four sessions or five or more sessions, suggesting that brief interventions can be effective in reducing drinking among people who do not have severe drinking problems requiring more intensive treatment (NIAAA 2005).

The appropriate intervention is influenced by factors such as the severity of the alcohol problem, the use of other drugs, or the co-occurrence of a medical or psychiatric problem. The choice of intervention is also based on the clinical setting, the clinician's skills and interest, and time constraints. A brief intervention usually includes personalized feedback and counseling based on patient risk for harmful drinking. Often, simply providing this feedback is enough to encourage those at risk to reduce their alcohol intake (Moyer and Finney 2004/2005).

Successful brief interventions share several elements that motivate the problem drinker to change his or her drinking, including an emphasis on personal responsibility for change, clear advice on change, a menu of alternative change options, empathy, and transmitting a sense of empowerment and optimism to the client (Bien, Miller, and Tonigan 1993).

Brief interventions can be successfully performed on problem drinkers in a variety of settings, including primary care, the emergency room, prenatal care, the criminal justice setting, and the college campus (NIAAA 2005). Brief interventions have consistently been found effective in reducing alcohol consumption or achieving treatment referral of problem drinkers. Among persons who are problem drinkers but not alcoholic, brief interventions are more effective than no counseling, and often as effective as more extensive treatment. Another benefit is increased effectiveness of subsequent treatment (Bien, Miller, and Tonigan 1993). Research shows that these interventions appear to be cost-effective (Moyer and Finney 2004/2005), but it should be emphasized that the long-term effectiveness of brief interventions may be limited (NIAAA 2004/2005)

*Note:*

*Brief interventions are not intended to help alcohol-dependent clients achieve abstinence, but instead are used with nondependent problem drinkers to reduce or prevent harm associated with their level of alcohol use. Brief interventions are effective in helping problem drinkers cut down or quit drinking, but the effect may not be long-lasting. Heavy alcohol abusers and problem drinkers with multiple consequences from drinking may not respond to this approach.*

## Other Psychosocial Approaches

### Confrontational Counseling

The use of confrontation in alcohol- and drug-dependent clients has a long tradition, and confrontation is used to break down the psychological defenses in order to overcome denial (SCCMHA 2007). Confrontational counseling approaches emerged through a confluence of cultural factors in U.S. history that predated the development of methods for reliably evaluating the effects of such treatment. Confrontational communication approaches varied from frank feedback to profanity-laden indictments, screamed denunciations of character, challenges and ultimatums, intense argumentation, ridicule, and purposeful humiliation. Confrontation marked a dramatic break from earlier therapeutic traditions that were guided by the importance of neutral exploration, empathy, compassionate support, and positive regard for clients. Originally practiced within voluntary peer-based communities, confrontational approaches soon extended to authority-based professional relationships where the potential for abuse and harm was greatly increased.

Four decades of research have not found a single clinical trial showing the effectiveness of confrontational counseling, whereas a number have documented harmful effects, particularly with more vulnerable populations. There are now numerous evidence-based alternatives to confrontational counseling, and clinical studies show that effective substance abuse counselors are those who practice with an empathic, supportive style. It is time to accept that the harsh confrontational practices of the past are ineffective, potentially harmful, and professionally inappropriate (White and Miller 2007).

### Psychodynamic Therapies

Psychodynamic therapies for alcoholism focus on several interpsychic processes, including the subconscious processes that drive client behavior, to facilitate change in drinking. The goals of psychodynamic therapy are increased self-awareness and identification of how the past influences the present behavior (Kaufman 1994). However, cure from alcoholism and other substance addiction does not come through psychodynamic insight.

In a prospective study of Harvard men (Vaillant 1995), twenty-six alcoholics received a total of 5,000 hours of psychotherapy, which is an average of 200 hours for each man. Only one man recovered from alcoholism while in psychotherapy (Vaillant 2005). The few studies reporting positive outcomes were conducted in institutions excelling in psychotherapy, by highly trained psychiatrists and psychologists, and in patients with more severe psychopathology. Thus, even if the research revealed consistent positive results, such an approach is unlikely to be cost-effective (Kaufman 1994).

### Health Realization

Health Realization (HR) addresses the nature of thought and how it influences experience. Students of HR are taught that they can change how they react to their circumstances by becoming aware that they are creating their own experience as they respond to their thoughts, and that problems stemming from thoughts can be countered by teaching the person to connect to his or her innate health and inner wisdom. With HR, all psychological phenomena are viewed as the manifestations of three operative principles (Pransky 2006; Mills and Spittle 2003; Mills 1995):

- Mind as the universal energy common to all life, and the source of innate health and well-being
- Consciousness as the ability to become aware
- Thought as the power to think and create one's experience of reality

According to the HR model, reality and circumstances are experienced through the continuous filter of one's thoughts, and this filter is what makes perception appear to be the truth. When thinking is changed, reality and one's reaction to events and circumstances change with it.

According to HR, a person's ability to control thoughts is limited, and counselors using HR encourage their clients to consider the premise that reality at any point in time is determined by the process of thought. HR views alcoholism as a response to a lack of a sense of self-efficacy, and not the result of disease. It believes that alcoholism and alcohol abuse can be overcome by showing the client that the negative and stressful emotions which compel the addictive use of alcohol are the self-generated products of their own thoughts. HR asserts that these thoughts can be self-quieted to provide a pathway to well-being that is not reliant on external circumstances (Pransky 2006; Mills and Spittle 2003; Mills 1995).

Published results of investigations into the effectiveness of HR in treating alcoholism are very limited. A single study comparing the effectiveness of HR with the Twelve Step approach among women in a residential substance abuse treatment program suggests comparable reductions between the two approaches in substance use and criminal justice involvement, and improvements in psychological health (Banerjee et al. 2007).

There is scant evidence that psychodynamic therapy alone has any lasting effect on reducing drinking in alcohol-dependent patients. Additional studies on Health Realization show some positive results are needed to support its use with alcohol-dependent clients.

## The Treatment Needs of Older Adults

Older adults with alcohol and other drug problems have specific medical, cognitive, and emotional treatment needs. Those who began drinking early in life are typically in worse health than later-onset drinkers and nondependent peers, have greater difficulty withdrawing from substances, require longer detoxification stays, and exhibit more severe emotional problems (Kraemer, Mayo-Smith, and Calkins 1997; Schonfeld and Dupree 1991). Compared to younger adults, older adults are at increased risk for cognitive and functional impairment during withdrawal (Kraemer, Mayo-Smith, and Calkins 1997). In addition, many older adults identify depression, grief, loneliness, and social pressure as common precursors to their drinking (Hazelden Dec. 2001).

A variety of treatment approaches work well for older adults, from brief interventions for at-risk drinkers to inpatient programs for those who are alcohol dependent (Blow and Barry 2000). Several treatment facilities around the country have designed elder-specific programming which includes a slower pace, accommodations for medical and ambulatory problems, supportive rather than confrontational approaches, and focus on specific issues such as grief, loneliness, boredom, and retirement (Hazelden Dec. 2001).

Research data show older adults tend to do well in age-specific programming (Blow and Barry 2000; Kashner et al. 1992). One study of men found that those who were randomly assigned to receive age-specific programming were three times more likely to report abstinence at six months and two times more likely to report abstinence at twelve months compared to peers who received treatment as usual in a mixed-age setting (Hazelden Dec. 2001).

Factors found to improve outcomes among older adults include lower pre-treatment alcohol consumption levels, having a social group that disapproves of drinking, and seeking help from mental health professionals (Moos, Brennan, and Moos 1991). Treatment for alcohol problems and regular AA participation are also associated with abstinence among older adults (Chermack et al. 1996). One study found no relationship between age of onset and inpatient treatment outcomes (Blow and Barry 2000; Hazelden Dec. 2001).

*Note:*

*Older adults benefit from the same treatment approaches as younger adults, but also need a tailored programming approach that addresses issues such as medical and pharmacological concerns; grief, loneliness, and retirement; and potential impairment in cognition and ability to live independently. The pace should also be slower, confrontation should be avoided, and support should be increased.*

## Treatment Outcome and Prognosis

This section looks at the history of research in the addiction field, its outcomes, and its prognosis for treatment success. The history of testing treatment programs and collecting data to validate outcomes is long and continues to lead the industry toward more effective treatment models.

### The History of Treatment Outcome Reporting

The reporting of addiction treatment outcomes has a long, problem-filled history. The first addiction treatment outcome study was conducted in 1874 by Dr. Joseph Turner, founder of the New York State Inebriate Asylum. Subsequent studies, some involving thousands of treated patients (Chamberlain 1891; Crothers 1893), became commonplace in the nineteenth century. The percentages of claimed cures declined as studies improved their methods, but honest reporting of these outcomes conflicted with business interests as new competitors (private addiction cure institutes, private sanatoria, and bottled home cures) entered the field claiming 90–100% cure rates.

The addictions treatment field in the late nineteenth century was plagued by the inherent conflict between the need for objective data to advance scientific knowledge and improve treatment protocols and the need to claim high success rates to market services and raise funds. More than a century later, discrepancies remain between addiction treatment outcomes reported in peer-reviewed scientific journals and the outcomes claimed by treatment industry representatives, especially those of particular treatment programs (White and Godley 2005).

Even today, it's not difficult to encounter treatment centers or addiction recovery programs that use deceptive promotion in their marketing approach. An obvious example of deception is when treatment centers promise a cure. Other examples of false and deceptive marketing include the use of these terms: *guaranteed, not a disease,* and *AA doesn't work* (BFICP 2007).

Claims of success rates of 50–70% and higher for specific programs are not uncommon when these figures are communicated by treatment program representatives. The Internet is filled with treatment claims of 70–100% success rates—rates that far exceed those reported at scientific conferences and in the scientific literature.

For example, a 2001 review of the largest and most scientifically rigorous treatment studies published up to that point (Miller, Walters, and Bennett 2001) reported an average one-year continuous abstinence rate of 24%.

There are several possible reasons for this discrepancy. Treatment outcomes do vary among different patient subpopulations and addiction treatment programs, and even across addiction counselors (Wilbourne and Miller 2003; McLellan et al. 1988). And some programs simply have superior treatment services and more highly competent professionals delivering care, clients with better prognoses for recovery, or a combination of these factors. However, the main reason for these discrepancies is probably the quality of the study methods and procedures used to report patient outcome (White and Godley 2005).

## What Is Successful Recovery?

The definition of recovery has changed over time from a focus on what has been removed to what has been added to one's life. AA co-founder Bill Wilson coined the phrase "emotional sobriety" to describe a state of emotional health that far exceeds the achievement of not drinking, which he defined as "real maturity . . . in our relations with ourselves, with our fellows and with God" (Wilson 1958; White and Kurtz 2006).

Because severe and chronic alcohol abuse impacts many areas of life functioning, recovery from such a problem should be measured across multiple domains of recovery, including the relationship with the drug of choice and other substance(s), physical health, psychological and emotional health, family and relationship health, and lifestyle health (White 1996). Thus, the goal of recovery can be referred to as *global health* (White and Kurtz 2006), and recovery from alcohol or other drug problems can be defined as "a process of change through which an individual achieves abstinence and improved health, wellness, and quality of life" (CSAT 2007).

A group of experts in the field of addictions met at the Betty Ford Center in order to further define successful recovery from alcoholism and substance dependence. The group's conclusions were published in 2007 (BFICP 2007) and include the following:

Recovery from substance dependence is a voluntarily maintained lifestyle characterized by these elements:

- *Sobriety*—Abstinence from alcohol and all other nonprescribed drugs (including nicotine, although this is controversial)
- *Personal health*—Improved quality of personal life reflected by physical health, psychological health, and spirituality
- *Citizenship*—Improved quality of social functioning and independent living

Other conclusions made by the panel of experts are as follows:

- Recovery is not simply abstinence from alcohol or other drugs.
- Personal health and citizenship are often achieved and maintained through peer support groups such as AA and practices consistent with the Twelve Steps and Twelve Traditions.
- Alcohol-dependent persons who take acamprosate or naltrexone as prescribed to reduce cravings for alcohol, but are abstinent from alcohol and all other nonprescribed drugs, meet the consensus definition of sobriety.

Regarding timeframes of sobriety, the panel concluded the following:

- Early sobriety = one month to one year
- Sustained sobriety = one to five years
- Stable sobriety = five years or more

An important point to make is that although many people recovering from alcohol and other drug dependence experience an improvement in many areas of life functioning with continued sobriety, early recovery can be marked by ongoing and substantial impairments in many life areas. Substantial levels of depression, anxiety, poor self-esteem, guilt, and impaired social functioning can challenge one's recovery (White and Kurtz 2006). There are also patterns of "high-bottom" recovery among people who got sober before they suffered severe losses related to their alcohol use, and patterns of "low-bottom" recovery achieved by persons who endured the advanced stages of addiction and experienced severe personal and social disintegration and anguish before achieving stable recovery ("High Bottom" 1949; White and Kurtz 2006).

### The Process Leading to Relapse

Just as the definition of successful recovery has been clarified over the last several decades, counselors working with recovering alcohol- and other drug-addicted clients have long observed a pattern of thinking and behavior that seems to ultimately lead to a relapse. This pattern was clarified and defined by Terence Gorski and Merlene Miller in 1982 as an unfolding eleven-step process. The eleven steps composing the relapse process include the following (Gorski and Miller 1982):

1.  Change in Attitude—Participating in a recovery program becomes viewed as unimportant, and is accompanied by a return to "stinking thinking," or unhealthy or addictive thinking. The person begins to slide in his or her effort at working a program of recovery, and may begin to feel something is wrong but can't identify the exact cause.

2.  Elevated Stress—Stress levels increase, due to either a major change in circumstances or just little things that keep building up. There is a risk of overreacting to these situations, and the development of mood swings or exaggerated positive or negative feelings represents a potentially serious concern.

3.  Reactivation of Denial—This is not denial over having an alcohol or other drug problem, but denial over being affected by the stress. The person may try to convince him- or herself that everything is okay. Fear and worry appear, which may be dismissed, and the person stops sharing those feelings with others.

4.  Recurrence of Post-acute Withdrawal Symptoms—Anxiety, depression, sleeplessness, and memory loss can return during times of stress, and are dangerous because of the temptation to self-medicate with alcohol or other drugs.

5.  Behavior Change—The person changes his or her daily routine developed in early sobriety that helped replace addictive behaviors with healthy alternatives, and begins to avoid situations

that might require an honest evaluation of their behavior. Poor judgment and problems from impulsive behavior may begin occurring.

6. Social Breakdown—Discomfort around others may begin, with avoidance of sober friends and support group meetings leading to social isolation.

7. Loss of Structure—The daily routine or schedule developed in early sobriety is now abandoned, and is replaced by sleeping late, ignoring personal hygiene, or skipping meals. Constructive planning stops, and overreaction occurs when plans don't work out.

8. Loss of Judgment—The person begins to have trouble making decisions, or makes unhealthy decisions, and may experience difficulty in managing thoughts and emotions. Thinking clearly may become difficult, confusion occurs easily, and the person may feel overwhelmed for no apparent reason, unable to relax, or easily annoyed and angered.

9. Loss of Control—Irrational decisions are made, which seem impossible to interrupt or alter. Supportive persons are cut off, and the person begins thinking of returning to social drinking or recreational drug use and controlling it. The person may begin to believe there is no hope and loses confidence in his or her ability to manage life.

10. Loss of Options—The person begins to limit available options as he or she stops attendance of all AA meetings and appointments with addiction professionals, and discontinues any medication treatments. The person may feel loneliness, frustration, anger, resentment, and tension, or feel helpless and desperate. He or she may conclude there are only three ways out: insanity, suicide, or self-medication with alcohol or other drugs.

11. Relapse—Social or short-term alcohol or other drug use is attempted, but the results are disappointing and shame and guilt

are immediately experienced. Loss of control over alcohol or other drug use spirals further out of control, causing increasing problems with relationships, employment, money, and mental and physical health.

The validity of this model of relapse is supported by the results of a study published in 2000 by Miller and Harris. In their study, thirty-seven questions that paralleled the steps toward relapse, as described above, were included in a test. The test was then given to alcoholic patients every two months throughout the first year of treatment completion. The authors found that a high score on this test was a strong predictor of relapse to drinking. Among the individual test items, the ones with the highest association with the total score, and therefore with risk of relapse, included the following:

- I have many problems in my life.
- I feel blue, down, listless, or depressed.
- I have trouble concentrating and prefer to dream about how things could be.
- Things don't work out well for me.
- I feel confused.
- I get irritated or annoyed with my friends.
- I feel angry or frustrated.
- I feel trapped and stuck, like there is no way out.
- I have long periods of serious depression.
- I feel like things are so bad that I might as well drink.
- I feel sorry for myself.
- I feel angry at the world in general.

Taken together, these test items reflect a general demoralization, depression, anxiety, and anger, and a feeling that life lacks purpose (Miller and Harris 2000).

Another interesting finding came from evaluating the test items that were most associated with a low overall score, and therefore with the lowest risk of relapse. The attributes represented by these test items included a sense of meaning in life, honesty, hope, low levels of emotional negativity, stable eating and sleeping patterns, clear thinking, absence of self-pity, and a sense of peace and stability. Alcoholics Anonymous has the viewpoint that more than just abstinence is required for sobriety, and from this perspective, low scores on this scale may be viewed as a measure of the quality of sobriety (Miller and Harris 2000).

*Note:*

*Successful recovery involves more than just abstinence from alcohol and other drugs of abuse. It also involves improving one's emotional well-being, relationships and family health, and lifestyle health. The use of medication to reduce alcohol cravings such as naltrexone or acamprosate is not a contradiction to successful recovery, if the person has achieved abstinence and an improved quality of life.*

## What Does the Research Show on Treatment Outcome?

Treatment has helped thousands of people obtain long-term abstinence and improved quality of life. A review of alcoholism treatment outcome studies arrived at three major conclusions:

1. The remission (persons no longer meeting the *DSM-IV* criteria for a substance use disorder following treatment) average is about one-third of those treated.

2. Substance use (measured by days of use and quantity used) decreased by an average of 87% following treatment.

3. Substance-related problems decreased by an average of 60% following treatment (Miller, Walters, and Bennett 2001).

Some patients do not attain total abstinence but achieve partial recovery, which means that they have fewer alcohol-related problems, improvement in health and social functioning, and significant reductions in the costs and hazards they pose to the larger community (Zweben 1996). These are important findings because patients not achieving total abstinence following treatment have traditionally been discounted, with treatment being regarded as ineffective or failed (Miller, Walters, and Bennett 2001).

Many studies (Hoffmann and Harrison 1991; Higgins et al. 1991; Hoffmann, Harrison, and Belille 1983) show a strong correlation between high abstinence rates and compliance with aftercare and/or participation in AA. These results help confirm that addiction needs to be treated as a chronic illness through long-term involvement in a recovery program such as AA.

McLellan et al. (1993) and other researchers (Institute of Medicine 1990; Gerstein and Harwood 1990; Morgenstern and McCrady 1992) have found significant differences in outcomes between different types of treatment programs, with the better six-month outcomes related to greater quantity and range of services delivered. Patient factors such as more severe substance dependence, poorer social and economic supports, and worse psychiatric problems are generally related to poorer outcomes after treatment (Institute of Medicine 1990; Gerstein and Harwood 1990; Hazelden June 1998).

Morgenstern and McCrady (1992) have studied the processes that promote good outcomes, and point to the trend of integrating behavioral treatment with traditional Twelve Step treatment. In traditional Twelve Step alcohol and other drug treatment, greater commitment to AA and belief in a Higher Power have been shown to predict reduced severity of relapse among those who do relapse (Morgenstern et al. 1996; Hazelden June 1998).

A review of cost-benefit, or cost-offset, studies of addiction treatment by Langenbucher et al. (1993) found that treatment is not a costly add-on to health care, but instead is an important cost-saving component. Other cost-benefit analyses support this conclusion (Holder and Hallan 1986; Jones and Vischi 1979; Finigan 1996), including one that found for each dollar invested in treatment in California, taxpayers saved $7 in reduced health and social costs (Gerstein and Johnson 1994; Hazelden June 1998).

*Note:*

*Although treatment is effective in helping some patients achieve abstinence, abstinence rates are significantly higher among those who become involved in AA and/or aftercare following treatment. Some patients even benefit from treatment without achieving complete abstinence. Alcoholism treatment saves taxpayer money in the long run. The importance of long-term involvement in a recovery program following treatment reflects the chronic, relapsing nature of alcohol dependence.*

## Patient Outcomes of Minnesota Model Treatment

Earlier efforts by Hazelden to evaluate patient outcomes consisted of data obtained from Hazelden alumni. One example was the results that were published by Laundergan in 1982. This study attempted to evaluate the outcome of 3,638 patients discharged during the mid-1970s. Only 52% of patients were reachable twelve months after treatment; of these, 50% reported continuous abstinence in the year following treatment, and 17.6% reported improved status. Another study of 1,531 patients published in 1985 (Gilmore 1985) found that 89% reported either abstinence or reduced alcohol use one year after treatment. And Higgins et al. (1991) found that among 1,655 patients, 66% reported being abstinent at both the six-month and one-year follow-ups (Slaymaker and Sheehan 2008).

These studies were helpful, but the conclusions drawn from their results were limited by problems with the nature of the study design. Refining the research methods used by earlier investigators, Stinchfield and Owen (1998) prospectively followed a group of 1,083 Hazelden patients at one, six, and twelve months following treatment, and used friends or relatives to verify the information given them by the subjects. At one year following treatment, 53% of this patient group reported continuous abstinence and an additional 35% reported substantially reduced alcohol and other drug use (Slaymaker and Sheehan 2008).

Additional studies became published with the increasingly widespread use of the Minnesota Model across the U.S. Hoffman and Harrison (1991) evaluated the outcomes of more than 3,000 patients entering Minnesota Model programs across the country during the mid-1980s. They found that roughly two-thirds reported abstinence in the year following treatment. The response rates were low, which led the authors to estimate that the actual one-year abstinence rate was 40%.

A study published in 1993 by McLellan et al. obtained high response rates (94%) and included urine and breath tests for verification. Of the 198 alcohol- and/or cocaine-dependent men who completed a Twelve Step inpatient or outpatient program, 59% were abstinent from alcohol and 84% were abstinent from drugs at six-month follow-up. Psychosocial functioning was also improved from pre- to post-testing (Slaymaker and Sheehan 2008).

*Note:*

*Evaluation of the Minnesota Model has found abstinence rates around 50% one year after treatment, with many more patients reducing their level of drinking and/or other drug use. Several issues make it difficult to obtain accurate figures of treatment outcome. These include how to report the treatment outcomes of patients who are unable to be reached, and the reliance on patient self-report without independent verification.*

*Specific treatment approaches and treatment centers for alcoholism have a long history of inflating their reported success rates, and any treatment that is promoted as a cure is using deceptive advertising. There are many differences in treatment outcome. These stem from differences in the level of skill of staff, the treatment approach used, and the makeup of the population being treated.*

CHAPTER 8

# Meditation and Recovery from Alcoholism

Stanislav Grof, a world-renowned psychiatrist and one of the founders of the field of transpersonal psychology, stated that addiction is a manifestation of a profound spiritual yearning, the "thirst for wholeness." Many people develop alcohol or other drug addictions in order to escape the pain of this unfulfilled desire and to fill the emptiness. Essentially, the real need of alcoholics and addicts is for wholeness, healing of the wounded psyche, and transcendence (Grof and Grof 1993).

Meditation has the potential to fulfill this need for the recovering alcohol- or other drug-dependent person. Mindfulness meditation in particular can provide the means to live more fully in the present, act with deliberation instead of reacting on impulse, and to develop a more inclusive universal awareness and a greater connection with the God of one's understanding. The founders of Alcoholics Anonymous realized the importance of meditation, along with prayer, and included both practices in their program of recovery.

# Background

The word *meditation* is derived from the Latin *meditari,* which means "to engage in contemplation or reflection" (Ospina et al. 2007), and meditation has been a spiritual and healing practice in some regions of the world for more than 5,000 years (Walters 2002). Many spiritual and religious traditions incorporate meditative practices as a key access point to the Divine (Linehan 1993; Appel and Kim-Appel 2009).

For example, there are many practices within Christianity that represent forms of meditation or mindfulness. Christian meditation is often expressed in the form of prayer. Monastic customs often seek a turn inward and involve practices of intense prayer, rosary, and adoration of the Eucharist. The Eastern Orthodoxy tradition of the hesychast, involving the practice of focusing one's attention on an individual object, represents a direct form of meditation or mindfulness. Philokalia is considered a form of meditation of the heart, which leads toward theosis, the goal of which is to ignore the senses and achieve an inner stillness (Hierotheos 1998). Similar to Christianity, Judaism encompasses several meditative practices. In the Tannach (the Hebrew Bible), meditation was a key practice of the prophets (Ribner 1998). Kabbalah is also inherently a meditative field of religious or mystical study.

Likewise, meditation is an important element of Islam and Muslim mystical traditions, especially Sufism. The Muslim prophet Muhammad reportedly spent long periods in contemplation and meditation, and during one such period received revelations that formed the Holy Qur'an (Nigosian 2004). Islamic meditation includes the concepts of *tafakkur* and *tadabbur,* which literally mean "reflection upon the universe" (Appel and Kim-Appel 2009).

Many contemplative religious and spiritual traditions speak of loving-kindness as the wish of happiness for others, and of compassion as the wish to relieve others' suffering. To cultivate these qualities, practitioners in a number of traditions have developed specific meditative practices that are believed essential in counteracting self-centered tendencies so that selfless altruistic behaviors might arise more frequently and spontaneously than selfish interests. These techniques include concentration exercises that train attention, behavioral training such as the practice of generosity, cognitive strategies that include reflection on the fleeting nature of the self, and empathic strategies such as shifting perspectives from self-oriented to other-oriented, or the visualization of the suffering of others (Gethin 1998; Nuchols 2006; Lutz et al. 2008).

The beneficial effects of meditation in helping alcoholics achieve sobriety first became known to the public with the publication of the first edition of *Alcoholics Anonymous* (the Big Book) in 1939. The practice of meditation, along with prayer, was considered so important to recovery from alcoholism by the founders of AA that it was incorporated into Step Eleven of the Twelve Steps, which reads: "Sought through prayer and meditation to improve our conscious contact with God *as we understood Him,* praying only for knowledge of His will for us and the power to carry that out."

One of the reasons that meditation is an appealing element of a recovery program relates to the motivation to use alcohol or other drugs by persons with chronic anxiety, upsetting trauma memories, and other psychiatric conditions. Termed self-medication, alcohol and other drugs are used to reduce symptoms and distress, which reflect the power of negative reinforcement as a motivation for substance abuse. From this perspective, meditation may serve as a useful alternative to alcohol use by producing some of the same positive benefits such as tension relief and relaxation (Marlatt and Chawla 2007).

Meditation and mindfulness may also serve as an intervention for alcohol or other drug cravings. The heightened state of present-focused awareness may counteract the conditioned automatic response to use alcohol during the experience of cravings and urges. With practice, meditative awareness may become a learned response to the urge itself, serving to pause and delay the impulse to act on the urge. Meditation can cultivate a greater understanding of the transience of all experience and an acceptance of one's current condition, including tension or craving. This is contrary to the thinking of a person in an addicted state, where there is often an inability to accept impermanence and a desire to alter one's current experience (Marlatt 1994; Marlatt and Chawla 2007).

The greater capacity for awareness and acceptance of one's immediate experience that comes with meditation may also reduce the risk for relapse in several ways. Some consider alcohol abuse as a form of experiential avoidance, or the unwillingness to remain in contact with one's experience (Hayes et al. 1996), a trait shared with other forms of psychiatric illness (Hayes, Strosahl, and Wilson 1999). Meditation can counter this experiential avoidance by encouraging the direct, nonjudgmental, moment-to-moment contact with one's experiences, without attempting to alter, manipulate, or judge the experience (Marlatt and Chawla 2007).

Two broad categories of meditation practices have been used with alcohol- and substance-abusing patients: relaxation or mantra meditation (Transcendental Meditation and Relaxation Response), and mindfulness meditation (vipassana, Zen Buddhist meditation, Mindfulness-Based Stress Reduction, and Mindfulness-Based Relapse Prevention) (Marlatt and Chawla 2007).

These meditative techniques can also be grouped according to the dominant attentional style, with relaxation/mantra meditations using a more concentrative method and mindfulness meditations using a more diffuse approach (Dakwar and Levin 2009). Although elements of Hindu and Buddhist meditation practices have been removed from their broader spiritual context and adapted for clinical use, persons in recovery from alcohol or other drug dependence are likely to achieve greater benefit when meditation is accompanied by the traditional spiritual component (Dakwar and Levin 2009).

## Relaxation and Mantra Meditations

Two forms of meditation discussed briefly here provide a more traditional mantra approach to meditation practices.

### Transcendental Meditation

Transcendental Meditation (TM) is a technique derived from the Vedic tradition of India that was described in the writings of Maharishi Mahesh Yogi on the nature of transcendental consciousness. TM strives to achieve a meditative state in which the repetition of a mantra no longer consciously occurs and instead the mind is quiet and without thought. During the practice of TM, the ordinary thinking process is said to be transcended (or gone beyond) as the awareness gradually settles down and is eventually freed of all mental content, remaining silently awake within itself, and producing a state of restful alertness. These periods, referred to as pure consciousness or transcendental consciousness, are said to be characterized by the experience of perfect stillness, rest, stability, and order, and by a complete absence of mental boundaries (Alexander 1994; Farrow and Hebert 1982; Ospina et al. 2007).

The TM meditation state is achieved by the repetition of a mantra. The mantra is a meaningless sound, typically a spiritual word derived from Hindu philosophy, and the meditator silently repeats the mantra during two twenty-minute periods daily with eyes closed. If the practitioner becomes distracted by thoughts or feelings during the meditation period, instruction is given to gently return one's attention to the mantra (Marlatt and Chawla 2007). No breath control procedures are used.

**Relaxation Response Meditation**

Sympathetic nervous system hyperactivity is associated with the fight-or-flight response that accompanies stress, and includes elevated heart rate, blood pressure, and respiration rate. The relaxation response (RR) refers to the self-induced calming of sympathetic nervous system activity. This response was believed to be common to many ancient meditation practices, which were integrated into a single technique with RR meditation. With RR, the individual is instructed to assume a comfortable position, close the eyes, and relax the muscles beginning at the feet and progressing upward to the scalp. Once relaxation is achieved, the meditator is instructed to breathe through the nose, focus on the breath, and to inhale and exhale while silently saying the word *one* with each exhalation. Should distracting thoughts occur, an attempt is made to ignore them and focus on the mantra; thus, the mantra is linked with the breath. Similar to TM, this repetition of a sound, word, or phrase is considered essential to RR meditation. When the practice is completed, the meditator sits quietly for several minutes with eyes closed and then with eyes open (Benson 1983; Keable 1985; Ospina et al. 2007).

## Mindfulness Meditations

Mindfulness approaches are not considered relaxation or mood management techniques, and differ from mantra or relaxation meditation in several ways. Although a focus on breath or bodily sensations is common to both, mindfulness meditation in contrast to mantra meditations teaches an attitude of acceptance toward the distracting thoughts and emotions that may emerge when one is still.

Even when the experience is unpleasant, one is taught to observe or investigate the experience instead of using avoidance or suppression to dispel it. The attitude of acceptance of an intense or unpleasant emotion or thought does not mean a passive resignation, but instead refers to being fully present and not preoccupied when such an event occurs. The process of mindfulness meditation involves the interplay of focusing on an object, acknowledging and accepting distraction, and gently returning the attention to breathing. In this process, the person learns not to take emotions and thoughts literally as facts but instead as transient mental events. In this way, mindfulness meditation transforms how one relates to dysfunctional thoughts and negative or unpleasant emotions instead of changing or eliminating the uncomfortable state. This type of responding has been referred to as taking a decentered perspective and as cognitive distancing (Breslin, Zack, and McMain 2002; Hayes, Strosahl, and Wilson 1999; Teasdale, Segal, and Williams 1995).

Many persons recovering from alcohol use disorders attempt to suppress cravings, which can paradoxically serve to increase intrusive, automatic alcohol-related thoughts (Palfai et al. 1997), dysphoria, and physiological stress (Wenzlaff and Wegner 2000). Larimer, Palmer, and Marlatt (1999) observed that mindfulness involves the acceptance of the present moment, whereas addiction involves the repeated desire to avoid the present moment, which contributes to the urge to use.

An example of how mindfulness meditation can be used to prevent relapse is referred to as *urge surfing* (Marlatt 2002). In this procedure, the meditator is taught to visualize the intense craving as an ocean wave that begins as a small wavelet and gradually increases in magnitude to culminate as a large cresting wave.

With instruction to become aware of one's breath as a surfboard, the client is given the goal of surfing the urge by allowing it to first rise up and decline without being wiped out by giving in to the urge. Clients are taught that most urges are conditioned learned responses that are triggered by environmental cues and emotional reactivity. Similar to an ocean wave, the conditioned response grows in intensity until it reaches a peak level of craving. By successfully surfing the urge, the addictive conditioning is weakened and self-efficacy and acceptance is developed and strengthened. This process is consistent with the approach of relapse prevention therapy, which emphasizes the importance of developing alternative coping strategies (Marlatt and Chawla 2007).

Mindfulness has been described as a process of bringing a certain quality of attention to moment-by-moment experience, and as a combination of the self-regulation of attention with an attitude of curiosity, openness, and acceptance toward one's experiences. Mindfulness meditation is the core practice of vipassana meditation, and various meditation techniques originating in Buddhist spiritual practices have been developed to evoke mindfulness.

Once learned, mindfulness increases the chances that activities or events will expand the perspective and understanding of oneself. In a state of mindfulness, thoughts and feelings are observed on par with objects of sensory awareness, and by breaking the pattern of reacting in an automatic, habitual way, mindfulness allows one to develop a response to situations that is reflective and not impulsive (Bishop et al. 2004; Salmon et al. 2004; Ospina et al. 2007).

Over the last two decades, mindfulness has gained wide acceptance in the mental health and addiction recovery fields, and is being used to help treat stress, anxiety, depression, and personality disorders (Kabat-Zinn et al. 1992; Hayes, Strosahl, and Wilson 1999; Fields 2009). For instance, Marsha

Linehan (1993) integrates mindfulness practices in her Dialectical Behavior Therapy (DBT) for the treatment of borderline personality disorder.

Here are the core features of mindfulness meditation (Fields 2009):

- Develops a broader awareness of the present moment
- Develops a curious, nonjudgmental acceptance of one's moment-to-moment experiences
- Develops an awareness of the transient nature of internal experience, allows one to let go of the need to control what comes next
- Frees one from rigid attitudes, cognitions, and behaviors, and reduces reactivity
- Cultivates the ability to let go of a desired outcome to more easily tolerate pain, without the need to avoid or fix it

Following are four meditative practices briefly discussed.

### Vipassana

Vipassana, or insight meditation, is the oldest of the Buddhist meditation techniques that also include Zen (Soto and Rinzai schools) and Tibetan Tantra, and is believed to be the form of meditation practiced by Gautama the Buddha more than 2,500 years ago. The Pali term *vipassana* is not directly translatable to English, but roughly means "looking into something with clarity and precision, seeing each component as distinct, and piercing all the way through so as to perceive the most fundamental reality of that thing" (Gunaratana 1993; Ahir 1999; Ospina et al. 2007).

Buddhist teachings, referred to as *dharma,* make several references to addiction, and offer considerable insight into the basic nature of addiction, what contributes to the development of addictive behavior, and how meditation can be used as a method of transcending a wide variety of addiction problems (Marlatt 2002).

Buddhism describes addiction as being a false refuge—a delusional place where alcohol or other drugs are used in an attempt to hide and escape from being present and aware. Buddhism also describes addiction in the context of grasping, resisting, and delusions. The grasping describes the craving, obsession, and compulsion to use alcohol or other drugs, and the accompanying addiction-related behaviors. Buddhist literature describes addiction as a problem related to ego-attachment, and emphasizes craving or grasping as the major motivational dynamic (Fields 2009).

Grasping is described in the three Cs in the functional definition of alcohol and other drug addiction—*compulsion* and obsession, inability to *control,* and continued use despite negative *consequences.* Resisting represents the pushing away, the isolation, the shutting down of normal human pleasures and displeasures, and the withdrawal from connection with others. Resistance is demonstrated through denial and delusion, and rejecting advice, help, and direction from others. The delusion component of addiction relates to how addicts deceive themselves from accepting suffering as part of their lives. In contrast, Buddhism strives to help the meditator become more aware and present by overcoming his or her deceptions (Fields 2009).

The goal of vipassana is the understanding of the three characteristics of nature, which are impermanence (*anicca*), sufferings (*dhuka*), and non-existence (*anatta*). Vipassana meditation helps its practitioners to become more highly attuned to their emotional states, to increase their awareness of the flow of their life experience, and to become more sensitive and more receptive to their perceptions and thoughts without becoming caught up in them. Vipassana meditation also teaches practitioners how to scrutinize their perceptual processes, to watch thoughts arise, and to react with calm detachment and clarity. This reduces impulsive reaction, and increases the capacity of deliberate action (Gunaratana 1993; Ospina et al. 2007).

The cultivation of several attitudes is expected of practitioners of vipassana meditation. These are (1) don't expect anything; (2) don't strain; (3) don't rush; (4) observe experience mindfully, that is, don't cling to or reject anything; (5) loosen up and relax; (6) accept all experiences that you have; (7) be gentle with yourself and accept who you are; (8) question everything; (9) view all problems as challenges; (10) avoid deliberation; and (11) focus on similarities rather than differences (Gunaratana 1993; Ospina et al. 2007).

The practice of vipassana meditation involves being in a seated position when focusing on the breath; otherwise, no specific posture is required and the meditator may sit, stand, walk, or lie down. Although practitioners of vipassana meditation were traditionally taught to not change a static position until the meditation has ended, Western teachers often allow students to move, though mindfully, to avoid discomfort from being in the same position for too long. The eyes are closed (Gunaratana 1993; Ospina et al. 2007).

There are four focal points of attention and awareness during vipassana meditation: body, emotions and feelings, thoughts, and mental processes. By focusing attention on the breath, novices attain a degree of shallow concentration, which differs from the deep absorption or pure concentration with mantra meditations. The focus of attention gradually shifts to the rims of the nostrils, to the feeling of the breath going in and out. When attention wanders from the breath, the meditator brings it back and anchors it there. The meditator notices the feeling of inhaling and exhaling and ignores the details of the experience. The movement of the abdominal wall while inhaling and exhaling may also be used as a focus of attention (Gunaratana 1993; Ahir 1999; Ospina et al. 2007).

The body scan is the primary technique for focusing on bodily sensations. Beginning with the top of the head, the practitioner observes the sensations as if for the first time, and then scans the scalp, the back of the head, and the face. When visualizations of the body distract the meditator, the thoughts are simply directed back to the sensations. The focus of attention is moved continuously over the body, moving down the neck, to the shoulders, arms, hands, trunk, legs, and feet. Throughout the entire scan, an attitude of nonanticipation and acceptance is maintained (Glickman 2002; Ospina et al. 2007).

Mindfulness can be practiced during any activity and practitioners are encouraged to practice being mindful and fully aware during other activities such as walking, stretching, and eating (Ahir 1999).

Many practitioners have described vipassana meditation as a profound religious practice; however, no particular spiritual or philosophical system is required for involvement in vipassana meditation (Gunaratana 1993).

### Zen Buddhist Meditation

Zen Buddhist meditation, also called Zazen, is a school of Mahayana Buddhism that uses meditation techniques originating in India several thousand years ago that were introduced to Japan from China in 1191 A.D. (Sogen 2001). Zen Buddhist meditation is typically divided into the Rinzai and Soto schools. A fundamental aspect of the practice of Zen is harmony of the body, breath, and mind, and physical preparation for the practice of Zen meditation traditionally involves eating nutritious food in modest portions (Sogen 2001; Kit 2001; Ospina et al. 2007).

Posture is greatly emphasized in Zen meditation, with traditional forms performed while seated on a cushion in either the full-lotus or half-lotus position. Breathing is active, and after the practitioner has learned to focus on breath by counting, counting is omitted and meditators practice *shikantaza,* which means "nothing but precisely sitting." Through practice, the frequency of breathing is reduced to around three to six breaths per minute, and the frequency of breathing is counted by either counting the cycles of inhalation and exhalation, inhalations only, or exhalations only. Attention can also be focused on a *koan,* which is a specific riddle that is unsolvable by logical analysis. Some koans have become famous in the West, such as, "What is the sound of one hand clapping?"

However, most beginners often silently repeat the sound "mu" while counting. Many additional koans can be introduced over several years as the meditator becomes more skilled. The silent repetition allows the meditator to become fully absorbed in the koan, and an essential aspect of the meditation is the concentration of the mind on the counting or on the koan, and not on respiration itself. The meditator sits, aware only of the present moment, and no attempt is made to direct or focus the mind on a single idea or experience (Thomson 2000; Sogen 2001; Ospina et al. 2007).

At a spiritual level, Zen is considered the constant participation of all beings in the reality of each being, with the meditation based on the compassionate desire to save all living beings by means of calming the mind. This belief is not essential to practice, and only the wish to save all sentient beings and the strength to be disciplined in practice are necessary (Thomson 2000; Sogen 2001; Ospina et al. 2007).

## Mindfulness-Based Stress Reduction

Mindfulness-Based Stress Reduction (MBSR) is a standardized meditation program created in 1979 out of the desire to integrate Buddhist mindfulness meditation with contemporary clinical and psychological practice. The foundation of MBSR is the cultivation of mindfulness, and the mindfulness component includes a sitting meditation, a body scan, and Hatha yoga. Patients are also taught diaphragmatic breathing, coping strategies and assertiveness, and receive education on stress (Greene 2004).

The foundation for the practice of MBSR is the cultivation of seven attitudes:

1. Nonjudgment—becoming an impartial witness to your own experience

2. Patience—allowing one's experiences to unfold in their own time

3. Beginner's mind—a willingness to see everything as if for the first time

4. Trust—in one's own intuition and authority, and being oneself

5. Nonstriving—having no goal other than meditation itself

6. Acceptance—of things as they actually are in the present moment

7. Free thinking—not censoring one's thoughts and allowing them to come and go

A high level of motivation and perseverance is considered essential to developing a strong meditation practice and a high degree of mindfulness. These attitudes are cultivated consciously during each meditation session. As with other mindfulness practices, whenever attention wanders from the breath, the practitioner will simply notice the distracting thought and then let it go as attention is returned to the breath. This process is repeated each time that attention wanders from the breath. In informal practice, practitioners are reminded to become mindful of their breath to help induce a state of physical relaxation, emotional calm, and insight (Kabat-Zinn 1990; Chiesa and Serretti 2009).

The body scan is the first formal mindfulness technique that meditators do for a prolonged period, and is practiced intensively for the first four weeks of the program. Body scanning involves lying on the back and moving the mind through the different regions of the body, starting with the toes of the left foot and moving slowly upwards to the top of the head. Scanning is done in silence and stillness (Kabat-Zinn 1990).

The second formal meditation technique used in the MBSR program is mindful Hatha yoga. This consists of slow and gentle stretching and strengthening exercises, along with mindfulness of breathing and of the sensations that arise as the practitioner assumes various postures (Kabat-Zinn 1990).

During sitting meditation, the attention is focused on the inhalation and exhalation of the breath or on the rising and falling of the abdomen. When the mind becomes distracted by other thoughts, the attention is gently but firmly returned to the breath or abdomen. During the body scan, attention is focused on the bodily sensations. When the mind wanders, attention is brought back to the part of the body that was the focus of awareness (Kabat-Zinn 1990).

### Mindfulness-Based Relapse Prevention

Mindfulness-Based Relapse Prevention (MBRP) is an eight-week mind–body approach created specifically for people recovering from substance abuse and addiction that merges G. Alan Marlatt's Relapse Prevention Therapy with Jon Kabat-Zinn's Mindfulness-Based Stress Reduction (Marlatt, Bowen, and Chawla 2010). MBRP is offered only to persons with at least thirty days of sobriety. Each class teaches mindfulness meditation, yoga, or chi gong, along with cognitive-behavioral strategies, to maintain and reinforce sobriety. Participants are expected to perform daily home practice throughout the eight-week period. The philosophy of MBRP is based on the qualities of authenticity, unconditional acceptance, empathy, humor, and present-moment experience, through which both teacher and student experience the group process and are changed as a result.

The MBRP program is structured according to the following parameters:

Session 1:  Automatic Pilot and Craving
Theme:      Introduce the idea of automatic pilot

Session 2:  Triggers, Thoughts, Emotions, and Cravings
Theme:      Observe thoughts, see how they affect emotions and behavior

Session 3:  Mindfulness in Everyday Life
Theme:      Increase awareness during everyday activities

Session 4:  Staying Present and Aware in High-Risk Situations
Theme:  Recognize temptations to seek and use alcohol or other drugs

Session 5:  Balancing Acceptance and Change
Theme:  Accept our experience, acting with awareness

Session 6:  Thoughts Are Not Facts
Theme:  Experience thoughts as merely thoughts, even when they feel like the truth

Session 7:  How Can I Best Take Care of Myself?
Theme:  Build support networks and coping cards

Session 8:  Balanced Living and Using What Has Been Learned
Theme:  Balance and the ability to manage different aspects of one's life

## How Meditation Works

A growing body of neuroscience research is showing that meditation produces changes in the function and structure of brain regions that are directly related to the positive benefits reported by practitioners. Some studies have used brain imaging technologies to compare the brains of persons actively meditating with those of persons who were nonmeditators, while other studies compared the brains of persons who were long-term meditators with those of either meditation novices or nonmeditators. The brain imaging research typically used functional magnetic resonance imaging, or fMRI. Most of this research used mindfulness meditation techniques. None of these brain imaging studies enrolled alcoholic-dependent participants. However, it seems reasonable that the same changes in brain structure and function, and the corresponding positive changes in thinking, emotion, and perception reported by the nonalcoholics, apply to recovering alcoholics as well. Studies reporting the results of meditation in recovering alcoholic patients will be discussed last.

## Changes in Brain Function

Several studies have examined the short-term effects of meditation by looking at changes in brain function in persons actively meditating. These studies found that meditation produced changes in brain function associated with the following areas of thought, emotion, behavior, and perception:

### Impulsivity

*Impulsivity* has been defined as the "decreased sensitivity to negative consequences of behavior; rapid, unplanned reactions to stimuli before complete processing of information; and a disregard for long-term consequences" (Moeller et al. 2001). As discussed earlier, impulsiveness is often a component of alcohol and other drug dependence, and can both precede and result from the development of addiction. The interface between impulsivity and emotion is a particularly important concern with alcohol- and other drug-dependent persons, and can manifest as emotional reactivity and poor emotional regulation (the capacity to control emotional experiences) (Stratton 2006). The area of the brain referred to as the prefrontal cortex has been called the supervisory management system of the brain, and impulsivity is a reflection of functional impairment in the prefrontal cortex.

Mindfulness has been described as "a way to pay attention, on purpose, in the present moment, and nonjudgmentally" (Kabat-Zinn 1992).

As mindfulness is cultivated, it displaces impulsive thought and behavior through the ability to maintain attention on the present moment, and with the qualities of acceptance, openness, and curiosity (Stratton 2006).

Meditation has been found to enhance the blood flow, and thus to increase the functioning of the prefrontal cortex, thalamus, and cingulate gyrus. Together, these brain areas are responsible for impulse control, thinking and planning, emotion, and goal-directed concentration and planning (Hölzel et al. 2007; Lazar et al. 2000; Hamer 2004).

### Emotional Regulation and Distress Reduction

Emotional regulation is also called affect regulation and emotional self-regulation. It is a term used (1) to describe one's ability to calm oneself when emotionally upset, (2) to control one's thought reactions to an un-settling event, and (3) to control or inhibit emotion-based behavior.

Emotional dysregulation describes an individual who does not respond to a person, place, thing, or event in a manner that would generally be considered within the normal range of emotions. Examples of poor emotional regulation/emotional dysregulation include rage over a broken fingernail, screaming or breaking something when frustrated, or frantically clinging to a romantic partner over the thought of being alone. The capacity for emotional regulation, as well as impulse control, is also strongly influenced by the integrity of the prefrontal cortex. The prefrontal cortex not only puts the brakes on the impulse to act on intense emotion, but also projects pathways of neurons into the more primitive brain regions that produce the intense emotions of anger and fear. These neurons serve to dampen the intensity of emotions so they are not experienced as overpowering.

The use of meditation to reduce emotional distress is consistent with the concept of mindfulness meditation that involves a letting go of upsetting emotional or mental thought content (Baer et al. 2006). Training in mind-fulness meditation can disrupt the ingrained, maladaptive, and automatic emotional reactions to situations. Davidson and colleagues (2003) found a significant increase in the activation of the left-sided anterior frontal lobe during meditation, which they concluded was the basis for the significant decreases in anxiety and increases in positive emotion that were observed in their study and by other investigators (Kabat-Zinn et al. 1992; Miller, Fletcher, and Kabat-Zinn 1995; Teasdale et al. 2000; Teasdale, Segal, and Williams 1995; Beauchamp-Turner and Levinson 1992).

*Transcendence*

While meditation increases blood flow to activate some areas of the brain, other areas of the brain are slowed down and exhibit a reduced blood flow during brain imaging. One such area is the called the posterior superior parietal lobe. This region is referred to as the orientation association area, and also functions to allow a person to distinguish between the self and the nonself. Through the slowing of activity in this brain region through meditation, the effect is the inability to distinguish between the self and the nonself (Hamer 2004), which can be understood by the descriptions of meditators of having a spiritual experience—"I feel at one with the universe" and "I feel a part of everything around me." Both descriptions reflect a loss of self and self-transcendence.

Practitioners of meditation also report a greater ability to "stay out of their heads." Many psychiatric conditions, and psychological distress in general, are associated with a heightened degree of self-focused attention and self-obsession. Evidence suggests that through activation of the prefrontal cortex, meditation helps to relieve the person of self-obsession by achieving a more balanced attention between self and others (Siegel 2007; Appel and Kim-Appel 2009).

### Changes in Brain Structure

Other research on meditation has investigated the long-term positive effects by examining potential changes in brain structure.

Until recently, the prevailing belief was that many brain functions were hard-wired in specific, localized regions that were unchangeable from early childhood. It was believed that brain dysfunction was not reversible and that incidents of brain recovery were rare and unexplainable events. Recent neuroscience research has demonstrated the capacity of neurons and neuron pathways in the brain to change their connections and behavior in response to new information or experience and, as a result, to reorganize in order to restore or improve brain function.

This ability of the brain to change in structure as the result of experience is termed *neuroplasticity* (Buonomano and Merzenich 1998). The results of recent research have also demonstrated that structural changes are possible through the repeated short-term activation of specific brain regions that comes with long-term involvement in meditation (Hölzel et al. 2008).

Meditation improves emotional regulation and decreases emotional distress by shifting the focus of attention in terms of how the mind is used to channel the flow of energy and information through various brain circuits. By disengaging from old, habitual, and ingrained patterns of activity in the brain, new neuron pathways and brain regions that were formerly underactive and lacked normal function now become activated, while other neuron pathways and brain regions that were overactive become quieted. Essentially, the long-term practice of meditation can re-map key areas of the brain, and it is this mechanism that accounts for the positive changes in emotion, thinking, behavior, and perspective that are reported by regular practitioners. With repeated practice over time, the temporary state that is induced by meditation transforms into an in-grained trait; this change from state to trait is reflected by the short-term changes in brain function that ultimately become changes in brain structure (Siegel 2007).

Positive changes in brain structure with long-term meditation were reported by Hölzel et al. (2008), who found enhanced concentrations of neurons that compose the right hippocampus, right anterior insula, left inferior temporal gyrus, and medial orbito-frontal cortex. Collectively, the enhanced function in these brain regions is associated with a heightened capacity to

- control and modify emotional response,
- control and modify attentional and emotional processes and emotional memory,
- alter one's response to situations that provoke a learned fear response,
- control and modify learned emotional responses, and
- reduce the likelihood of being overwhelmed by negative emotions (Hölzel et al. 2008).

The amygdala is the brain region that is involved in the fear response and the processing of threat in one's environment. It triggers other brain areas to induce a physiological and cognitive response to real or perceived threat; in persons with a history of experiences such as trauma, the amygdala will often generate an intense fear response when there is little or no actual threat (Nuchols 2006).

Creswell and colleagues (2007) found that regular mindfulness meditation led to a state they referred to as *dispositional mindfulness*. They found that this state of dispositional mindfulness was strongly associated with enhanced activation of the prefrontal cortex and reduced activity in the amygdala. Creswell et al. state that this represents a common brain pathway that links the repeated practice of mindfulness meditation with the substantial reductions in negative and distressing emotion, mood disturbance, and physical symptoms of stress that have been found in numerous studies with different patient populations.

They also suggest that this enhancement in prefrontal cortex activity and suppression of amygdala activity account for the ability of frequent meditators to alter their emotional and behavioral responses to a wide variety of situations encountered in their daily lives (Creswell et al. 2007). Similar results were found in a study by Chiesa involving long-term vipassana meditation (2010); greater enhancement of prefrontal lobe structures in long-term meditators led to the ability to dampen and suppress the responses of fear and emotional arousal originating from the amygdala. Consistent with these reports were the findings of Lazar et al. (2005) that long-term meditators possessed a thicker prefrontal cortex and right anterior insula than novice meditators.

In summary, regular meditation may be associated with structural changes in areas of the brain that are important for sensory, cognitive, and emotional processing.

## Research Involving Alcoholics

Earlier research evaluating the effects of meditation on alcohol use primarily focused on preventive effects with nondependent drinkers, and found that long-term TM practice led to a reduction or cessation of drinking (Shafil, Lavely, and Jaffe 1975; Monahan 1977). More recently, Bowen et al. (2009) published the results of 168 patients in treatment for alcohol or other drug dependence who were assigned to either eight weeks of Mindfulness-Based Relapse Prevention (MBRP) or conventional treatment (control group). Four months after completion of the trial, patients receiving MBRP had significantly lower rates of relapse, significantly briefer durations of relapse when it did occur, significantly fewer cravings, significant improvements in emotion regulation skills, and significant increases in mindfulness relative to those assigned to the control treatment. The decreased craving in the MBRP group was partially explained by changes in judgment and acceptance during the course of MBRP treatment. Based on results of this study, the authors describe the following effects of mindfulness meditation on alcohol- and other drug-dependent patients:

Immediate Effects

- Lowers heart rate
- Lowers blood pressure
- Activates the soothing relaxation response
- Dampens the fight-or-flight stress response
- Activates sensory awareness and the control of attention

Long-Term Effects

- Dampens reactivity to stress
- Increases positive emotions
- Enhances self-regulation
- Increases ability to pause before acting
- Enhances ability to feel empathy for others
- Increases insight and self-awareness
- Modulates fear
- Increases capacity to make moral choices

Recovering alcoholics tend to cope with drinking urges by attempting to suppress the cravings. Although this approach may work in the short run, the process can actually perpetuate and intensify these cravings by driving them within the cognitive unconscious. This coping response can ultimately worsen the cravings by amplifying the reactivity to people, places, and things associated with alcohol and drinking. Mindfulness training may serve to undo this process.

During the gradual practice of mindfulness, one learns to work with negative emotions in the context of *metacognition,* a term that refers to a level of thinking that involves active control over the process of thinking. This use of metacognition results in a marked decrease in emotional reactivity to difficult thoughts, such as cravings for alcohol, and in improved self-regulation in the face of stressors, such as alcohol-related cues. Through mindfulness training, alcohol cravings are attended to in a nonreactive, nonjudgmental manner, and since the need to suppress the urge to drink is removed, the cravings are more likely to be extinguished over time instead of intensifying as a result of suppression (Garland et al. 2010).

A ten-week course of mindfulness training was found to reduce stress and alcohol thought suppression in abstinent alcoholics attempting to maintain their sobriety. Mindfulness training also led to a significant reduction in psychiatric symptoms. Garland et al. (2010) concluded from their study that mindfulness meditation training appears to target several of the key mechanisms involved in alcohol dependence, including the cognitive, affective, and physiological mechanisms that underlie the vulnerability to stress-induced relapse.

A participant in the Garland et al. (2010) study described how mindfulness training helped her after she completed the training in the study and graduated from formal treatment. She describes how mindfulness training helped her not become overwhelmed by the rejection she encountered during the job-hunting process following treatment, and helped her cope with alcohol cravings when she became emotionally stressed after obtaining a job in an alcohol-serving restaurant:

I had to practice it [mindfulness] every day, when I went out looking for a job, and being rejected, because of my not working in two years, using the techniques that were being taught to me, in my everyday life . . . I use it every day . . . and it [mindfulness] played a very big part when I had to deal with some customers [who] were drinking . . . it played a big part in helping me get through it. I had to go outside and breathe. Well, by me using it every day, breathing, taking time to sit down and think about what I'm going to do before I react, not reacting on impulse. I was very self-destructive, and if something got in my way, I would hide behind the alcohol and the drugs to get past it, and so now instead of doing that, I take whatever time I need to sit down and collect my thoughts, and not stay in my head . . . (Garland et al. 2010).

Bowen et al. (2007) studied the outcome of an intensive ten-day course of vipassana meditation that enrolled alcohol- or other drug-dependent inmates in a correctional setting. The researchers found that compared with standard chemical dependency services offered in the prison, mindfulness training led to greater reductions in post-release substance use, substance-related problems, and psychiatric symptoms. Additional research involving mindfulness-based interventions with substance abusers have found significant reductions in distress, negative emotion, physiological markers of stress such as cortisol, and substance use (Marcus, Fine, and Kouzekanani 2001; Marcus, Fine, and Moeller 2003; Zgierska et al. 2009). Although the size of these studies were small and patients were followed for relatively brief periods of time, the collective evidence suggests that mindfulness interventions may reduce the risk of stress-related relapse and alcohol abuse (Garland et al. 2010).

## Mindfulness Meditation and Post-traumatic Stress

Many alcoholics have histories of trauma. Persons who have experienced emotional trauma may develop negative coping strategies to feel less overwhelmed. They may abuse alcohol or other drugs, or engage in distracting behaviors, dissociation, or denial. Although these coping strategies may temporarily reduce emotional distress, they ultimately serve to block recovery. Mindfulness meditation has direct relevance to recovery from trauma. Because mindfulness involves acceptance of the present without judgment, it can be immensely helpful to alcoholics in denial of past trauma. Mindfulness is a learnable set of skills that can be a useful component of trauma therapy for both the therapist and the client, and can be a helpful approach for a client processing traumatic material (Marlatt and Chawla 2007).

*Post-traumatic growth (PTG)* is a term that has been used to describe the positive outcomes with recovery from emotional trauma. PTG is defined as positive changes within a person determined by the gradual shaping of a new reality as a person processes the trauma disrupting one's world view and integrates the experience (Tedeschi and Calhoun 2004).

PTG can manifest as a greater appreciation for life, greater meaning in one's interpersonal relationships, and an increased sense of personal strength (Tedeschi and Calhoun 2004).

Certain aspects of mindfulness, such as observation and contact with the present moment, may be beneficial in facilitating PTG. Focusing on spiritual issues may also help trauma survivors achieve greater PTG. Spirituality in the context of PTG can simply refer to a greater sense of universal presence, an increased commitment to one's religion, a clearer understanding of one's spiritual or religious beliefs, a sense of being connected to something greater than was possible before the trauma, or a spiritual quest to seek answers to the existential questions that were evoked by the event (Tedeschi, Park, and Calhoun 1998).

Meditation may be productive with a client who is receptive to exploring spiritual growth by promoting in the client an understanding of how the traumatic experience may have led to a broader connection with forces larger than oneself (Chopko and Schwartz 2009).

Avoidance is not only one of the central components of post-traumatic stress disorder (PTSD), but is also related to the worsening of symptoms and is implicated in the relationship between PTSD and alcohol or other drug abuse. Mindfulness meditation is an approach that opposes the habitual coping strategies of escape and avoidance. Simpson et al. (2007) found that intensive mindfulness-based meditation was well tolerated and accepted by persons with PTSD symptoms, and that mindfulness may provide a reasonable treatment alternative for persons who are diagnosed with both PTSD and a substance use disorder. Another study employing eight weeks of mindfulness training in a group of adult survivors of childhood sexual abuse found that depressive symptoms and the PTSD symptoms of avoidance and/or numbing were substantially reduced (Kimbrough et al. 2010).

# Trends in the Treatment of Alcoholism

**A**lthough large surveys have found that treatment was a necessary first step for as many as 50% of persons with more severe alcohol and other drug addiction in achieving sustained recovery (Cunningham 1999; Cunningham 2000), these figures do not reflect the shortcomings in the current treatment system (White and Sanders 2006). A major criticism is that treatment of alcoholism uses an acute care model for a condition that is now increasingly regarded as a chronic illness.

## Shortcomings of the Current Acute Care Model of Alcohol Treatment

Today, most addiction professionals recognize alcohol and other drug dependence as a chronic disease. However, modern treatment approaches alcoholism as if it were an acute illness. The current acute care treatment to alcoholism generally consists of serial episodes of brief, intensive, high-cost care combined with a brief follow-up or aftercare with the expectation of sustained recovery or even cure (White, Boyle, and Loveland 2003).

Several factors contribute to the widespread use of this approach that has dramatically shortened both inpatient and outpatient treatment. These factors include

- the professionalization of treatment services;
- escalating medical and health care costs; and, most importantly,
- the emergence of an aggressive system of managed behavioral health care.

Even addiction treatment approaches that traditionally have used a long-term approach, such as methadone maintenance, have been restructured to conform to the short-term, acute care paradigm (White, Boyle, and Loveland 2003).

Most alcohol and other drug dependence treatment programs use an acute care model of treatment. It is characterized by the following elements:

- Services are delivered in a sequential and uniform series of activities—typically, screening, admission, assessment, treatment, discharge, and sometimes brief aftercare followed by termination of the provider relationship.
- Services occur over a brief period of time, often as a function of a pre-arranged, time-limited insurance payment.
- The message conveyed to the client and his or her family is that permanent remission can now be achieved by completing the treatment program.
- Relapse and re-admission to treatment are often viewed as a shortcoming of the client.

George Vaillant was one of the first researchers to dispute the effectiveness of the acute care model. With data from his 1983 long-term study of alcoholism and recovery, he challenged three primary assumptions about alcoholism treatment as it was and is currently practiced: (1) alcoholism can be effectively treated with a single episode of acute care, (2) relapse following treatment is a failure, and (3) multiple relapses following multiple acute treatment stays may indicate the patient is untreatable (Vaillant, 1983; White, Boyle, and Loveland 2003).

A landmark paper published in 2000 by McLellan and colleagues presented the most thorough and convincing argument up to that time of the concept of addiction as a chronic disease. In the paper, McLellan highlighted several factors that have resulted in a push away from an acute care model and toward a chronic disease (recovery management) model (White, Boyle, and Loveland 2003). Other supportive research in the field of addiction treatment has included the following:

1.  There is a growing recognition that managing severe and persistent alcohol and other drug problems with single or serial episodes of acute treatment is clinically ineffective and represents an inefficient or even wasteful use of individual, family, and community resources. A single, acute intervention is rarely sufficient to initiate stable and enduring recovery in those with severe and persistent alcohol and other drug problems. Multiple treatment episodes should be considered as incremental steps in the developmental process of recovery. The steps should not be viewed as failures but instead as treatment episodes that may have cumulative positive effects (Hser et al. 1997).

2.  Alcohol and other drug dependence is often chronic and relapsing in nature (Simpson, Joe, and Lehman 1986). It has much in common with other chronic diseases such as diabetes and hypertension (O'Brien and McLellan 1996) (see chapter 6). The approaches used in managing these chronic diseases should be adapted for the treatment of alcohol and other drug dependence (Lewis 1993; McLellan et al. 2000; White, Boyle, and Loveland 2003).

3.  The same managed care system that has slashed reimbursement for inpatient treatment and shifted the focus to one of cost-containment has spawned a new grassroots recovery advocacy (consumer) movement. These movements are developing a deeper understanding of the long-term addiction recovery process and how indigenous community resources may support this time-enduring process (White 2000) (White, Boyle, and Loveland 2003).

## The Recovery Management of Alcohol Dependence

Persons suffering from chronic, incurable disorders require models of intervention that focus on the management rather than the cure of these long-term disorders. Disease management, also called recovery management, provides an alternative to the traditional approach of reacting to life-impairing and life-threatening episodes of chronic disorders with unrelated, serial episodes of acute, high-intensity care. In the absence of a cure, recovery management implies a longer-term vision of influencing the course of a disorder to optimize personal and family health and enhance length and quality of life (White, Boyle, and Loveland 2003).

The shift from regarding addiction as an acute illness to treating it as a chronic condition has required a shift in focus from the pathology of addiction to the nature of long-term addiction recovery (Hser et al. 1997). Some of the core components of a recovery-oriented system of care for severe and persistent alcohol problems include the following (White, Boyle, and Loveland 2003):

- There are many pathways to recovery influenced by styles of recovery, sobriety-based support structures, and recovery capital (the inner, interpersonal, and community resources that can be accessed to initiate and maintain recovery) (Granfield and Cloud 1999).

- The mechanisms and processes that sustain recovery may be different than the factors that initiate recovery (Humphreys, Moos, and Finney 1995).

- Addiction recovery can be self-directed and incremental in nature (Prochaska, DiClemente, and Norcross 1992), or recovery can be a sudden, climactic transformation (Miller and C' de Baca 2001). Some persons undergo a series of minor incremental steps toward the readiness to change behaviors, eventually culminating in cessation of use or even in moderating their drinking.

- Recovery from alcohol dependence most often involves a process of developmental change for which stage-appropriate interventions can be designed and delivered (Brown 1985; DiClemente, Carbonari, and Velasquez 1992).

- Recovery can be professionally-guided, peer-guided, or done alone through efforts such as Internet-based support and information, reading of recovery literature, or listening to audio (Larimer and Kilmer 2000).
- Styles of recovery vary greatly. They are determined by whether one incorporates addiction or recovery as an element of personal identity and/or whether one maintains contact with other recovering people as a recovery maintenance activity.
- Recovery outcomes vary greatly in terms of primary and secondary alcohol or other drug use, and in the broader dimensions of global (cognitive, emotional, family, social, occupational) functioning.
- Post-treatment outcomes are characterized by subgroups who (1) continue using, (2) sustain abstinence, and (3) vacillate between problematic use, nonproblematic use, and abstinence. The fluid state of addiction or recovery in the third group offers significant opportunities to enhance outcomes with recovery management models of intervention.
- Long-term, staged recovery considers treatment and support services (e.g., harm reduction, motivational interviewing, pharmacological adjuncts, cognitive-behavioral therapies, mutual-aid groups) not as competing and mutually exclusive approaches but as interventions that can be matched or administered to the same persons at different stages of their addiction or recovery process (White, Boyle, and Loveland 2003).

## A New Approach: A Low-Cost Supportive and Educational Model of Treatment

At the beginning of this century, the field of alcoholism treatment entered a stage of maturity. This stage now has expanded programs for special populations, increased interest in bridging the gap between research and clinical practice, and moved treatment services into other social systems such as the child welfare system, the criminal justice system, and public health agencies (White 2004). A treatment renewal movement now strives to reintegrate addiction treatment providers back into the communities where they originated, and to integrate treatment into the enduring process of addiction recovery (White 2001b).

The confluence of several factors has resulted in the creation of low-cost, low-intensity residential treatment programs. Those factors include

- the lack of accessible and affordable treatment in the wake of the widespread elimination of chemical dependency benefits by the insurance industry,
- the recognition of the shortcomings of traditional inpatient treatment, and
- the desire among some older members of AA to get back to the basics.

One such program with these characteristics is The Retreat, located in the Minneapolis suburb of Wayzata. Opened in 1998, The Retreat is a thirty-day program that uses a supportive/educational model. The program consists of the use of the Twelve Steps and the Big Book of AA to help residents identify the problems associated with their alcohol or other drug dependence and understand the solution to these problems. All groups are run by alumni and volunteers from AA. There are no chemical dependency counselors, nor any nursing, medical, psychiatric, or psychological services. This keeps the cost low and removes the potential clinical influence. Residents are referred to these services in the community if needed. However, the president, program director, and spiritual care advisor are licensed and trained professionals (Curtiss, pers. comm.).

The Retreat program is consistent with the recognition of the importance of long-term, low-intensity disease and recovery management in the community (see next section). An important component is the integration of residents into community-based recovery resources such as sober living houses (average stay nine to twelve months). In addition, residents are assimilated into community AA meetings, linked with AA sponsors, and integrated into the community of alumni and recovering persons. Also consistent with the long-term recovery management model is the accessibility to readmission for clients who have relapsed. Retreat alumni who have relapsed can be readmitted for thirty days, or for briefer periods of seven to fourteen days, depending on client need and finances (Curtiss, pers. comm.).

The cost of The Retreat is a fraction of conventional multidisciplinary inpatient or resident treatment. As of 2009, residential programs replicating The Retreat model have been started in Hong Kong and South Dakota, with programs under development in New Zealand, Florida, Nashville, and Hawaii. Additionally, more than ninety sober living residences using The Retreat sober house model have been replicated in the Twin Cities, nationally, and internationally. As of 2009, The Retreat programs have served 7,800 clients (Curtiss, pers. comm.).

## Trends in AA and Self-Help Recovery

Differences between individual AA meetings were noted from the very beginning when AA started growing (e.g., differences between the original AA groups in Akron and those in New York City). An important trend in the current history of Twelve Step and self-help organizations is the growing varieties of recovery experience (White and Kurtz 2006). The varieties of AA experience are reflected in the diversity of AA meeting formats (for example, open vs. closed meetings, speaker meetings vs. discussion meetings). In addition, AA tends to organize around special populations and special needs, different regions of the country, and differences in the approach of working the AA program.

The AA meeting list of any medium-sized or larger city reflects this specialization, such as meetings organized by age (young people, old-timers), gender (women-only and men-only), sexual orientation (lesbian, gay, bisexual, transgender), language (Spanish, Polish, no profanity), profession (physicians, lawyers, airline pilots), social status (off-the-books meetings for celebrities and those in high-status positions), relationship status (single, couples), co-occurring problems (psychiatric illness, HIV/AIDS), and smoking status (nonsmoking), to name just a few.

There are also differences in AA that transcend particular types of categorical or cultural experience. Significant differences can be found in degree of religious orientation (from efforts to Christianize AA to AA groups for atheists and agnostics), meeting rituals, pre- and post-meeting activities, and basic interpretations of the nature of the AA program (Kurtz and White 2003).

Such varieties multiply exponentially when one examines the range of adaptations of AA's Twelve Steps to other drug problems (e.g., Narcotics Anonymous, Cocaine Anonymous, Marijuana Anonymous, Pills Anonymous, Methadone Anonymous) and to co-occurring problems (e.g., Dual Diagnosis Anonymous, Dual Recovery Anonymous, Double Trouble in Recovery) (White, Kurtz, and Sanders 2006). Also significant is that many people are simultaneously participating in two or more recovery support structures—suggesting people are using different groups to meet different recovery support needs (White, Kurtz, and Sanders 2006).

The explosive growth of AA in the 1970s and 1980s concerned AA old-timers. The addiction treatment industry and criminal justice system were influencing AA (via mandated AA attendance). Old-timers suspected the core of AA's program was somehow being corrupted. This concern led to efforts to define and recapture the historical AA. AA historian Ernest Kurtz (1999) proposed five criteria to distinguish real AA from meetings that had taken on the flavor of treatment groups: (1) AA vocabulary (defects of character, self-inventory, Higher Power) rather than treatment vocabulary; (2) humor and the appreciation of paradox; (3) a story style that "describes in a general way what we used to be like, what happened, and what we are like now"; (4) respect for and adherence to AA traditions; and (5) a conviction by those attending meetings that they *need* rather than *want* to be there (White and Kurtz 2006).

## Grassroots Recovery Movements

There are two grassroots movements currently working to make a significant impact in persons attempting to achieve and maintain recovery. They are the recovery advocacy movement and communities of recovery.

## The Recovery Advocacy Movement

In 1976, fifty-two prominent Americans publicly announced their long-term recovery from alcoholism as part of the National Council of Alcoholism's Operation Understanding. Their coming out was a landmark in the modern history of alcoholism recovery.

In September 2009, more than 70,000 people in recovery participated in public Rally for Recovery events in cities across the United States—an achievement that would have been unthinkable only a few years ago. This new recovery advocacy movement is being led by recovering people and their families and friends, and carries the objective of countering the restigmatization, demedicalization, and recriminalization of alcohol and other drug problems. These grassroots organizations are putting a face and a voice on recovery, pushing pro-recovery policies, and working to expand treatment and recovery support services within local communities (White 2001a; White 2004).

Addiction recovery advocacy organizations generally work to achieve their objectives through four core activities:

1. Political advocacy for pro-recovery laws and social policies

2. Public and professional recovery education

3. The provision of nonclinical (peer-based) recovery support services

4. Recovery celebration events

This recovery advocacy movement has grown and is not affiliated with any Twelve Step or any other self-help organization, and financial support comes from recovering people and public and private organizations (White 2006; White and Taylor 2006; White 2007).

An example of this grassroots-driven recovery advocacy movement is the Minnesota Recovery Connection (MRC), located in Saint Paul, Minnesota. The MRC strives to fulfill the needs of persons attempting to achieve and maintain sobriety through four functions:

1. Linking people seeking recovery to resources and organizations that help foster and sustain long-term recovery

2. Providing programs and services that help people achieve and sustain recovery

3. Advocating for recovery by rallying the community and putting a positive face on recovery

4. Offering service opportunities for those in recovery through involvement in running recovery support programs, providing recovery coaching, and providing telephone recovery support

The MRC is composed of three salaried program staff including the director, a board of directors, and volunteers (MRC 2010).

### Communities of Recovery

For almost three centuries, people recovering from severe alcohol and other drug problems have created healing sanctuaries to share their experiences, strength, and hope, and to meet specific needs they faced in initiating and sustaining their recovery journeys. History suggests that when a vacuum of unmet needs reaches critical mass, recovering people, their families, and progressive-minded professionals join forces to become movements that generate new structures of recovery support. That critical mass—spawned in great part by the restigmatization, demedicalization, and recriminalization of addiction in the 1980s and 1990s—has been reached again, and the resulting scope and depth of recovery community-building activities in America is without historical precedent (White 2008).

The growing cultural and political awakening of individuals and families in recovery is being spurred by several factors:

- Growth and diversification of communities of recovery
- Emergence of an identity (person in recovery) that unites members of diverse recovery fellowships and those in recovery outside those fellowships
- Rise of grassroots recovery advocacy movements such as Faces and Voices of Recovery and the Minnesota Recovery Connection
- International spread of the recovery advocacy movement

- Rise of recovery community institutions such as sober houses, industries, schools, ministries/churches, community centers, cafes, and recovery community service organizations and sports teams, as well as new genres of recovery literature, art, music, dance, theatre, and comedy (White 2010)

Several aspects of this broader movement include the following (White 2008):

a. Growth and diversification of recovery mutual-aid societies (see "Trends in AA and Self-Help Recovery")

b. Virtual recovery communities (see following section)

c. Recovery advocacy movement (see pages 269–270)

d. Sober living houses

As we discussed in a previous chapter, exposure to people, places, and things associated with alcohol or other drug use can place the recovering person at risk of relapse. Sober living houses provide a vital role in facilitating sobriety by allowing the resident to consolidate the progress made in treatment, and to continue to strengthen his or her recovery away from the environment that contributed to or maintained the addiction (Leshner 2001).

Sober living houses (SLH) operate with neither professional staff nor a treatment structure and function (Borkman 2008). Unlike residential recovery programs, SLH are financially self-sustained by resident fees and are usually not financed through insurance or public funding. Since they do not offer formal treatment, they are not licensed or monitored by most states or municipalities. This independence from funding sources and licensing bodies allows them to tailor their own model of recovery without external mandates. For example, instead of responding to rigid time lines or funding sources, SLH allow residents to stay as long as they wish. An example of this are the SLH run by the residential program The Retreat, where residents may stay as long as two years (Curtiss, pers. comm.).

Most SLH require that residents engage in some type of recovery program (usually AA meeting attendance) and obtain employment (although some allow residents to attend college). Involvement in management of the facility is especially important for longer-term as a way for them to give back to the community of residents (Polcin and Borkman 2008).

The growth of the SLH movement was fueled by two factors. The first was the Federal Anti-Drug Abuse Act of 1988 (P.L. 100-690), which required states to establish a revolving fund for loans to recovering persons to rent a house to establish a recovery home. The second influence was the accumulation of scientific studies documenting the high rates of continued abstinence within the Oxford Houses, which were founded in 1975 and have grown to more than 1,200 recovery homes in forty-eight states. Self-managed recovery homes are spreading rapidly in the U.S. (Oxford House 2006; Jason et al. 2001; Jason et al. 2006; Malloy and White 2009).

e. Recovery schools
A relatively recent institution in the recovery community is the recovery school. Between 1977 and 2000, collegiate recovery school programs were launched at nine colleges and universities. The first sober high school opened in 1986 in Minnesota as Ecole Nouvelle, which was renamed Sobriety High a few years later. The growth of high school programs specifically for recovering students has quickened. Recovery school programs vary widely but generally combine special recovery support services with an emphasis on academic excellence (White 2008).

f. Recovery industries
The growth of recovery industries strive to provide assistance and opportunities to persons who have never had legitimate employment or have lost their jobs or careers due to their addic-

tion. Emphasis is placed on helping these persons enter or re-enter the mainstream workforce. A recovery industry is a business that purposely recruits, trains, and employs people in recovery. Such jobs may constitute a permanent employment position or a transitional position that helps a person develop responsible work habits and behaviors, a current work history, and references to obtain employment with mainstream businesses and industries (White 2008).

g. Recovery ministries and churches
Special ministries to alcoholics and addicts began in the closing decades of the nineteenth century through religiously sponsored urban rescue missions, and by the creation of rural inebriate colonies. The involvement of churches in the problem of addiction is not new, but this involvement has taken some stunning new turns in recent years. Recent developments in the continuum of involvement include the following:
   - Recovery-friendly churches that welcome recovering people but offer no special recovery services
   - Churches spawning new religiously sponsored recovery mutual-aid groups such as Celebrate Recovery and Ladies Victorious
   - Mega-churches adding a recovery pastor to their staff
   - Small churches using lay leaders and volunteers to lead recovery support meetings
   - Church-sponsored, recovery-focused worship services, recovery churches, faith-based recovery colonies, and the growth of non-Christian recovery ministries and support groups (White 2008)

An example of a recovery church can be found in Saint Paul, Minnesota, with Central Park United Methodist Church, which in 2006 became known as The Recovery Church. The stated mission of the church is "to provide a spiritual community for people in search of growth, healing, and recovery." In addition to holding sermons, a wide range of Twelve Step and other self-help meetings, as well as special events related to recovery, are held in the church (The Recovery Church 2010).

These new recovery institutions serve as a conduit to Twelve Step programs such as AA by assertively linking people to these resources, and they also augment groups like AA by providing the means for some people unable to achieve abstinence in AA to achieve stable recovery (White 2010).

The opportunities emerging from this trend are twofold. First, we may well see elevated long-term recovery outcomes for persons with high problem severity/complexity and low recovery capital. People are now achieving stable recovery whose needs have transcended the time and emotional resources of both sponsors and professional addiction counselors. This achievement is likely to become magnified over time, and will result in aggregate membership growth of recovery mutual-aid societies. Second, the rise of new peer-based recovery support roles also promises, at personal and at systems levels, to reconnect acute addiction treatment to the larger and more enduring process of long-term community-based recovery (White 2010).

## Recovery in the Digital Era

The computer and Internet, even smart phones and computer tablets, all have the opportunity to provide key recovery services not only for the client but for the general consumer of recovery-related materials and clinicians who need continuing education credits. Each year increases the use of the Internet for recovery for professional services and for the individual in recovery.

### Professional Services

The use of electronic communication has permeated daily life in the United States. While the use of the telephone for health-related issues is not as new, administering treatment electronically is relatively novel in the

United States. Substance abuse treatment through electronic means (also known as e-therapy) is not used widely, but experts predict that its use will increase rapidly during the next several years. E-therapy has the potential to fulfill unmet needs among the general population. In a national survey on substance abuse (SAMHSA 2006), respondents identified that they needed treatment but reported that they did not receive substance abuse treatment because of barriers related to cost (44.4%), stigma (18.5%), and access (21.2%). This lack of access is even worse in some areas of the country where resources for treatment are limited by number of treatment facilities, transportation, and costs (McAuliffe and Dunn 2004; McAuliffe et al. 2003).

E-therapy provides opportunities for populations that would otherwise go without much-needed care. E-therapy can be used by treatment providers throughout the continuum of care to deliver referrals, education, assessment and diagnosis, direct care, aftercare, training, and supervision. Few studies have been performed on the effectiveness of substance abuse services delivered by e-therapy, although this is likely to change soon. Other challenges of e-therapy include the preservation of confidentiality with clients and the digital divide, the term used to describe disparity of access to computers and the Internet in certain groups (CSAT 2009).

### Twelve Step and Self-Help

Electronic communication has the potential to transcend many of the traditional barriers to face-to-face meeting participation, including geographical isolation, inconvenience, schedule conflicts, and lack of available transportation or child care. Special populations are more likely to use this medium of Twelve Step contact, such as persons with social anxiety or social phobia, persons with fears regarding physical or psychological safety, and fear of stigma and discrimination. Already apps are available for recovery people with smart phones. Addiction professionals receive continuing education credits online at a plethora of addiction websites. Many non-Twelve Step recovery support groups already have more participants online than those who meet in person, and that day could potentially arrive for AA and NA (White 2010).

The potential growth of virtual recovery raises many questions about the future of recovery and the future of Twelve Step and other abstinence-based self-help organizations (White 2010):

- How will the online experience for different populations compare to their experience of face-to-face meetings?
- How quickly will a media that seems particularly well-suited to special populations (e.g., women, status-conscious professionals, adolescents, persons with limited mobility, persons living in remote locations) spread through the mainstream cultures of AA and NA?
- Can key activities within self-help organizations be performed with little or no face-to-face contact? How will these activities be changed in this process?
- Will the Internet create a larger climate in which secular and religious alternatives will compete for access to particular groups of AA and NA people?
- How will regular contact with recovering people from other countries and cultures influence the culture of recovery in the U.S.?
- What would be the possible role of text messaging–based electronic communications?
- What areas of unforeseen harms are possible for individuals or groups?

Although there is the potential for anticipated and unforeseen risks, they seem overshadowed by the potential of this media to reach large numbers of new people in need of recovery support (White 2010).

## The Science of Recovery

At this time, addiction neuroscience is perhaps the most dynamic field of scientific investigation today. The quality as well as the quantity of information being generated by addiction research in general is impressive

(Goodman 2008). There are two primary ways in which the results of recently published studies on the neuroscience of alcoholism are benefiting addiction professionals and alcoholic patients alike. The first involves the federal investment in a research infrastructure, which is beginning to reap significant rewards in terms of new understandings of the neurobiology of alcohol dependence. This knowledge is beginning to result in the ability to distinguish the genetic variation and underlying disease processes of different alcoholism subtypes, to identify therapeutic targets based on this neurobiology, and to more effectively use currently existing medications (White and McGovern 2003).

The second benefit involves the significant number of studies published on AA in the past decade. This body of research has confirmed much of the internal AA folklore that has passed as conventional wisdom within the AA organization for decades. Examples of these include the positive effects of regular participation, the value of Step work, sponsorship, reading AA literature, and having a home AA group. Although AA old-timers may read the findings of expensive scientific studies and smugly reflect, "I could have told them that for the price of a cup of coffee," one of the critical functions of science is to confirm or disconfirm the tenets of subjective experience.

Science is revealing important knowledge, such as

- who responds and does not respond to AA,
- when is the most effective time to participate in AA,
- what is the best way to link addiction treatment and AA,
- what is the value of matching individuals to particular fellowships and meetings, and
- how to reintegrate AA dropouts back into affiliation with AA (White 2010; Kaskutas 2009).

Science is also certain to generate controversies by challenging some of the prevailing beliefs held by some members of self-help organizations. The results of research on the value of medication-assisted recovery is challenging but also softening the negative attitudes held by some AA members about medication (White 2010).

# Other Aspects of Recovery from Alcohol Dependence

## Spontaneous Recovery

Spontaneous remission may occur when a problem drinker is confronted with major life events such as graduating from college, achieving employment, getting married, or becoming a parent (Dawson et al. 2006). A wide range of recovery from alcohol dependence is observed in the general population, from partial remission to full abstinence. It also shows that the disease course of alcoholism is not always clear-cut, and that some people appear to recover from alcoholism without any intervention. Others may cycle into and out of dependence throughout their lifetimes despite repeated attempts to achieve sobriety (NIAAA 2006).

Although researchers have known for decades that many problem drinkers either quit or greatly reduce their drinking to nonproblem levels without treatment or Twelve Step contact, a more recent review of long-term follow-up studies suggests that only between 14% and 50% of these spontaneous remissions (defined as abstinence or nonproblem drinking) are maintained for six months or longer (Walters 2000).

Because spontaneous remission may be followed by a high likelihood of relapse, preventive interventions may be indicated to forestall future alcohol problems among individuals who have cut down or quit drinking on their own (Moos and Moos 2006).

A landmark study followed a group of Harvard undergraduates and a group of socially disadvantaged inner city youth for sixty years. In both groups, the predictors of recovery among those who developed alcoholism were different from the predictors related to the development of alcoholism. The essential factors associated with recovery from alcohol dependence included finding rewarding nondrug activities as a substitute for alcohol, compulsory supervision (immediate negative consequences for relapse), new relationships, and involvement in a spiritual program. As AA combines all four of these factors, it was not a surprising finding that the men who achieved stable abstinence attended roughly twenty times as many AA meetings as men who did not.

Another interesting finding was that the most and the least severe alcoholics appeared to enjoy the best, long-term chance of remission from alcohol. An important finding from this study was that alcohol abuse could persist for decades without remission or progression to alcohol dependence (Vaillant 2003).

### Late-Stage Relapse

As a field, very little is known about the pathways and processes of long-term recovery. Late-stage relapse (LSR) is defined as a lapse or relapse after an extended period of seemingly stable sobriety, typically defined as five years or more. Existing research suggests that the risk of future lifetime relapse declines to below 15% for persons who have achieved five years of continuous sobriety, but those people who do relapse after years of recovery remain a mystery within the worlds of addiction research, addiction treatment, and recovery mutual-aid fellowships (White and Schulstad 2009).

# EPILOGUE

The quality and abundance of scientific evidence presented here sheds light on the debate surrounding the disease basis of alcoholism, AA effectiveness, and whether medication to assist recovery is appropriate and legitimate. Changes in brain function and structure that may contribute to the development of alcohol dependence and account for changes in thinking, emotion, and behavior with progression into alcoholism are described. These alterations in the brain may persist into abstinence, helping to explain the chronically relapsing nature of alcoholism and forming the basis for defining alcohol dependence as a chronic disease.

For decades there has existed a degree of mutual antipathy and distrust between medical professionals treating alcoholism and recovering chemical dependency counselors and longtime AA members. Some physicians and psychologists have dismissed the importance of spirituality and the value of AA due to the sparse body of supportive research, while some traditional chemical dependency counselors and long-term AA members have been wary of the medical treatment of alcoholism, and especially of the use of medication to treat the symptoms of alcoholism.

There is now an abundance of empirical evidence that AA involvement is an effective and accessible means to achieve long-term sobriety. Many people drop out of AA after brief contact, and findings of research that have identified the approaches to AA involvement associated with positive outcomes are discussed. Many persons attempting sobriety through AA or psychological therapy repeatedly relapse due to overpowering urges to drink. Yet medication therapy can effectively and safely reduce alcohol cravings and other forms of psychological distress with early recovery, facilitate AA involvement and forward progress in recovery that were previously unattainable, and play a vitally important role as a short-term adjunct to long-term involvement in AA or other supportive therapies.

By reviewing and discussing the latest alcoholism research for this book, we sincerely hope to elevate the understanding of alcoholism, to increase awareness of the availability and effectiveness of a range of treatment approaches for alcohol dependence, and, in doing so, to benefit many different readers.

Recovering alcoholics might gain an understanding of the impact of their dependence on decision making and choices, both past and present. Children and the loved ones of alcoholics may gain a greater understanding that the alcoholic's self-centered behavior, unavailability, and neglect of personal needs did not stem in many cases from a conscious disregard for the welfare of self or others but from a progressive fixation on alcohol stemming from his or her dependence, and from the desperation for relief from the emotional state when not drinking. Persons with an early-stage alcohol problem may also benefit from this book, and possibly reconsider the wisdom of continued drinking after reading the discussion on the neurobiology of alcoholism. Physicians working with alcoholic patients can also gain an understanding of available medication therapies; the exact mechanism by which these drugs counteract the disturbances in brain function that generate the distressing symptoms of drinking urges, insomnia, agitation, or anxiety; and the strength of scientific evidence supporting their use.

Compiling relevant information on the vast subject of alcoholism and placing it in one book provides an invaluable reference on the subject for professionals, teachers, students, people in recovery, and anyone with the desire to learn about the nature of alcoholism and its treatment. And perhaps most importantly, we would like to instill hope in the actively alcoholic reader, the family member of an alcoholic, and the general public at large that recovery is possible and that many treatment and recovery approaches are available and effective. In some cases combining different treatment modalities improves patient outcomes, and to some degree, treatment should be tailored to the individual needs of the alcoholic.

Great advances in the understanding of alcoholism and its treatment have been achieved in recent years, and are described in this book. However, there remains a substantial gap between the need for treatment and the availability of treatment.

Current estimates indicate that 23.5 million Americans are addicted to alcohol and/or drugs, and are in need of treatment. Unfortunately, only one in ten receives the treatment he or she needs, resulting in a treatment gap of more than 20 million Americans.

Similar to diabetes and high blood pressure, addiction is a chronic disease that can be managed successfully over time with access to proper treatment services, integrated medical care, and ongoing community-based support. In addition to the potentially life-saving benefit of addiction treatment, numerous cost-effectiveness studies have consistently found that every dollar spent on treatment leads to a five- to seven-dollar cost savings to society, mostly accounted for by increased worker productivity and reduced worker absenteeism, and reductions in health care, criminal justice, and social services costs. Unfortunately, society in general and the health care system in particular have been slow to recognize and respond to addiction as a chronic but treatable condition, resulting in millions of Americans with alcohol or other drug addiction unable to access the treatment services they need (Open Society Foundations 2010).

The greatest contributors to the gap between the need for and access to treatment are the very large number of persons without health insurance, inadequate insurance coverage, and insufficient public funds. For instance, private insurance pays for approximately 37% of general medical costs but only 10% of addiction treatment costs, with government sources paying for 77% of addiction treatment expenses and the rest being paid out-of-pocket and by other private sources. And despite the enormous personal, societal, and economic costs of alcohol and other drug addiction, only 1.3% of all health care spending in 2003 went to alcohol or other drug addiction treatment (Open Society Foundations 2010).

A widely overlooked but essential population in great need of treatment access is inmates residing in correctional settings. The current approach of incarcerating addicted offenders incurs enormous taxpayer burden, does nothing to interrupt the cycle of recidivism and reincarceration, and unnecessarily exposes many addicted inmates who are not otherwise criminals to the abuses of the prison system.

Of the 2.3 million inmates in U.S. prisons, 1.9 million either have a diagnosable substance use disorder or were under the influence of a substance during commission of their crime. In 2005, federal, state, and local governments spent $74 billion on substance abuse–related incarceration, court proceedings, probation, and parole, and only $632 million on prevention and treatment for such offenders. Only 11% of inmates with substance use disorders receive any form of treatment during incarceration, little of which is evidence-based care. Substance-involved offenders are very likely to end up back in prison without treatment (CASA 2010).

Steps can be taken to reduce crime and taxpayer costs by addressing the treatment needs of offenders while holding them accountable for their crimes. The National Institute on Drug Abuse estimates a savings of $12 in reduced substance-related crime and criminal justice and health care costs for every dollar spent on treatment (CASA 2010). Effective treatment of substance use disorders in inmates is based on recognition that addiction is a chronic disease requiring a disease management approach, and is outlined in the practice guidelines published in 2006 by the National Institute on Drug Abuse titled *Principles of Drug Abuse Treatment for Criminal Justice Populations.*

In March 2010, legislation to reform health care was passed, which may greatly expand access to alcohol and other drug addiction treatment. Provisions in the bill may mean that millions of Americans will have insurance coverage for addiction treatment as part of their basic benefit package. This legislation represented a major step forward in making addiction treatment part of a comprehensive approach to integrated health care (Open Society Foundations 2010).

Measures have been identified that could substantially improve the quality of alcoholism treatment. As with many areas of health care, the field of alcoholism and addiction treatment experiences a significant gap between the scientific validation of new approaches to treatment and actual change in clinical practice. One of the best ways to address this disparity between knowledge and practice entails clinician training in the evidence-based practice of alcoholism and addiction treatment. An important element of clinician training would be to address potential negative attitudes toward implementing new approaches in the care of patients. This may be especially true regarding the use of medications to reduce alcohol craving and the symptoms of post-acute withdrawal.

Additionally, current figures indicate that fewer than 7% of patients admitted to treatment are referred by a health care provider. Although this figure reflects the failure to integrate addiction screening and treatment into the nation's health care delivery system, it does convey hope that educational and other efforts that target health care providers can potentially increase the rates of assessment and referral to treatment (Open Society Foundations 2010).

The current body of research on alcoholism is profound. Still, we are in need of more research, specifically investigating the neuroscience of recovery from alcoholism and addiction. This should include the extent of brain pathology and reverses in recovery, factors that influence this recovery, interventions that can facilitate or accelerate the process, and the extent to which specific brain pathologies influence the capacity to achieve recovery (White 2007). A recent study found that recovering alcoholics with six to seven weeks of sobriety showed substantial structural, metabolic, and neuropsychological regeneration compared with the results of their brain scans at treatment admission (Bartsch et al. 2007). This study represents the research focus that is most needed in the near future to fill in many of the missing pieces in the puzzle of alcoholism and recovery.

# REFERENCES

## Introduction

Anthony, J. C., L. A. Warner, and R. C. Kessler. 1994. "Comparative Epidemiology of Dependence on Tobacco, Alcohol, Controlled Substances, and Inhalants: Basic Findings from the National Comorbidity Survey." *Experimental and Clinical Psychopharmacology* 2:244–268.

Centers for Disease Control and Prevention (CDC). 2010. "Alcohol Use." Accessed January 14, 2011. www.cdc.gov/nchs/fastats/alcohol.htm.

Chen, C. Y., and J. C. Anthony. 2004. "Epidemiological Estimates of Risk in the Process of Becoming Dependent upon Cocaine: Cocaine Hydrochloride Powder versus Crack Cocaine." *Psychopharmacology* 172:78–86.

Hasin, D. S., F. S. Stinson, E. Ogburn, and B. F. Grant. 2007. "Prevalence, Correlates, Disability, and Comorbidity of DSM-IV Alcohol Abuse and Dependence in the United States: Results from the National Epidemiologic Survey on Alcohol and Related Conditions." *Archives of General Psychiatry* 64 (7): 830–842.

Hughes, J. R., J. E. Helzer, and S. A. Lindberg. 2006. "Prevalence of *DSM*/ICD-Defined Nicotine Dependence." *Drug and Alcohol Dependence* 85:91–102.

Thavorncharoensap, M., Y. Teerawattananon, J. Yothasamut, C. Lertpitakpong, and U. Chaikledkaew. 2009. "The Economic Impact of Alcohol Consumption: A Systematic Review." *Substance Abuse Treatment, Prevention, and Policy* 4:20:1–11.

## Chapter 1

Alcoholics Anonymous (AA). 1956. *AA Fact File.* New York: AA Publishing, Inc.

Alcoholics Anonymous (AA). n.d. *A.A. Guidelines for A.A. Members Employed in the Alcoholism Field.* In White and Kurtz 2008.

Alcoholics Anonymous World Services, Inc. 1957. *Alcoholics Anonymous Comes of Age.* New York: Alcoholics Anonymous World Services, Inc.

Alcoholics Anonymous World Services, Inc. n.d. *Three Talks to Medical Societies by Bill W., Co-founder of AA.* New York: Alcoholics Anonymous World Services, Inc. www.aa.org/pdf/products/p-6_threetalkstomed.pdf.

Black, J. R. 1889. "Advantages of Substituting the Morphia Habit for the Incurably Alcoholic." Cincinnati, OH: Cincinnati Lancet Clinic. In Lindesmith 1947.

**287**

Blair Historic Preservation Alliance. 2008. "Keeley Cure." Blair Historic Preservation Alliance. Accessed Aug. 18, 2010. www.blairhistory.com/archive/keeley_cure /default.htm.

Blassingame, J. 1972. *The Slave Community: Plantation Life in the Antebellum South.* New York: Oxford University Press.

Blocker, J. S., D. M. Fahey, and I. R. Tyrrell, eds. 2003. *Alcohol and Temperance in Modern History.* Santa Barbara, CA: ABC-CLIO / Greenwood.

Bluhm, A. C. 2006. "Verification of C. G. Jung's Analysis of Rowland Hazard and the History of Alcoholics Anonymous." *History of Psychology* 9 (4): 313–324.

Brecher, E. M., and Consumer Reports Editors. 1972. *Licit and Illicit Drugs: The Consumers Union Report on Narcotics, Stimulants Depressants, Inhalants, Hallucinogens, and Marijuana—Including Caffeine, Nicotine, and Alcohol.* Boston: Little, Brown, and Company.

Brigham, G. S. 2003. "Twelve Step Participation as a Pathway to Recovery: The Maryhaven Experience and Implications for Treatment and Research." *Clinical Perspectives: 12 Steps and Treatment* 46:43–52.

Brill, L., and C. Winick, eds. 1985. *Yearbook of Substance Use and Abuse.* Vol. III. New York: Human Sciences Press, Inc.

Bufe, C. 1998. *Alcoholics Anonymous: Cult or Cure?* Tucson, Arizona: Sharp Press.

Cherrington, E. 1920. *The Evolution of Prohibition in the United States.* Westerville, OH: The American Issue Press. In White 1999, 16–22.

Coombs, R. H., ed. 2004. *Addiction Counseling Review: Preparing for Comprehensive, Certification, and Licensing Exams.* New York: Lahaska Press, 81–104.

Courtwright, D. T. 2001. *Forces of Habit.* Cambridge, MA: Harvard University Press.

Coyhis, D. L., and W. L. White. 2006. *Alcohol Problems in Native America: The Untold Story of Resistance and Recovery.* Colorado Springs: White Bison, Inc.

Curtiss, John. 2010. President and Program Director, The Retreat. Communication on July 25.

Davies, J. B. 1992. *The Myth of Addiction.* 1st ed. New York: Harwood Academic Publishers.

Douglass, F. 1855. *My Bondage and My Freedom.* New York: Miller, Orton, and Mulligan. In White 1999, 16–22.

Dunlap, M. P. 2006. "Social History of Alcohol Use and Abuse." Accessed Aug. 12, 2010. www.michaeledunlap.com.

Dyck, E. 2005. "Flashback: Psychiatric Experimentation with LSD in Historical Perspective." *Canadian Journal of Psychiatry* 50:381–388.

Escohotado, A. 1999. *A Brief History of Drugs.* Rochester, VT: Park Street Press.

Fingarette, H. 1989. *Heavy Drinking: The Myth of Alcoholism as a Disease*. Berkeley, CA: University of California Press.

"Focus on the Neurobiology of Addiction." 2005. *Nature Neuroscience* 8 (11).

Foltz, A. Rev. 1891. "From Hell to Heaven and How I Got There: Being the Life History of a Saved Bar Keeper, with Stirring Addresses on the Temperance Question." Lincoln, NE: The Hunter Printing House. In Passetti and White 2009, 19–22.

Galanter, M., ed. 1989. *Recent Developments in Alcoholism* 7. New York: Plenum Publishing Corporation.

Galanter, M., and L. Kaskuta, eds. 2008. *Research on Alcoholics Anonymous and Spirituality in Addiction Recovery*. Vol. 18 of *Recent Developments in Alcoholism*, 37–57. New York: Springer.

Herd, D. 1985. "We Cannot Stagger to Freedom: A History of Blacks and Alcohol in American Politics." In Brill and Winick 1985.

Jensen, S. 1962. "A Treatment Program for Alcoholics in a Mental Hospital." *Quarterly Journal on Studies of Alcohol* 23:4–5.

Koerner, B. I. 2010. "Secret of AA: After 75 Years, We Don't Know How It Works." *Wired,* June 23.

Kolb, L. 1962. *Drug Addiction, A Medical Problem*. Springfield, IL: Charles C. Thomas. In Brecher 1972.

Kurtz, E. 1979. *Not-God: A History of Alcoholics Anonymous*. Center City, MN: Hazelden.

Kurtz, E. 1981. *Shame and Guilt: Characteristics of the Dependency Cycle*. Center City, MN: Hazelden.

Kurtz, E. 1991. *Not-God: A History of Alcoholics Anonymous*. Rev. ed. Center City, MN: Hazelden.

Kurtz, E., and W. L. White. 2003. "Alcoholics Anonymous (AA)." In Blocker, Fahey, and Tyrrell 2003, 27–31.

Lender, M., and J. Martin. 1982. *Drinking in America*. New York: The Free Press. In White 1999, 16–22.

Leshner, A. I. 1997. "Addiction Is a Brain Disease, and It Matters." *Science* 278 (5335): 45–47.

Levine, H. 1978. "The Discovery of Addiction: Changing Conceptions of Habitual Drunkenness in America." *Journal of Studies on Alcohol* 39 (2): 143–174. In White 2004.

Lindesmith, A. R. 1947. *Opiate Addiction*. Evanston, IL: Principia Press. In Brecher and Consumer Reports Editors 1972.

MacAndrew, C., and R. Edgerton. 1969. *Drunken Comportment*. Chicago: Aldine Publishing Company. In White 1999, 16–22.

Mancall, P. 1995. *Deadly Medicine: Indians and Alcohol in Early America.* Ithaca, NY: Cornell University Press. In White 1999, 16–22.

Mangini, M. 1998. "Treatment of Alcoholism Using Psychedelic Drugs: A Review of the Program of Research." *Journal of Psychoactive Drugs* 30:381–418.

Mann, M. 1944. "Formation of a National Committee for Education on Alcoholism." *Quarterly Journal of Studies on Alcohol* 5 (2): 354. In White 2004.

McCarthy, R. G. 1963. *Drinking and Intoxication.* New Haven, CT: New College and University Press.

"Medicine: Keeley Cure." *Time Magazine,* September 25, 1939.

Menninger, K. Quoted in Alcoholics Anonymous World Services, Inc., n.d.

Mosher, J. 1980. "The History of Youthful-Drinking Laws: Implications for Current Policy." In Wechsler 1980.

New York State OASAS (Office of Alcoholism and Substance Abuse Services). 2011. "A History of Recovery in New York State." Accessed June 21. www.oasas.state.ny.us/recovery/NYShistoryrecov.cfm.

NIAAA (National Institute on Alcohol Abuse and Alcoholism). 2009. "Apparent Per Capita Ethanol Consumption for the United States, 1850–2007." Accessed Sept. 1, 2010. www.niaaa.nih.gov/Resources/DatabaseResources/QuickFacts/AlcoholSales/consum01.html.

Pan, L. 1975. *Alcohol in Colonial Africa.* New Brunswick, NJ: The Finnish Foundation for Alcohol Studies.

Passetti, L. L., and W. L. White. 2009. "Recovery Support Meetings for Youths." *Student Assistance Journal* 29 (3): 19–22.

*Pass It On: The Story of Bill Wilson and How the A.A. Message Reached the World.* 1984. New York: Alcoholics Anonymous World Services, Inc. In White and Kurtz 2008.

Peele, S. 1989. *The Diseasing of America.* Lexington, MA: Lexington Books.

Pittman, B. 1988. *AA: The Way It Began.* Seattle: Glenn Abbey Books.

Rorabaugh, W. 1979. *The Alcoholic Republic: An American Tradition.* Oxford: Oxford University Press. In White 1999, 16–22.

Schaler, J. A. 2000. *Addiction Is a Choice.* Chicago: Open Court.

Sherratt, A. 1995. "Alcohol and Its Alternatives: Symbol and Substance in Pre-industrial Cultures." In *Consuming Habits,* edited by J. Goodman, P. E. Lovejoy, and A. Sherratt. London: Routledge.

Simonelli, R. 2006. Book review of D. L. Coyhis and W. L. White. 2006. *Alcohol Problems in Native America.* In *Winds of Change,* 73–75. Accessed Aug. 20, 2010. www.whitebison.org/2007pdf/WOCreview_alcohol.pdf.

Slaymaker, V. J., and T. Sheehan. 2008. "The Impact of AA on Professional Treatment." *Recent Developments in Alcoholism* 18:59–70.

Steinsapir, C. 1983. "The Ante-bellum Temperance Movement at the Local Level: A Case Study of Schenectady, New York." Ph.D. Dissertation: Rutgers University. In White 1999, 16–22.

Trice, H. M., and W. J. Staudenmeier. 1989. "A Sociocultural History of Alcoholics Anonymous." In Galanter 1989.

Vallee, B. 1998. "Alcohol in the Western World." *Scientific American* 278 (6): 80–84. In White 1999, 16–22.

Walton, S., and B. Glover. 1999. *The Ultimate Encyclopedia of Wine, Beer, Spirits, and Liqueurs.* Leicester, England: Hermes House.

Wechsler, H. 1980. *Minimum-Drinking Age Laws.* Lexington, MA: Lexington Books. In White 1999, 16–22.

Westermeyer, J. 1996. "Alcoholism among New World Peoples: A Critique of History, Methods, and Findings." *American Journal on Addictions* 5 (2): 110–123. In White 1999, 16–22.

White, W. L. 1998. *Slaying the Dragon: The History of Addiction Treatment and Recovery in America.* Bloomington, IL: Chestnut Health Systems.

White, W. L. 1999. "A History of Adolescent Alcohol, Tobacco and Other Drug Use in America." *Student Assistance Journal* 11 (5): 16–22.

White, W. L. 2000a. "Addiction as a Disease: Birth of a Concept." *Counselor* 1 (1): 46–51, 73.

White, W. L. 2000b. "The Rebirth of the Disease Concept of Alcoholism in the 20th Century." *Counselor* 1 (2): 62–66.

White, W. L. 2001a. "Addiction Disease Concept: Advocates and Critics." *Counselor* 2 (1): 42–46.

White, W. L., ed. 2001b. "The Combined Addiction Disease Chronologies of William White, MA, Ernest Kurtz, PhD, and Caroline Acker, PhD." Accessed Sept. 19, 2010. www.williamwhitepapers.com/papers/all/.

White, W. L. 2003. "Alcoholic Mutual Aid Groups (United States)." In Blocker, Fahey, and Tyrrell 2003, 24–27.

White, W. L. 2004. "History of Drug Problems and Drug Policies in America." In Coombs 2004.

White, W. L. 2007a. "Addiction Recovery: Its Definition and Conceptual Boundaries." *Journal of Substance Abuse Treatment* 33:229–241.

White, W. L. 2007b. "In Search of the Neurobiology of Addiction Recovery: A Brief Commentary on Science and Stigma." Accessed Sept. 17, 2010. www.facesandvoicesofrecovery.org/pdf/White/White_neurobiology_2007.pdf. (Also available at www.williamwhitepapers.com.)

White, W. L., and E. Kurtz. 2008. "Twelve Defining Moments in the History of Alcoholics Anonymous." In Galanter and Kaskutas 2008.

White, W. L., and M. Sanders. 2002. "Addiction and Recovery among African Americans Before 1900." *Counselor* 3 (6): 64–66.

White, W. L., M. Sanders, and T. Sanders. 2006. "Addiction in the African American Community: The Recovery Legacies of Frederick Douglass and Malcolm X." *Counselor* 7 (5): 53–58.

White, W. L., and M. Schulstad. 2009. "Relapse Following Prolonged Addiction Recovery: Time for Answers to Critical Questions." *Counselor* 10 (4): 36–39.

*Winds of Change* magazine, Summer 2006, 73–75. Accessed July 29, 2010. www.whitebison .org/2007pdf/WOCreview_alcohol.pdf.

## Chapter 2

Aisa, B., R. Tordera, B. Lasheras, J. Del Río, and M. J. Ramírez. 2008. "Effects of Maternal Separation on Hypothalamic-Pituitary-Adrenal Responses, Cognition and Vulnerability to Stress in Adult Female Rats." *Neuroscience* 154 (4): 1218–1226.

Anthony, J. C., L. A. Warner, and R. C. Kessler. 1994. "Comparative Epidemiology of Dependence on Tobacco, Alcohol, Controlled Substances, and Inhalants: Basic Findings from the National Comorbidity Survey." *Experimental and Clinical Psychopharmacology* 2:244–268.

APA (American Psychiatric Association). 2000. *Diagnostic and Statistical Manual of Mental Disorders.* 4th ed., Text Revision. Washington, DC: American Psychiatric Association.

Arias, A. J., and H. R. Kranzler. 2008. "Treatment of Co-Occurring Alcohol and Other Drug Use Disorders." *Alcohol Research and Health* 31:155–167.

Beauvais, F. 1998. "American Indians and Alcohol." *Alcohol Research and Health* 22:253–260.

Blow, F. C., M. A. Walton, K. L. Barry, J. C. Coyne, S. A. Mudd, and L. A. Copeland. 2000. "The Relationship between Alcohol Problems and Health Functioning of Older Adults in Primary Care Settings." *Journal of the American Geriatric Society* 48:769–774.

Book, S. W., and C. L. Randall. 2002. "Social Anxiety Disorder and Alcohol Use." *Alcohol Research and Health* 26:130–135.

Bottlender, M., U. W. Preuss, and M. Soyka. 2006. "Association of Personality Disorders with Type A and Type B Alcoholics." *European Archives of Psychiatry and Clinical Neuroscience* 256 (1): 55–61.

Branchey, L., W. Davis, and C. S. Lieber. 1984. "Alcoholism in Vietnam and Korea Veterans: A Long Term Follow-Up." *Alcoholism: Clinical and Experimental Research* 8 (6): 572–575.

Bray, R. M., and L. L. Hourani. 2007. "Substance Use Trends among Active Duty Military Personnel: Findings from the United States Department of Defense Health Related Behavior Surveys, 1980–2005." *Addiction* 102:1092–1101.

Bremner, J. D., S M. Southwick, A. Darnell, and D. S. Charney. 1996. "Chronic PTSD in Vietnam Combat Veterans: Course of Illness and Substance Abuse." *American Journal of Psychiatry* 153 (3): 369–375.

Brown, S. A., P. W. Vik, T. L. Patterson, I. Grant, and M. A. Schuckit. 1995. "Stress, Vulnerability, and Adult Alcohol Relapse." *Journal of Studies on Alcohol* 56:538–545.

Bulik, C. M., C. A. Prescott, and K. S. Kendler. 2001. "Features of Childhood Sexual Abuse and the Development of Psychiatric and Substance Use Disorders." *British Journal of Psychiatry* 179:444–449.

Bussey, K., and A. Bandura. 1999. "Social-Cognitive Theory of Gender Development and Differentiation." *Psychological Review* 106:676–713.

Caetano, R., C. L. Clark, and T. Tam. 1998. "Alcohol Consumption among Racial/Ethnic Minorities: Theory and Research." *Alcohol Research and Health* 22:233–237.

Caldji, C., J. Diorio, and M. J. Meaney. 2000. "Variations in Maternal Care in Infancy Regulate the Development of Stress Reactivity." *Biological Psychiatry* 48 (12): 1164–1174.

Castro, F. G., and K. Coe. 2007. "Traditions and Alcohol Use: A Mixed-Methods Analysis." *Cultural Diversity and Ethnic Minority Psychology* 13 (4): 269–284.

Chen, C. M., M. C. Dufour, and H. Yi. 2004. "Alcohol Consumption among Young Adults Ages 18–24 in the United States: Results from the 2001–2002 NESARC Survey." *Alcohol Research and Health* 28 (4): 269–280.

Chen, C. Y., and J. C. Anthony. 2004. "Epidemiological Estimates of Risk in the Process of Becoming Dependent upon Cocaine: Cocaine Hydrochloride Powder versus Crack Cocaine." *Psychopharmacology* 172:78–86.

Clark, D. B., M. Vanukov, and J. Cornelius. 2002. "Childhood Antisocial Behavior and Adolescent Alcohol Use Disorders." *Alcohol Research and Health* 26 (2): 109–116.

Cleck, J. N., and J. A. Blendy. 2008. "Making a Bad Thing Worse: Adverse Effects of Stress on Drug Addiction." *Journal of Clinical Investigation* 118 (2): 454–461.

Colvert, E., M. Rutter, J. Kreppner, C. Beckett, J. Castle, C. Groothues, A. Hawkins, S. Stevens, and E. J. S. Sonuga-Barke. 2008. "Do Theory of Mind and Executive Function Deficits Underlie the Adverse Outcomes Associated with Profound Early Deprivation? Findings from the English and Romanian Adoptees Study." *Journal of Abnormal Child Psychology* 36 (7): 1057–1068.

Cotton, N. S. 1979. "The Familial Incidence of Alcoholism: A Review." *Journal of Studies on Alcohol and Drugs* 40:89–116.

Dawson, D. A., B. F. Grant, and T. K. Li. 2005. "Quantifying the Risks Associated with Exceeding Recommended Drinking Limits." *Alcoholism: Clinical and Experimental Research* 29 (5): 902–908.

De Bellis, M. D. 2002. "Developmental Traumatology: A Contributory Mechanism for Alcohol and Substance Use Disorders." *Psychoneuroendocrinology* 27:155–170.

de Geus, E. J., D. van't Ent, S. P. Wolfensberger, P. Heutink, W. J. Hoogendijk, D. I. Boomsma, and D. J. Veltman. 2007. "Intrapair Differences in Hippocampal Volume in Monozygotic Twins Discordant for the Risk for Anxiety and Depression." *Biological Psychiatry* 61 (9): 1062–1071.

Deas, D., and S. Thomas. 2002. "Comorbid Psychiatric Factors Contributing to Adolescent Alcohol and Other Drug Use." *Alcohol Research and Health* 26:116–121.

Dick, D. M., and A. Agrawal. 2008. "The Genetics of Alcohol and Other Drug Dependence." *Alcohol Research and Health* 31:111–118.

Drake, R. E., and K. T. Mueser. 2002. "Co–Occuring Alcohol Use Disorder and Schizophrenia." *Alcohol Research and Health* 26:99–102.

Fergusson, D. M., and P. E. Mullen. 1999. *Childhood Sexual Abuse: An Evidence Based Perspective.* Vol. 40 of *Developmental Clinical Psychology and Psychiatry* series. Thousand Oaks, CA: Sage.

Finn, P. R., and A. Justus. 1997. "Physiological Responses in Sons of Alcoholics." *Alcohol Research and Health* 21:227–231.

Fothergill, K. E., and M. E. Ensminger. 2006. "Childhood and Adolescent Antecedents of Drug and Alcohol Problems: A Longitudinal Study." *Drug and Alcohol Dependence* 82:61–67.

Frank, J. W., R. S. Moore, and G. M. Ames. 2000. "Historical and Cultural Roots of Drinking Problems among American Indians." *American Journal of Public Health* 90:344–351.

Friedmann, P. D., L. Jin, T. Karrison, M. Nerney, D. C. Hayley, R. Mulliken, J. Walter, A. Miller, and M. H. Chin. 1999. "The Effect of Alcohol Abuse on the Health Status of Older Adults Seen in the Emergency Department." *American Journal of Drug and Alcohol Abuse* 25:529–542.

Fries, A. B. W., T. E. Ziegler, J. R. Kurian, S. Jacoris, and S. D. Pollak. 2005. "Early Experience in Humans Is Associated with Changes in Neuropeptides Critical for Regulating Social Behavior." *Proceedings of the National Academy of Sciences U.S.A.* 102 (47): 17237–17240.

Fromme, K., H. de Wit, K. E. Hutchison, L. Ray, W. R. Corbin, T. A. Cook, T. L. Wall, and D. Goodman. 2004. "Biological and Behavioral Markers of Alcohol Sensitivity." *Alcoholism: Clinical and Experimental Research* 28:247–256.

Ganry, O., A. Dubreuil, J. Joly, and M. Queval. 2000. "Prevalence of Alcohol Problems among Elderly Patients in a University Hospital." *Addiction* 95:107–113.

Gilbertson, R., R. Prather, and S. J. Nixon. 2008. "The Role of Selected Factors in the Development and Consequences of Alcohol Dependence." *Alcohol Research and Health* 31 (4): 389–400.

Goldberg, J., S. A. Eisen, W. R. True, and W. G. Henderson. 1990. "A Twin Study of the Effects of the Vietnam Conflict on Alcohol Drinking Patterns." *American Journal of Public Health* 80:570–574.

Goodman, A. 2009. "The Neurobiological Development of Addiction." *Psychiatric Times* 26:1–14.

Goodwin, D. W., F. Schulsinger, N. Moller, L. Hermansen, G. Winokur, and S. B. Guze. 1974. "Drinking Problems in Adopted and Nonadopted Sons of Alcoholics." *Archives of General Psychiatry* 31:164–169.

Grant, B. F., and D. A. Dawson. 2006. "Introduction to the National Epidemiologic Survey on Alcohol and Related Conditions." *Alcohol Research and Health* 29 (2): 74–79.

Grant, B. F., D. A. Dawson, F. S. Stinson, S. P. Chou, M. C. Dufour, and R. P. Pickering. 2004. "The 12-Month Prevalence and Trends in *DSM–IV* Alcohol Abuse and Dependence: United States, 1991–1992 and 2001–2002." *Drug and Alcohol Dependence* 74:223–234.

Grant, B. F., F. S. Stinson, D. A. Dawson, S. P. Chou, M. C. Dufour, R. P. Pickering, and K. Kaplan. 2004. "Prevalence and Co-occurrence of Substance Use Disorders and Independent Mood and Anxiety Disorders: Results from the National Epidemiologic Survey on Alcohol and Related Conditions." *Archives of General Psychiatry* 61 (8): 807–816.

Grant, B. F., F. S. Stinson, D. A. Dawson, S. P. Chou, W. J. Ruan, and R. P. Pickering. 2006. "Co-Occurrence of 12-Month Alcohol and Drug Use Disorders and Personality Disorders in the United States: Results From the National Epidemiologic Survey on Alcohol and Related Conditions." *Alcohol Research and Health* 29 (2): 121–130.

Grant, J. E., M. G. Kushner, and S. W. Kim. 2002. "Pathological Gambling and Alcohol Use Disorder." *Alcohol Research and Health* 26:143–150.

Grilo, C. M., R. Sinha, and S. S. O'Malley. 2002. "Eating Disorders and Alcohol Use Disorders." *Alcohol Research and Health* 26:151–156.

Hazelden. Jan. 1999. "Women and Substance Abuse." *Research Update.* Center City, MN: Hazelden.

Hazelden. Aug. 2001. "Genetic Factors in Alcohol Dependence." *Research Update.* Center City, MN: Hazelden.

Hazelden. Dec. 2001. "Alcohol Problems and Older Adults." *Research Update.* Center City, MN: Hazelden.

Holmes, A., A. M. le Guisquet, E. Vogel, R. A. Millstein, S. Leman, and C. Belzung. 2005. "Early Life Genetic, Epigenetic and Environmental Factors Shaping Emotionality in Rodents." *Neuroscience and Biobehavioral Reviews* 29 (8): 1335–1346.

Hughes, J. R., J. E. Helzer, and S. A. Lindberg. 2006. "Prevalence of *DSM*/ICD-Defined Nicotine Dependence." *Drug and Alcohol Dependence* 85:91–102.

Hunt, W. A., and S. Zakhari, eds. 1995. *Stress, Gender, and Alcohol-Seeking Behavior.* Research Monograph No. 29. Bethesda, MD: National Institute on Alcohol Abuse and Alcoholism.

Jacob, T., and S. Johnson. 1997. "Parenting Influences on the Development of Alcohol Abuse and Dependence." *Alcohol Research and Health* 21:204–210.

Johnston, L. D., P. M. O'Malley, J. G. Bachman, and J. E. Schulenberg. 2008. *Monitoring the Future National Survey Results on Drug Use, 1975–2007.* Vol. I: Secondary School Students. NIH Publication No. 08–6418A. Bethesda, MD: National Institute on Drug Abuse, 26.

Jones-Webb, R. 1998. "Drinking Patterns and Problems among African-Americans: Recent Findings." *Alcohol Research and Health* 22:260–264.

Kalinichev, M., K. W. Easterling, and S. G. Holtzman. 2003. "Long-Lasting Changes in Morphine-Induced Locomotor Sensitization and Tolerance in Long-Evans Mother Rats as a Result of Periodic Postpartum Separation from the Litter: A Novel Model of Increased Vulnerability to Drug Abuse?" *Neuropsychopharmacology* 28:317–328.

Keane, T. M., R. J. Gerardi, J. A. Lyons, and J. Wolfe. 1988. "The Interrelationship of Substance Abuse and Posttraumatic Stress Disorder: Epidemiological and Clinical Considerations." *Recent Developments in Alcoholism* 6:27–48.

Kendler, K. S., C. M. Bulik, J. Silberg, J. M. Hettema, J. Myers, and C. A. Prescott. 2000. "Childhood Sexual Abuse and Adult Psychiatric and Substance Use Disorders in Women: An Epidemiological and Cotwin Control Analysis." *Archives of General Psychiatry* 57:953–959.

LaBrie, J. W., J. Cail, J. F. Hummer, A. Lac, and C. Neighbors. 2009. "What Men Want: The Role of Reflective Opposite-Sex Normative Preferences in Alcohol Use among College Women." *Psychology of Addictive Behaviors* 23 (1): 157–162.

Ladd, C. O., R. L. Huot, K. V. Thrivikraman, C. B. Nemeroff, and P. M. Plotsky. 2004. "Long-Term Adaptations in Glucocorticoid Receptor and Mineralocorticoid Receptor mRNA and Negative Feedback on the Hypothalamo-Pituitary-Adrenal Axis Following Neonatal Maternal Separation." *Biological Psychiatry* 55 (4): 367–375.

Lamarine, R. J. 1988. "Alcohol Abuse among Native Americans." *Journal of Community Health* 13:143–155.

Ling, W., D. R. Wesson, and D. E. Smith. 2005. "Prescription Opiate Abuse." In Lowinson et al. 2005.

Lo, C. C., and T. C. Cheng. 2007. "The Impact of Childhood Maltreatment on Young Adults' Substance Abuse." *American Journal of Drug and Alcohol Abuse* 33:139–146.

Lowinson, J. H, P. Ruiz, R. B. Millman, and J. G. Langrod, eds. 2005. *Substance Abuse: A Comprehensive Textbook.* 4th ed. Philadelphia, PA: Lippincott, Williams, and Wilkins, 459–468.

Luczak, S. E., T. L. Wall, S. H. Shea, S. M. Byun, and L. G. Carr. 2001. "Binge Drinking in Chinese, Korean, and White College Students: Genetic and Ethnic Group Differences." *Psychology of Addictive Behavior* 15 (4): 306–309.

Makimoto, K. 1998. "Drinking Patterns and Drinking Problems among Asian-Americans and Pacific Islanders." *Alcohol Research and Health* 22:270–280.

Martin, C. S. 2008. "Timing of Alcohol and Other Drug Use." *Alcohol Research and Health* 31:96–100.

May, P. A., and J. R. Moran. 1995. "Prevention of Alcohol Misuse: A Review of Health Promotion Efforts among American Indians." *American Journal of Health Promotion* 9:288–299.

Miller, J. W., T. S. Naimi, R. D. Brewer, and S. E. Jones. 2007. "Binge Drinking and Associated Health Risk Behaviors Among High School Students." *Pediatrics* 119 (1): 76–85.

Mirand, A., and J. W. Welte. 1996. "Alcohol Consumption among the Elderly in a General Population, Erie County, New York." *American Journal of Public Health* 86:978–984.

Mokdad, A., J. Marks, D. Stroup, and J. Gerberding. 2004. "Actual Causes of Death in the United States, 2000." *Journal of the American Medical Association* 291:1238–1245.

Molina, B. S. G., and W. E. Pelham. 2003. "Childhood Predictors of Adolescent Substance Use in a Longitudinal Study of Children with ADHD." *Journal of Abnormal Psychology* 112 (3): 497–507.

Moore, A. A., R. D. Hays, G. A. Greendale, M. Damesyn, and D. B. Reuben. 1999. "Drinking Habits among Older Persons: Findings from the NHANES I Epidemiologic Followup Study (1982–84)." *Journal of the American Geriatric Society* 47 (6): 412–416.

Naimi, T. S., R. D. Brewer, A. Mokdad, C. Denny, M. K. Serdula, and J. S. Marks. 2003. "Binge Drinking among U.S. Adults." *Journal of the American Medical Association* 289 (1): 70–75.

NIAAA (National Institute on Alcohol Abuse and Alcoholism). 2000. "Why Do Some People Drink Too Much? The Role of Genetic and Psychosocial Influences." *Alcoholism Research and Health* 24:17–26.

NIAAA (National Institute on Alcohol Abuse and Alcoholism). 2003. "The Genetics of Alcoholism." *Alcohol Alert* 60. Accessed Oct. 2, 2010. http://pubs.niaaa.nih.gov /publications/aa60.htm.

NIAAA (National Institute on Alcohol Abuse and Alcoholism). 2004. "Neuroscience Research and Therapeutic Targets." *Alcohol Alert* 61. Accessed Oct. 2, 2010. http://pubs.niaaa.nih.gov/publications/aa61.htm.

NIAAA (National Institute on Alcohol Abuse and Alcoholism). 2006. "National Epidemiologic Survey on Alcohol and Related Conditions." *Alcohol Alert* 70:1–6.

NIAAA (National Institute on Alcohol Abuse and Alcoholism). 2007a. "Helping Patients Who Drink Too Much." NIH Publication No. 07–3769.

NIAAA (National Institute on Alcohol Abuse and Alcoholism). 2007b. "Family History." NIH Publication No. 03–5340.

NIAAA (National Institute on Alcohol Abuse and Alcoholism). 2008. "Alcohol: A Women's Health Issue." NIH Publication No. 03–4956.

Office of Applied Studies (OAS), Substance Abuse and Mental Health Services Administration. 2006. "Alcohol Dependence or Abuse: 2002, 2003, and 2004." *The NSDUH Report* 16. http://oas.samhsa.gov/2k6/AlcDepend/AlcDepend.htm.

O'Malley, P. M., and L. D. Johnston. 2002. "Epidemiology of Alcohol and Other Drug Use among American College Students." *Journal of Studies on Alcohol* (Supplement 14): 23–39.

Patterson, T. L., and D. V. Jeste. 1999. "The Potential Impact of the Baby-Boom Generation on Substance Abuse among Elderly Persons." *Psychiatric Services* 50:1184–1188.

Plotsky, P. M., K. V. Thrivikraman, C. B. Nemeroff, C. Caldji, S. Sharma, and M. J. Meaney. 2005. "Long-Term Consequences of Neonatal Rearing on Central Corticotropin-Releasing Factor Systems in Adult Male Rat Offspring." *Neuropsychopharmacology* 30 (12): 2192–2204.

Pohorecky, L. A. 1991. "Stress and Alcohol Interaction: An Update of Human Research." *Alcoholism: Clinical and Experimental Research* 15:438–459.

Prescott, C. A., and K. S. Kendler. 1999. "Genetic and Environmental Contributions to Alcohol Abuse and Dependence in a Population-Based Sample of Male Twins." *American Journal of Psychiatry* 156:34–40.

Pruessner, J. C., F. Champagne, M. J. Meaney, and A. Dagher. 2004. "Dopamine Release in Response to a Psychological Stress in Humans and Its Relationship to Early Life Maternal Care: A Positron Emission Tomography Study Using [11C]Raclopride." *Journal of Neuroscience* 24 (11): 2825–2831.

Pryce, C. R., and J. Feldon. 2003. "Long-Term Neurobehavioural Impact of the Postnatal Environment in Rats: Manipulations, Effects and Mediating Mechanisms." *Neuroscience and Biobehavioral Reviews* 27:57–71.

Randolph, W. M., C. Stroup-Benham, S. A. Black, and K. S. Markides. 1998. "Alcohol Use among Cuban-Americans, Mexican-Americans, and Puerto Ricans." *Alcohol Research and Health* 22 (4): 265–269.

Regier, D. A., M. E. Farmer, D. S. Rae, B. Z. Locke, S. J. Keith, L. L. Judd, and F. K. Goodwin. 1990. "Comorbidity of Mental Disorders with Alcohol and Other Drug Abuse: Results from the Epidemiologic Catchment Area (ECA) Study." *Journal of the American Medical Association* 264 (19): 2511–2518.

Research Society on Alcoholism (RSA). 2009. "Impact of Alcoholism and Alcohol Induced Disease on America." Accessed Aug. 2, 2010. www.rsoa.org /2009-01-12RSAWhitePaper.pdf.

SAMHSA (Substance Abuse and Mental Health Services Administration). 1999. "National Household Survey on Drug Abuse, 1999." Accessed Sept. 13, 2010. www.samhsa.gov/oas/NHSDA/1999.

SAMHSA (Substance Abuse and Mental Health Services Administration). 2008a. "Alcohol Use." Accessed Sept. 13, 2010. www.oas.samhsa.gov/alcohol.cfm.

SAMHSA (Substance Abuse and Mental Health Services Administration). 2008b. "Underage Alcohol Use: Findings from the 2002–2006 National Surveys on Drug Use and Health." Accessed Sept. 13, 2010. http://oas.samhsa.gov/underage2k8/toc.htm.

Schuck, A. M., and C. S. Widom. 2001. "Childhood Victimization and Alcohol Symptoms in Females: Causal Inferences and Hypothesized Mediators." *Child Abuse and Neglect* 25:1069–1092.

Schuessler, G. 2004. "Neurobiology and Psychotherapy." *Zeitschrift fur Psychosomatische Medizin und Psychotherapie* 50 (4): 406–429.

Seal, K. H., D. Bertenthal, C. R. Miner, S. Sen, and C. Marmar. 2007. "Bringing the War Back Home: Mental Health Disorders among 103,788 U.S. Veterans Returning from Iraq and Afghanistan Seen at Department of Veterans Affairs Facilities." *Archives of Internal Medicine* 167:476–482.

Sher, K. J., B. D. Bartholow, and S. Nanda. 2001. "Short- and Long-Term Effects of Fraternity and Sorority Membership on Heavy Drinking: A Social Norms Perspective." *Psychology of Addictive Behaviors* 15 (1): 42–51.

Sinha, R. "Chronic Stress, Drug Use, and Vulnerability to Addiction." 2008. *Annals of the New York Academy of Sciences* 1141:105–130.

Smith, B. H., B. S. G. Molina, and W. E. Pelham, Jr. 2002. "The Clinically Meaningful Link Between Alcohol Use and Attention Deficit Hyperactivity Disorder." *Alcohol Research and Health* 26:122–130.

Smith, G. T., M. S. Goldman, P. E. Greenbaum, and B. B. Christiansen. 1995. "Expectancy for Social Facilitation from Drinking: The Divergent Paths of High-Expectancy and Low-Expectancy Adolescents." *Journal of Abnormal Psychology* 104:32–40.

Sonne, S. C., and K. T. Brady. 2002. "Bipolar Disorder and Alcoholism." *Alcohol Research and Health* 26:103–108.

Stevens, S. E., E. J. S. Sonuga–Barke, J. M. Kreppner, C. Beckett, J. Castle, E. Colvert, C. Groothues, A. Hawkins, and M. Rutter. 2008. "Inattention/Overactivity Following Early Severe Institutional Deprivation: Presentation and Associations in Early Adolescence." *Journal of Abnormal Child Psychology* 36 (3): 385–398.

Straus, R., and S. D. Bacon. 1953. *Drinking in College.* New Haven, CT: Yale Univ. Press. In O'Malley and Johnston 2002.

Suwaki, H., H. Kalant, S. Higuchi, J. C. Crabbe, S. Ohkuma, M. Katsura, M. Yoshimura, R. C. Stewart, T. K. Li, and F. Weiss. 2001. "Recent Research on Alcohol Tolerance and Dependence." *Alcoholism: Clinical and Experimental Research* 25 (5 Suppl ISBRA): 189S–196S.

Tsigos, C., and G. P. Chrousos. 1995. "The Neuroendocrinology of the Stress Response." In Hunt and Zakhari 1995.

U.S. Department of Defense (DoD). 2005. "2005 Survey of Health Related Behaviors among Active Duty Military Personnel." Accessed Sept. 14, 2010. www.defense .gov/Releases/Release.aspx?ReleaseID=10395.

Walter, M., G. Dammann, G. A. Wiesbeck, and B. F. Klapp. 2005. "Psychosocial Stress and Alcohol Consumption: Interrelations, Consequences, and Interventions." *Fortschritte der Neurologie—Psychiatrie* 73:517–525.

Wechsler, H., J. E. Lee, M. Kuo, M. Seibring, T. F. Nelson, and H. Lee. 2002. "Trends in College Binge Drinking During a Period of Increased Prevention Efforts. Findings from Four Harvard School of Public Health College Alcohol Study Surveys: 1993–2001." *Journal of American College Health* 50 (5): 203–217.

WHO (World Health Organization). 2004. *Global Status Report on Alcohol 2004.* Geneva, Switzerland: World Health Organization.

WHO (World Health Organization). 2008. "Core Health Indicators: Per Capita Recorded Alcohol Consumption (Litres of Pure Alcohol) among Adults (>=15 Years)." Accessed Sept. 15, 2011. http://apps.who.int/whosis/database /core/core_select_process.cfm?strISO3_select=ALL&strIndicator_select =AlcoholConsumption&intYear_select=latest&language=english.

Wilk, J. E., P. D. Bliese, P. Y. Kim, J. L. Thomas, D. McGurk, and C. W. Hoge. 2010. "Relationship of Combat Experiences to Alcohol Misuse among U.S. Soldiers Returning from the Iraq War." *Drug and Alcohol Dependence* 108 (1–2): 115–121.

Yager, T., R. Laufer, and M. Gallops. 1984. "Some Problems Associated with War Experience in Men of the Vietnam Generation." *Archives of General Psychiatry* 41 (4): 327–333.

Zucker, R. A., C. R. Bingham, J. E. Schulenberg, J. E. Donovan, K. E. Leonard, M. A. Schuckit, and K. J. Sher. 1996. "Longitudinal Research on Alcohol Problems: The Flow of Risk, Problems and Disorder Over Time." *Alcoholism: Clinical and Experimental Research* 20 (Nov. Suppl.): 93A–95A.

## Chapter 3

Abbey, A., T. Zawacki, P. O. Buck, A. M. Clinton, and P. McAuslan. 2001. "Alcohol and Sexual Assault." *Alcohol Research and Health* 25 (1): 43–51.

Adams, W. L., Z. Yuan, J. J. Barboriak, and A. A. Rimm. 1993. "Alcohol-Related Hospitalizations of Elderly People." *Journal of the American Medical Association* 270 (10): 1222–1225.

Ames, G., C. Schmidt, L. Klee, and R. Saltz. 1996. "Combining Methods to Identify New Measures of Women's Drinking Problems Part I: The Ethnographic Stage." *Addiction* 91:829–844.

Anda, R. F., D. F. Williamson, and P. L. Remington. 1988. "Alcohol and Fatal Injuries among U.S. Adults." *Journal of the American Medical Association* 260 (17): 2529–2532.

Bagnardi, V., M. Blangiardo, C. La Vecchia, and G. Corrao. 2001. "Alcohol Consumption and the Risk of Cancer: A Meta-analysis." *Alcohol Research and Health* 25 (4): 263–270.

Beitel, G. A., M. C. Sharp, and W. D. Glauz. 2000. "Probability of Arrest while Driving Under the Influence of Alcohol." *Injury Prevention* 6 (2): 158–161.

Berman, S. M., S. C. Whipple, R. J. Fitch, and E. P. Noble. 1993. "P3 in Young Boys as a Predictor of Adolescent Substance Use." *Alcohol* 10:69–76.

Borges, G., C. J. Cherpitel, M. E. Medina-Mora, L. Mondragón, and L. Casanova. 1998. "Alcohol Consumption in Emergency Room Patients and the General Population: A Population-Based Study." *Alcoholism: Clinical and Experimental Research* 22 (9): 1986–1991.

Borkenstein, R. F., R. F. Crowther, R. P. Shumate, W. B. Ziel, and R. Zylman. 1964. *The Role of the Drinking Driver in Traffic Accidents.* Bloomington, IN: Department of Police Administration, Indiana University.

Brennan, P. L., R. H. Moos, and K. M. Kelly. 1994. "Spouses of Late-Life Problem Drinkers: Functioning, Coping Responses, and Family Contexts." *Journal of Family Psychology* 8:447–457.

Brinkmann, B., J. Beike, H. Köhler, A. Heinecke, and T. Bajanowski. 2002. "Incidence of Alcohol Dependence among Drunken Drivers." *Drug and Alcohol Dependence* 66 (1): 7–10.

Brismar, B., and B. Bergman. 1998. "The Significance of Alcohol for Violence and Accidents." *Alcoholism: Clinical and Experimental Research* 22 (Suppl 7): 299S–306S.

Butterworth, R. F. 2003. "Hepatic Encephalopathy—A Serious Complication of Alcoholic Liver Disease." *Alcohol Research and Health* 27:143–146.

Caspi, A., T. E. Moffitt, D. L. Newman, and P. A. Silva. 1996. "Behavioral Observations at Age 3 Years Predict Adult Psychiatric Disorders: Longitudinal Evidence from a Birth Cohort." *Archives of General Psychiatry* 53:1033–1039.

CDC (Centers for Disease Control and Prevention). 2005. "Annual Smoking—Attributable Mortality, Years of Potential Life Lost, and Productivity Losses—United States, 1997–2001." *Morbidity and Mortality Weekly Report* 54 (25): 625–628.

Chang, I., and S. C. Lapham. 1996. "Validity of Self-Reported Criminal Offenses and Traffic Violations in Screening of Driving-while-Intoxicated Offenders." *Alcohol and Alcoholism* 31 (6): 583–590.

Chen, W.-J. A., S. E. Maier, S. E. Parnell, and J. R. West. 2003. "Alcohol and the Developing Brain: Neuroanatomical Studies." *Alcohol Research and Health* 27 (2): 174–180.

Cherpitel, C. J. 1993. "Alcohol and Injuries: A Review of International Emergency Room Studies." *Addiction* 88:923–937.

Cherpitel, C. J. 1995. "Alcohol and Casualties: Comparison of County-Wide Emergency Room Data with the County General Population." *Addiction* 90 (3): 343–350.

Cherpitel, C. J. 2007. "Alcohol and Injuries: A Review of International Emergency Room Studies Since 1995." *Drug and Alcohol Review* 26 (2): 201–214.

Cherpitel, C. J., G. Borges, N. Giesbrecht, D. Hungerford, M. Peden, V. Poznyak, R. Room, and T. Tockwell, eds. 2009. *Alcohol and Injuries: Emergency Department Studies in an International Perspective.* Geneva, Switzerland: World Health Organization.

Cherpitel, C. J., G. L. G. Borges, and H. C. Wilcox. 2004. "Acute Alcohol Use and Suicidal Behavior: A Review of the Literature." *Alcoholism: Clinical and Experimental Research* 28 (5 Suppl.): 18S–28S.

Cherpitel, C. J., A. R. Meyers, and M. W. Perrine. 1998. "Alcohol Consumption, Sensation Seeking and Ski Injury: A Case-Control Study." *Journal of Studies on Alcohol* 59 (2): 216–221.

Children of Alcoholics Foundation. 1990. *Children of Alcoholics in the Medical System: Hidden Problems, Hidden Costs.* New York: Children of Alcoholics Foundation.

Collins, J. J., and P. M. Messerschmidt. 1993. "Epidemiology of Alcohol-Related Violence." *Alcohol Health and Research World* 17 (2): 93–100.

Cook, C. C., and A. D. Thomson. 1997. "B-complex Vitamins in the Prophylaxis and Treatment of Wernicke-Korsakoff Syndrome." *British Journal of Hospital Medicine* 57 (9): 461–465.

Crancer, A. April 1986. "The Myth of the Social Drinker–DUI Driver." Presented at the meeting of the American Medical Society on Alcoholism and Other Drug Dependencies (AMSAODD) and the Research Society on Alcoholism (RSA). San Francisco, CA.

Dahl, R. E. 2004. "Adolescent Brain Development: A Period of Vulnerabilities and Opportunities." Keynote address. *Annals of the New York Academy of Sciences* 1021:1–22.

Dahl, R., and A. Hariri. 2004. "Frontiers of Research on Adolescent Decision Making—Contributions from the Biological, Behavioral, and Social Sciences." Background paper prepared for the Planning Meeting on Adolescent Decision Making and Positive Youth Development: Applying Research to Youth Programs and Prevention Strategies, April 2004. National Research Council/Institute of Medicine Board on Children, Youth, and Families, Committee on Adolescent Health and Development.

De Bellis, M. D., D. B. Clark, S. R. Beers, P. H. Soloff, A. M. Boring, J. Hall, A. Kersch, and M. S. Keshavan. 2000. "Hippocampal Volume in Adolescent-Onset Alcohol Use Disorders." *American Journal of Psychiatry* 157 (5): 737–744.

Dees, W. L., V. K. Srivastava, and J. K. Hiney. 2001. "Alcohol and Female Puberty: The Role of Intraovarian Systems." *Alcohol Research and Health* 25: 271–276.

Emanuele, M. A., and N. Emanuele. 2001. "Alcohol and the Male Reproductive System." *Alcohol Research and Health* 25:282–288.

Erikkson, C. J. P., T. Fukunaga, T. Sarkola, H. Lindholm, and L. Ahola. 1996. "Estrogen-Related Acetaldehyde Elevation in Women During Alcohol Intoxication." *Alcoholism: Clinical and Experimental Research* 20:1192–1195.

Fazzone, P. A., J. K. Holton, and B. G. Reed. 1997. *Substance Abuse Treatment and Domestic Violence.* Treatment Improvement Protocol (TIP) Series 25. Rockville, MD: Substance Abuse and Mental Health Services Administration, Center for Substance Abuse Treatment.

Frintner, M. P., and L. Rubinson. 1993. "Acquaintance Rape: The Influence of Alcohol, Fraternity Membership, and Sports Team Membership." *Journal of Sex Education and Therapy* 19:272–284.

Gavaler, J. S. 1982. "Sex-Related Differences in Ethanol-Induced Liver Disease: Artificial or Real?" *Alcoholism: Clinical and Experimental Research* 6 (2): 186–196.

Gentilello, L. M., B. E. Ebel, T. M. Wickizer, D. S. Salkever, and F. P. Rivara. 2005. "Alcohol Interventions for Trauma Patients Treated in Emergency Departments and Hospitals: A Cost Benefit Analysis." *Annals of Surgery* 241 (4): 541–550.

Giesbrecht, N., R. González, M. Grant, E. Österberg, R. Room, I. Rootman, and L. Towle, eds. 1989. *Drinking and Casualties: Accidents, Poisonings and Violence in an International Perspective.* Vol. 1. London: Croom Helm, 21–66.

Gil-Rivas, V., R. Fiorentine, and M. D. Anglin. 1996. "Sexual Abuse, Physical Abuse, and Post-traumatic Stress Disorder among Women Participating in Outpatient Drug Abuse Treatment." *Journal of Psychoactive Drugs* 28:95–102.

Gmel, G., A. Bissery, R. Gammeter, J.-C. Givel, J.-M. Clames, B. Yersin, and J.-B. Daeppen. 2006. "Alcohol-Attributable Injuries in Admissions to a Swiss Emergency Room: An Analysis of the Link between Volume of Drinking, Drinking Patterns, and Preattendance Drinking." *Alcoholism: Clinical and Experimental Research* 30 (3): 501–509.

Gmel, G., S. Klingemann, R. Müller, and D. Brenner. 2001. "Revising the Preventive Paradox: The Swiss Case." *Addiction* 96 (2): 273–284.

Gmel, G., and J. Rehm. 2003. "Harmful Alcohol Use." *Alcohol Research and Health* 27 (1): 52–62.

Gordis, E. 2001. "Alcohol and Violence: Introduction." *Alcohol Research and Health* 25:1.

Grant, B. F. 2000. "Estimates of U.S. Children Exposed to Alcohol Abuse and Dependence in the Family." *American Journal of Public Health* 90 (1): 112–116.

Greenblatt, J. C. 2000. "Patterns of Alcohol Use Among Adolescents and Associations with Emotional and Behavioral Problems." Accessed August 27, 2010. www .oas.samhsa.gov/NHSDA/TeenAlc/teenalc.pdf.

Greenfield, L. R. 1998. "Alcohol and Crime: An Analysis of National Data on the Prevalence of Alcohol Involvement in Crime." Prepared for the Assistant Attorney General's National Symposium on Alcohol Abuse and Crime. Bureau of Justice Statistics, Washington, DC.

Gruenewald, P. J., P. R. Mitchell, and A. J. Treno. 1996. "Drinking and Driving: Drinking Patterns." *Addiction* 91 (11): 1637–1649.

Haberman, P. W., and M. M. Baden. 1974. "Alcoholism and Violent Death." *Quarterly Journal of Studies on Alcohol* 35 (1): 221–231.

Harburg, E., R. Gunn, L. Gleiberman, W. DiFranceisco, and A. Schork. 1993. "Psychosocial Factors, Alcohol Use, and Hangover Signs among Social Drinkers: A Reappraisal." *Journal of Clinical Epidemiology* 46 (5): 413–422.

Harwood, H. 2000. *Updating Estimates of the Economic Costs of Alcohol Abuse in the United States: Estimates, Update Methods, and Data.* Report prepared by The Lewin Group for the National Institute on Alcohol Abuse and Alcoholism.

Hazelden. Sept. 1998. "The Treatment Investment: Stemming the Cost of Addiction." *Research Update.* Center City, MN: Hazelden.

Hazelden. Jan. 1999. "Women and Substance Abuse." *Research Update.* Center City, MN: Hazelden.

Hazelden. Nov. 2000. "Alcohol Use and Domestic Violence." *Research Update.* Center City, MN: Hazelden.

Hazelden. Dec. 2000. "Substance Abuse and Crime." *Research Update.* Center City, MN: Hazelden.

Hazelden. Jan. 2002. "Youth Violence and Alcohol/Drug Abuse." *Research Update.* Center City, MN: Hazelden.

Hazelden. Mar. 2002. "Treatment in Criminal Justice Systems." *Research Update.* Center City, MN: Hazelden.

Hazelden. Sept. 2002. "Workplace Recovery Benefits Survey." *Research Update.* Center City, MN: Hazelden.

Hell, D., P. Six, and R. Salkeld. 1976. "Vitamin B1 Deficiency in Chronic Alcoholics and Its Clinical Correlation." *Schweiz Med Wochenschr* 106 (43): 1466–1470.

Hill, S. Y. 2004. "Trajectories of Alcohol Use and Electrophysiological and Morphological Indices of Brain Development: Distinguishing Causes from Consequences." *Annals of the New York Academy of Sciences* 1021:245–259. PMID: 15251894.

Hingson, R., T. Heeren, M. Winter, and H. Wechsler. 2005. "Magnitude of Alcohol-Related Mortality and Morbidity among U.S. College Students Ages 18–24: Changes from 1998 to 2001." *Annual Review of Public Health* 26:259–279.

Hingson, R., and J. Howland. 1993. "Alcohol and Non-traffic Unintended Injuries." *Addiction* 88:887–883.

Holder, H. D., and G. Edwards, eds. 1995. *Alcohol and Public Policy: Evidence and Issues.* New York, NY: Oxford University Press, 114–142.

Honkanen, R., L. Ertama, P. Kuosmanen, M. Linnoila, A. Alha, and T. Visuri. 1983. "The Role of Alcohol in Accidental Falls." *Journal of Studies on Alcohol* 44 (2): 231–245.

Howland, J., and R. Hingson. 1990. "Alcohol Use and Aquatic Activities in Massachusetts." *Journal of the American Medical Association* 264 (1): 19–20.

Howland, J., T. Mangione, R. Hingson, G. Smith, and N. Bell. 1995. "Alcohol as a Risk Factor for Drowning and Other Aquatic Injuries." In Watson 1995.

Hurst, P. M. 1973. "Epidemiological Aspects of Alcohol in Driver Crashes and Citations." *Journal of Safety Research* 5 (3): 130–148.

Hurst, P. M., D. Harte, and W. J. Frith. 1994. "The Grand Rapids DIP Revisited." *Accident Analysis and Prevention* 26 (5): 647–654.

Institute for Health Policy. 1993. *Substance Abuse: The Nation's Number One Health Problem: Key Indicators for Policy.* Princeton, New Jersey: Brandeis University for The Robert Wood Johnson Foundation.

Kim, D.-J., W. Kim, S.-J. Yoon, B.-M. Choi, J.-S. Kim, H. J. Go, Y.-K. Kim, and J. Jeong. 2003. "Effects of Alcohol Hangover on Cytokine Production in Healthy Subjects." *Alcohol* 31 (3): 167–170.

Klatsky, A. L., G. D. Friedman, and A. B. Siegelaub. 1981. "Alcohol and Mortality: A Ten Year Kaiser Permanent Experience." *Annals of Internal Medicine* 95 (2): 139–145.

Kochis, C. L. 1997. "Alcohol Expectancies and Personality Characteristics of Driving while Intoxicated Offenders as Compared to Other Legal Offenders: A Test of Problem Behavior Theory." *Dissertation Abstracts International* 57 (12): 5050–A.

Kodituwakku, P. W., W. Kalberg, and P. A. May. 2001. "The Effects of Prenatal Alcohol Exposure on Executive Functioning." *Alcohol Research and Health* 25 (3): 192–198.

Kovacs, E. J., and KAN Messingham. 2002. "Influence of Alcohol and Gender on Immune Response." *Alcohol Research and Health* 26 (4): 257–263.

Kramer, A. L. 1986. "Sentencing the Drunk Driver: A Call for Change." *Alcoholism Treatment Quarterly* 3 (2): 25–35.

Kyriacou, D. N., D. Anglin, E. Taliaferro, S. Stone, T. Tubb, J. Linden, R. Muelleman, E. Barton, and J. F. Kraus. 1999. "Risk Factors for Injury to Women from Domestic Violence." *New England Journal of Medicine* 341 (25): 1892–1898.

LaBrie, J. W., J. Cail, J. F. Hummer, A. Lac, and C. Neighbors. 2009. "What Men Want: The Role of Reflective Opposite-Sex Normative Preferences in Alcohol Use among College Women." *Psychology of Addictive Behaviors* 23 (1): 157–162.

Lapham, S. C., E. Smith, J. C'de Baca, I. Chang, B. J. Skipper, G. Baum, and W. C. Hunt. 2001. "Prevalence of Psychiatric Disorders among Persons Convicted of Driving while Impaired." *Archives of General Psychiatry* 58 (10): 943–949.

Larkby, C., and N. Day. 1997. "The Effects of Prenatal Alcohol Exposure." *Alcohol Research and Health* 21:192–199.

Leonard, K. E., and B. M. Quigley. 1999. "Drinking and Marital Aggression in Newlyweds: An Event-Based Analysis of Drinking and the Occurrence of Husband Marital Aggression." *Journal of Studies on Alcohol* 60:537–545.

Li, G., and S. P. Baker. 1994. "Alcohol in Fatally Injured Bicyclists." *Accident Analysis and Prevention* 26 (4): 543–548.

Li, G., S. P. Baker, S. Sterling, J. E. Smialek, P. C. Dischinger, and C. A. Soderstrom. 1996. "A Comparative Analysis of Alcohol in Fatal and Nonfatal Bicycling Injuries." *Alcoholism: Clinical and Experimental Research* 20 (9): 1553–1559.

Li, G., P. M. Keyl, G. S. Smith, and S. P. Baker. 1997. "Alcohol and Injury Severity: Reappraisal of the Continuing Controversy." *Journal of Trauma* 42:562–569.

Lieber, C. S. 2001. "Alcohol and Hepatitis C." *Alcohol Research and Health* 25:245–255.

Lieber, C. S. 2003. "Relationships between Nutrition, Alcohol Use, and Liver Disease." *Alcohol Research and Health* 27:220–232.

Luke, L. I., and M. E. Levy. 1982. "Exposure-Related Hypothermia Deaths—District of Columbia 1972–1982." *Morbidity and Mortality Weekly Report* 31 (50): 669–671.

Magura, M., and E. Shapiro. 1988. "Alcohol Consumption and Divorce: Which Causes Which?" *Journal of Divorce* 12:127–136.

Maier, S. E., and J. R. West. 2001. "Drinking Patterns and Alcohol-Related Birth Defects." *Alcohol Research and Health* 25 (3): 168–174.

Mangione, T. W., J. Howland, and M. Lee. 1998. *New Perspectives for Worksite Alcohol Strategies: Results from a Corporate Drinking Study.* Boston, MA: JSI Research and Training Institute.

Mann, K., A. Batra, A. Gunthner, and G. Schroth. 1992. "Do Women Develop Alcoholic Brain Damage More Readily Than Men?" *Alcoholism: Clinical and Experimental Research* 16:1052–1056.

Mann, R. E., R. G. Smart, and R. Govoni. 2003. "The Epidemiology of Alcoholic Liver Disease." *Alcohol Research and Health* 27 (3): 209–219.

Martin, P. R., C. K. Singleton, and S. Hiller-Sturmhöfel. 2003. "The Role of Thiamine Deficiency in Alcoholic Brain Disease." *Alcohol Research and Health* 27:134–143.

Masten, A. S., G. I. Roisman, J. D. Long, K. B. Burt, J. Obradović, J. R. Riley, K. Boelcke-Stennes, and A. Tellegen. 2005. "Developmental Cascades: Linking Academic Achievement and Externalizing and Internalizing Symptoms Over 20 Years." *Developmental Psychology* 41 (5): 733–746.

Mattson, S. N., A. M. Schoenfeld, and E. P. Riley. 2001. "Teratogenic Effects of Alcohol on Brain and Behavior." *Alcohol Research and Health* 25 (3): 185–191.

McCrady, B. S., and W. Hay. 1987. "Coping with Problem Drinking in the Family." In Orford 1987, 86–116.

McKinney, A., and K. Coyle. 2004. "Next Day Effects of a Normal Night's Drinking on Memory and Psychomotor Performance." *Alcohol and Alcoholism* 39 (6): 509–513.

Miller, J. W., T. S. Naimi, R. D. Brewer, and S. E. Jones. 2007. "Binge Drinking and Associated Health Risk Behaviors Among High School Students." *Pediatrics* 119 (1): 76–85.

Moeller, F. G., and D. M. Dougherty. 2001. "Antisocial Personality Disorder, Alcohol, and Aggression." *Alcohol Research and Health* 25 (1): 5–11.

Mokdad, A. H., J. S. Marks, D. F. Stroup, and J. L. Gerberding. 2004. "Actual Causes of Death in the United States, 2000." *Journal of the American Medical Association (JAMA)* 291:1238–1245.

Mukamal, K. J., and E. B. Rimm. 2001. "Alcohol's Effects on the Risk for Coronary Heart Disease." *Alcohol Research and Health* 25:255–263.

Mumola, C. J. 1999. *Substance Abuse and Treatment, State and Federal Prisoners, 1997.* NCJ 172871. Washington, DC: U.S. Department of Justice, Bureau of Justice Statistics.

National Highway Traffic Safety Administration (NHTSA), U.S. Department of Transportation. 1997. *U.S. Department of Transportation Fatal Accident Reporting System.* Washington, DC: NHTSA.

NIAAA (National Institute on Alcohol Abuse and Alcoholism). 1990. *Seventh Special Report to the U.S. Congress on Alcohol and Health from the Secretary of Health and Human Services.* DHS Publication No. 90–1656. Rockville, MD: NIAAA.

NIAAA (National Institute on Alcohol Abuse and Alcoholism). 2008. *Alcohol: A Women's Health Issue.* NIH Publication No. 03–4956. Rockville, MD: NIAAA.

O'Farrell, T. J., V. Van Hutton, and C. M. Murphy. 1999. "Domestic Violence Before and After Alcoholism Treatment: A Two-Year Longitudinal Study." *Journal of Studies on Alcohol* 60:317–321.

ONDCP (Office of National Drug Control Policy). 2004. *The Economic Costs of Drug Abuse in the United States: 1992–2002.* Washington, DC: Executive Office of the President (Publication No. 207303).

Orford, J., ed. 1987. *Coping with Disorder in the Family.* London: Croom and Helm.

Oscar-Berman, M., and K. Marinkovic. 2003. "Alcoholism and the Brain: An Overview." *Alcohol Research and Health* 27:125–134.

Parks, K. A., and W. Fals-Stewart. 2004. "The Temporal Relationship between College Women's Alcohol Consumption and Victimization Experiences." *Alcoholism: Clinical and Experimental Research* 28:625–629.

Perrine, M. W., R. C. Peck, and J. C. Fell. 1989. "Epidemiologic Perspectives on Drunk Driving." In *Surgeon General's Workshop on Drunk Driving: Background Papers.* Washington DC: U.S. Department of Health and Human Services, 35–76.

Pettinati, H. M., J. D. Pierce, A. L. Wolf, M. R. Rukstalis, and C. P. O'Brien. 1997. "Gender Differences in Comorbidly Depressed Alcohol Dependent Outpatients." *Alcoholism: Clinical and Experimental Research* 21:1742–1746.

Quigley, B. M., and K. E. Leonard. 2000. "Alcohol and the Continuation of Early Marital Aggression." *Alcoholism: Clinical and Experimental Research* 24 (7): 1003–1010.

Regier, D. A., M. E. Farmer, D. S. Rae, B. Z. Locke, S. J. Keith, L. L. Judd, and F. K. Goodwin. 1990. "Comorbidity of Mental Disorders with Alcohol and Other Drug Abuse: Results from the Epidemiologic Catchment Area (ECA) Study." *Journal of the American Medical Association* 264:2511–2518.

Rehm, J., M. J. Ashley, R. Room, E. Single, S. Bondy, R. Ferrence, and N. Giesbrecht. 1996. "On the Emerging Paradigm of Drinking Patterns and Their Social and Health Consequences." *Addiction* 91 (11): 1615–1621.

Roberts, L. J., C. F. Roberts, and K. E. Leonard. 1999. "Alcohol, Drugs, and Interpersonal Violence." In Van Hasselt and Hersen 1999.

Roizen, J. 1982. "Estimating Alcohol Involvement in Serious Events: Alcohol Consumption and Related Problems." *Alcohol and Health* Monograph 1, DHHS Publication (ADM) 82-1190. Bethesda, MD: National Institute on Alcohol Abuse and Alcoholism, 179–219.

Roizen, J. 1989. "Alcohol and Trauma." In Giesbrecht et al. 1989.

Romelsjö, A. 1995. "Alcohol Consumption and Unintentional Injury, Suicide, Violence, Work Performance, and Inter-generational Effects." In Holder and Edwards 1995.

Rose, M. E., and J. E. Grant. 2010. "Alcohol-Induced Blackout: Phenomenology, Biological Basis, and Gender Differences." *Journal of Addiction Medicine* 4:61–73.

Rosenbloom, M., E. V. Sullivan, and A. Pfefferbaum. 2003. "Using Magnetic Resonance Imaging and Diffusion Tensor Imaging to Assess Brain Damage in Alcoholics." *Alcohol Research and Health* 27:146–153.

Roy, A. 1993. "Risk Factors for Suicide among Adult Alcoholics." *Alcohol Health and Research World* 17 (2): 133–136.

RSA (Research Society on Alcoholism). 2009. "Impact of Alcoholism and Alcohol Induced Disease on America." Accessed Sept. 22, 2010. www.rsoa.org/2009-01-12 RSAWhitePaper.pdf.

Ryan, L. C., and S. R. Mohler. 1979. "Current Role of Alcohol as a Factor in Civil Aircraft Accidents." *Aviation, Space, and Environmental Medicine* 50 (3): 275–279.

SAMHSA (Substance Abuse and Mental Health Services Administration). 1998. *The Costs and Effects of Parity for Substance Abuse Insurance Benefits.* Rockville, MD: SAMHSA.

SAMHSA (Substance Abuse and Mental Health Services Administration). 2004. "Substance Use: Dependence or Abuse among Full-Time Workers." *The National Household Survey on Drug Abuse.* Rockville, MD: SAMHSA.

Schuckit, M. A., R. M. Anthenelli, K. K. Bucholz, V. M. Hesselbrock, and J. Tipp. 1995. "The Time Course of Development of Alcohol-Related Problems in Men and Women." *Journal of Studies on Alcohol* 56:218–225.

Sinha, R., J. Robinson, K. Merikangas, G. T. Wilson, J. Rodin, and S. O'Malley. 1996. "Eating Pathology among Women with Alcoholism or Anxiety Disorders." *Alcoholism: Clinical and Experimental Research* 20:1184–1191.

Smart, R., F. Glasser, and Y. Israel, eds. 1983. *Research Advances in Alcohol Drug Problems.* Vol. 7. New York: Plenum Press, 299–342.

Smith, G. S., and J. F. Kraus. 1988. "Alcohol and Residential, Recreational, and Occupational Injuries: A Review of the Epidemiologic Evidence." *Annual Review of Public Health* 9:99–121.

Smith-Warner, S. A., D. Spiegelman, S. S. Yaun, P. A. van den Brandt, A. R. Folsom, A. Goldbohm, S. Graham, L. Holmberg, G. R. Howe, J. R. Marshall, A. B. Miller, J. D. Potter, F. E. Speizer, W. C. Willet, A. Wolk, and D. J. Hunter. 1998. "Alcohol and Breast Cancer in Women: A Pooled Analysis of Cohort Studies." *Journal of the American Medical Association* 279 (7): 535–540.

Soderstrom, C. A., M. F. Ballesteros, P. C. Dischinger, T. J. Kerns, R. D. Flint, and G. S. Smith. 2001. "Alcohol/Drug Abuse, Driving Convictions, and Risk-Taking Dispositions among Trauma Center Patients." *Accident Analysis and Prevention* 33 (6): 771–782.

Stallones, L., and J. F. Kraus. 1993. "The Occurrence and Epidemiologic Features of Alcohol-Related Occupational Injuries." *Addiction* 88:945–951.

Stickel, F., B. Hoehn, D. Shuppan, and H. K. Seitz. 2003. "Review Article: Nutritional Therapy in Alcoholic Liver Disease." *Alimentary Pharmacology and Therapeutics* 18 (4): 357–373.

Tapert, S. F., and A. D. Schweinsburg. 2005. "The Human Adolescent Brain and Alcohol Use Disorders." *Recent Developments in Alcoholism* 17:177–189.

Taxman, F. S., and A. Piquero. 1998. "On Preventing Drunk Driving Recidivism: An Examination of Rehabilitation and Punishment Approaches." *Journal of Criminal Justice* 26 (2): 129–143.

Thavorncharoensap, M., Y. Teerawattananon, J. Yothasamut, C. Lertpitakpong, and U. Chaikledkaew. 2009. "The Economic Impact of Alcohol Consumption: A Systematic Review." *Substance Abuse Treatment, Prevention, and Policy* 4:20:1–11.

Treno, A. J., and H. D. Holder. 1997. "Measurement of Alcohol-Involved Injury in Community Prevention: The Search for a Surrogate III." *Alcoholism: Clinical and Experimental Research* 21 (9): 1695–1703.

Urbano-Marquez, A., R. Estruch, J. Fernandez-Sola, J. Micolas, J. Carlos Pare, and E. Rubin. 1995. "The Greater Risk of Alcoholic Cardiomyopathy and Myopathy in Women Compared with Men." *Journal of the American Medical Association* 274:149–154.

Urschel, J. D. 1990. "Frostbite: Predisposing Factors and Predictors of Poor Outcome." *Journal of Trauma* 30 (3): 340–342.

USDHHS (U.S. Department of Health and Human Services). 2007. *The Surgeon General's Call to Action To Prevent and Reduce Underage Drinking.* Rockville, MD: USDHHS, Office of the Surgeon General.

Van Hasselt, V. B., and M. Hersen, eds. 1999. *Handbook of Psychological Approaches with Violent Criminal Offenders: Contemporary Strategies and Issues.* New York: Plenum Press, 493–519.

Verster, J. C., D. van Duin, E. R. Volkerts, A. H. Schreuder, and M. N. Verbaten. 2003. "Alcohol Hangover Effects on Memory Functioning and Vigilance Performance after an Evening of Binge Drinking." *Neuropsychopharmacology* 28 (4): 740–746. Epub 2002 Oct 8.

Vingilis, E. 1983. "Drinking Drivers and Alcoholics: Are They from the Same Population?" In Smart, Glasser, and Israel 1983.

Voas, R. B., and D. A. Fisher. 2001. "Court Procedures for Handling Intoxicated Drivers." *Alcohol Research and Health* 25 (1): 32–42.

Voas, R. B., and J. Hause. 1987. "Deterring the Drinking Driver: The Stockton Experience." *Accident Analysis and Prevention* 19 (2): 81–90.

Vyrostek, S. B., J. L. Annest, and G. W. Ryan. 2004. "Surveillance for Fatal and Nonfatal Injuries—United States, 2001." *Morbidity and Mortality Weekly Report* 53 (SS–7): 1–59.

Waller, J. 1988. "Methodological Issues in Hospital-Based Injury Research." *Journal of Trauma* 28:1632–1636.

Walters, E. E., and K. S. Kendler. 1995. "Anorexia Nervosa and Anorexic-Like Syndromes in a Population-Based Female Twin Sample." *American Journal of Psychiatry* 152:64–71.

Watson, R. R., ed. 1995. "Alcohol, Cocaine, and Accidents." *Drug and Alcohol Abuse Reviews.* Vol. 7. Totowa, NJ: Humana Press Inc., 85–104.

Welsh, D. M., ed. 1994. "Alcohol-Related Birth Defects." *Alcohol, Health, and Research World* 18 (1).

White, W., and D. Gasperin. 2007. "The 'Hard Core Drinking Driver': Identification, Treatment and Community Management." *Alcoholism Treatment Quarterly* 25 (3): 113–132.

Wiese, J. G., M. G. Shlipak, and W. S. Browner. 2000. "The Alcohol Hangover." *Annals of Internal Medicine* 132 (11): 897–902.

Wilsnack, S. C., N. D. Vogeltanz, A. D. Klassen, and T. R. Harris. 1997. "Childhood Sexual Abuse and Women's Substance Abuse: National Survey Findings." *Journal of Studies on Alcohol* 58:264–271.

Windle, M., R. C. Windle, D. M. Scheidt, and G. B. Miller. 1995. "Physical and Sexual Abuse and Associated Mental Disorders among Alcoholic Inpatients." *American Journal of Psychiatry* 152:1322–1328.

World Health Organization (WHO). 2004. *Global Status Report on Alcohol 2004.* Geneva, Switzerland: World Health Organization.

Yesavage, J. A., and V. O. Leirer. 1986. "Hangover Effects on Aircraft Pilots 14 Hours after Alcohol Ingestion: A Preliminary Report." *American Journal of Psychiatry* 143 (12): 1546–1550.

Yi, H., G. D. Williams, and M. C. Dufour. 2002. *Surveillance Report #61: Trends in Alcohol-Related Fatal Traffic Crashes, United States, 1977–2000.* Rockville, MD: National Institute on Alcohol Abuse and Alcoholism.

Ylikahri, R. H., T. Leino, M. O. Huttunen, A. R. Pösö, C. J. Eriksson, and Nikkilä. 1976. "Effects of Fructose and Glucose on Ethanol-Induced Metabolic Changes and on the Intensity of Alcohol Intoxication and Hangover." *European Journal of Clinical Investigation* 6 (1): 93–102.

Yoon, Y.-H., F. S. Stinson, H. Yi, and M. C. Dufour. 2003. "Accidental Alcohol Poisoning Mortality in the United States, 1996–1998." *Alcohol Research and Health* 27 (1): 110–118.

## Chapter 4

Addolorato, G., L. Leggio, L. Abenavoli, and G. Gasbarrini. 2005. "On Behalf of the Alcoholism Treatment Study Group Neurobiochemical and Clinical Aspects of Craving in Alcohol Addiction: A Review." *Addictive Behaviors* 30:1209–1224.

Alcoholics Anonymous. 1939. *Alcoholics Anonymous: The Story of How More Than One Hundred Men Have Recovered from Alcoholism.* New York: Works Publishing Company.

Angres, D. H., and K. Bettinardi-Angres. 2008. "The Disease of Addiction: Origins, Treatment, and Recovery." *Disease-a-Month* 54:696–721.

APA (American Psychiatric Association). 2000. *Diagnostic and Statistical Manual of Mental Disorders.* 4th ed., Text Revision. Washington, DC: American Psychiatric Association.

Babor, T. F., and R. Caetano. 2006. "Subtypes of Substance Dependence and Abuse: Implications for Diagnostic Classification and Empirical Research." *Addiction* 101:104–110.

Babor, T. F., M. Hofmann, F. K. DelBoca, V. Hesselbrock, R. E. Meyer, Z. S. Dolinsky, and B. Rounsaville. 1992. "Types of Alcoholics, I. Evidence for an Empirically Derived Typology Based on Indicators of Vulnerability and Severity." *Archives of General Psychiatry* 49:599–608.

Barron, S., A. White, H. S. Swartzwelder, R. L. Bell, A. Z. Rodd, C. J. Slawecki, C. L. Ehlrs, E. D. Levin, A. H. Rezvani, and L. P. Spear. 2005. "Adolescent Vulnerabilities to Chronic Alcohol or Nicotine Exposure: Findings from Rodent Models." *Alcoholism: Clinical and Experimental Research* 29:1720–1725.

Bates, M. E., S. C. Bowden, and D. Barry. 2002. "Neurocognitive Impairment Associated with Alcohol Use Disorders: Implications for Treatment." *Experimental and Clinical Psychopharmacology* 10 (3): 193–212.

Bates, M. E., G. T. Voelbel, J. F. Buckman, E. R. Labouvie, and D. Barry. 2005. "Short-Term Neuropsychological Recovery in Clients with Substance Use Disorders." *Alcoholism: Clinical and Experimental Research* 29:367–377.

Beeder, A. B., and R. B. Millman. 1997. "Patients with Psychopathology." In Lowinson, et al. 1997.

Bernstein, J., E. Bernstein, K. Tassiopoulos, T. Hereen, S. Levenson, and R. Hingson. 2005. "Brief Motivational Intervention at a Clinic Visit Reduces Cocaine and Heroin Use." *Drug and Alcohol Dependence* 77:49–59.

Bien, T., W. Miller, and J. Tonigan. 1993. "Brief Intervention for Alcohol Problems: A Review." *Addiction* 88 (3): 315–336.

Blum, K., E. R. Braverman, J. M. Holder, J. F. Lubar, V. J. Monastra, D. Miller, J. O. Lubar, T. J. Chen, and D. E. Comings. 2000. "Reward Deficiency Syndrome: A Biogenetic

Model for the Diagnosis and Treatment of Impulsive, Addictive, and Compulsive Behaviors." *Journal of Psychoactive Drugs* 32 (Suppl): i–iv.

Bogenschutz, M. P., J. S. Tonigan, and H. M. Pettinati. 2009. "Effects of Alcoholism Typology on Response to Naltrexone in the COMBINE Study." *Alcoholism: Clinical and Experimental Research* 33 (1): 10–18.

Bozarth, M. 1990. "Drug Addiction as a Psychobiological Process." In Warburton 1990.

Breese, G. R., K. Chu, C. V. Dayas, D. Funk, D. J. Knapp, G. F. Koob, D. A. Lê, L. E. O'Dell, D. H. Overstreet, A. J. Roberts, R. Sinha, G. R. Valdez, and F. Weiss. 2005. "Stress Enhancement of Craving during Sobriety: A Risk for Relapse." *Alcoholism: Clinical and Experimental Research* 29 (2): 185–195.

Burman, S. 1997. "The Challenge of Sobriety: Natural Recovery without Treatment and Self-Help Programs." *Journal of Substance Abuse* 9:41–61.

Chen, K., and D. B. Kandel. 1995. "The Natural History of Drug Use from Adolescence to the Mid-thirties in a General Population Sample." *American Journal of Public Health* 85:41–47.

Clapp, P., S. V. Bhave, and P. L. Hoffman. 2008. "How Adaptation of the Brain to Alcohol Leads to Dependence: A Pharmacological Perspective." *Alcohol Research and Health* 31:310–340.

Clay, S. W., J. Allen, and T. Parran. 2008. "A Review of Addiction." *Postgraduate Medicine* 120 (2): E01–7.

Cleck, J. N., and J. A. Blendy. 2008. "Making a Bad Thing Worse: Adverse Effects of Stress on Drug Addiction." *Journal of Clinical Investigation* 118:454–462.

Cloninger, C. R. 1987. "Neurogenetic Adaptive Mechanisms in Alcoholism." *Science* 236:410–416.

Cloninger, C. R., S. Sigvardsson, and M. Bohman. 1996. "Type I and Type II Alcoholism: An Update." *Alcohol Health and Research World* 20:18–24.

Comings, D. E., and K. Blum. 2000. "Reward Deficiency Syndrome: Genetic Aspects of Behavioral Disorders." *Progress in Brain Research* 126:325–341.

Cotton, N. S. 1979. "The Familial Incidence of Alcoholism: A Review." *Journal of Studies on Alcohol* 40:89–116.

Crews, F. T. 2008. "Alcohol-Related Neurodegeneration and Recovery: Mechanisms From Animal Models." *Alcohol Research and Health* 31:377–389.

Crews, R. T., T. Buckley, P. R. Dodd, G. Ende, N. Foley, D. Harper, J. He, D. Innes, E. W. Loh, A. Pfefferbaum, J. Zou, and E. V. Sullivan. 2005. "Alcoholic Neurobiology: Changes in Dependence and Recovery." *Clinical and Experimental Research* 29:1504–1513.

Cruz, M. T., M. Bajo, P. Schweitzer, and M. Roberto. 2008. "Shared Mechanisms of Alcohol and Other Drugs." *Alcohol Research and Health* 31:137–148.

Dackis, C. A., and M. S. Gold. 1985. "New Concepts in Cocaine Addiction: The Dopamine Depletion Hypothesis." *Neuroscience and Biobehavioral Reviews* 9:469–477.

Dawson, D. A., B. F. Grant, F. S. Stinson, P. S. Chou, B. Huang, and W. J. Ruan. 2005. "Recovery from DSM–IV Alcohol Dependence: United States, 2001–2002." *Addiction* 100:281–292.

Di Chiara, G., and A. Imperato. 1988. "Drugs Abused by Humans Preferentially Increase Synaptic Dopamine Concentrations in the Mesolimbic System of Freely Moving Rats." *Proceedings of the National Academy of Sciences U.S.A.* 85:5274–5278.

Eckardt, M. J., and P. R. Martin. 1986. "Clinical Assessment of Cognition in Alcoholism." *Alcoholism: Clinical and Experimental Research* 10:123–127.

Ende, G., H. Welzel, S. Walter, W. Weber-Fahr, A. Diehl, D. Hermann, A. Heinz, and K. Mann. 2005. "Monitoring the Effects of Chronic Alcohol Consumption and Abstinence on Brain Metabolism: A Longitudinal Proton Magnetic Resonance Spectroscopy Study." *Biological Psychiatry* 58:974–980.

Fama, R., A. Pfefferbaum, and E. V. Sullivan. 2004. "Perceptual Learning in Detoxified Alcoholic Men: Contribution from Explicit Memory, Executive Function, and Age." *Alcoholism: Clinical and Experimental Research* 28:1657–1665.

Feltenstein, M. W., and R. E. See. 2008. "The Neurocircuitry of Addiction: An Overview." *British Journal of Pharmacology* 154:261–274.

Fingarette, H. 1989. *Heavy Drinking: The Myth of Alcoholism as a Disease.* Berkeley: University of California Press.

Gilbertson, R., R. Prather, and S. J. Nixon. 2008. "The Role of Selected Factors in the Development and Consequences of Alcohol Dependence." *Alcohol Research and Health* 31 (4): 389–399.

Gill, K., Z. Amit, and B. K. Koe. 1988. "Treatment with Sertraline: A New Serotonin Uptake Inhibitor, Reduces Voluntary Ethanol Consumption in Rats." *Alcohol* 5:349–554.

Gilpin, N. W., and G. F. Koob. 2008. "Neurobiology of Alcohol Dependence: Focus on Motivational Mechanisms." *Alcohol Research and Health* 31:185–196.

Goldstein, R. Z., and N. D. Volkow. 2002. "Drug Addiction and Its Underlying Neurobiological Basis: Neuroimaging Evidence for the Involvement of the Frontal Cortex." *American Journal of Psychiatry* 159:1642–1652.

Gonzales, R. A., M. O. Job, and W. M. Doyon. 2004. "The Role of Mesolimbic Dopamine in the Development and Maintenance of Ethanol Reinforcement." *Pharmacology and Therapeutics* 103 (2): 121–146.

Goodman, A. 2008. "Neurobiology of Addiction: An Integrative Review." *Biochemical Pharmacology* 75 (1): 266–322.

Goodman, A. 2009. "The Neurobiological Development of Addiction." *Psychiatric Times* 26:1–14.

Goodwin, D. W., F. Schulsinger, N. Moller, L. Hermansen, G. Winokur, and S. B. Guze. 1974. "Drinking Problems in Adopted and Nonadopted Sons of Alcoholics." *Archives of General Psychiatry* 31:164–169.

Gorski, T. T. 2001. *Best Practice Principles in the Treatment of Substance Use Disorders.* Independence, MO: GORSKI-CENAPS Web Publications.

Granfield, R., and W. Cloud. 1999. *Coming Clean: Overcoming Addiction without Treatment.* New York: New York University Press.

Halpern, J. H. 2002. "Addiction Is a Disease." *Psychiatric Times* 19:1–5.

Hazelden. Aug. 1998. "Addiction: A Disease Defined." *Research Update.* Center City, MN: Hazelden.

Hazelden. July 2001. "Alcohol, Drugs, and the Brain." *Research Update.* Center City, MN: Hazelden.

Hazelden. Aug. 2001. "Genetic Factors in Alcohol Dependence." *Research Update.* Center City, MN: Hazelden.

Hazelden. Nov. 2006. "Cognitive Improvement and Alcoholism Recovery." *Research Update.* Center City, MN: Hazelden.

Heinz, A., K. Mann, D. R. Weinberger, and D. Goldman. 2001. "Serotonergic Dysfunction, Negative Mood States, and Response to Alcohol." *Alcoholism: Clinical and Experimental Research* 25 (4): 487–495.

Henderson, E. C. 2000. *Understanding Addiction.* Jackson, MS: University Press of Mississippi.

Herrera, D. G., A. G. Yague, S. Johnsen-Soriano, F. Bosch-Morell, L. Collado-Morente, M. Muriach, F. J. Romero, and J. M. Garcia-Verdugo. 2003. "Selective Impairment of Hippocampal Neurogenesis by Chronic Alcoholism: Protective Effects of an Antioxidant." *Proceedings of the National Academy of Sciences* 100:7919–7924.

Hillemacher, T., and S. Bleich. 2008. "Neurobiology and Treatment in Alcoholism— Recent Findings Regarding Lesch's Typology of Alcohol Dependence." *Alcohol and Alcoholism* 43 (3): 341–346.

Hyytia, P., and G. F. Koob. 1995. "GABA-A Receptor Antagonism in the Extended Amygdala Decreases Ethanol Self-Administration in Rats." *European Journal of Pharmacology* 283:151–159.

Iacono, W. G., S. M. Malone, and M. McGue. 2008. "Behavioral Disinhibition and the Development of Early-Onset Addiction: Common and Specific Influences." *Annual Review of Clinical Psychology* 4:325–348.

Jellinek, E. M. 1960. *The Disease Concept of Alcoholism*. New Brunswick, NJ: Hillhouse Press.

Jentsch, K., and J. Taylor. 1999. "Impulsivity Resulting from Frontostriatal Dysfunction in Drug Abuse: Implications for the Control of Behavior by Reward-Related Stimuli." *Psychopharmacology* 146:373–390.

Kalivas, P. W., and C. O'Brien. 2008. "Drug Addiction as a Pathology of Staged Neuroplasticity." *Neuropsychopharmacology* 33 (1): 166–180.

Kalivas, P. W., and N. D. Volkow. 2005. "The Neural Basis of Addiction: A Pathology of Motivation and Choice." *American Journal of Psychiatry* 162:1403–1413.

Kauer, J. A., and R. C. Malenka. 2007. "Synaptic Plasticity and Addiction." *Nature Reviews Neuroscience* 8:844–858.

Kenna, G. A., J. E. McGeary, and R. M. Swift. 2004. "Pharmacotherapy, Pharmacogenomics, and the Future of Alcohol Dependence Treatment, Part 2." *American Journal of Health System Pharmacy* 61:2380–2388.

Kiefer, F., and A. Barocka. 1999. "Secondary Depression in Weaned Alcoholics: Implications of Lesch's Typology of Chronic Alcoholism." *Alcohol and Alcoholism* 34:916–917.

Koob, G. F. 2003. "Alcoholism: Allostasis and Beyond." *Alcoholism: Clinical and Experimental Research* 27 (2): 232–243.

Koob, G. F. 2006. "The Neurobiology of Addiction: A Neuroadaptational View Relevant for Diagnosis." *Addiction* 101 (Suppl. 1): 23–30.

Koob, G. F., and N. D. Volkow. 2010. "Neurocircuitry of Addiction." *Neuropsychopharmacology* 35 (1): 217–238.

Lesch, O. M., J. Kefer, S. Lentner, R. Mader, B. Marx, M. Musalek, A. Nimmerrichter, H. Preinsberger, H. Puchinger, and A. Rustembegovic, et al. 1990. "Diagnosis of Chronic Alcoholism: Classificatory Problems." *Psychopathology* 23 (2): 88–96.

Lesch, O. M., and H. Walter. 1996. "Subtypes of Alcoholism and Their Role in Therapy." *Alcohol and Alcoholism* 31 (Suppl 1): 63–67.

Leshner, A. I. 1997. "Addiction Is a Brain Disease, and It Matters." *Science* 278 (5335): 45–47.

Leshner, A. I. 2001. "Addiction Is a Brain Disease." *Issues in Science and Technology Online*. Accessed July 3, 2010. www.issues.org/17.3/leshner.htm.

Lewis, D. C. 1994. "A Disease Model of Addiction." In Miller 1994, 1–7.

Lowinson, J. H., P. Ruiz, R. B. Millman, and J. G. Langrod, eds. 1997. *Substance Abuse: A Comprehensive Textbook*. Baltimore, MD: Williams and Wilkins.

Lubman, D. I., M. Yucel, and C. Pantelis. 2004. "Addiction, A Condition of Compulsive Behavior? Neuroimaging and Neuropsychological Evidence of Inhibitory Dysregulation." *Addiction* 99:1491–1502.

Mann, K., K. Ackermann, B. Croissant, H. Mundle, H. Nakovics, and A. Diehl. 2005. "Neuroimaging of Gender Differences in Alcohol Dependence: Are Women More Vulnerable?" *Alcoholism: Clinical and Experimental Research* 29:896–901.

Mann, K., A. Batra, A. Gunthner, and G. Schroth. 1992. "Do Women Develop Alcoholic Brain Damage More Readily than Men?" *Alcoholism: Clinical and Experimental Research* 16:1052–1056.

McLellan, A. T., D. C. Lewis, C. P. O'Brien, and H. D. Kleber. 2000. "Drug Dependence, a Chronic Medical Illness: Implications for Treatment, Insurance, and Outcomes Evaluation." *Journal of the American Medical Association* 284 (13): 1689–1695.

Miller, N. S., ed. 1994. *Principles of Addiction Medicine.* Chevy Chase, MD: American Society of Addiction Medicine.

Moss, H. B., C. M. Chen, and H. Yi. 2007. "Subtypes of Alcohol Dependence in a Nationally Representative Sample." *Drug and Alcohol Dependence* 91 (2–3): 149–158.

Nestler, E. J. 2005. "Is There a Common Molecular Pathway for Addiction?" *Nature Neuroscience* 8:1445–1449.

NIAAA (National Institute on Alcohol Abuse and Alcoholism). 2000. *Tenth Special Report to Congress: Highlights from Current Research.* Bethesda, Maryland: U.S. Department of Health and Human Services.

NIAAA (National Institute on Alcohol Abuse and Alcoholism). 2004. "Neuroscience Research and Therapeutic Targets." *Alcohol Alert* 61.

NIAAA (National Institute on Alcohol Abuse and Alcoholism). 2009. "Neuroscience: Pathways to Alcohol Dependence." *Alcohol Alert* 77.

Nixon, K., and F. T. Crews. 2004. "Temporally Specific Burst in Cell Proliferation Increases Hippocampal Neurogenesis in Protracted Abstinence from Alcohol." *Journal of Neuroscience* 24:9714–9722.

O'Brien, C. P. 2005. "Anticraving Medications for Relapse Prevention: A Possible New Class of Psychoactive Medications." *American Journal of Psychiatry* 162:1423–1431.

O'Brien, C. P., and A. T. McLellan. 1996. "Myths about the Treatment of Addiction." *The Lancet* 347:237–240.

Pierce, R. C., and V. Kumaresan. 2006. "The Mesolimbic Dopamine System: The Final Common Pathway for the Reinforcing Effect of Drugs of Abuse?" *Neuroscience and Biobehavioral Reviews* 30:215–238.

Pombo, S., and O. M. Lesch. 2009. "The Alcoholic Phenotypes among Different Multi-dimensional Typologies: Similarities and Their Classification Procedures." *Alcohol and Alcoholism* 44 (1): 46–54.

Pombo, S., P. Levy, M. Bicho, F. Ismail, and J. M. Neves Cardoso. 2008. "Neuropsychological Function and Platelet Monoamine Oxidase Activity Levels in Type I Alcoholic Patients." *Alcohol and Alcoholism* 43 (4): 423–430.

Prescott, C. A., and K. S. Kendler. 1999. "Genetic and Environmental Contributions to Alcohol Abuse and Dependence in a Population-Based Sample of Male Twins." *American Journal of Psychiatry* 156 (1): 34–40.

Pulvirenti, L., and M. Diana. 2001. "Drug Dependence as a Disorder of Neural Plasticity: Focus on Dopamine and Glutamate." *Review Neuroscience* 12:41–59.

Rosenbloom, M. J., A. Pfefferbaum, and E. V. Sullivan. 2004. "Recovery of Short-Term Memory and Psychomotor Speed but Not Postural Stability with Long-Term Sobriety in Alcoholic Women." *Neuropsychology* 18:589–597.

Schuessler, G. 2004. "Neurobiology and Psychotherapy." *Zeitschrift fur Psychosomatische Medizin und Psychotherapie* 50 (4): 406–429.

Simpson, D. D., G. W. Joe, and W. E. Lehman. 1986. "Addiction Careers: Summary of Studies Based on the DARP 12-Year Follow-Up." *Treatment Research Report* (ADM 86–1420). Bethesda, MD: National Institute on Drug Abuse.

Sinha, R., T. Fuse, L. R. Aubin, and S. S. O'Malley. 2000. "Psychological Stress, Drug-Related Cues and Cocaine Craving." *Psychopharmacology* (Berl) 152: 140–148.

Spaminato, M., M. D. Vittoria, M. Castillo, R. Rojas, E. Palacios, L. Frascheri, and F. Descartes. 2005. "Magnetic Resonance Imaging Findings in Substance Abuse: Alcohol and Alcoholism and Syndromes Associated with Alcohol Abuse." *Topics in Magnetic Resonance Imaging* 16:223–230.

Spanagel, R., and F. Kiefer. 2008. "Drugs for Relapse Prevention of Alcoholism: Ten Years of Progress." *Trends in Pharmacological Sciences* 29:109–115.

Sullivan, E. V., and A. Pfefferbaum. 2005. "Neurocircuitry in Alcoholism: A Substrate of Disruption and Repair." *Psychopharmacology* 180:583–594.

Sullivan, E. V., M. J. Rosenbloom, A. Pfefferbaum, and K. O. Lim. 2000. "Longitudinal Changes in Cognition, Gait, and Balance in Abstinent and Relapsed Alcoholic Men: Relationships to Changes in Brain Structure." *Neuropsychology* 14:178–188.

Vaillant, G. 1983. *The Natural History of Alcoholism: Causes, Patterns, and Paths to Recovery.* Cambridge, MA: Harvard University Press.

Vaillant, G. E. 2003. "A 60-Year Follow-Up of Alcoholic Men." *Addiction* 98:1043–1051.

Valdez, G. R., and G. F. Koob. 2004. "Allostasis and Dysregulation of Corticotropin-releasing Factor and Neuropeptide Y Systems: Implications for the Development of Alcoholism." *Pharmacology Biochemistry and Behavior* 79:671–689.

Vengeliene, V., A. Bilbao, A. Molander, and R. Spanagel. 2008. "Neuropharmacology of Alcohol Addiction." *British Journal of Pharmacology* 154:299–315.

Warburton, D. M., ed. 1990. *Addiction Controversies.* London: Harwood Academic Publishers, 112–134.

Weiss, F., R. Ciccocioppo, L. H. Parsons, S. Katner, X. Liu, E. P. Zorrilla, G. R. Valdez, O. Ben-Shahar, S. Angeletti, and R. R. Richter. 2001. "Compulsive Drug-Seeking Behavior and Relapse: Neuroadaptation, Stress, and Conditioning Factors." *Annals of the New York Academy of Sciences* 937:1–26.

White, W. L. 2007. "In Search of the Neurobiology of Addiction Recovery: A Brief Commentary on Science and Stigma." Accessed Oct. 5, 2010. www.facesandvoices ofrecovery.org/pdf/White/White_neurobiology_2007.pdf. (Also available at www.williamwhitepapers.com.)

White, W., M. Boyle, and D. Loveland. 2003. "Addiction as Chronic Disease: From Rhetoric to Clinical Application." *Alcoholism Treatment Quarterly* 3/4:107–130.

White, W. L., and A. T. McLellan. 2008. "Addiction as a Chronic Disorder." *Counselor* 9 (3): 24–33.

Winger, G., J. H. Woods, C. M. Galuska, and T. Wade-Galuska. 2005. "Behavioral Perspectives on the Neuroscience of Drug Addiction." *Journal of the Experimental Analysis of Behavior* 84 (3): 667–681.

Wise, R. A. 1980. "Action of Drugs of Abuse on Brain Reward Systems." *Pharmacology Biochemistry and Behavior* 13:213–223.

Wise, R. A. 2002. "Brain Reward Circuitry: Insights from Unsensed Incentives." Neuron 36:229–240.

Wolffgramm, J., and A. Heyne. 1995. "From Controlled Drug Intake to Loss of Control: The Irreversible Development of Drug Addiction in the Rat." *Behavioural Brain Research* 70 (1): 77–94.

Wrase, J., N. Makris, D. F. Braus, K. Mann, M. N. Smolka, D. N. Kennedy, V. S. Caviness, S. M. Hodge, L. Tang, M. Albaugh, D. A. Ziegler, O. C. Davis, C. Kissling, G. Schumann, H. C. Breiter, and A. Heinz. 2008. "Amygdala Volume Associated with Alcohol Abuse Relapse and Craving." *American Journal of Psychiatry* 165 (9): 1179–1184.

## Chapter 5

Alcoholics Anonymous. 1976. *Alcoholics Anonymous.* 3rd ed. New York: Alcoholics Anonymous World Services, Inc.

Allen, J. 1999. "Biology and Transactional Analysis: Integration of a Neglected Area." *Transactional Analysis Journal* 29 (4): 250–259.

Bogerts, B. 1996. "Plasticity of Brain Structure and Function as the Neurobiological Principle of Psychotherapy." *Zeitschrift für Klinische Psychologie, Psychiatrie und Psychotherapie* 44 (3): 243–252.

Centonze, D., A. Siracusano, P. Calabresi, and G. Bernardi. 2005. "Removing Pathogenic Memories: A Neurobiology of Psychotherapy." *Molecular Neurobiology* 32:123–132.

CSAT (Center for Substance Abuse Treatment). 2006. *Detoxification and Substance Abuse Treatment.* Treatment Improvement Protocol (TIP) Series 45. DHHS Publication No. (SMA) 06-4131. Rockville, MD: Substance Abuse and Mental Health Services Administration.

CSAT (Center for Substance Abuse Treatment). 2010. "Protracted Withdrawal." *Substance Abuse Treatment Advisory.* Vol. 9, issue 1. Rockville, MD: CSAT.

Etkin, A., C. Pittenger, H. J. Polan, and E. R. Kandel. 2005. "Toward a Neurobiology of Psychotherapy: Basic Science and Clinical Applications." *Journal of Neuropsychiatry and Clinical Neuroscience* 17:145–158.

Frewen, P. A., D. J. Dozois, and R. A. Lanius. 2008. "Neuroimaging Studies of Psychological Interventions for Mood and Anxiety Disorders: Empirical and Methodological Review." *Clinical Psychology Review* 28 (2): 228–246.

Gorski, T., and M. Miller. 1986. *Staying Sober: A Guide for Relapse Prevention.* Independence, MO: Herald House/Independence Press.

Heilig, M., M. Egli, J. C. Crabbe, and H. C. Becker. 2010. "Acute Withdrawal, Protracted Abstinence and Negative Affect in Alcoholism: Are They Linked?" *Addiction Biology* 15:169–184.

Kranzberg, M. 2000/2001. "Words Change the Brain." *The Group Circle* (Dec./Jan.).

Liggan, D. Y., and J. Kay. 1999. "Some Neurobiological Aspects of Psychotherapy: A Review." *Journal of Psychotherapy Practice and Research* 8:103–114.

Martinotti, G., M. D. Nicola, D. Reina, S. Andreoli, F. Focà, A. Cunniff, F. Tonioni, P. Bria, and L. Janiri. 2008. "Alcohol Protracted Withdrawal Syndrome: The Role of Anhedonia." *Substance Use and Misuse* 43 (3–4): 271–284.

NIAAA (National Institute on Alcohol Abuse and Alcoholism). 2005. *Helping Patients Who Drink Too Much: A Clinician's Guide.* Updated ed. Bethesda, MD: NIAAA. www.niaaa.nih.gov/Publications/EducationTrainingMaterials/Pages/guide.aspx.

Owen, P., and G. A. Marlatt. 2001. "Should Abstinence Be the Goal of Alcohol Treatment?" *The American Journal on Addictions* 10:289–295.

Pendery, M. L., I. M. Maltzman, and L. J. West. 1982. "Controlled Drinking by Alcoholics? New Findings and a Reevaluation of a Major Affirmative Study." *Science* 217:169–175.

Porto, P. R., L. Oliveira, J. Mari, E. Volchan, I. Figueira, and P. Ventura. 2009. "Does Cognitive Behavioral Therapy Change the Brain? A Systematic Review of Neuroimaging in Anxiety Disorders." *Journal of Neuropsychiatry and Clinical Neurosciences* 21 (2): 114–125.

Pozzi, G., G. Martinotti, D. Reina, T. Dario, A. Frustaci, L. Janiri, and P. Bria. 2008. "The Assessment of Post-detoxification Anhedonia: Influence of Clinical and Psychosocial Variables." *Substance Use and Misuse* 43 (5): 722–732.

Rolfe, W. 2000. "Rethinking Feelings: Integrating the Biology of Emotion with Redecision Therapy." *Journal of Redecision Therapy* 2 (1): 13–31.

Satel, S. L., T. R. Kosten, M. A. Schuckit, and M. W. Fischman. 1993. "Should Protracted Withdrawal from Drugs Be Included in *DSM-IV*?" *American Journal of Psychiatry* 150:695–704.

Schuessler, G. 2003. "Neurobiology and Psychotherapy." Lecture Given at the Congress in Innsbruck in July.

Seidel, J. A. 2005. "Experience Is a Biochemical Intervention: Reconceptualizing the 'Biologically Based Mental Illness'." *Bulletin of the Menninger Clinic* 69:157–171.

Sobell, M. B., and L. C. Sobell. 1976. "Second Year Treatment Outcome of Alcoholics Treated by Individualized Behavior Therapy: Results." *Behavior Research and Therapy* 14:195–215.

Trevisan, L. A., B. Nashaat, I. L. Petrakis, and J. H. Krystal. 1998. "Complications of Alcohol Withdrawal." *Alcohol Health and Research World* 22:61–67.

Vaillant, G. E. 2005. "Alcoholics Anonymous: Cult or Cure?" *Australian and New Zealand Journal of Psychiatry* 39 (6): 431–436.

## Chapter 6

Alcoholics Anonymous. 1939. *Alcoholics Anonymous: The Story of How More Than One Hundred Men Have Recovered from Alcoholism.* New York: Works Publishing Company.

Alcoholics Anonymous. 1952. *Twelve Steps and Twelve Traditions.* New York: Alcoholics Anonymous World Services, Inc.

Alcoholics Anonymous. 1975. *Living Sober.* New York: Alcoholics Anonymous World Services, Inc.

Alcoholics Anonymous. 1976. *Alcoholics Anonymous.* 3rd ed. New York: Alcoholics Anonymous World Services, Inc.

Alcoholics Anonymous. 2008. *Alcoholics Anonymous 2007 Membership Survey.* New York: Alcoholics Anonymous World Services, Inc. Accessed July 14, 2010. www.aa.org/pdf/products/p-48_07survey.pdf.

Alcoholics Anonymous. 2010. *AA Fact File.* New York: Alcoholics Anonymous World Services, Inc.

Alcoholics Anonymous World Services, Inc. n.d. *Three Talks to Medical Societies by Bill W., Co-founder of AA.* New York: Alcoholics Anonymous World Services, Inc. Accessed July 8, 2010. www.aa.org/pdf/products/p-6_threetalkstomed.pdf.

B., Nancy. 2010. "Maryland General Service Delegate Report, October 16, 2010." Accessed Nov. 4, 2010. www.marylandaa.org/docs.

Bickel, W. K., and R. E. Vuchinich, eds. 2000. *Reframing Health Behavior Change with Behavior Economics.* Mahwah, NJ: Erlbaum.

Blocker, J. S., D. M. Fahey, and I. R. Tyrrell, eds. 2003. *Alcohol and Temperance in Modern History.* Santa Barbara, CA: ABC-CLIO / Greenwood, 27–31.

Bogenschutz, M. P. 2007. "Twelve Step Approaches for the Dually Diagnosed: Mechanisms of Change." *Alcoholism: Clinical and Experimental Research* 31:64s–66s.

Bogenschutz, M. P., J. S. Tonigan, and W. R. Miller. 2006. "Examining the Effects of Alcoholism Typology and AA Attendance on Self Efficacy as a Mechanism of Change." *Journal of Studies on Alcohol and Drugs* 67 (4): 562–567.

Bond, J., L. A. Kaskutas, and C. Weisner. 2003. "The Persistent Influence of Social Networks and Alcoholics Anonymous on Abstinence." *Quarterly Journal of Studies on Alcohol* 64 (4): 579–588.

Borkman, T. 2008. "The Twelve-Step Recovery Model of AA: A Voluntary Mutual Help Association." In Galanter and Kaskutas 2008b, 9–35.

Brandsma, J. M., M. C. Maultby, and R. I. Welsh. 1980. "Outpatient Treatment of Alcoholism: A Review and Comparative Study." Baltimore, MD: University Park Press.

Brown, H. P., and J. H. Peterson. 1987. "Alternate Explanations of How Alcoholics Anonymous Works." Paper presented at the 22nd Annual Meeting of the Southern Anthropological Society, Atlanta, GA.

Brown, H. P., and J. H. Peterson. 1990. "Values and Recovery from Alcoholism to Alcoholics Anonymous." *Counseling and Values* 35:63–68.

Brown, H. P., and J. H. Peterson. 1991. "Assessing Spirituality in Addiction Treatment and Followup: Development of the Brown-Peterson Recovery Progress Inventory (B-PRPI)." *Alcoholism Treatment Quarterly* 8:21–50.

Caldwell, P. E., and H. S. G. Cutter. 1998. "Alcoholics Anonymous Affliction During Early Recovery." *Journal of Substance Abuse Treatment* 15 (1): 221–228.

Carroll, S. 1993. "Spirituality and Purpose in Life in Alcoholism Recovery." *Journal of Studies on Alcohol and Drugs* 54:297–301.

Connors, G. J., J. S. Tonigan, and W. R. Miller. 2001. "A Longitudinal Model of AA Affiliation, Participation, and Outcome: Retrospective Study of the Project

MATCH Outpatient and Aftercare Samples." *Journal of Studies on Alcohol and Drugs* 62 (6): 817–825.

Connors, G. J., K. S. Walitzer, and J. S. Tonigan. 2008. "Spiritual Change in Recovery." In Galanter and Kaskutas 2008b, 209–228.

Dawson, D. A., B. F. Grant, F. S. Stinson, et al. 2006. "Recovery From DSM–IV Alcohol Dependence: United States, 2001–2002." *Alcohol Research and Health* 29:131–144.

Del Boca, F. K., and M. E. Mattson. 1994. "Developments in Alcoholism Treatment Research: Patient-Treatment Matching." *Alcohol* 11:6.

DDA (Dual Diagnosis Anonymous). 1996. "12 Steps + 5: Original Concept Paper." Dual Diagnosis Anonymous of Oregon Inc. website. Accessed Apr. 8, 2011. www.ddaoregon.com/about.htm.

Doe, J. 1955. *Sobriety and Beyond*. Indianapolis, IN: Sons of Matt Talbot Guild.

Emrick, D. C., J. S. Tonigan, H. Montgomery, and L. Little. 1993. "Alcoholics Anonymous: What Is Currently Known?" In McCrady and Miller 1993.

Fiorentine, R., and M. P. Hillhouse. 2000. "Drug Treatment and Twelve Step Program Participation: The Additive Effects of Integrated Recovery Activities." *Journal of Substance Abuse Treatment* 18:65–74.

Forman, R. F., K. Humphreys, and J. S. Tonigan. 2003. "Response: The Marriage of Drug Abuse Treatment and 12-Step Strategies." *Science and Practice Perspectives* 2 (1): 52–54.

Galanter, M., ed. 2003. *Research on Alcoholism Treatment*. Vol. 16 of *Recent Developments in Alcoholism*. New York: Kluwer Academic / Plenum Publishers, 149–164.

Galanter, M. 2006. "Innovations: Alcohol and Drug Abuse: Spirituality in Alcoholics Anonymous: A Valuable Adjunct to Psychiatric Services." *Psychiatric Service* 57:307–309.

Galanter, M., and L. A. Kaskutas, eds. 2008a. *Alcoholism Research: Alcoholics Anonymous and Spirituality* 18. New York: Kluwer Academic / Plenum.

Galanter, M., and L. A. Kaskutas, eds. 2008b. *Research on Alcoholics Anonymous and Spirituality in Addiction Recovery*. Vol. 18 of *Recent Developments in Alcoholism*. New York: Springer.

Gilbert, F. S. 1991. "Development of a Steps Questionnaire." *Journal of Studies on Alcohol and Drugs* 52 (4): 353–360.

Green, L. L., M. T. Fullilove, and R. E. Fullilove. 1998. "Stories of Spiritual Awakening: The Nature of Spirituality in Recovery." *Journal of Substance Abuse Treatment* 15 (4): 325–331.

Hazelden. 1993. *The Dual Diagnosis Recovery Book*. Center City, MN: Hazelden.

Hazelden. Dec. 2004. "Alcoholics Anonymous." *Research Update*. Center City, MN: Hazelden.

Hazelden. June 2010. "Project MATCH: A Study of Alcoholism Treatment Approaches." *Research Update*. Center City, MN: Hazelden.

Hirschi, T. 1969. *Causes of Delinquency*. Berkeley: University of California Press.

Humphreys, K. 1999. "Professional Interventions that Facilitate Twelve Step Self-Help Group Involvement." *Alcoholism Research and Health* 23:93–98.

Humphreys, K. 2003. "Alcoholics Anonymous and Twelve Step Alcoholism Treatment Programs." In Galanter 2003.

Humphreys, K., P. D. Huebsch, J. W. Finney, and R. H. Moos. 1999. "A Comparative Evaluation of Substance Abuse Treatment: Substance Abuse Treatment Can Enhance the Effectiveness of Self-Help Groups." *Alcoholism: Clinical and Experimental Research* 23 (3): 558–563.

Humphreys, K., L. A. Kaskutas, and C. Weisner. 1998. "The Alcoholics Anonymous Affiliation Scale: Development, Reliability, and Norms for Diverse Treated and Untreated Populations." *Alcoholism: Clinical and Experimental Research* 23 (3): 974–978.

Humphreys, K., and E. Klaw. 2001. "Can Targeting Nondependent Problem Drinkers and Providing Internet-Based Services Expand Access to Assistance for Alcohol Problems? A Study of the Moderation Management Self-Help/Mutual Aid Organization." *Journal of Studies on Alcohol and Drugs* 62 (4): 528–532.

Humphreys, K., E. S. Mankowski, R. H. Moos, and J. W. Finney. 1999. "Do Enhanced Friendship Networks and Active Coping Mediate the Effect of Self-Help Groups on Substance Abuse?" *Annals of Behavioral Medicine* 21 (1): 54–60.

Humphreys, K., and R. H. Moos. 1996. "Reduced Substance-Abuse-Related Health Care Costs among Voluntary Participants in Alcoholics Anonymous." *Psychiatric Services* 47 (7): 709–713.

Humphreys, K., and R. Moos. 2001. "Can Encouraging Substance Abuse Patients to Participate in Self-Help Groups Reduce Demand for Health Care: A Quasi-experimental Study." *Alcoholism: Clinical and Experimental Research* 25:711–716.

Humphreys, K., S. Wing, D. McCarty, J. Chappel, L. Gallant, B. Haberle, A. T. Horvath, L. A. Kaskutas, T. Kirk, D. Kivlahan, A. Laudet, B. S. McCrady, A. T. McLellan, J. Morgenstern, M. Townsend, and R. Weiss. 2004. "Self-Help Organizations for Alcohol and Drug Problems: Toward Evidence-Based Practice and Policy." *Journal of Substance Abuse Treatment* 26 (3): 151–158.

Institute of Medicine. 1990. *Broadening the Base of Treatment for Alcohol Problems*. Washington, DC: National Academy Press.

Kaplan, H. B. 1996. "Psychosocial Stress from the Perspective of Self Theory." *Psychosocial Stress: Perspectives on Structure, Theory, Life Course, and Methods*. New York: Academic Press, 175–244.

Kaskutas, L. A. 1994. "What Do Women Get Out of Self-Help? Their Reasons for Attending Women for Sobriety and Alcoholics Anonymous." *Journal of Substance Abuse Treatment* 11 (3): 185–195.

Kaskutas, L. A. 2009. "Alcoholics Anonymous Effectiveness: Faith Meets Science." *Journal of Addictive Diseases* 28 (2): 145–157.

Kaskutas, L. A., M. S. Subbaraman, J. Witbrodt, and S. E. Zemore. 2009. "Effectiveness of Making Alcoholics Anonymous Easier (MAAEZ): A Group Format Twelve Step Facilitation Approach." *Journal of Substance Abuse Treatment* 37 (3): 228–239.

Kaskutas, L. A., Y. Ye, T. K. Greenfield, J. Witbrodt, and J. Bond. 2008. "Epidemiology of Alcoholics Anonymous Participation." *Recent Developments in Alcoholism* 18:261–282.

Kelly, J. F., and J. D. Yeterian. 2008. "Mutual-Help Groups." In O'Donohue and Cunningham 2008.

Khantzian, E. J., and J. E. Mack. 1989. "Alcoholics Anonymous and Contemporary Psychodynamic Theory." *Recent Developments in Alcoholism* 7:67–89.

Kranzler, H. R., G. Koob, D. R. Gastfriend, R. M. Swift, and M. L. Willenbring. 2006. "Advances in the Pharmacotherapy of Alcoholism: Challenging Misconceptions." *Alcoholism: Clinical and Experimental Research* 30:272–281.

Kurtz, E. 1979. *Not-God: A History of Alcoholics Anonymous.* Center City, MN: Hazelden.

Kurtz E. 1991. *Not-God: A History of Alcoholics Anonymous.* Rev. ed. Center City, MN: Hazelden.

Laudet, A. B. 2008. "The Impact of Alcoholics Anonymous on Other Substance Abuse Related Twelve Step Programs." In Galanter and Kaskutas 2008a, 71–89.

Laudet, A. B., J. B. Becker, and W. L. White. 2009. "Don't Wanna Go through That Madness No More: Quality of Life Satisfaction as Predictor of Sustained Remission from Illicit Drug Misuse." *Substance Use and Misuse* 44 (2): 227–252.

Laudet, A. B., S. Magura, H. S. Vogel, and E. Knight. 2000. "Support, Mutual Aid and Recovery from Dual Diagnosis." *Community Mental Health Journal* 36:457–476.

Laudet, A. B., K. Morgen, and W. L. White. 2006. "The Role of Social Supports, Spirituality, Religiousness, Life Meaning and Affiliation with Twelve Step Fellowships in Quality of Life Satisfaction Among Individuals in Recovery from Alcohol and Drug Problems." *Alcohol Treatment Quarterly* 24:33–73.

Laudet, A., V. Stanick, and B. Sands. 2007. "The Effect of Onsite Twelve Step Meetings on Post-treatment Outcomes among Polysubstance-Dependent Outpatient Clients." *Evaluation Review* 31 (6): 613–646.

Leonard, K. E., and H. T. Blane, eds. 1999. *Psychological Theories of Drinking and Alcoholism*. 2nd ed. New York: Guilford, 106–163.

Longabaugh, R., D. M. Donovan, M. P. Karno, B. S. McCrady, J. Morgenstern, and J. S. Tonigan. 2005. "Active Ingredients: How and Why Evidence-Based Alcohol Behavioral Treatment Interventions Work." *Alcoholism: Clinical and Experimental Research* 29:235–247.

Magura, S., A. Rosenblum, C. L. Villano, H. S. Vogel, C. Fong, and T. Betzler. 2008. "Dual-Focus Mutual Aid for Co-occurring Disorders: A Quasi-experimental Outcome Evaluation Study." *American Journal of Drug and Alcohol Abuse* 34 (1): 61–74.

Maisto, S. A., K. B. Carey, and C. M. Bradizza. 1999. "Social Learning Theory." In Leonard and Blane 1999.

Mankowski, E. S., K. Humphreys, and R. H. Moos. 2001. "Individual and Contextual Predictors of Involvement in Twelve Step Self-Help Groups after Substance Abuse Treatment." *American Journal of Community Psychology* 29:537–563.

Mann, R. E., R. G. Smart, B. R. Rush, R. F. Zalcman, and H. Suurvali. 2005. "Cirrhosis Mortality in Ontario: Effects of Alcohol Consumption and Alcoholics Anonymous Participation." *Addiction* 100 (11): 1669–1679.

Mann, R. E., R. F. Zalcman, R. G. Smart, B. R. Rush, and H. Suurvali. 2006a. "Alcohol Consumption, Alcoholics Anonymous Membership, and Homicide Mortality Rates in Ontario 1968 to 1991." *Alcoholism: Clinical and Experimental Research* 30 (10): 1743–1751.

Mann, R. E., R. F. Zalcman, R. G. Smart, B. R. Rush, and H. Suurvali. 2006b. "Alcohol Consumption, Alcoholics Anonymous Membership, and Suicide Mortality Rates, Ontario, 1968–1991." *Journal of Studies on Alcohol and Drugs* 67 (3): 445–453.

Mattson, M. E., and J. P. Allen. 1991. "Research on Matching Alcoholic Patients to Treatments: Findings, Issues, and Implications." *Journal of Addictive Diseases* 11:33–49.

McCrady, B., and W. R. Miller, eds. 1993. *Research on Alcoholics Anonymous: Opportunities and Alternatives*. Brunswick, NJ: Rutgers Center of Alcohol Studies, 41–78.

McGee, E. M. 2000. "Alcoholics Anonymous and Nursing: Lessons in Holism and Spiritual Care." *Journal of Holistic Nursing* 18:11–26.

McKellar, J., E. Stewart, and K. Humphreys. 2003. "Alcoholics Anonymous Involvement and Positive Alcohol-Related Outcomes: Cause, Consequence, or Just a Correlate? A Prospective 2-Year Study of 2,319 Alcohol-Dependent Men." *Journal of Consulting and Clinical Psychology* 71:302–308.

Miller, W. 1998. "Researching the Spiritual Dimensions of Alcohol and Other Drug Problems." *Addiction* 93:979–990.

Miller, W. R., and J. C'de Baca. 2001. *Quantum Change: When Epiphanies and Sudden Insights Transform Ordinary Lives.* New York: Guilford Press.

Miller, W., and E. Kurtz. 1994. "Models of Alcoholism Used in Treatment: Contrasting AA and Other Perspectives with which It Is Often Confused." *Journal of Studies on Alcohol* 55 (2): 159–166.

Moos, R. H. 2008. "How and Why Twelve-Step Self-Help Groups Are Effective." In Galanter and Kaskutas 2008b, 393–412.

Moos, R. H., and B. S. Moos. 2004. "Long-Term Influence of Duration and Frequency of Participation in Alcoholics Anonymous on Individuals with Alcohol Use Disorders." *Journal of Consulting and Clinical Psychology* 72:81–90.

Moos, R. H., and B. S. Moos. 2006. "Participation in Treatment and Alcoholics Anonymous: A 16-Year Follow-Up of Initially Untreated Individuals." *Journal of Clinical Psychology* 62 (6): 735–750.

Morgenstern, J., and M. E. Bates. 1999. "Effects of Executive Treatment." *Journal of Studies on Alcohol* 60:846–855.

Morgenstern, J., E. Labouvie, B. S. McCrady, C. W. Kahler, and R. M. Frey. 1997. "Affiliation with Alcoholics Anonymous after Treatment: A Study of Its Therapeutic Effects and Mechanisms of Action." *Journal of Consulting and Clinical Psychology* 65 (5): 768–777.

Nowinski, J., S. Baker, and K. Carroll. 1992. "Twelve Step Facilitation Therapy Manual: A Clinical Research Guide for Therapists Treating Individuals with Alcohol Abuse and Dependence." *Project MATCH Monograph Series.* DHHS Publication No. (ADM) 92–1893. Vol. 1. Rockville, MD: National Institute on Alcohol Abuse and Alcoholism.

NREPP (National Registry of Evidence-based Programs and Practices). 2007. "Double Trouble in Recovery." Accessed Apr. 11, 2011. www.nrepp.samhsa.gov /ViewIntervention.aspx?id=13.

O'Donohue, W., and J. R. Cunningham, eds. 2008. *Evidence-Based Adjunctive Treatments.* New York: Elsevier, 61–105.

Owen, P. L., V. Slaymaker, J. S. Tonigan, B. S. McCrady, E. E. Epstein, L. A. Kaskutas, K. Humphreys, and W. R. Miller. 2003. "Participation in Alcoholics Anonymous: Intended and Unintended Change Mechanisms." *Alcoholism: Clinical and Experimental Research* 27 (3): 524–533.

Pettinati, H. M., A. A. Sugerman, N. DiDonato, and H. S. Maurer. 1982. "The Natural History of Alcoholism Four Years after Treatment." *Journal of Studies on Alcohol* 43:201–215.

Project MATCH Research Group. 1993. "Project MATCH: Rationale and Methods for a Multisite Clinical Trial Matching Patients to Alcoholism Treatment." *Alcoholism: Clinical and Experimental Research* 17 (6): 1130–1145.

Project MATCH Research Group. 1997. "Matching Alcoholism Treatments to Client Heterogeneity: Project MATCH Posttreatment Drinking Outcomes." *Journal of Studies on Alcohol* 58 (1): 7–29.

Project MATCH Research Group. 1998. "Matching Alcoholism Treatments to Client Heterogeneity: Project MATCH Three-Year Drinking Outcomes." *Alcoholism: Clinical and Experimental Research* 22 (6): 1300–1311.

Riessman, F. 1965. "The 'Helper Therapy' Principle." *Social Work* 10 (2): 27–32.

Room, R., and T. Greenfield. 1993. "Alcoholics Anonymous, Other Twelve Step Movements and Psychotherapy in the U.S. Population, 1990." *Addiction* 88 (4): 555–562.

Sandoz, C. J. 1999. "Exploring the Spiritual Experience of the Twelve Steps of Alcoholics Anonymous." *Journal of Ministry in Addiction and Recovery* 6:99–107.

Saginaw County Community Mental Health Authority (SCCMHA). 2007. "A Guide to Evidence-Based Practices for Individuals with Substance Use Disorders." Accessed Oct. 15, 2010. www.sccmha.org/quality/A%20Guide%20to%20Evidence-Based %20Practices%20for%20Individuals%20with%20Substance%20Use%20Disorders% 20v%201%200.pdf.

Schneider, R., M. Burnette, and C. Timko. 2008. "History of Physical or Sexual Abuse and Participation in Twelve Step Self-Help Groups." *American Journal of Drug and Alcohol Abuse* 34 (5): 617–625.

Sheeren, M. 1988. "The Relationship between Relapse and Involvement in Alcoholics Anonymous." *Journal of Studies on Alcohol* 49:104–106.

Smart, R. G., and R. E. Mann. 1993. "Recent Liver Cirrhosis Declines: Estimates of the Impact of Alcohol Abuse Treatment and Alcoholics Anonymous." *Addiction* 88 (2): 193–198.

Steigerwald, F., and D. Stone. 1999. "Cognitive Restructuring and the Twelve Step Program of Alcoholics Anonymous." *Journal of Substance Abuse Treatment* 16 (4): 321–327.

Tiebout, H. M. 1961. "Alcoholics Anonymous: An Experiment in Nature." *Quarterly Journal of Studies on Alcohol* 22:52–68.

Timko, C. 2008. "Outcomes of AA for Special Populations." In Galanter and Kaskutas 2008b, 373–392.

Timko, C., and A. Debenedetti. 2007. "A Randomized Controlled Trial of Intensive Referral to Twelve Step Self-Help Groups: One-Year Outcomes." *Drug and Alcohol Dependence* 90:270–279.

Timko, C., J. W. Finney, and R. H. Moos. 2005. "The 8-Year Course of Alcohol Abuse: Gender Differences in Social Context and Coping." *Alcoholism: Clinical & Experimental Research* 29 (4): 612–621.

Timko, C., R. H. Moos, J. W. Finney, and M. D. Lesar. 2000. "Long-Term Outcomes of Alcohol Use Disorders: Comparing Untreated Individuals with Those in Alcoholics Anonymous and Formal Treatment." *Journal of Studies on Alcohol* 61:529–540.

Tonigan, J. S. 2003. "Spirituality and AA Practices Three and Ten Years after Project MATCH." *Alcoholism: Clinical and Experimental Research* 26 (5 Supplement) 660A (Abstract).

Tonigan, J. S. 2007. "Spirituality and Alcoholics Anonymous." *Southern Medical Journal* 100 (4): 437–440.

Tonigan, J. S. 2008. "Alcoholics Anonymous Outcomes and Benefits." In Galanter and Kaskutas 2008b, 357–372.

Tonigan, J. S., M. P. Bogenschutz, and W. R. Miller. 2006. "Is Alcoholism Typology a Predictor of Both AA Affiliation and Disaffiliation after Treatment?" *Journal of Substance Abuse Treatment* 30:323–330.

Tonigan, J. S., and G. J. Connors. 2003. "Considerations When Assessing the Nature and Benefits of Long-Term Participation." *Alcoholism: Clinical and Experimental Research* 26 (5 Supplement) 650A (Abstract).

Tonigan, J. S., G. Connors, and W. R. Miller. 1996. "The Alcoholic Anonymous Involvement Scale (AAI): Reliability and Norms." *Psychology of Addictive Behavior* 10 (2): 75–80.

Tonigan, J. S., G. J. Connors, and W. R. Miller. 1998. "Special Populations in Alcoholics Anonymous." *Alcohol Health and Research World* 22 (4): 281–285. Review.

Tonigan, J. S., W. R. Miller, and C. Schermer. 2002. "Atheists, Agnostics, and Alcoholics Anonymous." *Journal of Studies on Alcohol and Drugs* 63:534–541.

Tonigan, J. S., W. R. Miller, and D. H. Vick. 2000. "Psychometrics on the General Alcoholics Anonymous Tools of Recovery (GAATOR 2.1)." *Alcoholism: Clinical and Experimental Research* 24 (5 Supplement) (Abstract).

Tonigan, J. S., R. Toscova, and W. R. Miller. 1996. "Meta-analysis of the Literature on Alcoholics Anonymous: Sample and Study Characteristics Moderate Findings." *Journal of Studies on Alcohol and Drugs* 57:65–72.

Trice, H. M. 1959. "Alcoholics Anonymous." *Annals of the American Academy of Political and Social Science* 315:108–116.

Vaillant, G.E. 2005. "Alcoholics Anonymous: Cult or Cure?" *Australian and New Zealand Journal of Psychiatry* 39 (6): 431–436.

Veach, T. L., and J. N. Chappel. 1992. "Measuring Spiritual Health: A Preliminary Study." *Substance Abuse* 13:139–147.

Vogel, H. S., E. Knight, A. B. Laudet, and S. Magura. 1998. "Double Trouble in Recovery: Self-Help for the Dually Diagnosed." *Psychiatric Rehabilitation Journal* 21:356–364.

Walsh, D. C., R. W. Hingson, D. M. Merrigan, S. M. Levenson, L. A. Cupples, T. Heeren, G. A. Coffman, C. A. Becker, T. A. Barker, S. K. Hamilton, T. G. McGuire, and C. A. Kelley. 1991. "A Randomized Trial of Treatment Options for Alcohol-Abusing Workers." *New England Journal of Medicine* 325 (11): 775–782.

Westphal, V. K., L. M. Worth, and J. S. Tonigan. 2003. "Nature and Stability of AA Participation Over a 10-Year Period in Project MATCH." *Alcoholism: Clinical and Experimental Research* 26 (5 Supplement) 652A (Abstract).

White, W. L. 2003. "Alcoholic Mutual Aid Groups (United States)." In Blocker, Fahey, and Tyrrell 2003, 24–27.

White, W. L. 2010. "The Future of AA, NA and Other Recovery Mutual Aid Organizations." *Counselor* 11 (2): 10–19.

White, W., and E. Kurtz. 2006. "The Varieties of Recovery Experience." *International Journal of Self-Help and Self Care* 3 (1–2): 21–61.

White, W. L., E. Kurtz, and M. Sanders. 2006. *Recovery Management.* Chicago, IL: Great Lakes Addiction Technology Transfer Center (ATTC) Network. www.nattc.org /recoveryresourc/docs/RecMgmt.pdf.

White, W., and M. Nicolaus. 2005. "Styles of Secular Recovery." *Counselor* 6 (4): 58–61.

Willenbring, M. L., and M. E. Rose. 1993. "How Sponsors in Alcoholics Anonymous Help Their Newcomers." Unpublished data.

Wilson, B. 1944. "Basic Concepts of Alcoholics Anonymous." (Presentation to the Medical Society of the State of New York.) In Alcoholics Anonymous World Services, Inc., n.d.

Wilson, B. 1958. "Alcoholics Anonymous—Beginnings and Growth." Presented to the New York Medical Society on Alcoholism, April 28. In Alcoholics Anonymous World Services, Inc., n.d.

Wilson, W. G. 1944. "Basic Concepts of Alcoholics Anonymous." *New York State Journal of Medicine* 44:1805–1810.

Winzelberg, A., and K. Humphreys. 1999. "Should Patients' Religiosity Influence Clinicians' Referral to Twelve Step Self-Help Groups? Evidence from a Study of 3,018 Male Substance Abuse Patients." *Journal of Consulting and Clinical Psychology* 67:790–794.

Witbrodt, J., and L. A. Kaskutas. 2005. "Does Diagnosis Matter? Differential Effects of Twelve Step Participation and Social Networks on Abstinence." *American Journal of Drug and Alcohol Abuse* 31:685–707.

WSASHO (Workgroup on Substance Abuse Self-Help Organizations). 2003. *Self-Help Organizations for Alcohol and Drug Problems: Towards Evidence-Based Practice and Policy.* Rockville, MD: Substance Abuse and Mental Health Services Administration (SAMHSA).

Zemansky, T. R. 2005. "The Risen Phoenix, Psychological Transformation within the Context of Long-Term Sobriety in Alcoholics Anonymous." Doctoral dissertation, Fielding Graduate University.

Zemore, S. E. 2007. "A Role for Spiritual Change in the Benefits of Twelve Step Involvement." *Alcoholism: Clinical and Experimental Research* 31 (S3): 76S–79S.

Zemore, S. E. 2008. "An Overview of Spirituality in AA (and Recovery)." In Galanter and Kaskutas 2008b, 111–124.

Zemore, S., and L. Kaskutas. 2004. "Helping, Spirituality and Alcoholics Anonymous in Recovery." *Journal of Studies on Alcohol and Drugs* 65 (3): 383–391.

Zemore, S. E., L. A. Kaskutas, and L. N. Ammon. 2004. "In Twelve Step Groups, Helping Helps the Helper." *Addiction* 99 (8): 1015–1023.

## Chapter 7

"A Pill to Cure Alcoholism." 2008. *U.S. News and World Report.* June 13.

AHCPR (Agency for Health Care Policy and Research) Consensus Panel. 1999. *Brief Interventions and Brief Therapies for Substance Abuse.* Treatment Improvement Protocol (TIP) Series 34. DHHS Publication No. (SMA) 99–3353. Accessed Sept. 9, 2010. www.ncbi.nlm.nih.gov/books/bv.fcgi?rid=hstat5.chapter.59192.

Anton, R. F., D. H. Moak, L. R. Waid, P. K. Latham, R. J. Malcolm, and J. K. Dias. 1999. "Naltrexone and Cognitive Behavioral Therapy for the Treatment of Outpatient Alcoholics: Results of a Placebo-Controlled Trial." *American Journal of Psychiatry* 156 (11): 1758–1764.

Anton, R. F., S. S. O'Malley, D. A. Ciraulo, R. A. Cisler, D. Couper, D. M. Donovan, D. R. Gastfriend, J. D. Hosking, B. A. Johnson, J. S. LoCastro, R. Longabaugh, B. J. Mason, M. E. Mattson, W. R. Miller, H. M. Pettinati, C. L. Randall, R. Swift, R. D. Weiss, L. D. Williams, and A. Zweben, for the COMBINE Study Research Group 2006. "Combined Pharmacotherapies and Behavioral Interventions for Alcohol Dependence: The COMBINE Study: A Randomized Controlled Trial." *Journal of the American Medical Association* 295:2003–2017.

Babor, T. F., M. Hofmann, F. K. DelBoca, V. Hesselbrock, R. E. Meyer, Z. S. Dolinsky, and B. Rounsaville. 1992. "Types of Alcoholics: Evidence for an Empirically Derived Typology Based on Indicators of Vulnerability and Severity." *Archives of General Psychiatry* 49 (8): 599–608.

Banerjee, K., M. Howard, K. Mansheim, and M. Beattie. 2007. "Comparison of Health Realization and Twelve Step Treatment in Women's Residential Substance Abuse Treatment Programs." *American Journal of Drug and Alcohol Abuse* 33:207–215.

Berlim, M. T., V. D. Neto, and G. Turecki. 2009. "Transcranial Direct Current Stimulation: A Promising Alternative for the Treatment of Major Depression?" *Revista Brasileira de Psiquiatria* 31 (Suppl I): S34–S38.

BFICP (Betty Ford Institute Consensus Panel). 2007. "What Is Recovery? A Working Definition from the Betty Ford Institute." *Journal of Substance Abuse Treatment* 33:221–228.

Bien, T., W. Miller, and J. Tonigan. 1993. "Brief Intervention for Alcohol Problems: A Review." *Addiction* 88 (3): 315–336.

Blow, F. C., and K. L. Barry. 2000. "Older Patients with At-Risk and Problem Drinking Patterns: New Developments in Brief Interventions." *Journal of Geriatric Psychiatry and Neurology* 13:115–123.

Bogenschutz, M. P., J. S. Tonigan, and H. M. Pettinati. 2009. "Effects of Alcoholism Typology on Response to Naltrexone in the COMBINE Study." *Alcoholism: Clinical and Experimental Research* 33 (1): 10–18.

Carter, A., and W. Hall. 2011. "Proposals to Trial Deep Brain Stimulation to Treat Addiction Are Premature." *Addiction* 106:235–237.

Centre for Genetics Education. 2007. "Fact Sheet 25:Pharmacogenetics/ Pharmacogenomics." *Australasian Genetics Resource Book*. Accessed July 29, 2010. www.genetics.edu.au/factsheet/fs25.

Chamberlain, H. 1891. "Modern Methods of Treating Inebriety." *Chautaquan* 13:494–499. Reported in White and Godley 2005.

Chatterjee, S., and S. E. Bartlett. 2010. "Neuronal Nicotinic Acetylcholine Receptors as Pharmacotherapeutic Targets for the Treatment of Alcohol Use Disorders." *CNS and Neurological Disorders—Drug Targets* 9 (1): 60–76.

Chermack, S. T., F. C. Blow, E. S. L. Gomberg, S. A. Mudd, and E. M. Hill. 1996. "Older Adult Controlled Drinkers and Abstainers." *Journal of Substance Abuse* 8:453–462.

Cooney, N. L., M. D. Litt, P. A. Morse, L. O. Bauer, and L. Gaupp. 1997. "Alcohol Cue Reactivity, Negative-Mood Reactivity, and Relapse in Treated Alcoholic Men." *Journal of Abnormal Psychology* 106 (2): 243–250.

Croissant, B., A. Diehl, O. Klein, S. Zambrano, H. Nakovics, A. Heinz, and K. Mann. 2006. "A Pilot Study of Oxcarbazepine versus Acamprosate in Alcohol-Dependent Patients." *Alcoholism: Clinical and Experimental Research* 30 (4): 630–635.

Crothers, T. D. 1893. *The Disease of Inebriety from Alcohol, Opium and Other Narcotic Drugs: Its Etiology, Pathology, Treatment and Medico-legal Relations*. New York: E. B. Treat, Publisher. Reported in White and Godley 2005.

CSAT (Center for Substance Abuse Treatment). 2007. *National Summit on Recovery: Conference Report.* DHHS Publication No. (SMA) 07–4276. Rockville, MD: Substance Abuse and Mental Health Services Administration.

De Sousa, A. 2010. "The Role of Topiramate and Other Anticonvulsants in the Treatment of Alcohol Dependence: A Clinical Review." *CNS and Neurological Disorders— Drug Targets* 9 (1): 45–49.

DiClemente, C. C., L. E. Bellino, and T. M. Neavins. 1999. "Motivation for Change and Alcoholism Treatment." *Alcoholism Research and Health* 23:86–92.

Dole, V. 1991. "Addiction as a Public Health Problem." *Alcoholism: Clinical and Experimental Research* 15 (5): 749–752.

Drummond, D. C., S. Glautier, B. Remington, and S. Tiffany, eds. 1995. *Addiction: Cue Exposure Theory and Practice.* London: Wiley and Sons, 169–196.

Durbin, P., T. Hulot, and S. Chabac. 1996. "Pharmacodynamics and Pharmacokinetics of Acamprosate: An Overview." In Soyka 1996, 47–64.

Fals-Stewart, W., K. Klostermann, B. T. Yates, T. J. O'Farrell, and G. R. Birchler. 2005. "Brief Relationship Therapy for Alcoholism: A Randomized Clinical Trial Examining Clinical Efficacy and Cost-Effectiveness." *Psychology of Addictive Behavior* 19 (4): 363–371.

Finigan, M. 1996. "Societal Outcomes and Cost Savings of Drug and Alcohol Treatment in the State of Oregon." Northwest Professional Consortium. Conducted for the Office of Alcohol and Drug Abuse Programs, Oregon Department of Human Resources.

Forman, R. F., K. Humphreys, and J. S. Tonigan. 2003. "Response: The Marriage of Drug Abuse Treatment and 12-Step Strategies." *Science and Practice Perspectives* 2 (1): 52–54.

Galanter, M., and L. A. Kaskutas, eds. 2008. *Research on Alcoholics Anonymous and Spirituality in Addiction Recovery.* Vol. 18 of *Recent Developments in Alcoholism.* New York: Springer.

Garbutt, J. C. 2009. "The State of Pharmacotherapy for the Treatment of Alcohol Dependence." *Journal of Substance Abuse Treatment* 36 (1): S15–S23.

Garbutt, J. C., H. R. Kranzler, S. S. O'Malley, D. R. Gastfriend, H. M. Pettinati, B. L. Silverman, J. W. Loewy, E. W. Ehrich, and Vivitrex Study Group. 2005. "Efficacy and Tolerability of Long-Acting Injectable Naltrexone for Alcohol Dependence: A Randomized Controlled Trial." *Journal of the American Medical Association* 293 (13): 1617–1625.

Gerstein, D., and H. Harwood, eds. 1990. *Treating Drug Problems.* Vol. 1. Washington, DC: National Academy Press.

Gerstein, D. R., and R. A. Johnson. 1994. "Evaluating Recovery Services: The California Drug and Alcohol Treatment Assessment (CALDATA)." Chicago, IL: National Opinion Research Center.

Gilmore, K. 1985. *Hazelden Primary Treatment Program: 1985 Profile and Patient Outcome* (unpublished research report). Center City, MN: Hazelden.

Gorski, T. T., and M. Miller. 1982. *Counseling for Relapse Prevention.* Independence, MO: Independence Press.

Grant, J. E., S. W. Kim, and B. L. Odlaug. 2007. "N-Acetyl Cysteine, a Glutamate-Modulating Agent, in the Treatment of Pathological Gambling: A Pilot Study." *Biological Psychiatry* 62 (6): 652–657.

Grant, J. E., B. L. Odlaug, and S. W. Kim. 2009. "N-Acetylcysteine, a Glutamate Modulator, in the Treatment of Trichotillomania: A Double-blind, Placebo-Controlled Study." *Archives of General Psychiatry* 66 (7): 756–763.

Grant, J. E., B. L. Odlaug, and S. W. Kim. 2010. "A Double-Blind, Placebo-Controlled Study of N-acetyl Cysteine Plus Naltrexone for Methamphetamine Dependence." *European Neuropsychopharmacology* 20:823–828.

Hazelden. Dec. 2001. "Alcohol Problems and Older Adults." *Research Update.* Center City, MN: Hazelden.

Hazelden. June 1998. "Outcomes of Alcohol/Other Drug Dependency Treatment." *Research Update.* Center City, MN: Hazelden.

Heilig, M., and G. F. Koob. 2007. "A Key Role for Corticotropin-Releasing Factor in Alcohol Dependence." *Trends in Neurosciences* 30 (8): 399–406.

Heinze, H.-J., M. Heldmann, J. Voges, H. Hinrichs, J. Marco-Pallares, J.-M. Hopf, U. J. Müller, I. Galazky, V. Sturm, B. Bogarts, and T. F. Münte. 2009. "Counteracting Incentive Sensitization in Severe Alcohol Dependence Using Deep Brain Stimulation of the Nucleus Accumbens: Clinical and Basic Science Aspects." *Frontiers in Human Neuroscience* 3:22.

Higgins, P., R. Bauemler, J. Fisher, and V. Johnson. 1991. "Treatment Outcomes for Minnesota Model Programs." In Spicer 1991.

Higgins, S. T., A. J. Budney, W. K. Bickel, F. E. Foerg, R. Donham, and G. J. Badger. 1994. "Incentives Improve Outcome in Outpatient Behavioral Treatment of Cocaine Dependence." *Archives of General Psychiatry* 51 (7): 568–576.

Higgins, S. T., and N. M. Petry. 1999. "Contingency Management: Incentives for Sobriety." *Alcoholism Research and Health* 23:122–127.

"High Bottom." 1949. *A.A. Grapevine.* New York: Alcoholics Anonymous.

Hoffmann, N., and P. Harrison. 1991. "The Chemical Abuse Treatment Outcome Registry (CATOR): Treatment Outcome from Private Programs." In Spicer 1991.

Hoffmann, N. G., P. A. Harrison, and C. A. Belille. 1983. "Alcoholics Anonymous after Treatment." *International Journal of Addictions* 18:311–318.

Holder, H. D., and J. B. Hallan. 1986. "Impact of Alcoholism Treatment on Total Health Care Costs: A Six-Year Study." *Advances in Alcohol and Substance Abuse* 6 (1): 1–15.

Humphreys, K. 1999. "Professional Interventions That Facilitate Twelve Step Self-Help Group Involvement." *Alcoholism Research and Health* 23:93–98.

Hutchison, K. E., L. Ray, E. Sandman, M. C. Rutter, A. Peters, D. Davidson, and R. Swift. 2006. "The Effect of Olanzapine on Craving and Alcohol Consumption." *Neuropsychopharmacology* 31 (6): 1310–1317.

Institute of Medicine. 1990. *Broadening the Base of Treatment for Alcohol Problems.* Washington, DC: National Academy Press.

Johnson, B. A., N. Rosenthal, J. A. Capece, F. Wiegand, L. Mao, K. Beyers, A. McKay, N. Ait-Daoud, R. F. Anton, D. A. Ciraulo, H. R. Kranzler, K. Mann, S. S. O'Malley, R. M. Swift, Topiramate for Alcoholism Advisory Board, and Topiramate for Alcoholism Study Group. 2007. "Topiramate for Treating Alcohol Dependence: A Randomized Controlled Trial." *Journal of the American Medical Association (JAMA)* 298 (14): 1641–1651.

Jones, K., and T. Vischi. 1979. "Impact of Alcohol, Drug Abuse and Mental Health Treatment on Medical Care Utilization." *Medical Care* 17 (Suppl. 12): 1–82.

Kadden, R. M. 2001. "Behavioral and Cognitive-Behavioral Treatments for Alcoholism: Research Opportunities." *Addictive Behavior* 26:489–507.

Kampman, K. M., H. M. Pettinati, K. G. Lynch, T. Whittingham, W. Macfadden, C. Dackis, C. Tirado, D. W. Oslin, T. Sparkman, and C. P. O'Brian. 2007. "A Double-Blind, Placebo-Controlled Pilot Trial of Quetiapine for the Treatment of Type A and Type B Alcoholism." *Journal of Clinical Psychopharmacology* 27 (4): 344–351.

Kashner, T. M., D. E. Rodel, S. R. Ogden, F. G. Guggenheim, and C. N. Karson. 1992. "Outcomes and Costs of Two VA Inpatient Treatment Programs for Older Alcoholic Patients." *Hospital and Community Psychiatry* 43:985–989.

Kaufman, E. 1994. *Psychotherapy of Addicted Persons.* New York: Guilford Press.

Kenna, G. A. 2010. "Medications Acting on the Serotonergic System for the Treatment of Alcohol Dependent Patients." *Current Pharmaceutical Design* 16 (19): 2126–2135.

Kenna, G. A., T. L. Lomastro, A. Schiesl, L. Leggio, and R. M. Swift. 2009. "Review of Topiramate: An Antiepileptic for the Treatment of Alcohol Dependence." *Current Drug Abuse Reviews* 2 (2): 135–142.

Kenna, G. A., J. E. McGeary, and R. M. Swift. 2004. "Pharmacotherapy, Pharmaco-genomics, and the Future of Alcohol Dependence Treatment, Part 2." *American Journal of Health System Pharmacy* 61:2380–2388.

Kraemer, K. L., M. F. Mayo-Smith, and D. R. Calkins. 1997. "Impact of Age on the Severity, Course, and Complications of Alcohol Withdrawal." *Archives of Internal Medicine* 157:2234–2240.

Krahn, D. 2009. "Pharmacotherapy for Alcohol Use Disorders." Wisconsin Public Psychiatry Network Teleconference Series. October 29.

Kranzler, H. R., and A. Gage. 2008. "Acamprosate Efficacy in Alcohol-Dependent Patients: Summary of Results from Three Pivotal Trials." *American Journal on Addictions* 17 (1): 70–76.

Kranzler, H. R., G. Koob, D. R. Gastfriend, R. M. Swift, and M. L. Willenbring. 2006. "Advances in the Pharmacotherapy of Alcoholism: Challenging Misconceptions." *Alcoholism: Clinical and Experimental Research* 30:272–281.

Krystal, A. D., H. H. Durrence, M. Scharf, and P. Jochelson. 2010. "Efficacy and Safety of Doxepin 1 mg and 3 mg in a 12-Week Sleep Laboratory and Outpatient Trial of Elderly Subjects with Chronic Primary Insomnia." *Sleep* 33 (11): 1553–1561.

Kuhn, J., D. Lenartz, W. Huff, S. Lee, A. Koulousakis, J. Klosterkoetter, and V. Sturm. 2007. "Remission of Alcohol Dependency following Deep Brain Stimulation of the Nucleus Accumbens: Valuable Therapeutic Implications?" *Journal of Neurology, Neurosurgery, and Psychiatry* 78 (10): 1152–1153.

Langenbucher, J. W., B. S. McCrady, J. Brick, and R. Esterly. 1993. *Socioeconomic Evaluations of Addictions Treatment.* New Brunswick, NJ: Rutgers University, Center of Alcohol Studies.

LaRowe, S. D., H. Myrick, S. Hedden, P. Mardikian, M. Saladin, A. McRae, K. Brady, P. W. Kalivas, and R. Malcolm. 2007. "Is Cocaine Desire Reduced by N-acetylcysteine?" *American Journal of Psychiatry* 164 (7): 1115–1117.

Laundergan, J. C. 1982. *Easy Does It: Alcoholism Treatment Outcomes, Hazelden, and the Minnesota Model.* Center City, MN: Hazelden.

Leggio, L., J. C. Garbutt, and G. Addolorato. 2010. "Effectiveness and Safety of Baclofen in the Treatment of Alcohol Dependent Patients." *CNS and Neurological Disorders—Drug Targets* 9 (1): 33–44.

Leggio, L., G. A. Kenna, M. Fenton, E. Bonenfant, and R. M. Swift. 2009. "Typologies of Alcohol Dependence: From Jellinek to Genetics and Beyond." *Neuropsychology Review* 19 (1): 115–129.

Litt, M. D., R. M. Kadden, N. L. Cooney, and E. Kabela. 2003. "Coping Skills and Treatment Outcomes in Cognitive-Behavioral and Interactional Group Therapy for Alcoholism." *Journal of Consulting and Clinical Psychology* 71:118–128.

Longabaugh, R., and J. Morgenstern. 1999. "Cognitive-Behavioral Coping-Skills Therapy for Alcohol Dependence: Current Status and Future Directions." *Alcoholism Research and Health* 23:78–85.

Maccioni, P., G. Colombo, and M. A. Carai. 2010. "Blockade of the Cannabinoid CB1 Receptor and Alcohol Dependence: Preclinical Evidence and Preliminary Clinical Data." *CNS and Neurological Disorders—Drug Targets* 9 (1): 55–59.

Mahowald, Mark, M.D. 2011. Former director, Regional Sleep Disorder Center, Hennepin County Medical Center, Minneapolis, MN. Communication on January 10.

Mardikian, P. N., S. D. LaRowe, S. Hedden, P. W. Kalivas, and R. J. Malcolm. 2007. "An Open-Label Trial of N-acetylcysteine for the Treatment of Cocaine Dependence: A Pilot Study." *Progress in Neuro-Psychopharmacology and Biological Psychiatry* 31 (2): 389–394.

Marinelli-Casey, P., C. P. Domier, and R. A. Rawson. 2002. "The Gap Between Research and Practice in Substance Abuse Treatment." *Psychiatric Services* 53 (8): 984–987.

Marlatt, G. A. 1985. "Relapse Prevention: Theoretical Rationale and Overview of the Model." In Marlatt and Gordon 1985.

Marlatt, G. A., and J. R. Gordon, eds. 1985. *Relapse Prevention.* New York: Guilford Press, 250–280.

Martinotti, G., S. Andreoli, D. Reina, M. Di Nicola, I. Ortolani, D. Tedeschi, F. Fanella, G. Pozzi, E. Iannoni, S. D'Iddio, and L. J. Prof. 2011. "Acetyl-L-Carnitine in the Treatment of Anhedonia, Melancholic, and Negative Symptoms in Alcohol-Dependent Subjects." *Progress in Neuro-Psychopharmacology and Biological Psychiatry* 35 (4): 953–958.

Martinotti, G., D. Reina, M. Di Nicola, S. Andreoli, D. Tedeschi, I. Ortolani, G. Pozzi, E. Iannoni, S. D'Iddio, and L. Janiri. 2010. "Acetyl-L-carnitine for Alcohol Craving and Relapse Prevention in Anhedonic Alcoholics: A Randomized, Double-Blind, Placebo-Controlled Pilot Trial." *Alcohol and Alcoholism* 45 (5): 449–455.

Mason, B. J., and A. M. Goodman. 1997. *Brief Intervention and Medications Compliance Procedures: Therapies Manual.* New York: Lipha Pharmaceuticals, Inc.

Mason, B. J., and C. J. Heyser. 2010a. "Acamprosate: A Prototypic Neuromodulator in the Treatment of Alcohol Dependence." *CNS and Neurological Disorders—Drug Targets* 9 (1): 23–32.

Mason, B. J., and C. J. Heyser. 2010b. "The Neurobiology, Clinical Efficacy and Safety of Acamprosate in the Treatment of Alcohol Dependence." *Expert Opinion on Drug Safety* 9 (1): 177–188.

Mason, B. J., J. M. Light, L. D. Williams, and D. J. Drobes. 2009. "Proof-of-Concept Human Laboratory Study for Protracted Abstinence in Alcohol Dependence: Effects of Gabapentin." *Addiction Biology* 14:73–83.

Mason, B. J., F. R. Salvato, L. D. Williams, E. C. Ritvo, and R. B. Cutler. 1999. "A Double-Blind, Placebo-Controlled Study of Oral Nalmefene for Alcohol Dependence." *Archives of General Psychiatry* 56 (8): 719–724.

McCaul, M. E., and N. M. Petry. 2003. "The Role of Psychosocial Treatments in Pharmacotherapy for Alcoholism." *American Journal of Addiction* 12 (Suppl 1): S41–S52.

McKee, S. A., E. L. Harrison, S. S. O'Malley, S. Krishnan-Sarin, J. Shi, J. M. Tetrault, M. R. Picciotto, I. L. Petrakis, N. Estevez, and E. Balchunas. 2009. "Varenicline Reduces Alcohol Self-Administration in Heavy-Drinking Smokers." *Biological Psychiatry* 66 (2): 185–190.

McKenna, D. J. 2004. "Clinical Investigations of the Therapeutic Potential of Ayahuasca: Rationale and Regulatory Challenges." *Pharmacology and Therapeutics* 102: 111–129.

McLellan, A. T., G. R. Grissom, P. Brill, J. Durell, D. S. Metzger, and C. P. O'Brien. 1993. "Private Substance Abuse Treatments: Are Some Programs More Effective Than Others?" *Journal of Substance Abuse Treatment* 10 (3): 243–254.

McLellan, A. T., G. E. Woody, L. Luborsky, and L. Goehl. 1988. "Is the Counselor an 'Active Ingredient' in Substance Abuse Rehabilitation? An Examination of Treatment Success among Four Counselors." *Journal of Nervous and Mental Disease* 176 (7): 423–430.

Miller, W. R., and R. J. Harris. 2000. "Simple Scale of Gorski's Warning Signs for Relapse." *Journal of Studies on Alcohol* 61:759–765.

Miller, W. R., R. J. Meyers, and S. Hiller-Sturmhofel. 1999. "The Community-Reinforcement Approach." *Alcoholism Research and Health* 23:116–121.

Miller, W. R., S. T. Walters, and M. E. Bennett. 2001. "How Effective Is Alcoholism Treatment in the United States?" *Journal of Studies on Alcohol and Drugs* 62 (2): 211–220.

Mills, R. 1995. *Realizing Mental Health: Toward a New Psychology of Resiliency.* Sulberger and Graham Publishing, Ltd.

Mills, R., and E. Spittle. 2003. *The Health Realization Primer.* Lone Pine Publishing.

Mishra, B. R., S. H. Nizamie, B. Das, and S. K. Praharaj. 2010. "Efficacy of Repetitive Transcranial Magnetic Stimulation in Alcohol Dependence: A Sham-Controlled Study." *Addiction* 105:49–55.

Monti, P. M., and D. J. Rohsenow. 1999. "Coping-Skills Training and Cue-Exposure Therapy in the Treatment of Alcoholism." *Alcoholism Research and Health* 23:107–115.

Moos, R. H., P. L. Brennan, and B. S. Moos. 1991. "Short-Term Processes of Remission and Nonremission among Late-Life Problem Drinkers." *Alcoholism: Clinical and Experimental Research* 15:948–955.

Morgenstern, J., R. M. Frey, B. S. McCrady, E. Labouvie, and C. J. Neighbors. 1996. "Examining Mediators of Change in Traditional Chemical Dependency Treatment." *Journal of Studies on Alcohol* 57 (1): 53–64.

Morgenstern, J., and R. Longabaugh. 2000. "Cognitive-Behavioral Treatment for Alcohol Dependence: A Review of Evidence for its Hypothesized Mechanisms of Action." *Addiction* 95:1475–1490.

Morgenstern, J., and B. S. McCrady. 1992. "Curative Factors in Alcohol and Drug Treatment: Behavioral and Disease Model Perspectives." *British Journal of Addiction* 87:901–912.

Moyer, A., and J. W. Finney. 2004/2005. "Brief Interventions for Alcohol Problems: Factors That Facilitate Implementation." *Alcohol Research and Health* 28 (1): 44–50.

Müller, U. J., V. Sturm, J. Voges, H. J. Heinze, I. Galazky, M. Heldmann, H. Scheich, and B. Bogerts. 2009. "Successful Treatment of Chronic Resistant Alcoholism by Deep Brain Stimulation of Nucleus Accumbens: First Experience with Three Cases." *Pharmacopsychiatry* 42 (6): 288–291.

NASADAD (National Association of State Alcohol and Drug Abuse Directors). 2001. "State Issue Brief No. 1: Current Alcohol Research in the Use of Medications as an Adjunct to Alcohol Treatment and Implications for State Alcohol Treatment Systems." Washington, DC: NASADAD. http://pubs.niaaa.nih.gov/publications /NASADAD/NIAAA1stBrief.htm.

NIAAA (National Institute on Alcohol Abuse and Alcoholism). 2000. "Why Do Some People Drink Too Much? The Role of Genetic and Psychosocial Influences." *Alcoholism Research and Health* 24 (1): 17–26.

NIAAA (National Institute on Alcohol Abuse and Alcoholism). 2004/2005. "Screening and Brief Intervention." *Alcohol Research and Health* 28 (1).

NIAAA (National Institute on Alcohol Abuse and Alcoholism). 2005. "Brief Interventions." *Alcohol Alert.* Bethesda, MD: NIAAA.

NREPP (National Registry of Evidence-based Programs and Practices). 2007. "Motivational Interviewing." Rockville, MD: NREPP. http://nrepp.samhsa.gov/ViewIntervention .aspx?id=107.

NREPP (National Registry of Evidence-based Programs and Practices). 2008. "Relapse Prevention Therapy." Rockville, MD: NREPP. http://nrepp.samhsa.gov /ViewIntervention.aspx?id=97.

O'Brien, C. P. 2005. "Anticraving Medications for Relapse Prevention: A Possible New Class of Psychoactive Medications." *American Journal of Psychiatry* 162:1423–1431.

Odlaug, B. L., and J. E. Grant. 2007. "N-acetyl Cysteine in the Treatment of Grooming Disorders." *Journal of Clinical Psychopharmacology* 27 (2): 227–229.

O'Farrell, T. J., K. A. Choquette, and H. S. Cutter. 1998. "Couples Relapse Prevention Sessions after Behavioral Marital Therapy for Male Alcoholics: Outcomes During the Three Years after Starting Treatment." *Journal of Studies on Alcohol* 59:357–370.

O'Farrell, T. J., and W. Fals-Stewart. 2001. "Family-Involved Alcoholism Treatment: An Update." *Recent Developments in Alcoholism* 15:329–356.

O'Farrell, T. J., and W. Fals-Stewart. 2003. "Alcohol Abuse." *Journal of Marital Family Therapy* 29:121–146.

O'Malley, S. S., R. S. Croop, J. M. Wroblewski, D. F. Labriola, and J. R. Volpicelli. 1995. "Naltrexone in the Treatment of Alcohol Dependence: A Combined Analysis of Two Trials." *Psychiatric Annals* 25 (11): 681–688.

O'Malley, S. S., A. J. Jaffe, G. Chang, R. S. Schottenfeld, R. E. Meyer, and B. Rounsaville. 1992. "Naltrexone and Coping Skills Therapy for Alcohol Dependence: A Controlled Study." *Archives of General Psychiatry* 49 (11): 881–887.

Owen, R. T. 2009. "Selective Histamine H(1) Antagonism: A Novel Approach to Insomnia Using Low-Dose Doxepin." *Drugs of Today* (Barcelona) 45 (4): 261–267.

Paille, F. M., J. D. Guelfi, A. C. Perkins, R. J. Royer, L. Steru, and P. Parot. 1995. "Double-Blind Randomized Multicentre Trial of Acamprosate in Maintaining Abstinence from Alcohol." *Alcohol and Alcoholism* 30:239–247.

Parantainen, J. 1983. "Prostaglandins in Alcohol Intolerance and Hangover." *Drug and Alcohol Dependence* 11:239–248.

Pransky, J. 2006. *Somebody Should Have Told Us*. Martinsville, IN: Airleaf Publishing.

Prochaska, J. O., C. C. DiClemente, and J. C. Norcross. 1992. "In Search of How People Change: Applications to Addictive Behaviors." *American Psychologist* 47:1102–1114.

Project MATCH Research Group. 1997a. "Matching Alcoholism Treatments to Client Heterogeneity: Project MATCH Posttreatment Drinking Outcomes." *Journal of Studies on Alcohol* 58:7–29.

Project MATCH Research Group. 1997b. "Project MATCH Secondary a Priori Hypotheses." *Addiction* 92:1671–1698.

Ressler, K. J., and H. S. Mayberg. 2007. "Targeting Abnormal Neural Circuits in Mood and Anxiety Disorders: From the Laboratory to the Clinic." *Nature Neuroscience* 10:1116–1124.

Richardson, H. N., Y. Zhao, E. M. Fekete, C. K. Funk, P. Wirsching, K. D. Janda, E. P. Zorrilla, and G. F. Koob. 2008. "MPZP: A Novel Small Molecule Corticotropin-Releasing Factor Type 1 Receptor (CRF1) Antagonist." *Pharmacology, Biochemistry and Behavior* 88 (4): 497–510.

Roache, J. D., Y. Wang, N. Ait-Daoud, and B. A. Johnson. 2008. "Prediction of Serotonergic Treatment Efficacy Using Age of Onset and Type A/B Typologies of Alcoholism." *Alcoholism: Clinical and Experimental Research* 32 (8): 1502–1512.

Rohsenow, D. J., P. M. Monti, and D. B. Abrams. 1995. "Cue Exposure Treatment of Alcohol Dependence." In Drummond et al. 1995.

Roth, T., H. Heith Durrence, P. Jochelson, G. Peterson, E. Ludington, R. Rogowski, M. Scharf, and A. Lankford. 2010. "Efficacy and Safety of Doxepin 6 mg in a Model of Transient Insomnia." *Sleep Medicine* 11 (9): 843–847.

SCCMHA (Saginaw County Community Mental Health Authority). 2007. *A Guide to Evidence-Based Practices for Individuals with Substance Abuse Disorders*. Saginaw, MI: SCCMHA.

Schonfeld, L., and L. W. Dupree. 1991. "Antecedents of Drinking for Early- and Late-Onset Elderly Alcohol Abusers." *Journal of Studies on Alcohol* 52:587–592.

Slaymaker, V. J., and T. Sheehan. 2008. "The Impact of AA on Professional Treatment." In Galanter and Kaskutas 2008, 59–70.

Soyka, M., ed. 1996. *Acamprosate in Relapse Prevention of Alcoholism*. Berlin, Germany: Springer-Verlag, 47–64.

Spicer, J., ed. 1991. *Does Your Program Measure Up? An Addiction Professional's Guide to Evaluating Treatment Effectiveness*. Center City, MN: Hazelden, 93–114.

Stinchfield, R., and P. Owen. 1998. "Hazelden's Model of Treatment and Its Outcome." *Addictive Behaviors* 23: 669–683.

Substance Abuse and Mental Health Services Administration (SAMHSA). 2005. "Acamprosate: A New Medication for Alcohol Use Disorders." *Substance Abuse Treatment Advisory* 4 (1): 1–8.

Swift, R. 2007. "Emerging Approaches to Managing Alcohol Dependence." *American Journal of Health-System Pharmacy* 64 (5 Suppl 3): S12–S22.

Swift, R., and H. M. Pettinati. 2005. "Choosing Pharmacotherapies for the COMBINE Study—Process and Procedures: An Investigational Approach to Combination Pharmacotherapy for the Treatment of Alcohol Dependence." *Journal of Studies on Alcohol and Drugs* (Suppl. 15): 141–147.

Vaillant, G. E. 1995. *Natural History of Alcoholism Revisited*. Cambridge, MA: Harvard University Press.

Vaillant, G. E. 2005. "Alcoholics Anonymous: Cult or Cure?" *Australian and New Zealand Journal of Psychiatry* 39 (6): 431–436.

Vergne, D. E., and R. F. Anton. 2010. "Aripiprazole: A Drug with a Novel Mechanism of Action and Possible Efficacy for Alcohol Dependence." *CNS and Neurological Disorders—Drug Targets* 9 (1): 50–54.

Volpicelli, J. R. 2001. "Alcohol Abuse and Alcoholism: An Overview." *Journal of Clinical Psychiatry* 62 (Suppl 20): 4–10.

Volpicelli, J. R., A. I. Alterman, M. Hayashida, and C. P. O'Brian. 1992. "Naltrexone in the Treatment of Alcohol Dependence." *Archives of General Psychiatry* 49:876–880.

Volpicelli, J. R., N. T. Watson, A. C. King, C. E. Sherman, and C. P. O'Brian. 1995. "Effect of Naltrexone on Alcohol 'High' in Alcoholics." *American Journal of Psychiatry* 152 (4): 613–615.

Weber, J., M. A. Siddiqui, A. J. Wagstaff, and P. L. McCormack. 2010. "Low-Dose Doxepin: In the Treatment of Insomnia." *CNS Drugs* 24 (8): 713–720.

Weiss, R. D., and K. D. Kueppenbender. 2006. "Combining Psychosocial Treatment with Pharmacotherapy for Alcohol Dependence." *Journal of Clinical Psychopharmacology* 26 (Suppl. 1): S37–S42.

West, S. L., J. C. Garbutt, T. S. Carey, et al. 1999. *Pharmacotherapy for Alcohol Dependence*. Evidence report number 3. AHCPR Publication No. 99–E004. Accessed April 20, 2006. www.ahrq.gov/clinic/epcsums/alcosumm.htm.

White, W. L. 1996. *Pathways from the Culture of Addiction to the Culture of Recovery: A Travel Guide for Addiction Professionals*. 2nd ed. Center City, MN: Hazelden.

White, W. L., and M. Godley. 2005. "Addiction Treatment Outcomes: Who and What Can You Believe?" *Counselor* 6 (3): 52–55.

White, W. L., and E. Kurtz. 2006. "The Varieties of Recovery Experiences." In White, Kurtz, and Sanders 2006.

White, W. L., E. Kurtz, and M. Sanders. 2006. "Recovery Management." Great Lakes Addiction Technology Transfer Center (ATTC) Network. Accessed Jan. 13, 2011. www.nattc.org/recoveryresourc/docs/RecMgmt.pdf.

White, W. L., and W. R. Miller. 2007. "The Use of Confrontation in Addiction Treatment: History, Science and Time for Change." *Counselor* 8 (4): 12–30.

Wilbourne, P., and W. Miller. 2003. "Treatment of Alcoholism: Older and Wiser?" *Alcoholism Treatment Quarterly* 20 (3/4): 41–59.

Wilde, M. I., and A. J. Wagstaff. 1997. "Acamprosate: A Review of Its Pharmacology and Clinical Potential in the Management of Alcohol Dependence after Detoxification." *Drugs* 53 (6): 1038–1053.

Wilson, B. 1958. "The Next Frontier: Emotional Sobriety." *A.A. Grapevine*. New York: Alcoholics Anonymous, 2–5.

Witkiewitz, K., and G. A. Marlatt. 2004. "Relapse Prevention for Alcohol and Drug Problems: That Was Zen, This Is Tao." *American Psychologist* 59:224–235.

Zweben, J. E. 1996. "Psychiatric Problems among Alcohol and Other Drug Dependent Women." *Journal of Psychoactive Drugs* 28 (4): 345–366.

## Chapter 8

Ahir, D. C., ed. 1999. *Vipassana: A Universal Buddhist Meditation Technique.* New Delhi: Sri Satguru Publications.

Alexander, C. N. 1994. "Transcendental Meditation." In Corsini 1994.

Appel, J., and D. Kim-Appel. 2009. "Mindfulness: Implications for Substance Abuse and Addiction." *International Journal of Mental Health and Addiction.* Accessed Feb. 11, 2011. www.slideshare.net/pharho/mindfulness-implications-for-substance-abuse-and-addiction.

Baer, R. A., J. Hopkins, J. Krietemeyer, G. T. Smith, and L. Toney. 2006. "Using Self-Report Assessment Methods to Explore Facets of Mindfulness." *Assessment* 13 (1): 27–45.

Beauchamp-Turner, D. L., and D. M. Levinson. 1992. "Effects of Meditation on Stress, Health, and Affect." *Medical Psychotherapy: An International Journal* 5:123–131.

Benson, H. 1983. "The Relaxation Response: Its Subjective and Objective Historical Precedents and Physiology." *Trends in Neurosciences* 6 (7): 281–284.

Bishop, S. R., M. Lau, S. Shapiro, L. Carlson, N. D. Anderson, J. Carmody, Z. V. Segal, S. Abbey, M. Speca, D. Velting, and G. Devins. 2004. "Mindfulness: A Proposed Operational Definition." *Clinical Psychology: Science and Practice* 11 (3): 230–241.

Bowen, S., N. Chawla, S. E. Collins, K. Witkiewitz, S. Hsu, J. Grow, S. Clifasefi, M. Garner, A. Douglass, M. E. Larimer, and A. Marlatt. 2009. "Mindfulness-Based Relapse Prevention for Substance Use Disorders: A Pilot Efficacy Trial." *Substance Abuse* 30 (4): 295–305.

Bowen, S., K. Witkiewitz, T. Dillworth, and G. A. Marlatt. 2007. "The Role of Thought Suppression in the Relationship between Mindfulness, Meditation, and Alcohol Use." *Addictive Behaviors* 32 (10): 2323–2328.

Breslin, F. C., M. Zack, and S. McMain. 2002. "An Information-Processing Analysis of Mindfulness: Implications for Relapse Prevention in the Treatment of Substance Abuse." *Clinical Psychology: Science and Practice* 9:275–299.

Buonomano, D. V., and M. M. Merzenich. 1998. "Cortical Plasticity: From Synapses to Maps." *Annual Review of Neuroscience* 21:149–186.

Chiesa, A. 2010. "Vipassana Meditation: Systematic Review of Current Evidence." *Journal of Alternative and Complementary Medicine* 16 (1): 37–46.

Chiesa, A., and A. Serretti. 2009. "Mindfulness-Based Stress Reduction for Stress Management in Healthy People: A Review and Meta-Analysis." *Journal of Alternative and Complementary Medicine* 15:593–600.

Chopko, B. A., and R. C. Schwartz. 2009. "The Relation Between Mindfulness and Posttraumatic Growth: A Study of First Responders to Trauma-Inducing Incidents." *Journal of Mental Health Counseling* 31 (4): 363–376.

Corsini, R. J., ed. 1994. *Encyclopedia of Psychology*. 2nd ed., vol. 3. New York: John Wiley and Sons, 545–546.

Creswell, J. D., B. M. Way, N. I. Eisenberger, and M. D. Lieberman. 2007. "Neural Correlates of Dispositional Mindfulness During Affect Labeling." *Psychosomatic Medicine* 69:560–565.

Dakwar, E., and F. R. Levin. 2009. "The Emerging Role of Meditation in Addressing Psychiatric Illness, with a Focus on Substance Use Disorders. *Harvard Review of Psychiatry* 17:254–267.

Davidson, R. J., J. Kabat-Zinn, J. Schumacher, M. Rosenkranz, D. Muller, S. F. Santorelli, F. Urbanowski, A. Harrington, K. Bonus, and J. F. Sheridan. 2003. "Alterations in Brain and Immune Function Produced by Mindfulness Meditation." *Psychosomatic Medicine* 65 (4): 564–570.

Farrow, J. T., and J. R. Hebert. 1982. "Breath Suspension during the Transcendental Meditation Technique." *Psychosomatic Medicine* 44 (2): 133–153.

Fields, R. 2009. "Enhancing Recovery with Meditation and Mindfulness." *Counselor Magazine*. Accessed Feb. 11, 2011. www.counselormagazine.com/component /content/article/29-alternative/891-enhancing-recovery-with-meditation-and-mindfulness.

Garland, E. L., S. A. Gaylord, C. A. Boettiger, and M. O. Howard. 2010. "Mindfulness Training Modifies Cognitive, Affective, and Physiological Mechanisms Implicated in Alcohol Dependence: Results of a Randomized Controlled Pilot Trial." *Journal of Psychoactive Drugs* 42:177–192.

Gethin, R. 1998. *The Foundations of Buddhism*. Oxford: Oxford University Press.

Glickman, M. 2002. *Beyond the Breath: Extraordinary Mindfulness through Whole-Body Vipassana Meditation*. 1st ed. Boston: Journey Editions.

Greene, P. B. 2004. "Stress Reactivity, Health, and Meditation: A Path Analytic Approach." Dissertation. Boston: Boston University.

Grof, S., and C. Grof. 1993. "Addiction As a Spiritual Emergency." In Walsh and Vaughan 1993, 144–146.

Gunaratana, H. 1993. *Mindfulness in Plain English*. Boston: Wisdom Publications.

Hamer, D. 2004. *The God Gene*. New York: Doubleday.

Hayes, S. C., K. D. Strosahl, and K. G. Wilson. 1999. *Acceptance and Commitment Therapy: An Experiential Approach to Behavior Change*. New York: Guilford Press.

Hayes, S. C., K. G. Wilson, E. V. Gifford, V. M. Follette, and K. Strosahl. 1996. "Experimental Avoidance and Behavioral Disorders: A Functional Dimensional Approach to Diagnosis and Treatment." *Journal of Consulting and Clinical Psychology* 64 (6): 1152–1168.

Hierotheos, M. Translated by E. Williams. 1998. *The Mind of the Orthodox Church.* Levadia, Greece: The Theotokos Monastery.

Hölzel, B. K., U. Ott, T. Gard, H. Hempel, M. Weygandt, K. Morgen, and D. Vaitl. 2008. "Investigation of Mindfulness Meditation Practitioners with Voxel-Based Morphometry." *Social Cognitive and Affective Neuroscience* 3 (1): 55–61.

Hölzel, B. K., U. Ott, H. Hemphel, A. Hackl, K. Wolf, R. Stark, and D. Vaitl. 2007. "Differential Engagement of Anterior Cingulate and Adjacent Medial Frontal Cortex in Adept Meditators and Non-meditators." *Neuroscience Letters* 421 (1): 16–21.

Kabat-Zinn, J. 1990. *Full Catastrophe Living: Using the Wisdom of Your Body and Mind to Face Stress, Pain, and Illness.* New York: Delacorte Press.

Kabat-Zinn, J., et al. 1992. Quoted in Segal, Williams, and Teasdale 2002.

Kabat-Zinn, J., A. O. Massion, J. Kristeller, L. G. Peterson, K. E. Fletcher, L. Pbert, W. R. Lenderking, and S. F. Santorelli. 1992. "Effectiveness of a Meditation-Based Stress Reduction Program in the Treatment of Anxiety Disorders." *American Journal of Psychiatry* 149:936–943.

Keable, D. 1985. "Relaxation Training Techniques: A Review: What Is Relaxation?" *British Journal of Occupational Therapy* 48 (4): 99–102.

Kimbrough, E., T. Magyari, P. Langenberg, M. Chesney, and B. Berman. 2010. "Mindfulness Intervention for Child Abuse Survivors." *Journal of Clinical Psychology* 66:17–33.

Kit, W. K. 2001. *The Complete Book of Zen.* Boston: Tuttle Publishing.

Larimer, M. E., R. S. Palmer, and G. A. Marlatt. 1999. "Relapse Prevention: An Overview of Marlatt's Cognitive-Behavioral Model." *Alcohol Research and Health* 23 (2): 151–160.

Lazar, S. W., G. Bush, R. L. Gollub, G. L. Fricchione, G. Khalsa, and H. Benson. 2000. "Functional Brain Mapping of the Relaxation Response and Meditation." *NeuroReport* 11:1581–1585.

Lazar, S. W., C. E. Kerr, R. H. Wasserman, J. R. Gray, D. N. Greve, M. T. Treadway, M. McGarvey, B. T. Quinn, J. A. Dusek, H. Benson, S. L. Rauch, C. I. Moore, and B. Fischl. 2005. "Meditation Experience Is Associated with Increased Cortical Thickness." *NeuroReport* 16 (17): 1893–1897.

Linehan, M. M. 1993. *Skills Training Manual for Treating Borderline Personality Disorder.* New York: Guilford Press.

Lutz, A., J. Brefczynski-Lewis, T. Johnstone, and R. J. Davidson. 2008. "Regulation of the Neural Circuitry of Emotion by Compassion Meditation: Effects of Meditative Expertise." *Public Library of Science (PLoS) One* 3 (3): 1–10.

Marcus, M. T., M. Fine, and K. Kouzekanani. 2001. "Mindfulness-Based Meditation in a Therapeutic Community." *Journal of Substance Use* 5:305–311.

Marcus, M. T., P. M. Fine, and F. G. Moeller. 2003. "Change in Stress Levels following Mindfulness-Based Stress Reduction in a Therapeutic Community." *Addictive Disorders and Their Treatment* 2 (3): 63–68.

Marlatt, G. A. 1994. "Addiction, Mindfulness, and Acceptance." In Hayes et al. 1994, 175–197.

Marlatt, G. A. 2002. "Buddhist Philosophy and the Treatment of Addictive Behavior." *Cognitive and Behavioral Practice* 9:44–50. Quoted in Fields 2009.

Marlatt, G. A., S. Bowen, and N. Chawla. 2010. "Mindfulness-Based Relapse Prevention (MBRP)." Accessed January 30, 2010. www.drbolger.com/mbrp.htm.

Marlatt, G. A., and N. Chawla. 2007. "Meditation and Alcohol Use." *Southern Medical Journal* 100 (4): 451–453.

Miller, J. J., K. Fletcher, and J. Kabat-Zinn. 1995. "Three-Year Follow-Up and Clinical Implications of a Mindfulness Meditation-Based Stress Reduction Intervention in the Treatment of Anxiety Disorders." *General Hospital Psychiatry* 17:192–200.

Moeller, G., E. Barratt, D. Dougherty, J. Schmitz, and A. Swann. 2001. "Psychiatric Aspects of Impulsivity." *American Journal of Psychiatry* 158:1783–1793.

Monahan, R. J. 1977. "Secondary Prevention of Drug Dependence through the Transcendental Meditation Program in Metropolitan Philadelphia." *International Journal of the Addictions* 12 (6): 729–754.

Nigosian, S. A. 2004. *Islam. Its History, Teaching, and Practices.* Bloomington, IN: Indiana University Press.

Nuchols, C. C. 2006. "The Neuroscience Behind Making Human and Spiritual Connections in Recovery." *Counselor* 7:12–22.

Ospina, M. B., K. Bond, M. Karkhaneh, L. Tjosvold, B. Vandermeer, Y. Liang, L. Bialy, N. Hooton, N. Buscemi, D. M. Dryden, and T. P. Klassen. 2007. "Meditation Practices for Health: State of the Research." *Evidence Report/Technology Assessment* 155. Rockville, MD: Agency for Healthcare Research and Quality.

Palfai, T. P., P. M. Monti, S. M. Colby, and D. J. Rohsenow. 1997. "Effects of Suppressing the Urge to Drink on the Accessibility of Alcohol Outcome Expectancies." *Behaviour Research and Therapy* 35:59–65.

Ribner, M. 1998. *Everyday Kabbalah: A Practical Guide to Jewish Meditation, Healing, and Personal Growth.* Citadel Yucca Valley, CA: Ribner.

Salmon, P. G., S. E. Sephton, I. Weissbecker, K. Hoover, C. Ulmer, and J. L. Studts. 2004. "Mindfulness Meditation in Clinical Practice." *Cognitive and Behavioral Practice* 11 (4): 434–446.

Segal, Z. V., J. M. G. Williams, and J. D. Teasdale. 2002. *Mindfulness-Based Cognitive Therapy for Depression.* New York: Guilford.

Shafil, M., R. Lavely, and R. Jaffe. 1975. "Meditation and the Prevention of Alcohol Abuse." *American Journal of Psychiatry* 132 (9): 942–945.

Siegel, D. J. 2007. "Mindfulness Training and Neural Integration: Differentiation of Distinct Streams of Awareness and the Cultivation of Well-Being." *Social Cognitive and Affective Neuroscience* 2 (4): 259–263.

Simpson, T. L., D. Kaysen, S. Bowen, L. M. MacPherson, N. Chawla, A. Blume, G. A. Marlatt, and M. Larimer. 2007. "PTSD Symptoms, Substance Use, and Vipassana Meditation among Incarcerated Individuals." *Journal of Traumatic Stress* 20 (3): 239–249.

Sogen, O. 2001. *An Introduction to Zen Training: A Translation of Sanzen Nyumon.* Boston: Tuttle Publishing. Cited in Ospina, Bond, Karkhaneh, et al. 2007.

Stratton, K. J. 2006. "Mindfulness-Based Approaches to Impulsive Behaviors." *New School Psychology Bulletin* 4:49–73.

Teasdale, J. D., Z. V. Segal, J. M. Williams, V. A. Ridgeway, J. M. Soulsby, and M. A. Lau. 2000. "Prevention of Relapse/Recurrence in Major Depression by Mindfulness-Based Cognitive Therapy." *Journal of Consulting and Clinical Psychology* 68 (4): 615–623.

Teasdale, J. D., Z. Segal, M. G. Williams. 1995. "How Does Cognitive Therapy Prevent Depressive Relapse and Why Should Attentional Control (Mindfulness) Training Help?" *Behaviour Research and Therapy* 33:25–39.

Tedeschi, R. G., and L. G. Calhoun. 2004. "Posttraumatic Growth: Conceptual Foundations and Empirical Evidence." *Psychological Inquiry* 15:1–18.

Tedeschi, R. G., C. L. Park, and L. G. Calhoun, eds. 1998. "Posttraumatic Growth: Conceptual Issues." *Posttraumatic Growth: Positive Changes in the Aftermath of Crisis.* Mahwah, NJ: Erlbaum, 1–22.

Thomson, R. F. 2000. "Zazen and Psychotherapeutic Presence." *American Journal of Psychiatry* 54:531–548.

Walters, J. D. 2002. *The Art and Science of Raja Yoga: Fourteen Steps to Higher Awareness.* Delhi: Motilal Banarsidass Publishers.

Wenzlaff, R. M., and D. M. Wegner. 2000. "Thought Suppression." *Annual Review of Psychology* 51:59–91.

Zgierska, A., D. Rabago, N. Chawla, K. Kushner, R. Koehler, and A. Marlatt. 2009. "Mindfulness Meditation for Substance Use Disorders: A Systematic Review." *Substance Abuse* 30 (4): 266–294.

## Chapter 9

Anti-Drug Abuse Act of 1988. Pub. L. No. 100-690, 102 Stat. 4181. Approved November 18, 1988.

Blocker, J. S., D. M. Fahey, and I. R. Tyrrell, eds. 2003. *Alcohol and Temperance in Modern History.* Santa Barbara, CA: ABC-CLIO / Greenwood, 27–31.

Borkman, T. 2008. "Introduction: The Twelve-Step Program Model of AA." In Galanter and Kaskutas 2008b, 3–8.

Brown, S. 1985. *Treating the Alcoholic: A Developmental Model of Recovery.* New York: Wiley.

Center for Substance Abuse Treatment (CSAT). 2009. *Considerations for the Provision of E-Therapy.* HHS Publication. No. (SMA) 09–4450. Rockville, MD: Center for Substance Abuse Treatment, Substance Abuse and Mental Health Services Administration.

Central Park United Methodist Church. 2010. Accessed Sept. 9. www.therecoverychurch.org.

Cunningham, J. A. 1999. "Resolving Alcohol-Related Problems With and Without Treatment: The Effects of Different Problem Criteria." *Journal of Studies on Alcohol* 60:463–466.

Cunningham, J. A. 2000. "Remissions from Drug Dependence: Is Treatment a Prerequisite?" *Drug and Alcohol Dependence* 59:211–213.

Curtiss, John. 2010. President and Program Director, The Retreat. Communication on July 25.

Dawson, D. A., B. F. Grant, F. S. Stinson, and P. S. Chou. 2006. "Estimating the Effect of Help-Seeking on Achieving Recovery from Alcohol Dependence." *Addiction* 101 (6): 824–834.

DiClemente, C. C., J. P. Carbonari; and M. M. Velasquez. 1992. "Treatment Mismatching from a Process of Change Perspective." In Watson 1992.

Galanter, M., and L. A. Kaskutas, eds. 2008a. *Alcoholism Research: Alcoholics Anonymous and Spirituality* 18. New York: Kluwer Academic / Plenum.

Galanter, M., and L. A. Kaskutas, eds. 2008b. *Research on Alcoholics Anonymous and Spirituality in Addiction Recovery.* Vol. 18 of *Recent Developments in Alcoholism.* New York: Springer.

Goodman, A. 2008. "Neurobiology of Addiction: An Integrative Review." *Biochemical Pharmacology* 75 (1): 266–322.

Granfield, R., and W. Cloud. 1999. *Coming Clean: Overcoming Addiction without Treatment.* New York: New York University Press.

Hser, Y.-I., M. D. Anglin, C. Grella, D. Longshore, and M. L. Prendergast. 1997. "Drug Treatment Careers: A Conceptual Framework and Existing Research Findings." *Journal of Substance Abuse Treatment* 14 (6): 543–558.

Humphreys, K., R. H. Moos, and J. W. Finney. 1995. "Two Pathways Out of Drinking Problems without Professional Treatment." *Addictive Behaviors* 20:427–441.

Jason, L. A., M. I. Davis, J. R. Ferrari, and P. D. Bishop. 2001. "Oxford House: A Review of Research and Implications for Substance Abuse Recovery and Community Research." *Journal of Drug Education* 31 (1): 1–27.

Jason, L., J. Ferrari, M. Davis, and B. Olson. 2006. *Creating Communities for Addiction Recovery.* New York: Haworth Press.

Kaskutas, L. A. 2009. "Alcoholics Anonymous Effectiveness: Faith Meets Science." *Journal of Addictive Diseases* 28 (2): 145–157.

Kurtz, E. 1999. *The Collected Ernie Kurtz.* Wheeling, WV: The Bishop of Books.

Kurtz, E., and W. L. White. 2003. "Alcoholics Anonymous (AA)." In Blocker, Fahey, and Tyrrell 2003, 27–31.

Larimer, M. E., and J. R. Kilmer. 2000. "Natural History." In Zernig et al. 2000.

Leshner, A. I. 2001. "Addiction Is a Brain Disease." *Issues in Science and Technology.* Accessed July 26, 2010. www.issues.org/17.3/leshner.htm.

Lewis, D. C. 1993. "A Disease Model of Addiction." In Miller 1994.

Malloy, P. J., and W. L. White. 2009. "Oxford Houses: Support for Recovery without Relapse." *Counselor* 10:1–6.

McAuliffe, W. E., and R. Dunn. 2004. "Substance Abuse Treatment Needs and Access in the USA: Interstate Variations." *Addiction* 99:999–1014.

McAuliffe, W. E., R. LaBrie, R. Woodworth, C. Zhang, and R. P. Dunn. 2003. "State Substance Abuse Treatment Gaps." *The American Journal on Addictions* 12:101–121.

McLellan, A. T., D. C. Lewis, C. P. O'Brien, and H. D. Kleber. 2000. "Drug Dependence, a Chronic Medical Illness: Implications for Treatment, Insurance, and Outcomes Evaluation." *Journal of the American Medical Association* 284 (13): 1689–1695.

Miller, N. S., ed. 1994. *Principles of Addiction Medicine.* Chevy Chase, MD: American Society on Addiction Medicine, 1–7.

Miller, W., and J. C' de Baca. 2001. *Quantum Change: When Epiphanies and Sudden Insights Transform Ordinary Lives.* New York: Guilford Press.

Moos, R. H., and B. S. Moos. 2006. "Participation in Treatment and Alcoholics Anonymous: A 16-Year Follow-Up of Initially Untreated Individuals." *Journal of Clinical Psychology* 62 (6): 735–750.

MRC (Minnesota Recovery Connection). 2010. "Who We Are." Accessed October 18, 2010. www.minnesotarecovery.org/who_are_we/index.html.

NIAAA (National Institute on Alcohol Abuse and Alcoholism). 2006. "National Epidemiological Survey of Alcohol and Related Conditions." *Alcohol Alert* 70. Accessed Aug. 1, 2010. http://pubs.niaaa.nih.gov/publications/AA70/AA70.htm.

O'Brien, C., and T. McLellan. 1996. "Myths about the Treatment of Addiction." *Lancet* 347:237–240.

Oxford House. 2006. "Oxford House Comes of Age: Oxford House—The Model." Presented at the 8th Oxford House World Convention, Wichita, KS, September 21–24, 2006.

Polcin, D., and T. Borkman. 2008. "The Impact of A.A. on Non-professionalized Substance Abuse Recovery Programs and Sober Living Houses." In Galanter and Kaskutas 2008a, 91–108.

Prochaska, J. O., C. C. DiClemente, and J. C. Norcross. 1992. "In Search of How People Change: Applications to Addictive Behaviors." *American Psychologist* 47:1102–1114.

The Recovery Church. 2010. "About Us." Accessed Nov. 2. www.therecoverychurch .org/about.html.

SAMHSA (Substance Abuse and Mental Health Services Administration). 2006. *Results from the 2005 National Survey on Drug Use and Health: National Findings.* HHS Publication No. SMA 06–4194. Rockville, MD: SAMHSA.

Simpson, D. D., G. W. Joe, and W. E. Lehman. 1986. "Addiction Careers: Summary of Studies Based on the DARP 12-Year Follow-Up." National Institute on Drug Abuse. Treatment Research Report (ADM 86–1420).

Vaillant, G. E. 1983. "Natural History of Male Alcoholism: Is Alcoholism the Cart or the Horse to Sociopathy?" *British Journal of Addiction* 78:317–326.

Vaillant, G. E. 2003. "A 60-Year Follow-Up of Alcoholic Men." *Addiction* 98:1043–1051.

Walters, G. D. 2000. "Spontaneous Remission from Alcohol, Tobacco, and Other Drug Abuse: Seeking Quantitative Answers to Qualitative Questions." *American Journal of Drug and Alcohol Abuse* 26 (3): 443–460.

Watson, R. R., ed. 1992. "Alcoholism Treatment Mismatching from a Process of Change Perspective." *Drug and Alcohol Abuse Reviews, Vol. 3: Alcohol Abuse Treatment.* Totowa, NJ: The Humana Press, 115–142.

White, W. L. 2000. "Toward a New Recovery Movement: Historical Reflections on Recovery, Treatment and Advocacy." Presented at the Center for Substance Abuse Treatment Recovery Community Support Program Conference, April 3–5, 2000. Accessed Aug. 17, 2010. www.facesandvoicesofrecovery.org/pdf/toward_new_recovery.pdf.

White, W. L. 2001a. "The New Recovery Advocacy Movement: A Call to Service." *Counselor* 2 (6): 64–67.

White, W. L., ed. 2001b."The Combined Addiction Disease Chronologies of William White, MA, Ernest Kurtz, PhD, and Caroline Acker, PhD." Accessed July 15, 2010. www.williamwhitepapers.com/papers/all/.

White, W. L. 2004. "Recovery: The Next Frontier." *Counselor* 5:18–21.

White, W. L. 2006. "Let's Go Make Some History: Chronicles of the New Addiction Recovery Advocacy Movement." Washington, DC: Johnson Institute and Faces and Voices of Recovery.

White, W. L. 2007. "Addiction Recovery: Its Definition and Conceptual Boundaries." *Journal of Substance Abuse Treatment* 33:229–241.

White, W. L. 2008. "Recovery: Old Wine, Flavor of the Month or New Organizing Paradigm?" *Substance Use and Misuse* 43 (12&13): 1987–2000.

White, W. L. 2010. "The Future of AA, NA and Other Recovery Mutual Aid Organizations." *Counselor* 11 (2): 10–19.

White, W. L., M. Boyle, and D. Loveland. 2003. "Recovery Management: Transcending the Limitations of Addiction Treatment." *Behavioral Health Management* 23 (3): 38–44.

White, W. L., and E. Kurtz. 2006. "The Varieties of Recovery Experience." In White, Kurtz, and Sanders 2006.

White, W. L., E. Kurtz, and M. Sanders. 2006. "Recovery Management." Chicago, IL: Great Lakes Addiction Technology Transfer Center (ATTC) Network. Accessed Aug. 27, 2010. www.attcnetwork.org/regcenters/generalContent.asp?rcid=3&content=STCUSTOM1.

White, W. L., and T. McGovern. 2003. "Treating Alcohol Problems: A Future Perspective." *Alcoholism Treatment Quarterly* 3/4:233–239.

White, W. L., and M. Sanders. 2006. "Recovery Management and People of Color." In White, Kurtz, Sanders 2006.

White, W. L., and M. Schulstad. 2009. "Relapse following Prolonged Addiction Recovery: Time for Answers to Critical Questions." *Counselor* 10 (4): 36–39.

White, W. L., and P. Taylor. 2006. "A New Recovery Advocacy Movement." Accessed Sept. 8, 2010. www.facesandvoicesofrecovery.org/pdf/White/a_new_recovery_advocacy_movement.pdf.

Zernig, G., A. Saria, M. Kurz, and S. S. O'Malley, eds. 2000. *Handbook of Alcoholism.* Boca Raton, FL: CRC Press.

## Epilogue

Bartsch, A. J., G. Homola, A. Biller, S. M. Smith, H.-G. Weijers, G. A. Wiesbeck, M. Jenkinson, N. De Stefano, L. Solymosi, and M. Bendszus. 2007. "Manifestations of Early Brain Recovery Associated with Abstinence from Alcoholism." *Brain* 130 (1): 36–47.

CASA (National Center on Addiction and Substance Abuse at Columbia University). 2010. "Behind Bars II: Substance Abuse and America's Prison Population." Accessed Feb. 14, 2011. www.casacolumbia.org/download.aspx?path= /UploadedFiles/tw0t55j5.pdf.

National Institute on Drug Abuse. 2006. *Principles of Drug Abuse Treatment for Criminal Justice Populations: A Research-Based Guide.* NIH Pub. No. 06–5316. Washington, DC: U.S. Department of Health and Human Services, National Institutes of Health, National Institute on Drug Abuse.

Open Society Foundations. 2010. "Defining the Addiction Treatment Gap." Accessed Feb. 11, 2011. www.soros.org/initiatives/treatmentgap/articles_publications /publications/data-summary-20100916.

White, W. L. 2007. "In Search of the Neurobiology of Addiction Recovery: A Brief Commentary on Science and Stigma." Accessed Feb. 15, 2011. www.facesandvoicesofrecovery.org/pdf/White/White_neurobiology _2007.pdf. (Also available at www.williamwhitepapers.com.)

# INDEX

**A**

AA. *See* Alcoholics Anonymous (AA)

abstinence

  AA participation and, 151–152, 168–169, 170–174

  brain healing after, 129–130

  craving after, 125–126

  as goal for alcohol-dependent, 143

  sobriety and, 232

  spirituality and, 167–168

abstinence-based mutual-aid societies, 17–18, 24

acamprosate (Campral), 197–198, 228

accidents and injuries

  domestic violence, 86–88

  dose-response relationship, 75

  hangovers and, 78

  home, 72

  intentional, 74

  motor vehicle, 71–72, 75

  occupational, 74

  overview of, 70–71

  recovery from, and alcohol abuse, 79–80

  recreational, 73

acetyl-L-carnitine (ALC), 204

action and behavior change, 218

acute care treatment model, shortcomings of, 261–263

addiction

  biological origin, 108

  brain and, 107, 113–120

  Buddhism and, 244–245

  delusions and, 244, 245

  denial and, 100

  development and speed of, 113–114, 116–120

  lifetime rates to various substances, 47

  need for wholeness and, 237

  number of Americans with, 283

  substitutes for, 123–124

  theories of development of, 113

addiction to alcohol. *See* alcohol dependence

addictive voice recognition technique (AVRT), 182–183

adolescents

  ADHD and, 59

  binge drinking by, 91–92

  comorbid conditions among, 58–59

  crime and violence by, 88–89

  deaths and injuries, 69

  drinking patterns, 50–51

  nineteenth-century alcoholic, 17

African Americans

  AA participation levels, 152

  alcohol use among, 15–16, 52–53

age

  alcohol use by elderly, 56

  alcohol use disorders rates by, 46

  brain healing after abstinence and, 129–130

  Cloninger Types I and II and, 133

  drinking by college students, 51–52, 69–70

  treatment programs for specific, 224–225

  *See also* adolescents

# ABOUT THE AUTHORS

**Mark Edmund Rose, M.A.**

has been extensively involved in the field of addiction for more than fifteen years as a licensed psychologist and addiction researcher. He has authored scientific papers published in peer-reviewed psychiatry and addiction journals, developed and written courses for physicians on addiction, testified in criminal trials as a court-validated expert on addiction, conducted research studies investigating the processes related to addiction and recovery, and performed numerous psychological evaluations of criminal defendants and disability claimants where substance use was an issue. He also co-authored *Prescription Painkillers: History, Pharmacology, and Treatment,* which was published by Hazelden in 2010.

**Cheryl J. Cherpitel, Dr.P.H.**

is a prominent alcoholism researcher in public health, the associate director of the National Alcohol Research Center, and a senior scientist at the Alcohol Research Group (ARG). She currently serves as an adjunct professor at the University of California at Berkeley's School of Public Health. She has been appointed to the National Institute on Alcohol Abuse and Alcoholism (NIAAA) National Advisory Council and Initial Review Group of the Clinical and Treatment Subcommittee. As a consultant, she has served the National Institutes of Health, the World Health Organization, and the Pan American Health Organization.